PRAISE FOR
THE 7 GRACES OF M

'At last—here's **a brilliant reframe of marketing and selling. Lynn Serafinn offers a brave new world,** where competition and scarcity give way to collaboration, abundance and greater connection among all humanity-- and **we still profit and prosper as we help each other. I love it!'**

~ DR. JOE VITALE
Author of bestsellers *The Attractor Factor, Buying Trances* and more

'*The 7 Graces of Marketing* offers **unique and powerful perspectives** that deliver a **much-needed message for consumers and marketers alike.'**

~ GREG S. REID
Co-author of bestseller *Think and Grow Rich: Three Feet from Gold*
www.gregsreid.com

'**This is what the world has been waiting for!** Finally a marketing book that guides us out of **fear, lack and limitation** into **love, prosperity and abundance.'**

~ ERIC PEARL
Author of bestseller *The Reconnection: Heal Others, Heal Yourself*
www.TheReconnection.com

'**The world NEEDS this book!** Lynn is ahead of the curve, and leading us toward **how we will ALL look at marketing in the future.'**

~ RICHARD S. GALLAGHER
Author of bestsellers *How to Tell Anyone Anything* and
What to Say to a Porcupine
www.pointofcontactgroup.com

'**Natural, fresh and original,** *The 7 Graces of Marketing* is **the defining organic approach to marketing**. Lynn Serafinn brings to marketing what Whole Foods brought to food! Go ahead and take a juicy bite!'

~ LIZ GOODGOLD
Branding Expert and author of *Red Fire Branding:
How to Create a Hot Personal Brand to Have Customers for Life!*
www.redfirebranding.com

'The question you must always ask yourself in a good marketing campaign is, "Do I like booby traps, hype and buffoonery, or prefer something **more honest and rewarding**?" *The 7 Graces of Marketing* **exemplifies and expands** upon this idea, asking you to reflect upon **the integrity of your marketing strategies** in a way that is **good for sales, for business, for your customers and the world.'**

~ **DAN HOLLINGS**
Internet and Mobile Marketing Consultant
Strategist for mega-hit *The Secret*
www.DanHollings.com

'Why is Lynn's book what we (marketers) and the world needs? Here's an anecdote: Yesterday I was listening to a radio interview with a famous photographer talking about Bob Dylan and his CD covers. At some point he said, 'That particular CD cover was so true, so authentic, so real. Do you know why? Because it was NOT chosen by marketers but by Bob Dylan himself!' I felt a sting in my true, authentic, marketing heart. Like that, The 7 Graces of Marketing **brings authenticity back into our marketing**. Marketeers of all ages, experiences, regions and specialisms: **read this book and take care not only of our customers and our planet, but also our profession and image.'**

~ **WARD VANDORPE**
Founder of Expert Marketeer
www.expertmarketeer.com

'People who effect great change in the world are usually courageous individuals...For them, it is not enough just to see the paradigm shift; they know a personal commitment to that change is essential. In The 7 Graces of Marketing, **Lynn Serafinn courageously follows in the path of those who have stood up for what was once the contrarian view.** She asks a huge question, and answers it with the precision of the academic she is, pointing the way to **what will surely become the new paradigm of marketing.'**

~ **SHELAGH JONES**
Founder of Spiritus the Spiritual Marketing Directory
www.spiritus.co

'Bringing our goods and services into the marketplace is an art to be celebrated, rather than manipulated. Lynn Serafinn has **brilliantly pulled the deceptive curtain back on marketing** and **returned grace and dignity to this ancient practice.** The 7 Graces of Marketing eloquently teaches us **how to be authentically visible** and, at the same time, **make a positive impact on humanity. A must-read for all entrepreneurs.'**

~ **ALLISON MASLAN**
Author of bestseller *Blast Off!*
The Surefire Success Plan to Launch Your Dreams into Reality
www.myblastoff.com

'Reading Lynn Serafinn's list of the marketing graces is **a liberating experience.** It reminds us that marketing can be either a thing of beauty or a source of our collective discontent. It reminds us that the choice is not 'Do I market or do I keep my integrity?' but rather, 'How can I make my marketing more gracious and graceful every day? **How can my own marketing be a part of the healing of the world?' Lynn paints it out so clearly**—for each virtue, there is a toxic mimic (twice the calories and none of the nutrition)...Marketing shouldn't feel like we're holding our breath just waiting to be discovered as frauds. It should feel like easy breathing. **Lynn's astounding contrast of virtues and vices is such an excellent guide.** I can't wait to dive deeper into it.'

~ TAD HARGRAVE
www.MarketingforHippies.com

'In a world where selling your products and services can feel like you are selling your soul, Lynn Serafinn's 7 Graces of Marketing provides **a forward-thinking, heart-felt, and healing perspective that turns marketing on it heels.** Imagine a world where marketing feels like you are giving gifts to your soul and the soul of humanity. This is **essential reading for entrepreneurs in the new millennium.'**

~ MISA HOPKINS
Author of The Root of All Healing: 7 Steps to Healing Anything
www.NewDreamFoundation.com

'**An antidote to the fear-based marketing** tactics of salespeople, The 7 Graces of Marketing **defines a new paradigm** for those committed to the health of people and the planet. **Lynn Serafinn lifts our consciousness** and our spirits in her **brilliant book.'**

~ STEPHANIE GUNNING
Author of Audacious Creativity and co-author of You Are a Spirit

'**First, I have to say this: "Wow."** The 7 Graces of Marketing is a blend of business and marketing practices **for a new economy and a new world,** plus **spiritual principles for a well-lived life,** and storytelling that pulls it all together. As you read this book, you will see your business, your beliefs, and your habits as a consumer reflected in the pages and called into question. **This book inspires me to think that we can truly create change** that is not promoted by fear, acquiescence, lack and addictions. Imagine the possibilities! **What Lynn has created here is nothing short of brilliant! Extraordinary!'**

~ TAMBRA HARCK
Author of Sacred Truths and Soulful Living by Design
www.TambraHarck.com

'We've sought for alternatives to business as usual, but there have been none—until now. In The 7 Graces of Marketing, Lynn takes us into **a completely new and evolved paradigm of marketing,** one which redefines the purpose and function of marketing as the expression of who we are and what we value. If you are interested in how to be **more intentional and thoughtful** when you engage in commerce, be it as a consumer or as a seller of goods or services, **read this book.** If you are **committed to bringing more connection and healing** into our world, **read this book.** If you are **ready for the paradigm shift to an enlightened, expansive, inclusive way of marketing and doing business, read this book. You will be transformed.'**

~ **PAULA TARRANT**
Life and Career Design Coach
www.InspiredWomenWork.com

'The 7 Graces of Marketing is **an inspirational guide for marketing's evolution.** I had always looked at marketing as a necessary evil. Reading Lynn's book **allowed me to release some unconscious guilt** surrounding the work I do in getting my own and my clients' messages out to the world. She provides **a neat checklist to make sure conscious marketers don't fall into old methods.** I now see that many influential corporations adhere to some of the "graces," while they still can't let go of some of the "sins." Only we, as consumers can help nudge them into compliance.'

~ **RENEE DURAN**
Duran Web Development
www.duranwd.com

'This book allows us the opportunity to **lift "marketing" out of the gutter** and **elevate it into a thing of integrity.'**

~ **KATE OSBORNE**
Esoteric writer, mentor and founder of Solarus Ltd.
www.solarusfoundation.com

The 7 Graces of Marketing

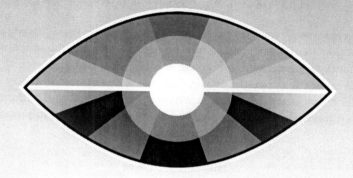

How to Heal Humanity and the Planet by Changing the Way We Sell

Lynn Serafinn

humanity1press.com

humanity1 press.com

Published in Great Britain by Humanity 1 Press

Copyright © Lynn Serafinn, 2011

Proofreading by Jessica Keet
Cover design by Renee Duran
Author's photograph by Andy Adams, Bedfordshire, UK

Humanity 1 Press
Unit 36, 88-90 Hatton Garden,
London, EC1N 8PN
England

Any queries relating to this publication or author may be sent to
info@humanity1press.com

This book may also be available in electronic format.
Please visit www.the7gracesofmarketing.com for details.

ISBN: 978-0-9568-5780-4

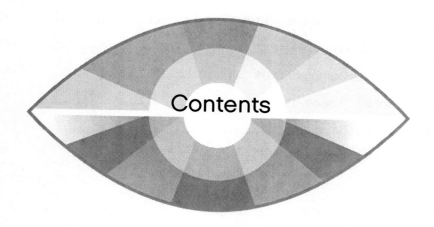

Contents

The 7 Deadly Sins of Marketing	The 7 Graces of Marketing
1: Disconnection	1: Connection
2: Persuasion	2: Inspiration
3: Invasion	3: Invitation
4: Distraction	4: Directness
5: Deception	5: Transparency
6: Scarcity	6: Abundance
7: Competition	7: Collaboration

For my grandson, Percy:
may your future be always full of grace.

Prologue:
Is Marketing Making Us Ill?

> '*A single ray of light from a distant star falling upon*
> *the eye of a tyrant in bygone times may have altered*
> *the course of his life, may have changed the destiny*
> *of nations, may have transformed the surface of the globe,*
> *so intricate, so inconceivably complex*
> *are the processes in Nature.*'
> **~ Nikola Tesla**[1]

T his is a book of questions, not a manual of answers. And I shall make no apologies for the fact that you are quite likely to have many more questions after you have finished reading this book than when you began. For it is my belief that wisdom comes much less from finding answers than it does from formulating the right questions. Nor shall I pretend to be able to guess all the questions that might arise in your mind as you read, or to know the answers to any of them. For while I might be a marketer by profession, it does not mean I am an expert on this or any other subject. And while I shall openly share my thoughts, experiences and beliefs with you as we ask these questions together, in no way will I ever assume that my beliefs are yours, or that I could ever tell you what is true for you.

Instead of needing to find all the answers, let us agree to engage in the free dialogue of ideas. Let us unlock any barriers that may lie between us. Let us see and respect each other for what we all are— sentient, intelligent beings, who are made of the same 'stuff' and who share the same planet. Let us see and hear each other. Let us allow ourselves to be seen and heard.

And now, with that in mind, let us begin with the first question of this book, and the one that will underpin all the other questions to follow:

'Is marketing making us ill?'

It is my belief it is. Marketing is making us ill. It is making us ill not only as individuals, but also as a society. At an almost non-stop pace, from the cradle to the grave, marketing has been feeding us a steady diet of fear, inadequacy, urgency, rage, panic, helplessness and, ultimately, disconnection—from ourselves, from each other and from our planet. What this does to us is unbounded. It culminates in crime, a pandemic array of serious stress-related health issues, and an obsessive entanglement with debt and dependency that has all but destroyed our economic system.

And as we mere mortals are part of the intricate eco-system known as Planet Earth, this illness has inevitably impacted the world around us, making our beautiful planet ill as well. If we stop running at our breakneck speed long enough to take a look at what's really happening, we will be able to see how every environmental issue around us today can be traced back to the way we have marketed and conducted our businesses over the past century, especially since the rise of mass media.

Yes, marketing is making humanity—and our planet—ill.

But like any illness, if we can probe deeply enough to find the root cause, rather than simply focussing on treating the symptoms, we can find a permanent cure. It is my belief that a fundamental shift in our marketing paradigm can not only heal us of this global affliction, it can also help us rise to a new pinnacle of human connection and wellbeing. If we commit ourselves to this change, we can not only save ourselves from ourselves, we can also restore the essence of our humanity—and ultimately our Divinity.

In short, marketing (a new kind of marketing) can save our world.

And that is what this book is about.

That is not how the book started out, however. The original intention of *The 7 Graces of Marketing* was to serve as a handbook for small-business owners who didn't 'like' marketing and didn't seem to be 'good' at it for reasons they couldn't quite understand. I had wanted to redefine the whole concept of marketing by taking the emotion out of the word, and to explore why a redefinition was needed. I also wished to offer a new paradigm for marketing along with practical ways for conscious business owners to apply this paradigm so their businesses could flourish.

But as I got into the crux of the subject, I started to realise the issues surrounding marketing went much deeper than I had ever imagined. Those sensitive souls who had come to me saying how much they didn't like marketing were really only the messengers to point me in the direction to examine an antiquated model that wasn't working for *anyone* anymore, if it ever did. And the more I explored, the more I came to understand how the social structures we call marketing, media and the economy were reflecting a cosmology that had gone seriously off-course for us as a society, taking us further and further away from ourselves.

This isn't a story about small-business people not knowing how to promote themselves; this is the story about how we lost connection to our own being-ness, and how we can re-establish it through a shift of perspective and personal practice. This is a story about how our own remarkable achievements in the 20th Century have sent us into an oblique orbit outside our own humanity, where we have become the proverbial prodigal sons of Creation, dreaming of finding the way home, and hoping we will be welcomed when we finally are courageous enough to knock on the door that leads back to who we really are.

This book is *not* about marketing inasmuch as it will not tell you how to advertise, master the art of social networking or close a deal.

But it *is* about marketing inasmuch as it takes the stance that marketing performs a vital role in our society: *the communication of our values.*

In the following pages, we will define marketing at its bare-bones level, and look far beneath the surface to explore the root causes of how we human beings came to create the very thing that is doing us so much harm. We'll explore how our relationships with ourselves, each other, our planet, our businesses and our economic system have created a sociological disease of global proportions. We'll explore the distorted value system that has arisen as a result of these relationships, and offer a new paradigm—which I call 'The 7 Graces of Marketing'—that can serve as a foundation upon which the healing process may begin.

Kindly note:

This book is not only a call-to-action for business owners and marketing professionals; it is intended for *every* person on the planet. We are all 'consumers' whether we like it or not. We are all part of our intricate socioeconomic system—comprised of people, planet, economy, technology and belief systems—that is both creating the problem and is ultimately going to be the source of the solution. No one is 'outside looking in.' No one is immune to the effects of this ubiquitous human creation we call marketing. And because of this, I humbly request everyone who reads this book to commit to ceasing to tolerate anything that falls beneath the standards of the value system to which your heart resounds—and hopefully which you will find within the pages of this book—and lead the way for the healing to begin.

Each and every one of us is a vital part of that process.

So let the dialogue begin...

Part One

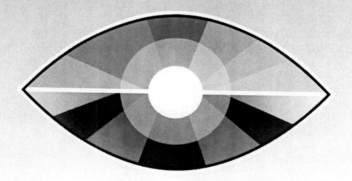

Where Are We
and How Did We Get Here?

Why Nice People HATE Marketing

July 6, 2010, 4:08pm BST
Phone rings. I answer. There is dead silence for a moment.
Then, a pre-recorded voice of a dire-sounding man comes
onto the line saying (in a sombre voice):
'Every year, thousands of people die without a valid Will.'

I hang up.

I spent most of my early adult life as a 'starving artist.' I was a freelance musician who chucked in my burgeoning career as a classical violinist at age 26 when I fell head over heels for a drummer who hated classical music. We married and together we formed many bands over the 20-plus years we spent together. Our division of labour was pretty clearly defined right from the start: he banged on the drums all day while I took care of what you might call the 'marketing.' Those being the days before the Internet, 'marketing' meant making and distributing lots of flyers, putting together lots of demo tapes and promo kits, and contacting lots of newspapers and magazines to see if they would run a feature on us. It was a non-stop job that resulted in mostly short-term results. And ironically, the one and only time the fruit of my marketing efforts resulted in attracting the attention of a major record label, when we actually came face-to-face with their A&R rep, we somehow couldn't pull it together to deliver what they wanted. Needless to say, we didn't get signed. I wasn't really sure at the time why we had failed to land a record deal after so many years of dreaming about it. It wasn't until years later I came to understand it was largely due to an underlying and somewhat unconscious resistance to relinquishing our proud 'starving artist' identity to 'the corporation.'

There is a widespread belief (sometimes conscious, sometimes not) amongst musicians that commercial success requires a compromise of artistic integrity—'selling out' they call it. And so, sadly, many gifted artists go their entire lives without any true career success, often financially destitute and/or working at 'day jobs' they loathe, not because they lack talent, but because they stubbornly resist the very thing that has the ability to bring them fame, fortune and the worldwide acknowledgement of their artistry: the business world. But it would be highly unfair simply to dub this attitude as mere 'self-sabotage;' there are actually many logical reasons why so many artists and other sensitive souls push away 'success,' as we'll see in the following pages.

By age 46, and after over 30 years in the music industry, being a starving artist had lost its lustre for me and I left both my marriage and my career. For the next few years I worked in the educational sector, eventually ascending the corporate ladder to become an Assistant Director at a large college. But somehow I never felt completely comfortable as a 'company man' (or woman), and at age 52, I returned to my freelance lifestyle to begin an entirely new career as a life coach and author.

Once again I came face-to-face with the challenges of marketing and self-promotion. Not being satisfied with my former level of success in the music business, I wanted to do it 'right' this time. Like many new business owners, I started by joining local business networks—mostly the kinds that meet at 6:45 A.M. for a horrible, greasy breakfast (that, being vegetarian, I could never eat), where you have to do a '60-second pitch.' I hated this environment. Not just disliked—hated. Don't get me wrong; many of the *people* in these networks were lovely. In fact, several became my clients. But there was something about the meetings themselves that made me feel positively alien. Slogging my morning coffee as I waited for my turn to do my pitch, I'd invariably sit at the meetings silently arguing with myself:

Voice 1 (yawning): *I wish I could leave. I just don't fit in here.*

Voice 2 (brashly): *Oh, get over yourself! Quit the 'starving artist' act and start acting like a grown-up. You'll have to learn how to fit in.*

Voice 1 (pleading): *But I can't be ME here.*

Voice 2 (chiding): *Ach! For once in your life, be responsible! If you want to be a REAL businesswoman, you have to act like one.*

Voice 1 (whining): *But I don't fit. I don't fit. I don't fit...*

Voice 2 (fed up): *Loser!*

Week after week, I would come home from these breakfast meetings stressed, suffering from indigestion and drained of energy to such a degree I would need to sleep for three hours before I could face my day. Nonetheless, I returned to the breakfast meetings week after week, partially because I had paid a small fortune in membership dues, and partially because 'Voice 2' was constantly bullying me into submission, and making me feel inadequate if I could not somehow learn how to 'fit' in to the business world.

But as the months progressed, no matter how much I tried, I felt worse and worse after every meeting. And the worse I felt, the fewer clients were referred to me via my business network. And really, who *would* refer clients to a coach who looked so bloody miserable? Naturally, the lack of referrals only made me feel even worse, which in turn made me more miserable, which led to even fewer referrals. It was a vicious cycle. The unhappier I became with the environment, the more I contributed to making it worse. But I was so 'in' the situation, I couldn't understand WHY I was so miserable. I started to ask myself: *Am I incapable of being a 'real' businesswoman? Am I destined to be a starving coach for the rest of my life, just as I had been a starving artist? Am I a failure at 'real' life?*

Tired of feeling like an alien being, I decided I needed a social outlet. At a local coffee shop, I saw many flyers of people in the area who were in holistic professions. Being into a holistic lifestyle, I started contacting some of these people and began meeting them for coffee. I made many wonderful new friends, and to my surprise and delight some of them also wanted to become my clients. Working with them made me feel enlivened, confident and peaceful. Now I was happy. Now I fit in.

Organically, and with little effort, I soon developed a small but identifiable niche of clients with a specific profile: small-business owners in the fields of homeopathy, Reiki, massage therapy, Reflexology, nutrition, etc. And what I found so interesting was that dozens of my newfound clients were now echoing the very same 'voices' back to me that I myself had been hearing in my own head. They complained of not feeling comfortable in business networks, but were at a loss to know how else to market their businesses other than distributing leaflets. They said, almost unanimously, they 'hated' marketing and 'dreaded' whenever they were faced with self-promotion. They said they didn't feel like they 'fit' in the business world, but if they didn't find a solution quickly, they would have to give up their businesses and go back to employment.

These people sounded an awful lot like the artists' crowd I had known for years. There seemed to be a whole sub-culture of business owners comprised of highly-sensitive, intuitive, creative and even spiritual people who just couldn't click with mainstream business culture, and whose values and motivators were far more intrinsic than financial. Most had a genuine passion for wanting to 'do good' in the world, but they had no idea how to communicate to their potential clients and customers, what to speak of when communicating with 'real' businesspeople in the networks.

In short, they were all 'nice' people who 'hated' marketing.

Furthermore, *I* was one of them.

No longer was I a lone wolf braving the howling masses; I was actually part of an emerging group of entrepreneurs who, without knowing, were calling for change. How could I facilitate that change?

DID YOU KNOW...?

Now on a mission, I decided to get out of my self-pitying bubble and start paying attention to what was actually going on around me at the breakfast meetings. Perhaps if I could figure out exactly what it was that was making me feel so drained and miserable, I could also help my clients. I began listening very closely to the 60-second pitches people delivered, and noticed there were invariably striking similarities in the pitches of the networkers who received the greatest number of referrals week after week. Here are some paraphrases of the highlights I recall:

- *'Did you know that break-ins increased last year by 11%? Let me give you a free quote for a household security system.'*

- *'Did you know that mortgage rates are predicted to rise to an all-time high next month? Take out a new mortgage with me today.'*

- *Did you read the story about the father of four who was killed by a drunk driver last week? Did you know he had no life insurance policy? Don't leave your family unprotected. Book an appointment and get covered today!'*

- *'Did you know that without a Will, your children might not inherit your property? You just heard from the guy right before me about how that father of four got killed by a drunk driver. It just goes to show you never know what's going to happen. Call me to get your Will made today.'*

And so on.

Can you see the pattern? No, it's not that each one starts with 'Did you know' (although, that is a marketing strategy we were 'taught' during our network training). If you look at these pitches carefully, you will notice that every one induces a feeling of urgency, anxiety and lack of safety.

In short, they trigger one of the most primal of all human emotions—*fear.*

FEAR AS A MOTIVATOR

When we are anxious or afraid, our endocrine system becomes flooded with stress hormones, such as adrenaline and cortisol, to enable us to respond to danger. These hormones help keep us safe in genuinely dangerous situations, as well as help us deal with daily stresses. But the body interprets danger very liberally. There doesn't have to be a tiger in the room; we merely have to *believe* there *might* be one. When we imagine there's a monster under the bed as children, we are afraid even though there is no monster. When we hear a loud noise, there may be no imminent danger, but our body jumps nonetheless, getting us ready to respond, just in case. Similarly, when we hear marketing messages that create doubt, fear, anxiety or confusion, our bodies respond even if our intellect says there's nothing to worry about. This makes fear a great motivator, and marketers know this. It gets us to move quickly, which is the very reason why fear-based pitches invariably evoked rapid responses from the people in my business network.

But fear can only ever be a *short-term* motivator. Once triggered, the body stays in a heightened state for some time, until it is satisfied the perceived danger has subsided. Over a period of *several hours*, the body very gradually returns to a balanced state and stress hormones return to normal levels. One nutritionist I consulted says it takes about 8 hours for cortisol levels in the body to return to a completely balanced state after a mere 5-minute period of stress.[1]

Knowing that, let's take a closer look at the impact of those sale pitches. Our network had about 40 members, meaning we listened to 40 one-minute pitches in a row at every weekly meeting. Now imagine that of these 40 messages, at least half of them are using anxiety or fear as a marketing motivator. At 60 seconds a pop, one after the other, there is absolutely *no physical possibility* for the mind and body to return to a completely balanced state as we move continuously from one pitch to the next. This and all the cups of coffee we drank to stay awake must have turned our endocrine systems into Gatlin guns of stress hormones every Thursday morning.

Could that have been why my messages of 'empowerment and overcoming limiting beliefs' seemed to land like a lead balloon every week? Were people simply not 'in the space' to receive such off-the-radar messages? Maybe. But I think there's more to the story. It had to do with the space *I* was in. The fact is that every time I stood up to speak to the group, I too had been unconsciously affected by the previous marketing pitches. And no matter how intellectually confident I might have felt, if I had been inwardly 'triggered' by the fear and negative beliefs around money, illness or death of those pitches, there would be no chance whatsoever I could inspire confidence and courage in my listeners. I'd have to be either the best actress or the most disingenuous person in the world.

I made a shocking confession to myself—I had indeed been 'hooked.' I was not standing in power. I was standing in muck. Finally, I began to comprehend not only why I had always left the meetings feeling so drained, but also why I had failed to communicate my message effectively to my audience.

While fear is a powerful incentive to quick action, it was never designed to be a *long-term* motivator. It cannot. Our bodies are not designed to withstand long-term fear and anxiety without some ramifications. When our brains are continually fed a stream of stress-inducing, 'urgent' messages, our bodies never get the chance to recover. The next 'dose' of cortisol gets fired through our system before our hormones have a chance to stabilise, and the vicious cycle of chronic stress begins. Our endocrine, metabolic and immune systems all become compromised. For many, it may affect their cardiovascular and digestive systems as well.

We compensate our exhaustion with caffeine and other stimulates, and our worries with a variety of diversions and intoxicants. Overworked and underpaid, our adrenal glands become like tired horses being whipped to carry a heavy load. We become susceptible not only to emotional and physical stress, but also to a plethora of other chronic conditions and auto-immune diseases plaguing our society at an alarmingly rapid and widespread level today. For me, this isn't just theory. I know it first-hand. It happened to me, and let me tell you it took me a long, painful time to recover.

Fear makes sales, but comes at a heavy price.

FIGHTERS, FLIGHTERS AND FREEZERS

Many of us have heard about the three classic responses to fear: fight, flight or 'freezing.' It seemed to me that many people in my business network were engaged in a constant, albeit unconscious, battle of reacting to their anxieties. When responding to marketing and media messages they were being fed, they sometimes used humour and sarcasm to push it away, attempting to make it look like they had it all together. Invariably these stoic types were the kinds of people who bought the insurance policies, purchased the Wills, made sure they had the best deal on their mortgages, ensured they had good credit ratings and paid their taxes early. They watched the news, read the newspaper and talked a lot about current affairs. They viewed their responses to marketing and media as signs of being a 'responsible' adult. These people were the 'fighters.'

Conversely, we have the 'flight-ers.' These are people with an unconscious aversion for aggressive marketing, such as those holistic professionals and creative artists I mentioned earlier. They 'fly' by resisting the whole idea of marketing (and sometimes business) altogether. They tend to live more peripherally and frequently feel 'outside' the status quo. They tend to be sensitive and idealistic, and justify their resistance to business and marketing by citing their values. They live with less, and get overwhelmed when they have to keep accounts.

To the 'fighters,' the 'flighters' are frequently viewed as being irresponsible or childish. To the flighters, the fighters are frequently deemed materialistic or aggressive. Sometimes you'll find flighter children have fighter parents; this can cause decades of family battles where the adult children feel judged and rejected by their parents, and the parents feel judged and let down by their children.

And then, there are the 'freezers.' Freezing happens when we go physically, emotionally or mentally numb and cannot move or make a decision. It is at those times we might yield to someone else, allowing them to make up our minds for us because our numbness cuts us off from the higher functions of the brain, including our own creativity. Artists in all fields know that fear is probably the most common inhibitor in their capacity to be productive, as anyone who has suffered from stage fright or writer's block can tell you. When we respond to fear in this way, it stops us dead in our tracks and renders us useless at responding to a situation, no matter how talented or intelligent we are.

Thus, freezers are neither towards nor against; they are blasé and dissociated from what they see and hear in the media, and are unlikely to realise the effect it is having on them. They have become so overloaded with emotionally charged information they no longer react, but operate almost autonomously, without questioning their own motivations. They become the compliant consumer. They overspend. They use their credit cards—a lot. They go into debt. They look for ways to transfer their balance from one card to a lower interest card. Unfortunately, this describes the majority of consumers in the world. And like it or not, most of us have been there at one time or another.

Now it all started to make sense to me. Fear seemed to be running the show. The 'nice' people I knew who seemed like they were 'no good' at marketing were the 'flighters.' To them, fear in marketing conflicted with their core values of healing, serving and creative freedom. I could see where I fit into all of this. As a business person, I was a dreamy 'flighter' at heart trying to pretend I was a responsible 'fighter'—and it simply wasn't working. That explained the battle between Voice 1 and Voice 2 in my head (furthermore, I realised that Voice 2 was the voice of my parents, and they had been dead for years!).

But while I might have been a 'flighter' in my business, in terms of my consumer habits, I realised I was pretty much a 'freezer.' I had become an unconscious consumer who had unknowingly bought into the myth that our ability to consume was in some way a measurement of our normalcy. I, like so many other people I knew, worked like a fiend every month counting every penny hoping I'd have enough to pay my credit card payments.

This is absurd, I thought.

I looked around my modest flat and started to wonder, *What do I have to show for all this debt? How did I get to this place? I don't remember spending all that money.*

Something...something...had made me spend. Could it be marketing? If so, what is it about marketing that has made me such an unconscious consumer? Could it be fear? What else might it be? Were there other things about marketing that unconsciously programmed me to act, to spend, to fear?

But what if this was not the only way to 'do' marketing? What if we eliminated fear and these other factors (whatever they were) from marketing? How would this change the way people responded to marketing?

How would it change our businesses?

How would it change our economy?

How would it change our health?

How would it change our world?

Early next Thursday morning, I awoke as usual for my business network meeting. And as I opened my eyes, I heard myself saying:

I don't fit?

...Hallelujah! I don't fit!

How a Broken TV Changed the World

It was February 2008. The word on the street was that we had just entered the biggest recession our world had known since the Great Depression of the 1930s. Every day, everywhere I went, people were talking about money and their fears about the future. Businesses and banks were closing. At my business network meetings (I was still attending them at the time), the 60-second pitches were even more riddled with messages of fear than before. A few months prior to my 'epiphany' in my business network, I was just as stressed over money that February as everyone else. My clients were cutting back on sessions, fearful of their own financial future. Fear was only generating more fear.

But we were not the only ones panicking. The banks were panicking too, as evidenced by the sudden rise in interest rates by nearly all credit card companies. Between that and my dwindling number of clients, my monthly interest payments alone were sometimes more than I was pulling in as income. And then I met this knee-jerk reaction of the banks with another knee-jerk reaction that is something you should NEVER do—I took out an emergency loan to pay my credit card bills, optimistically believing I could turn this situation around within the next three months. But when that didn't happen, I found myself with yet another high-interest debt to pay.

But then...my television blew up.

TV OR NOT TV?

Like most of us born after 1950, I had grown up with television. Since living alone after my daughter grew up, I had slowly settled into the same TV-watching pattern I had inherited from my parents—finish your work for the day, have dinner and then spend the rest of the evening watching television until it was time to go to bed (if you hadn't already fallen asleep in front of it, which was more often than not). Without being aware of it, television had become my drug of choice. My brain had come to accept it as the way I would 'wind down' for the day. It had become something of an unconscious addiction.

When I first moved into my Victorian flat in Bedford in 2006, I had picked up a very old tube set through the local *Freecycle* service. The old (and VERY clunky) tube set had served me well for those two years, but I wasn't completely surprised when I turned it on one evening and, instead of illuminating the room, it simply went 'poof!' I stared vacantly at a black screen with the white squiggly line running across it, somewhat pathetically waiting to see if the picture would come on. But after a few minutes, it was obvious the television was truly dead.

I said aloud (as you do when you live alone), 'Oh shit. Now I have to buy another TV. That just about takes the cake. That'll set me back yet another 300 quid. Yeah, right. As if I didn't have enough money problems already. That's really the Universe taking the Mick.'

Grumbling to myself, and with nothing to do, I decided to find a 'misery mate' and I called up my friend Linda in Wales. I moaned to her about my broken TV. But to my surprise, rather than commiserating, the always-looking-for-a-bargain Linda said, 'It broke? That's great! Now you can cancel your TV licence!'[2]

At first, I was slightly taken aback by her response. *Cancel my TV license? Do without television? What will I do in the evenings all by myself?* But then, I realised how absurd these questions were and I gradually began to think that perhaps she had a brilliant idea.

Ok, I thought, *so let's say I didn't replace my TV. What would happen? It would mean I would no longer have my weekly fix of X-Factor, Lost, Grey's Anatomy, America's Top Model or...*

America's Top Model?? Are you kidding me?

*Hmmm...*I considered. *Ok, point taken.*

Why was I watching TV anyway? Was it even a *conscious* choice anymore? What was I gaining from it? I had fallen into a pattern of stopping work at 7 P.M. every night and thinking, *Right. Time for telly.* I would lie down with a cup of peppermint tea (or glass of Pinot Grigio) by my side and lean my head on the arm of my sofa. Invariably, I would end up with a stiff neck. I cannot tell you how much money I had spent on visits to the Osteopath. And if I fell asleep while 'watching,' I'd wake up at 1 or 2 A.M. feeling semi-sedated and exhausted as I stumbled to my bedroom.

Yup. I could see there were lots of negative aspects to having a television. And if I didn't replace my set I would attain the absence of those negative things. But was there more than this? Where there some practical or even *financial* advantages to not having a TV?

Well first of all, yes, I would save on the license, which was then about £140 a year.

But then, I could also cancel my cable TV service. Heck, that's easily another £250 a year.

And then of course, I'd save the cost of buying a new TV itself. I had told myself it would cost £300, but really, once I was in the shop, how sure could I be that I wouldn't get seduced into buying the most high-tech one on the market? You know what I mean. Flat-screen, HD, digital stereo, digital radio, Internet access...

Ooh...Ooh...Don't stop! It's all so...sexy!

No, no, no, no...you must RESIST that sexy, new television...

And then, of course, I'd save on all those Osteopath visits at £35 a pop. How many times had I visited her in the past two years? Six times? Seven times? How much would that save me?

And what about all that Pinot Grigio?

Hmmm...

Five minutes ago I was thinking, *Oh shit. Yet another thing I can't afford.* Now I was thinking, *Wow, that broken TV just GAVE me over £1,000!*

'Yes,' I said to Linda, 'You are SO right. I'm NOT buying a new television.'

While this decision seemed like a small thing at the time, little could I have known this was the start of a 'butterfly effect' that would not only change my own life, but also the lives of others around me.

WHEN BEING A COUCH POTATO IS NOT AN OPTION

My TV gone and my evenings now free, I needed to find something new to do with my time. I figured it might as well be something useful that could help both my business and my upcoming book *The Garden of the Soul*, which I had hoped to bring out the following year. No longer waking groggily in the middle of the night after falling asleep on the sofa in front of the telly, I rose brightly every morning to write for at least two hours, resulting in a massive 1600% increase in my writing productivity. Every evening, I spent time learning. I became fully absorbed (some might even say obsessed) building my online network and researching information on how to do all kinds of techie things. Social networking, blogging and podcasting became a rich creative canvas in which I was meeting new people, getting new ideas and inventing new ways to communicate.

Within one year, my network grew from a few hundred random strangers, to many thousands of targeted subscribers, many of whom were becoming close network partners. I took dozens of seminars on marketing and book promotions, and learned many strategies for creating book launch campaigns. When my book came out in April 2009, it became a bestseller, which attracted the attention of other authors, laying the foundation for my now successful marketing company with several members of staff and a steady stream of bestselling mind-body-spirit author clients.

Another curious 'bonus' effect of not sitting in front of the TV all night was that my alcohol consumption had decreased significantly. Having a glass of Pinot Grigio as I sat down to relax in front of the set had become a frequent ritual three or four times a week. *It helps me sleep,* I'd tell myself. But when I was sitting working at my desk, I'd get so absorbed I just didn't bother to go pour myself that glass of wine. Soon I kicked the habit completely, and only drank if I was out to dinner with friends, and even then not very often.

But there's still more. Having come to terms with my 'not fitting' in my business networks, in April I decided to create a place in which I did. I established my own holistic community organisation called the Global Wellness Circle, which rapidly grew to 400 members in five chapters throughout central England. Instead of spending my evenings at home watching television, I was now travelling around to different towns once or twice a week, hosting and speaking at live events. This felt so right for me, by June I had quit my other business networks. While the Global Wellness Circle was never a profitable venture, in replacing my business networks it saved me thousands in networking fees, and over its two-year lifespan it gave dozens of holistic practitioners the chance to stand up and speak to the public in their own manner, rather than having to conform to the unnatural formula of a 60-second business pitch.

That summer, my increased exposure to people of a holistic mindset had the knock-on effect of inspiring me to make all kinds of lifestyle changes. Ever since I moved to the UK, I had learned how to live without an automobile, either walking or using public transport everywhere I went. But now I wanted to find more ways to cut my carbon footprint, such as insulating my loft, changing to a green energy company, buying organic produce from a local farm instead of from the supermarket. I also joined the Transition Town initiative and started a 'garden share' for the purpose of growing food in my backyard.

By July much of my life had already changed. I was getting a lot more done, saving money, leading a healthier life, meeting new people and feeling a lot better about myself in general. I also noticed I *was spending significantly less*, which made me feel like I had more money than before. But I could sense I was still holding on to something else I no longer needed. So one morning I woke up and decided if I could live a wonderful life without either a car or a television, I could live an even better life if I eliminated something I now had no urge whatsoever to use—my credit cards.

Since my divorce, I had gotten caught in a vicious cycle of debt. Putting a daughter through university, doing a Masters degree, paying for training for my new career and starting a new business had all contributed. Now I wanted to eliminate the false economy of spending what I didn't have and struggling just to pay the banks the minimum monthly payments. I found a company to help me work out a repayment scheme with my creditors, which would give me the breathing space to be able to save up the money I needed to pay these debts off (which I have since done). Yes, this decision meant I could kiss my credit rating goodbye, but as I moved through the process of letting go, a shocking revelation came to me:

It was the *fear* of not having a good credit rating
that had *gotten* me into the vicious cycle of debt in the first place.

How so? Because even when times were tough and I could scarcely pay the bills for my subsistence needs, I held onto those credit cards and my debts for dear life rather than admit defeat. Something had 'programmed' me to believe that losing a credit rating was the equivalent of being a social outcast, and that a bad credit rating would effectively ruin your life. That programming had also convinced me I 'needed' a credit card for 'emergencies.' What if something horrible happened and I needed money right away? I was living on 'what ifs' and not on 'what's here now.'

All this had made me hold on not only to my credit cards, but also to *the debts*, as I deluded myself into thinking I could manage the payments. But when the 'credit crunch' hit, and my interest rates skyrocketed from a cosy 4% to an extortionate 24%, my payments scarcely made a dent in my principle, and over time the balance went up, up, up rather than down. *Why* was I so obsessive about preserving my credit rating? How had I allowed it to control me to the degree that I willingly worked like a slave just to pay my debts rather than lose it?

Which brought me to the even bigger question:

Who *said* we needed credit anyway?

Where had that 'story' come from? *Why* was the story made up in the first place? *Why* did I believe it? *Why* did I think it was perfectly acceptable to spend money I didn't have, struggle to pay it back and then absurdly want to hold onto this arrangement because I thought my survival depended upon it?

Why did it seem the entire world believed this was normal?

Don't You Think You Should Be Worried?

Seven months had now passed. One afternoon in late September 2008, I was standing in the queue for the teller at the bank. As I stood waiting, I mindlessly allowed my eyes to fall upon the image on a very large flat-screen TV hanging on the wall, broadcasting BBC World News. The headline, scrolling over and over, was about how many major banks were on the verge of collapse, merging or being bought out by other banks.[3, 4, 5] These headlines was followed by a stream of one-liners elaborating on the impact this collapse would have upon the world economy. Everyone in the queue was watching the report, their ears lingering on every word. I could see the worried looks on their faces; the mood in the room felt so thick you could almost slice it with a knife. Some of the bank tellers looked so tense you might have thought they were being robbed at gunpoint.

But to my surprise, I felt no anxiety whatsoever. Everyone else around me was looking glum, desperate and worried, but I felt...um...fine.

Am I imagining this or does everyone around me feel really tense? How come I don't? Should I be feeling something?

After I left the bank, I started to wonder whether or not it was all in my imagination. Perhaps the people around me were not really as stressed as I was making them out to be? But apparently, they were. According to NHS statistics, prescriptions for anti-depressants had a sudden and sharp increase by 3.18 million in 2008, more than twice the typical annual rise. And while there are many things that could contribute to this disproportionate rise in anti-depressant use, many UK doctors cited the recession as being a major factor.[6]

No, it was not my imagination. For many weeks thereafter, I began to notice that just about everyone seemed to be stressed about the banks closing. The nightly news predicted all kinds of impending financial doom, and people were genuinely nervous about their investments, their jobs and the stability of the country. Many of these people had far more money than I did. I was still living on a fairly modest income.

But I, on the other hand, shrugged my shoulders and felt positively serene. I admit it was bewildering.

When friends or colleagues saw my lack of anxiety about the global economy, they'd react in interesting ways. Some would say, 'Boy, I wish I could be as calm as you. I'm losing sleep over this.'

But others were far more excitable. They'd say things like 'What? What do you *mean* you're not worried? The entire world banking system is about to collapse and you're not worried? Why *aren't* you worried? Don't you think you *should* be?'

Good questions, I thought. *Why* wasn't *I worried? Was I crazy? It's not like I'm rich or something. Not long ago I was totally stressed out over money. Last winter I'd have been climbing the walls over this...*

And then, it hit me like a brick.

This wasn't about money at all. This had to do with *me*.

Something had happened *within* me over the past seven months:

I had become de-toxed.

TV was the toxin...or rather, the carrier of the toxin. The toxin was the non-stop stream of urgent and distressing information coming mainly via television adverts and the nightly news. But unlike most of the nation, I wasn't watching the nightly news. I wasn't seeing those depressing daytime TV adverts about being in debt. In fact, I wasn't even thinking about my debts anymore. I wasn't watching night time adverts that made me want to spend money on things I didn't really need, or feel inadequate when I couldn't afford to buy them. I wasn't commuting into London anymore, glancing randomly over someone's shoulder reading the tabloids or the *Metro* on the train to work, and filling my brain with alarmist headlines. I wasn't seeing *anything* everyone else was seeing on a daily, hourly and even minute-to-minute basis. And because I wasn't seeing it, I wasn't thinking about it. It wasn't taking up any space in my brain or my life.

Of course, around this same time, the very same folks who said, 'Don't you think you *should* be worried?' also said things to me like, 'What do you *mean* you don't watch the news? Don't you think it's everyone's *responsibility* to stay informed?'

As I said earlier, wisdom is born of asking the right questions, not in knowing the right answers. And while the people who asked these kinds of questions thought they were challenging my beliefs, what they actually did was open the door to my being able to understand theirs:

1. That we are dependent upon the banks/credit system for our survival (i.e., safety)
2. That we are dependent upon the media for our information (i.e., truth)
3. That if we do not maintain a dependent relationship with them, we become irresponsible adults (i.e., social failures)

I suspect there is an alarming amount of people in our society today who unconsciously share these same powerful—and very dangerous—underlying beliefs. If my suspicions are correct, how are these beliefs impacting our society, our economy and our happiness? We humans formulate beliefs to give us feelings of order, safety and security. How well are these particular beliefs serving us in this way? Any belief based upon dependence (rather than *inter-dependence,* which we will explore later) makes us utterly vulnerable and positively *unsafe.* And the more we cling to such beliefs, the more dependent and vulnerable we become, and the more challenging it becomes to break free of them.

When we combine a fundamental belief in dependency with a continual flow of *messages of fear and lack,* we open ourselves to social instability. It generates stress not only at an individual level, but at a societal one. Conversely, freedom from fear and stresses allows us to think creatively and find solutions for whatever challenges, including financial, we invariably face in life. Fear and feelings of scarcity—*not actual financial crisis*—are the true causes of the epidemic of economic instability in our world...and marketing was the carrier of this virus.

But 'marketing' is a shape-shifter. It does not only incarnate in our world as advertising for the purpose of selling products or services. The nightly news, the newspaper headlines, a political speech may all rightly be called 'marketing' in the sense that they 'sell' us on a way of thinking. Some media pride themselves for their 'objectivity' and 'impartiality' but in reality there are no such things. No one, me included, can deliver information without skewing it, even if quite innocently, according to the picture of the world as they see it. In the broadest sense, I think it is accurate to say:

> 'Marketing,' in whatever form,
> is the business of *selling ideas.*

SATORI IN NANDO'S ON A SUNDAY EVENING

Throughout 2009, I had watched many businesses, both large and small, fail and disappear. Perhaps one of the most iconic events representing the economic frenzy in the UK in 2008 was the collapse of Woolworths retail stores who, after 100 years of an ubiquitous presence on Britain's high streets, shut the doors of 815 retail outlets by January 2009, having finally collapsed under the weight of debt amounting to £385 million, resulting in the loss of 27,000 jobs.[7, 8] A full year after our Bedford chain had closed, the storefront in which it had operated still stood empty and unused. No one was taking the risk of renting such a large storefront. The empty shell of our former local Woolies was like some sort of ruin from a bygone era, and its presence seemed to send out the message that the world was in crisis. Everywhere I went people were expressing their fears about the economy. Many of the self-employed holistic professionals in my Global Wellness Circle had also gotten caught in this web of anxiety, and I saw all too many talented and sensitive people leave their practices to return to employment just to make ends meet.

But my own experiences of the past two years had taught me that far from being helpless victims in an overwhelming Universe, we are typically the active creators of the very problem against which we believe we are struggling. Unlike so many people I knew, the year 2009 had actually been a fruitful one for me. And while the success of my book had raised my credibility significantly as both a coach and an author, it had also established my reputation as a *marketer.*

And somehow, the time was absolutely right for me to become a marketer for other business owners. What better way to try to change the face of marketing than to step into the occupation with both feet? After all, if marketing and media could impact us so negatively, could it also be used to create the opposite effect? Could it be possible to define and implement a completely different kind of marketing that created a positive impact on the world? Could marketing uplift us, feed us and heal us instead?

These seemed like such simple questions, but I knew there was a lot more I needed to understand before I could answer them. I did what I always do when I've got a lot on my mind—I went for a walk along the River Great Ouse. The walk was lovely, and my mind and lungs felt clear in the winter air, but flashes of insight into marketing did not seem to be forthcoming. I walked for half an hour or so until the sun started to set over the blue-black waters and the moon started to rise. It was getting dark and I was getting hungry. I decided to forget about marketing and head over to Nando's Restaurant for dinner.

Savouring my usual order of veggie pita, peri-peri chips and a bottle of Sagres beer, I was totally absorbed in my own little world. But sometimes the Universe just puts you in the right place at the right time. For as I was biting into my pita, my ears randomly picked up the word 'marketing' coming from somewhere behind where I was sitting. I stopped eating for a moment and listened. Was I hearing right or was I just imagining it? Yes, I had heard correctly. Not three feet away from me, seated at the table directly behind me and amidst screaming children and with samba music playing in the background, two young lads were having an animated discussion— about marketing.

It seemed bizarre and totally out of context. And how utterly ironic it was that I of all people was sitting within earshot of what was being said, considering all I had been thinking that day. But sometimes, the Universe drops you into a situation that is so offbeat you have to pay attention to it. So, without turning around, and without missing a bit of my dinner, I began to eavesdrop on their conversation:

Young Man #1: 'You shoulda been there, bro. I'm tellin' you, this seminar I went to today was awesome. Our business it gonna take off. I used to worry about marketing, but today, yeah, this guy showed us a marketing formula. I couldn't believe how simple it all is. I tell you, we've got it made.'

Young Man #2: 'Really? What is it? Waddawe have to do?'

Young Man #1: 'It's dirt simple. All we have to remember is three things...'

They lean in closer to one another.

Young Man #1: '...fear, sex and humour!'

Young Man #2: (leans back again) 'That's it?'

Young Man #1: 'That's it, bro.'

Young Man #2: 'Fear, sex and humour. Waddaya mean? Waddawe do with that?'

Young Man #1: 'All we have to do is put fear, sex or humour in our marketing. I'm tellin' you, we'll make the sale every time. This guy today was showing us example after example, and it's all true. I couldn't believe it. It's been around us in marketing all the time and I never saw it before. It's so simple. I'm tellin' you, our business is going to take off. We're going to be rich, mate.'

Young Man #2: 'All we have to do is use fear, sex and humour...'

Young Man #1: Yup. That's all we'll ever need to know about marketing. That's it.'

I tried very hard not to choke on my peri-peri chips.

In Zen Buddhism, there is a concept known as *satori*, which refers to 'a flash of sudden awareness' that has been described as being 'similar to awakening one day with an additional pair of arms, and only later learning how to use them.' Well, if ever I had experienced a 'satori moment' in my life, it was that moment. Sure, I had already 'discovered' the link between *fear* and marketing over the past couple of years, but I had never imagined it was actually the foundation of a marketing strategy that was actually *taught* by marketing experts, with apparently no ethical dilemma attached to it whatsoever! But not only that, fear was just the tip of the iceberg...

Fear...sex...AND humour?

You mean this triad is some sort of 'formula' being taught to marketers? How could I have missed that? It's been right in front of my face all along. And if fear in marketing can do so much damage to us, what about sex and humour? How much have I, and the rest of the world, been influenced by these Three Furies of Marketing throughout our lives? And, more importantly, how has it impacted our world in ways we might possibly not have noticed?

These young men seemed to believe they had found the magic bullet that was going to skyrocket them to financial success. But what they did not appear to have yet acquired was knowledge of one vital thing—the knowledge of human beings. They seemed to assume all humans operated at a primitive, base-level survival instinct, where they simply react to stimuli they are given. Furthermore, their marketing mentors, whoever they might have been, seemed to be reinforcing this assumption.

Fear, as we've seen, is only a short-term motivator at best, and while I hadn't yet explored it, I imagined sex and humour had their limitations as well. And certainly, none of these stimuli empowered people or brought them to knowledge of a higher level of Self. In other words, this was a model that catered only to the lower instincts in human beings; they might induce people to spend their money in the short-term, but they did not serve humanity or society as a whole.

As I listened to their conversation, I could hardly contain the sense of urgency running through my body like an electric current. I desperately wanted to turn around and say something like, 'Yeah, sure, all of that is ok if you only want to appeal to people's lower chakras! It will NEVER reach their higher consciousness!' (I later related these thoughts to a friend of mine, and she burst into uncontrollable fits of laughter).

But I said nothing. Instead, I sat there nursing the last few gulps of my slightly warm beer and reasoned that blurting out such a mad statement to two complete strangers who didn't even know I was eavesdropping would be a bit extreme, even for me. Did I really think I'd 'enlighten' them? Did I think they'd reply with, 'Wow! Thanks, lady. You've helped us see the light! Please tell us more'?

Or would they more likely say, 'Uhhh...yeah...whatever...'?

So I did what most women would do in this situation.

I got up to go to the ladies' room.

As I stood in the loo, splashing cold water on my face, I assessed the situation. I still hadn't yet seen the faces of the two young men who were sitting behind me, but I knew that on my way back to my table, I would come face-to-face with them. What would I do? Would I follow my urge and blurt out my thoughts to them? If I did, would they engage in conversation with me or just stare at me like I was some kind of middle-aged weirdo? In the grand design of the Universe, was it my 'moral obligation' to share my insights with them? Wouldn't I be helping them in the long-term success of their business venture? Shouldn't I ignore my own fears and act for the greater good? Or was I just a hopeless dreamer, on the verge of creating a scene that would embarrass me for many years to come?

As I started walking back into the restaurant, I could finally see the faces of the two young males. They were probably no more than 19 or 20 years old. Just kids, really. Perhaps they were students at the very college at which I used to teach a few years earlier. Seeing their youth and their innocence, I suddenly felt a wave of maternal compassion.

Then, my Inner Voice spoke up.

'Leave them alone. They're on their own journey,' the Voice said. 'Go home and write a book.'

I chugged down the last drop of Sagres, gathered my belongings and left, my brain swirling with ideas as I walked back home along the river, now shimmering in the darkness like a black satin sheet beneath the sliver of the crescent moon.

Fear, Sex and Humour
- OR -
How S-E-L-L Became a
4-Letter Word

> *'Fear is the mind-killer.*
> *Fear is the little-death that brings total obliteration.'*
> **~ Frank Herbert, *Dune*[1]**

One summer afternoon when I was 19 years old, I was backing my parents' car out of their driveway on my way to a friend's house. Just before I pulled up to the street, I noticed a small blur on the lawn to the left side of my line of vision. I stopped the car to take a closer look and saw an adult female robin floundering in the grass, apparently with one wing broken. Knowing that our neighbourhood was full of cats that would happily take advantage of this injured bird and finish it off, I got out of the car with the intention of 'rescuing' her. I walked over very gently, talking to the robin in a soft voice. The bird saw me coming and started flapping helplessly. I paused for a moment and spoke to her again, saying something like, 'It's ok. I won't hurt you.'

I leant down very gently to pick her up, at which point the look of terror in her eyes actually frightened me. I had no time to react, however, for within a split-second after I had managed to scoop her flailing little form into my well-intentioned hands, her entire body stiffened and her chest expanded to such a size I thought it would explode. In fact, her heart probably did explode beneath her ribcage, because suddenly I went from holding an injured robin to a limp, dead robin. I had never before thought a living creature could literally be 'scared to death,' but that afternoon I saw it with my own eyes, and held it in my own two hands.

Fear is quite possibly the most primordial of all emotions. It is present in both humans and animals. Controversial studies by scientists like Jagdish Chandra Bose and many others have suggested fear and other feelings are also experienced by plants, and even more controversial studies by Dr Masaru Emoto of *The Hidden Messages in Water* fame suggest emotions such as fear can even be observed in water molecules.[2] It would appear that fear is woven into the very fabric of our physical makeup.

Living in fear doesn't feel very good, but the fact that fear makes us so uncomfortable is the very reason why it is so useful and effective. If fear were not there to get us to react quickly to danger, most of us would probably end up dead at a very early age. Fear requires no thought. When we are afraid, it bypasses our 'thinking' brain by triggering a part of our brain known as the amygdala. The function of the amygdala is to ensure survival; it is not concerned with logic, reasoning or creativity. When we are in imminent danger, we are not supposed to think things through; we are supposed to MOVE as fast as we can. While many of us humans wish we could overcome our fears, fear at its essential level is Nature's way of protecting us. Fear is a good thing.

Our endocrine system is ingeniously designed to work with the brain when dealing with fear. If something threatens our safety, our body becomes flooded with stress hormones such as adrenaline or cortisol, to enable us to be stronger, faster and more focused than we ordinarily need to be in normal day-to-day situations. This triggers the amygdala, which in turn ensures that the 'higher functions' of the brain, such as reasoning, logic or creativity, are temporarily put on hold. You might think of your stress hormones as a team of construction workers doing road works, holding up big flashing signs that say, 'Road Closed. Follow Detour.' After the immediate danger has subsided, your system stays on alert for a while longer, just in case you need to react quickly again. Again, it's another safety precaution. Only after the body is quite certain the danger has passed, it settles down again, and the stress hormone levels go back to normal. Then, our logical and creative thinking returns and we become those wonderful, intelligent creatures we humans are known to be. And all of this happens without any effort or reasoning from us. We humans are brilliantly engineered.

We humans are also fairly resilient. Fear doesn't bother us too much when we are exposed to it in small doses and short spurts. But when fear gets more intense, the body's reaction can last far longer than really needed. Anyone who has been involved in a severe car accident might have experienced the jitters whenever you heard a loud noise anytime from days to months afterwards. But when such intense fear also becomes *continuous,* it is no longer simple fear, but *trauma.*

Most of us tend to associate trauma with extreme cases such as war veterans or victims of violent crime, but I believe trauma is much more common than most people realise. I myself was diagnosed with post-traumatic stress disorder (PTSD) some years ago, owing to decades of severe domestic traumas. I have personally experienced how trauma can get so lodged in the body that it can be reignited even with the smallest provocation. It took me years to understand why this was happening and to learn how to unravel the layers of fear that had gotten 'stuck' in my system. Later, when I became a coach, I witnessed trauma in my clients more frequently than I ever could have imagined. Traumas arising from abuse, bullying or violence (whether physical, sexual or verbal) get stored not only within the memory cells of our brains, but also within the very cells of our bodies, often for years after the original stimuli have passed. Most of us have no idea just how much fear we have stored up over time, carrying it around with us day in and day out, even though we appear to be living relatively 'normal' lives.

And in this case, what we don't know *can* hurt us.

How Fear in Marketing Makes Us Ill

Given all this evidence, it stands to reason that the continual, nagging, long-term exposure to fear triggered by marketing and media must certainly have an impact on us, whether we realise it or not. We might be tempted to think we are too clever to allow marketing to make us ill, but the constant drip-feed of fear-based messages in marketing keeps our system on alert, rendering us reactive rather than reasoning. Every day, we face an onslaught of urgent messages from television, radio, newspapers, magazines, billboards and email where we are being told to 'act now' or something undesirable will happen. 'Act now' before it's all gone. 'Act now' or you will no longer qualify. 'Act now' or you will suffer, get ill, lose money, be rejected, be too old or (ultimately) die. Any time we hear an 'act now' message in marketing, it automatically pushes our 'act now' buttons—our fears—whether we take the action or not.

Because fear is by nature meant to be a fast, short-term stimulus to 'act now,' when used in marketing its effect is that it disempowers consumers, driving them to buy impulsively without necessarily knowing why. Perhaps you have heard the term 'buyer's remorse,' which refers to what we feel when we have made a purchase due to impulse that we later wish we had not made. Conversely, because our daily environment keeps us in a continually heightened emotional state of alarm, many of us react by going out to buy something else to soothe the emptiness, hence the term 'retail therapy.'

When we receive a message to 'act now,' subliminally we are being sent a message of *scarcity*. Unconsciously, we are being told there isn't enough to go around, whether it is referring to 'limited product,' 'limited availability' or 'limited time.' And because everything has a feeling of being 'limited,' ultimately we find that nothing in our consumer culture is ever capable of filling the emotional void created by these feelings in the first place. And the great, sad irony is that had our fears of scarcity never been triggered by marketing, we would never have felt we were lacking in the first place. This conscious manipulation of the illusion of scarcity is a topic we will examine in detail when we talk about the 'Deadly Sin of Scarcity' later in this book.

Because the fear conjured by marketing is ultimately an illusion, what such marketing promises to deliver is also an illusion. And because it can never deliver, using fear in marketing can never build loyalty, connection or trust. And when these precious things are absent in a society, we become dissociative, cynical, apathetic and unhappy souls, wrapped up in our own worries, feeling devoid of support from the rest of the world. Emotionally, fear can trigger both hypersensitivity in which people are constantly 'on edge' and defensive, and hyposensitivity in which people become emotionally numb.

Chronic fear also impairs us physically. And when that impairment spreads at a societal level, we see pandemic amounts of stress, anxiety, aggression, impaired immune and metabolic systems, chronic health issues and even chronic physical pain.[3] This can drive people towards a widespread dependency on prescription and non-prescription painkillers, anti-depressants, stimulants, sedatives, alcohol, cannabis and other substances.

For all these reasons, fear in marketing is possibly the primary reason why so many sensitive people regard S-E-L-L to be a four-letter word, even if they are unaware of why they feel this way. And while historically it is quite clear that marketers, media, politicians and public relations experts have long been fully aware of the power of fear as a means to motivate people into action (and we'll be looking at some examples of this in the next chapter), it is now time for us also to become aware of the devastating impact this is having upon our society and our planet, and begin to take responsibility both for how we do business, and what we are willing to tolerate from businesses.

Fear is the mind-killer. And marketing is slowly scaring us to death.

LET'S TALK ABOUT SEX

Sex in marketing has become so ubiquitous it has become nearly a cliché. Like fear, sex is one of the most primordial of human instincts, as it is necessary for the survival of the species. On the other hand, sex at its best can also be one of the highest forms of intimacy between two human beings. But in addition to these two aspects, sex is also at the foundation of our *social identity*. A great many of our self-beliefs are entangled within our sexual identity, such as our degree of desirability, beauty, strength, power, nurturing capability and many others. It is this multi-faceted quality of sex that gives it the potential to become a powerful marketing tool.

This potential was first exploited in the early 20th Century as the result of the concurrent emergence of two major human developments at the turn of the 20th Century—mass production and psychoanalysis.

SEX, PSYCHOLOGY AND MANIPULATION

Sigmund Freud (1856-1939) was the father of psychoanalysis. His ideas on psychosexual development and drive theory propose that sexual drive is one of the primary motivators of all human behaviour, as well as the origin of many of our neuroses. While as controversial as he was influential, Freud's theories formed the backbone of much of early 20th Century thought, not only amongst psychologists, but also amongst sociologists, anthropologists, educators, politicians, businesspeople and, of course, marketers, journalists and PR agents. Hence, it might come as no surprise to you that the widely recognised 'father' of public relations and modern advertising was a man named Edward L. Bernays, who was in fact the nephew of Sigmund Freud himself.

Having been highly influenced by his uncle's ideas, especially those in the book *General Introductory Lectures*, wherein Freud proposed that human behaviour is essentially driven by 'irrational' forces, Bernays believed public behaviour could be manipulated without the public even realising it. All that was necessary, he felt, was an understanding of what he called 'the mass mind.'[4] Having already gained repute (if not notoriety) as one of the spin doctors who contributed greatly to the shaping of public opinion during World War I, in the 1920s Bernays was looking for a way to create a real 'movement' that would actually alter people's *behaviour* en masse.

Bernays was finally able to realise that ambition in 1929, the year after the publication of his book *Propaganda,* when he teamed up with the president of the American Tobacco Company (manufacturers of Lucky Strike brand cigarettes) to create a campaign that would alter public behaviour by convincing women to smoke cigarettes. This would be no small challenge. In that era, high society frowned upon women smoking in public, and viewed such women to be of questionable character.

But Bernays was convinced of his uncle Sigmund's hypothesis that people will act irrationally if you find the right way to push their emotional buttons. Consulting with one of Freud's disciples, Bernays asked what he felt cigarettes 'symbolised' to women. Drawing upon Freud's theories of psychosexual development, the disciple said they symbolised 'male power' (while it's hard for the 21st Century woman not to laugh at this blatant phallic cliché today, based upon what you're about to read about what happened next, who's to say Bernays wasn't right?).

Armed with this information, Bernays created a campaign for Lucky Strike he called 'Torches of Freedom' (again, blatantly phallic) in which he assembled an array of reputable and well-known women in New York to 'light up' their Luckies during the Easter Parade on 5th Avenue in the centre of Manhattan. The event, which took place on April 1, 1929, received international attention from the press (all pre-arranged). A major coup for the tobacco industry, the female market had now been firmly established, and the use of cigarettes by American women more than tripled in the decade to follow.[5] While surely this was a victory for both the American Tobacco Company and Bernays, whether or not this was an actual victory for women, society or the American economy is pretty questionable, as we'll see when we return to look at the impact of the rise of the tobacco industry later in this book.

Sex and Cigarettes

When we think of sexual stereotypes in cigarette advertising, most people will cite the infamous 'Marlboro Man,' who was used to portray a somewhat bizarre association between cigarette smoking and male virility in the 1960s. But while the Marlboro Man surely was busy manipulating the sexual identities (if not insecurities) of a whole generation of unsuspecting men, many of the more outrageous advertising campaigns for cigarettes throughout the 20th Century were targeted specifically at women and their ever-changing sexual identity in society.

The late 1940s through early 1960s was a markedly different era for women in America (I am citing America primarily because these

are where the advertising campaigns were based and whom they were targeting). After a long period of economic hardship followed by war, in which millions of young men had either been out of the country for an extended period of time or killed in combat, it was now the era of the post-war housewife—slightly sexy, but highly 'tame' compared to her 'liberated' counterpart in the decades on either side of them. These years of the housewife brought us some of the most extreme examples of marketing imaginable, in which cigarettes were blatantly marketed to women as a *weight loss aid*. This advert from Lucky Strike[6] shows two women in bathing suits standing ready to dive into a pool. One is a slender, young woman in full colour, and the other (who is also standing slightly back from the edge of the board, subtly implying she is not as confident as the other woman) is a distinctly overweight, older woman in black and white. The words on the advert ask, 'Is this you five years from now?' and then go on to advise, 'When tempted to over-indulge, reach for a Lucky instead.' According to the US Centers for Disease Control (CDC), Lucky Strike's campaign to convince women to 'Reach for a Lucky instead of a sweet' 'led to a greater than 300% increase in sales for this brand in the *first year* of the advertising campaign.'[7]

Another advert from the same era shows a woman dressed in a wedding gown, with a slightly devilish expression on her face, packing away a carton of Chesterfield's in anticipation of her

honeymoon.[8] Across the advert are the words, 'Packed with Pleasure' playing to the stereotype of lighting up a cigarette after having sex (within marriage of course...this was the 50s after all).

As women's sexual identity changed, advertising changed with it, although it is sometimes difficult to say which influenced which. Many Baby Boomers alive today will remember the famous Virginia Slims advertising campaigns in the late 1960s and early 1970s aiming to capture the 'Women's Lib' sector with their iconic slogan, 'You've come a long way, baby,' inferring that cigarettes were symbolic of social equality for women, putting them on par with men. I remember when I was about 15, lured by this marketing campaign, my friend Karen and I bought a pack of Virginia Slims and took them to Central Park in New York City to try them out. I took two puffs and hated it. I knew I was probably 'uncool' but I decided I didn't want to smoke, ever. Karen, on the other hand, liked it, and went on to smoke for decades, eventually managing to quit when she was well into her 40s, after smoking over a pack a day for more than 30 years.

If you do the maths, you'll see that in the case of my friend Karen, the 'You've come a long way, baby,' campaign resulted in her consuming *almost a quarter of a million cigarettes* (a pack a day equals 219,000 cigarettes over 30 years)—and that was just *one* customer. In other words, a mere 5,000 customers smoking a pack a day over 30 years would consume a *over a billion* cigarettes, and every 5 million customers would consume in excess of a whopping *trillion* cigarettes in their lifetime.

And even back then, there were a heck of a lot more than 5 million smokers in the US. According to the annual reports by the US Federal Trade Commission, US cigarette manufacturing suddenly shot up to over 600 billion cigarettes manufactured per year during the span of years from 1970 to 1975, representing an overall increase of more than 12% since 1969.[9] At a pack a day, that represents over 82 million smokers. Did the Virginia Slims campaign have anything to do with this? We can only assume it did. The US Surgeon General said, 'Initiation rates among girls aged 14 though 17 years rapidly increased in parallel with the combined sales of the leading women's-niche brands (Virginia Slims, Silva Thins, and Eve) during this period' [i.e., after 1968].[10] By 1978, cigarette manufacturing had reached 615.3 billion cigarettes a year and was still rising (it peaked at 636.5 billion in 1981, before it began its continuous decline to this day), with Virginia Slims representing 2.5% of all US sales[11], or approximately 15.4 billion cigarettes (yes, that's 15,400,000,000) sold almost exclusively to women.

To give you some visual perspective on what this actually means, if we took all the 100mm Virginia Slims that were consumed in just 1978 alone and lined them up end-to-end, they would stretch a distance of 1,540,000 kilometres (10,000 cigarettes = 1 kilometre), which is more than the distance of two round-trip journeys to the Moon and back. Multiply that by a 30-year habit (whether or not they continued to smoke Virginia Slims), and the cigarettes would stretch 46,200,000 kilometres, which is about a third of the distance to the Sun.

If we are evaluating marketing based solely upon sales, you've got to admit the 'You've come a long way, baby' was one heck of an effective campaign. But if we are looking at the bigger picture, it can only be viewed as a social *and* economic catastrophe.

THE REAL COST OF SEX IN MARKETING

While the tobacco industry is by no means the only industry to use sex in its marketing (nor does it use sex to target women only), these examples provide us with an easy way to understand why marketing success doesn't necessarily bring *holistic* success in the bigger picture of life. In America, widespread lung cancer, a disease which takes about 30 years to manifest, did indeed begin to appear in medical journals just about 30 years after the rise of the mass production of cigarettes.[12] But lung cancer is certainly not the only health risk from smoking. CDC reports on the impact of tobacco use upon women's health indicate a link between smoking and cancers of the oropharynx, pancreas, kidney, larynx, oesophagus, liver, colon/rectum, cervix and breast, as well as cardiovascular disease, stroke, reproductive disorders, menopausal abnormalities and a range of other diseases.[13]

Statistics can sometimes seem too abstract, but the story of my mother brings this home for me. Born in Manhattan in 1923, my mother would have been nearly six years old during the 'Torches of Freedom' campaign. Being a New Yorker, she might even have seen the event in person walking on 5th Avenue that Easter Day, although she never mentioned it to me. Mom started smoking 11 years later, having grown up in the years to follow when smoking became increasingly socially acceptable for women. A little over thirty years later, in the early 1970s, her emphysema was so bad she could not walk a city block without chest pains and having to gasp for breath. Travelling to the mountains or anyplace much above sea level was a painful, if not impossible, experience for her. She quit smoking when she was around 50, but never fully recovered the use of her lungs.

Mom eventually died of colorectal cancer on her 69th birthday. Tragically, with the exception of my father, every single relative in my parents' generation (and most of their friends) also died from cancer—mostly from lung cancer. Born between 1914 and 1928, they grew up in the era when cigarette marketing promoted smoking as something associated with sex, power and sophistication—for both men and women. Most died in their 60s and 70s. All of them, except my father, smoked cigarettes for many years, even if they quit later in life.

In sharp contrast, not a *single* relative in my grandparents' generation died from cancer of any kind. They all lived well into their 80s and 90s. None of them smoked cigarettes. Born 40 to 50 years before the 'Torches of Freedom' campaign—and indeed before the mass marketing of cigarettes in general—they were already much too set in their ways (and sexual identity) to be swayed by such marketing, no matter how clever.

And what about the young women and teenage girls who succumbed to the feminist-oriented cigarette marketing in the late 1960s and early 1970s? Again, bearing in mind that cancer trends only become visible about 30 years after a change in societal behaviour, CDC released these shocking statistics in 2001, just a little over 30 years after the 'You've come a long way, baby' campaign was first launched:

- In 1950, lung cancer accounted for only 3% of all cancer deaths among women; however, by 2000, it accounted for an estimated 25% of cancer deaths.
- Since 1950, lung cancer mortality rates for US women have increased an estimated 600%.
- In 1987, lung cancer surpassed breast cancer to become the leading cause of cancer death among US women.
- In 2000, about 27,000 more women died from lung cancer (67,600) than breast cancer (40,800).[14]

While these statistics are shocking enough, the ultimate irony of all this is that the 'success' of these marketing campaigns isn't even *economically* justifiable. According to the CDC, consumers spent an estimated $83.7 billion on cigarettes in 2006. In addition, the tobacco industry spent about *$12.5 billion in advertising* that year alone (that's $34,000,000 a day, by the way), which reduces their intake in 2006 to around $71.2 billion. But CDC also report, 'tobacco use costs the United States approximately $193 billion annually,' which includes 'about $97 billion from loss of productivity due to premature death and another $96 billion in smoking-related health care costs, as well as yet another $10 billion on expenses related to second-hand smoke.[15]

Thus, even without the cost of materials, production, salaries, insurance and other expenses figured in, we can estimate that the tobacco industry was responsible for an overall *loss* in the American economy of over $132,000,000,000 in 2006—a one-hundred-thirty-two-billion-dollar loss (that's a loss of over $360,000,000 *a day!*), not to speak of the inestimable cost of loss of life, in a single year. I cannot imagine what the statistics would be if we were to look at a global level, and over a longer period of time.

I'm no economist, but to me this just doesn't add up.

HUMOUR—A THIEF WE ALLOW IN WILLINGLY

Back in 1972, when I was still in high school on Long Island, the music department at our school took us to New York City to see the brand-new play *Jesus Christ Superstar* on Broadway.[16] For me, one of the most memorable moments in the show was 'King Herod's Song.' The actor playing Herod was brilliant. He was dressed in true 'glam rock' fashion of the day, in a silver lamé toga (I think) and enormously high platform shoes (I definitely remember that clearly). He sang the song in a very affected, exaggeratedly camp fashion which brought the audience (including myself) nearly rolling in the aisles with laughter as he sang:

> *Prove to me that you're no fool.*
> *Walk across my swimming pool...*

For many minutes, the audience continued to laugh and be thoroughly entertained as King Herod and his court danced around the stage in a clear 'homage' to the days of vaudeville.

But then, the entire tone of the show changed (and masterfully done, I might add, Lord Webber!) when Herod suddenly sang:

> *You're a joke, you're not the Lord*
> *You are nothing but a fraud*
> *Take him away*
> *He's got nothing to say!*
> *...Get out you King of the Jews!*[17]

These words from Herod were spat out with so much venom and contempt that my stomach felt gripped by them. I suddenly realised that this clever 'Herod' had been manipulating my emotions for the past several minutes without my knowing it. And it didn't feel good. Only a minute earlier, the entire audience was 'with' this witty Herod character, everyone laughing together, but the reality of the situation was that he was using humour (you might call it bullying) to curry public favour, so as to justify his decision to condemn the man who stood before him to a brutal execution. Of course this was a fictitious portrayal of an historic event, and we don't really know what exactly happened in Herod's court 2,000 years ago (and I seriously doubt he wore a lamé toga); nevertheless, the realisation that I could be 'suckered' by humour to accept what I would not normally accept was truly shocking to me.

I was only 17 years old when I saw this play, but it was my first lesson in how humour could be used as a tool for propaganda, powerful enough to influence public opinion to such a degree that they might tolerate (or even embrace) something they would ordinarily be against. I felt robbed by this thief called humour, even though I had let him in willingly. I'm not sure whether that was the underlying message Andrew Lloyd Webber had in mind when he penned this song, but it certainly was the message I took from it. Even after nearly 40 years, this lesson has stayed with me, and I am grateful to Lord Webber for helping me gain a greater awareness of which thoughts and feelings were my own, and which ones had entered my consciousness through the doorway of the 'distraction' of humour.

WHY HUMOUR IS NO LAUGHING MATTER

Just like fear and sex, laughter is one of the most precious assets of humankind. Studies by researchers such as Dr Lee S. Berk[18, 19] have shown that laughter not only releases endorphins that make us feel good, it also stimulates the immune system by increasing natural painkillers (NK) and stimulating T-cells. It also reduces stress hormones like adrenaline, dopamine and cortisol, lowers blood pressure and is good for cardiovascular health. More and more doctors are 'prescribing' laughter for their chronically and even terminally ill patients. In other words, scientific evidence is bringing us back to the old adage 'laughter is the best medicine' for whatever ails us. Many shamanic cultures use laughter for healing, and it is also being used in some yoga systems. In Indian culture, it is seen as one of the nine human emotions in classical *Bharata Natyam* dance. Humour is an integral ingredient of our humanity. It defines our cultures. It brings us together. It heals us. It feels good. You could even look at humour as a gift from the Divine.

Because we love humour and it plays such an important part in our lives, it also has the greatest potential to be exploited. Because we are generally open and inviting towards humour when it appears, it is also imbued with tremendous power to influence public thought at an unconscious level. And because of its ability to influence public thought, it is one of the most commonly used tools in marketing, appearing most often as what I call a 'Distraction.' Later in this book, when we look at 'The 7 Deadly Sins of Marketing,' we will examine the 'sin' of 'Distraction' in marketing in greater detail, but for now we will just get an overview of what it means.

When humour is used as a 'distracter' in marketing, its purpose is to lure you into paying attention, taking notice, remembering or becoming favourable towards a brand or product, not by focusing on the merits of the commodity itself, but rather upon the merits of the *way you felt when you interacted with the marketing piece.* In other words, you are 'buying' the marketing, not necessarily the product.

How many adverts can you recall simply because they made you laugh? Can you remember the brand they represented? Yes? Then you have responded precisely as was intended when the advert was conceived. You might think this is clever and 'good marketing.' You might also think, *What's the harm in a little humour?* After all, in the context of a world where the nightly news and other advertisers are bombarding us with fear, couldn't we use a little humour?

Of course, but when humour influences consumers mentally and emotionally to accept (and buy) brands based upon the 'feel good' factor of the advertising rather than the merits of the products or services themselves, it becomes insidious. When we relinquish our powers of discernment, it can lead to serious ramifications for our health, economy and natural environment.

But there's an impact upon our culture as well, as we become a society used to being continually hurtled back and forth between the two polarities of stress and escapism. Our bodies are reacting, whether we are aware of it or not. Our moods are affected. Our health is compromised. Our attention span is challenged. Humour no longer becomes the precious gift of laughter, but merely an escape from what we have called 'reality.' It becomes an anaesthesia that makes us feel numb and undiscerning instead of the nourishing delight it is meant to be.

But even more profound than that, when we finally realise we have been manipulated by humour, we begin to lose trust. Just as I felt in the audience during *Jesus Christ Superstar*, we feel we are being duped into feeling feelings and thinking thoughts that are not our own. When our trust begins to crumble, the fabric of our relationships begins to unravel. And when humanity no longer has strong relationships, very little truly healing laughter can be heard.

SUMMARY: HOW S-E-L-L BECAME A 4-LETTER WORD

Many of us have used the term 'used car salesman' to conjure up a cliché image of someone who is fast-talking, coercive, urgent and possibly dishonest. Nevertheless, this cliché doesn't seem to have had any negative impact upon used car sales over the decades. We can only conclude, therefore, that as a culture we both dislike marketing and selling, but we also accept it as a necessary part of our lives.

If that's the case, it might be useful to understand *why* we have agreed to live within this paradoxical human invention. Throughout this chapter, we looked at the first layer of that understanding by exploring how marketers consciously utilise fear, sex and humour in their advertising, and the impact this has upon us. It is important to remember that our human responses to these 'Three Furies' are largely unconscious and spontaneous. But what is equally important to remember is that while our conscious mind may be unaware of what is going on, our unconscious mind, our bodies, our communities and our planet are all being affected in a big way.

Many, if not most, of us are not even aware we are being affected. Many have become so numb to the information being thrown at them that they no longer realise their thoughts and emotions are being manipulated. They have bought into the game, and have either become addicted to it, or have learned how to exploit it for their own gain.

Those who have become addicted become the unwitting prey of consumer culture, and become trapped in so many ways that we will discuss in the next chapter. But the so-called 'exploiters' are not necessarily in any better position. I have worked with corporate executives who were very good at 'playing the game,' but it didn't mean they were 'winning' it. Some of the most successful people I have coached also exhibited some of the greatest amounts of fear and loneliness. For these people, a deeper level of healing is needed that restores hope, connection, trust and self-worth. It does no good for society to marginalise corporates or marketers and make them 'the enemy.'

The 'fear-sex-humour' model we have looked at so far is really only the tip of the very large marketing iceberg. This 'unholy trinity' trigger only what might be regarded as our base-level instincts. They operate from a mechanistic view of humanity in which we are powerless and reactive machines; and because of this, they cannot possibly bring society to a higher good. In my background as a teacher, if students believed they could only achieve a certain level, they indeed would only achieve that level at best. As a coach, if my clients do not believe they are capable of greatness, the quality of their lives never rises above mediocre. And if I, as a teacher or coach, believe these people are incapable of greatness, even at the most subtle level, I will never be able to help them see past their own limiting beliefs. So too, if marketers operate from the perspective that human beings are simply reactive machines as Bernays did (and as apparently did the mentor of those boys in Nando's Restaurant), they will never be able to communicate anything of value to us as human beings. In fact, they can *only* diminish the quality of our lives.

Creating the space for healing starts with shifting the way we see both ourselves and each other. Of course, healing at a global level is admittedly a challenge, especially when our dependence upon the media is just so relentless. We keep watching the media because we intuitively want to see the ending to whatever story we are following. But the conclusion never comes. There is no end. There are so many simultaneous threads of information that we feel we are climbing a mountain, but whenever we look up the summit is always just as far away as it was the day before. We fear there is simply no way to reach the top and get off this mountain altogether. And when we look down, we see we have left the world below so far behind us that there is also no way to return to where we started.

This is how consumer culture feels.

This is why we need to change it.

If marketers help start the process of healing by ceasing to operate from a mechanistic view of humanity, and learn how to speak to the higher levels of who we really are, that will at least be a good start.

The Rise and Fall of Consumer Culture

'Machinery that gives us abundance has left us in want.'
~ **Charlie Chaplin in *The Great Dictator***[1]

Many people in the West have heard the term 'caste system' used to describe the indigenous social structure of India. In my experience, the majority of Westerners (and many Indians as well) misinterpret the original intent of this *varnashrama* system (as it is called in Sanskrit), believing it to be inherently a system created for the oppression of the lower classes. And while there might be some truth to this rumour in that it has been misused throughout various times in history to that effect, the actual design of the *varnashrama* system reveals a fascinating model of human social organisation.

In this system, there are four *'varnas'* (or classes) and four *'ashramas'* (or stages of life). The *ashramas* progress first from childhood/student life to householder life, then on to retired life, and ultimately to spending one's final days removed from society, making the gradual transition to leaving the world altogether. Every human being, regardless of their social status (or *varna*), is advised to move through these four *ashramas* in order to complete the cycle of life.

Unlike the *ashramas,* the four *varnas* are not progressive stages, but rather interrelated components of society that work together to make a complete entity. In fact, in the *varnashrama* system, the different *varnas* are often compared allegorically to different parts of the human body, with the body representing society as a whole.

The first *varna* is the *Brahmin* class, who are the intellectuals, mentors, teachers and advisors of society. They are compared to the 'head' of the body of society.

The second *varna* is the *Kshatriya* class, which is the administrative and military class. This includes all government officials (whether kings or presidents), soldiers and all other supporting divisions of public service. This class is seen as the 'arms' of society, because their role is to protect and serve all who reside within his kingdom. This not only refers to human beings but also to the Earth, plants, animals and even supernatural entities.

What is so interesting about the *varnashrama* system is that there are checks and balances built into it to prevent it from becoming dysfunctional. For example, the *Brahmins*, while the possessors of the highest knowledge in a society, are expected to be financially humble and are not supposed to own property. They depend upon the charitable support of the rest of society for their sustenance. This prevents them from abusing their intelligence for their own gain. The *Kshatriyas*, on the other hand, can own land and amass wealth, but even the king is expected not to make decisions without the advice of respected *Brahmins*. This minimises the possibility of a king or military leader becoming a dictator or tyrant.

At the bottom of the social 'body' are the legs and feet. In the *varnashrama* system, these are represented by the fourth *varna*—the *Shudras*. The *Shudra* class is comprised of the labourers, craftsmen, artists and service providers of all kinds. They support the other three *varnas* by using their talents and physical strength to generate all the products, services and artefacts society needs for its health, happiness and entertainment. Far from being the least important, if you remove the 'legs' of the *Shudra* class, a society becomes very shaky indeed, and it may feel impelled to seek a replacement for its *Shudras* elsewhere, possibly leading to invasion, exploitation, warfare, serfdom and even slavery.

I intentionally left the third *varna*—the *Vaishya* class—until last. The *Vaishyas* are comprised of both the mercantile and the agricultural class. Together, they are seen as the 'torso' of the body of society because they literally provide its sustenance. The agriculturists produce the food and, in much the same way as the digestive system works, the mercantile class ensures that food, clothing and other needs are circulated and consumed efficiently throughout the rest of the 'body.' Basically, if you were to remove the *Vaishya* class, society would starve and civilisation itself would disintegrate, returning to a more 'primitive' type of existence wherein everyone would have to do everything for themselves.

If you look at the *varnashrama* system objectively rather than through any pre-conceived notions you might have had about it from the past, you will see it is not really a caste or class system at all—it is a socioeconomic model created to ensure cultural stability. Although we'd be hard-pressed to find any modern nation authentically implementing the *varnashrama* system today, I am citing it to highlight the fundamental principles it demonstrates that ensure the stability of any society. The *varnashrama* system assumes:

- That any solid social structure is comprised of many mutually interdependent components
- That certain checks and balances must be in place to ensure the integrity of this interdependence is maintained
- That everyone within a system must respect and value the contributions each of the components bring to the whole
- That a healthy mercantile (or business) sector is one of the vital components of a functional society

It's important to remember that in Vedic culture, the term 'mutually interdependent components' does not just refer to social creations of human beings alone (i.e., economies, governments, industries, etc), but also to plants, animals, land, water, air and inorganic resources. Like any other paradigm of this sort, whether communist or capitalist, dictatorship or democracy, its success is dependent upon the maintenance of the checks and balances between these mutually interdependent components. When things go unchecked and out of balance, any system, no matter how sound it is in theory, can result in corruption and/or collapse. If any of the above principles is missing or weak in a culture, its economy cannot possibly survive in any healthy form.

If you look at any economic or political system that has collapsed within our own lifetime—including the economic recession that started in 2008 in the West—you will be able to trace its roots back to one or more of these four pillars becoming 'diseased.' In fact, generally if you see evidence of one of these principles being compromised, you will see evidence of them all to one degree or another. But just as it takes up to 30 years for cancer to manifest in the body of a long-term smoker, socioeconomic systems also do not collapse overnight (even if it sometimes appears that way). If that is the case, why is our economy wobbling now? How and when did the imbalance within our own society begin, and how do we unravel this tangled web we've woven and return to stability? And finally, what role, if any, has marketing played in the recent rumblings within our economy?

To answer these questions, we have to go back at least 200 years.

LIVING INSIDE THE COSMIC CLOCK

As I write these words, it is only two days after a catastrophic earthquake and tsunami devastated the northeast coast of Japan on 11 March 2011. Video images of this natural disaster seemed to spread around the globe over the Internet even more rapidly than the 500-mile-an-hour lethal waves that claimed thousands of lives within what seemed the blink of an eye. Geophysicists explained that the quake had been caused by a sudden 1.5-metre drop of a tectonic plate that ran under the Pacific Ocean. For several days before this event, the volcano Kilauea in Hawaii had started emitting dramatic plumes of lava into the sky. Clearly, the Earth herself was busy relieving pressure that had been building up within her for who knows how long. In planetary terms, this was a natural and healthy thing. In human terms, it is beyond tragic.

It is during events like this that we humans are reminded of our intimate connection to the planet on which we live. When life moves smoothly along for us, we can easily lose sight of how intricately woven our very existence is with the delicate balance of what she gives us. The air has exactly the right blend of oxygen for us to breathe. Plants breathe out the oxygen for animals like us and we breathe out carbon dioxide for them. The Earth provides our food, our water and indeed the very ground upon which we walk. Everything we depend upon, create for ourselves and delight in comes from the Earth.

Furthermore, our Earth is dancing in a delicate balance of her own. The gravitational forces within the solar system are so precise that all the planets (at least within the microscopically small span of our human time-keeping) maintain regular orbits and exhibit stable behaviour. We are being held, as if within a pair of great arms, in an orbit that is exactly the right distance from the Sun where we have just enough heat and just enough cold to manifest the conditions to support all the beautiful and variegated life forms that surround us.

And then, our tiny solar system is engaged in still a bigger dance with our stunning galaxy.

And our galaxy is also in the great dance with all the other galaxies throughout the Universe.

And perhaps our Universe is also in a dance with many other Universes. Perhaps they breathe in and out for all eternity.

We are living within a Cosmic Clock of never-ending Time.

It is hard for us to imagine eternity. To us who live a mere hundred years or so, a few million years seem like a very long time. A few billion years are hard enough to visualise, but the concept of eternity—time without end—is almost beyond our ability to comprehend. With our limited vision, it is sometimes easy for us to walk through life under the impression everything around us is unchanging. But in fact, everything is in a state of continual change and movement.

Within that enormity, it is also easy for us to lose sight of our own significance. Things look so vast, so immense that we cannot imagine how we might have any power within this system. But we do. We are a part of this intricate system. We are not outside looking in, or inside looking out at it. Everything we do both influences and is influenced by the world around us. Every decision we make has an impact upon the whole, even if we cannot see it. Universal Time is not the same as human time.

Our ancestors understood this. Every culture on the planet understood that life itself is a tapestry of *interdependence.* No species on Earth, no element—whether organic or inorganic—is separate from the whole, and the human ability to reason gives us not so much a privilege amongst species, but rather a *responsibility* towards all life. The cosmology of so many ancient cultures was that we humans were put here to take care of the planet, and it would in turn take care of us.

But somewhere along the line, we lost the plot. While many of us regard the onset of the so-called 'scientific revolution' in the 17th Century as marking the beginning of the split between Man and planet, some scholars believe there was a shift in Western thinking several centuries earlier. Eloquently explained in his book *Harmony,* in a chapter appropriately entitled 'The Age of Disconnection,' HRH Prince Charles shares the research of Dr Joseph Milne of the University of Kent, which suggests sometime during the 13th Century thinkers of the day started to embrace a new view of God, Nature and mankind:

> Slowly but surely God began to be defined as something that lay outside of creation and was separate from Nature and, as that happened, so Nature itself came to be seen more and more as an unpredictable force; something likely to be unruly, without inherent order and capable of going on its own, sometimes dark, way...At the heart of things, within a very short space of time, that all-important, timeless principle of *participation* in the 'being' of things was eliminated from mainstream Western thinking. Or, to put it more graphically, with God separate from His Creation, humanity likewise became separate from Nature.[2]

What we can learn from this new historical information is that it was not science or technology that created the split between Man and Planet, but rather, it was our *belief system* that enabled us to create the scientific models and technological advancements that came afterwards. These belief systems were already centuries old when the period of time we refer to as the 'Age of Enlightenment' took place, when we embraced the cosmology of a mechanistic and impersonal Universe, and the view of Man as an observer rather than as a participant in his world had become the norm.

Our creations and manifestations in the world are only ever a mirror of what we believe. In the worldview of traditional Native American cultures, for example, the idea of land ownership was completely foreign. If you are an interdependent part of the Earth, how could you possibly 'own' a piece of her? Because of their worldview, their socioeconomic models were constructed in such a way that tribes agreed on the 'use' of lands for hunting, but there was no such thing as property ownership.

We can learn from this example that all cultural artefacts, and most especially our socioeconomic systems, are always the reflections of our current cosmology. Actually, they're apt to be slightly behind the times, in that it takes time for our social systems to catch up with our ideas. Whatever we create in this world has its origins in our beliefs. The idea of 'ownership' of anything, whether of land or anything else, can only arise when we hold the following three beliefs:

1. That we are separate from the thing being owned
2. That we are entitled to own it (i.e., superior to it)
3. That we are entitled to change, direct and use that entity according to our will

It's very simple. If we do not have these three beliefs, the question of ownership will never arise. Conversely, if we have these beliefs, the notion of ownership is inevitable.

OWNERSHIP, EXPLOITATION AND DISCONNECTION

The belief in ownership and privilege is ultimately a precursor to exploitation. In fact, it cannot help but produce exploitation in some form or another. At its most extreme, it is at the foundation of political totalitarianism and the practice of slavery—whether of humans or animals. But the belief in ownership and privilege is also a precursor to the exploitation of natural resources, both organic and inorganic.

When, however, we believe we are connected to and interdependent upon someone or something, it would simply not occur to us to exploit that entity. The notion of 'loving thy neighbour as thyself' has a completely different meaning when we understand this interdependence. When we believe we are separate, we *cannot* love another as ourselves. It is simply a moral obligation and not truly *love*. It is only when we feel, at the deepest level, that we are interdependently connected to the whole of Creation that we can truly love. And when we truly love, exploitation is unthinkable.

In Western society, the shift towards mechanistic thinking over the past 800 years—where we view ourselves as separate from our planet—has since become mirrored in our modern governments and economies. The notion of 'interdependence' gave way to the 'buzz word' of 'independence,' especially towards the end of the 18th Century. Even to this day, the word 'independence' has become virtually synonymous with the idea of 'freedom,' and the two have become fused into a single underpinning value that informs our political and economic structures.

But true independence removes us from 'the whole;' and as we became more separate from that 'whole,' our socioeconomic models became less and less able to maintain the checks and balances needed to maintain their integrity. And actions taken in isolation of the bigger picture have the potential to reap disastrous long-term results for the entire world. But because we have come to believe that independence also means freedom, we cling to this cosmology while trying to find patchy political solutions to our economic and environmental problems, unaware it is our belief system that is creating them.

Here's an example of what I mean: For the past 150 years or so, we humans have been relentlessly pumping oil from the Earth. Such behaviour can only arise when a culture embraces the triad of beliefs of 'ownership' as listed above. After more than a century of this behaviour, most of us have now become aware of the negative impact our addiction to fossil fuels is having upon the quality of our water, air, soil and overall health in the form of pollution. But fewer people seem to be thinking about how the rate of our consumption of petroleum products in the form of plastics is creating waste at a far faster rate than the Earth is designed to recycle naturally back into her system. Fewer still seem to be thinking about the fact we are extracting oil from within the Earth faster than the Earth produces it (although there are widespread controversies about just how long that process is), which will inevitably find us in a situation of 'peak oil' where we will have extracted all the economically viable sources of oil on the planet, and the easy flow of oil will simply stop. In fact, many people scoff when they hear the words 'peak oil,' saying it's all baloney. And to my knowledge, hardly anyone out there is daring to wonder whether or not the very act of drilling into the Earth's crust might be creating unknown disturbances deep beneath our feet. I'm not a scientist, but in my little brain, the idea of releasing uncountable amounts of pent-up pressure of gasses that might have been stored there for hundreds, or possibly even millions, of years every day over the course of a single century is like opening the biggest bottle of champagne imaginable; we are lapping up the champagne without any thought of what is happening to the bottle. The fact is, in spite of what we might have been taught in school, scientists don't actually *know* the truth about oil—what actually causes it, how long it takes to form and what purpose it serves in the ecosystem of the Earth—but we seem nonetheless willing to risk creating a potentially catastrophic time bomb, on the chance we won't live long enough to see the consequences of our recklessness.

Yet we continue to exploit petroleum as a 'resource.' To address the issues that are arising (or perhaps to make us feel less guilty), we devise stop-gap solutions such as recycling and 'cutting back' on our usage of said resources. In their book *Cradle to Cradle,* Michael Braungart and William McDonough call such solutions 'less bad,' as they cannot ever solve our problems, but only slow down the damage we are causing to the delicate balance of our planetary ecosystem.[3]

What we don't ever seem to do is stop exploiting altogether. Why not? Because the fissure of disconnection between us, our planet and our socioeconomic system has become as wide as the gap on Mount Kilauea. While petroleum dependency is a big issue, it's really just a symptom of our underlying condition. The real illness from which we suffer is *Disconnection* (one of the 'Deadly Sins' we will explore later), and the vehicle driving that disconnection further and further is our belief in (and the confusion between) our severely distorted and outdated ideas of capitalism and democracy that in turn perpetuate our unconscious addiction to consumerism.

THE DANGER OF COLLAPSED BELIEFS

Neither capitalism nor democracy is an invention of the modern Western world. Early capitalist models have been cited as long ago as 200 B.C in Assyria, and 'democracy' as a concept was first coined by the ancient Athenians, as documented by the great thinkers of the day such as Plato and Aristotle. More recent origins of modern capitalism started in the aftermath of the Great Famine and Black Plague that swept Europe during the 14th Century. These social catastrophes caused a complete shake-up of social classes, resulting in one class of people who owned land, resources and means, and another class of people who had skills, strength and labour. These skilled labourers could help the property owners profit from their property. These conditions, coupled with an increasingly mechanistic view of the world that had started in the previous century, were the seeds for early European capitalistic society that was to emerge in the Netherlands and England over the coming centuries.

The precise meaning of the term 'capitalism' has been the subject of hot debate for more than a century now. But the two key words that seem to be consistent in all definitions are 'property' and 'profit.' Unless a society collectively holds the belief that property and resources can be owned in the first place, capitalism cannot arise. What is 'property'? Originally 'property' meant land and resources, but in more recent times it can also include the structure of a business itself (i.e., the means of production, distribution, etc). In other words, capitalism is an economic system wherein a property owner can create the means to make a profit. Those who are not 'property owners' get paid for their skills and labour, but they do not profit from the property. Really at its core, it's as simple as that.

Democracy is a system of government that is 'by the people.' Although we toss the word around liberally to mean any country wherein there is the right to vote, technically, a 'pure democracy' means that all decisions are made directly by a small group of citizens created for that purpose. In this sense, there is no purely democratic state amongst the major nations in the world today. The United States is not a 'pure democracy' at all, but a 'democratic republic.' In fact, the founding forefathers had no desire to create a 'pure democracy.' In his *Federalist Papers,* James Madison explains why, citing how historical attempts to create a pure democracy typically ended in violence, and concluding they were 'incompatible with personal security or the rights of property.'[4]

What is so interesting about all this is that capitalism has absolutely nothing whatsoever to do with corporate culture, global economies, the stock market, or anything else so many of us tend to equate with the word 'capitalism.' Yet today, the general public seems to have fused these terms together in their minds. And what is also so very interesting about what Madison wrote is that democracy as a concept really has absolutely nothing whatsoever to do with 'the rights of property.' That is an element of capitalism, not democracy. Yet, most of us seem to accept that these two entities are intrinsically linked. And if you listen to our media, especially whenever there is a political or civil uprising in another country, you would think democracy and our somewhat 'enhanced' definition of capitalism were one and the same.

We have become the unconscious inheritors of a 'collapsed belief': two or more disparate beliefs that have become so fused that they have morphed into an idea that is neither really one nor the other, kind of like the creepy man-insect creature in the old film *The Fly.* Capitalism and democracy are not the same. Nor are capitalism, corporatism and consumerism the same. But the fact that we subconsciously hold them to be so means we will accept and even *defend* things within our economic system that might not actually be working for us, because we believe they hold the cornerstone to our basic human freedom. And when this collapsed belief gets really out of control, we might even find ourselves locking horns in warfare with other nations who have a whole range of other 'collapsed beliefs.'

Because these beliefs are so powerful, we hold fast to trying to make old systems 'work' rather than considering the possibility that some fundamental changes are needed. And changes are indeed needed, because something has changed the face of our economic system in ways that ensured both its success as well as its downfall—technology.

IT SOUNDED LIKE A GOOD IDEA AT THE TIME

The idea of capitalism is great. Someone has something and makes it grow bigger. You make something, sell it at a profit, and you have more wealth. It's a simple idea. But to make a profit, you also need three big things: a supply of resources, a means of production, and a market in which to sell. Of course there are many 'little' things that make up these three big things, but if we look at each of these 'big things' individually, we can see how marketing has played a key role in the progress of capitalism over the past century or so.

First of all are your resources. Resources can include anything from natural resources to human resources. In the latter half of 19th Century America, both were booming. Expansion to the 'Wild West' brought metals, timber, coal, oil, water and nearly limitless amounts of land to the ambitious entrepreneur. As the Native North American cultures generally did not believe in land ownership, they designed their societies to be mobile, never building permanent towns and cities. Thus, the wide-open spaces truly appeared to be wide and open to the new American entrepreneurs. Waves of immigration from the late 19th Century through the early 20th Century provided a more than ample workforce that could make these new enterprises grow. Job opportunities seemed endless as industry grew. Never before in history had so much come to so few in such a short period of time. The seeds of the notion of the so-called 'American Dream' and 'land of opportunity' were beginning to sprout.

But viewed at a holistic level, this seeming opportunity was largely an illusion, as it was entirely dependent upon an underlying socioeconomic imbalance between different ethnic strata in the emerging American society. The Native American peoples (what was left of them) were driven to take up residence in self-contained reservations, and African Americans during the Reconstruction Period, although technically 'freed' from slavery after the American Civil War, had no access to education and virtually no civil rights.

Most Black Americans who lived in the south continued to work within the agricultural sector, providing a work force of cheap labour, especially for the rising tobacco and textile (cotton) industries. Race and class distinctions extended to the non-agricultural industries, where cheap labour was plentifully provided by Asian (primarily Chinese) and European immigrants, especially from Ireland.

My own maternal great-grandfather, like so many other Irishmen who came across the Atlantic in the aftermath of the Great Irish Famine (1845–1852)[5], found work as a labourer on the great railroad construction projects spreading across the North American continent in the latter decades of the 19th Century. After that, his family (and the generation to follow) lived in inner-city Irish ghettos where they worked for poverty-level wages in factories. My paternal grandfather, a skilled craftsman from the South Tyrol, moved to the United States in the early 1920s hoping to find freedom from ethnic discrimination rising in his country, only to find his lack of ability to speak English restricted his employment opportunities to a highly dangerous, poverty-level and illness-causing job in the gruelling coal mines of Pennsylvania. While he lived into his 80s, he lost his larynx to occupationally-induced cancer when still a relatively young man.

So basically, when you get right down to it, the rise of industry in the decades around the turn of the 20th Century could only have occurred by dint of:

- An over-efficient extraction of natural resources, resulting in...
- An ever-increasing imbalance in Nature, made possible by...
- A severe imbalance in human rights and...
- The rise of new technologies

This brings us to the second 'big thing' needed to make capitalism work—the means of production. The turn of the 20th Century saw a rapid increase of new technologies that changed the world completely. The rise of machinery in industry and Henry Ford's new innovation, the assembly line, now meant that what once took weeks might take a single day. Suddenly there was more 'product' to go around than we had ever had before.

But—and here's the big 'but'—a fundamental principle of capitalism is the balance between supply and demand. The Industrial Revolution was responsible for a rapid increase in supply. But what about the demand? While you might be led to believe that as commodities became more plentiful, the increased supply automatically generated a proportionate amount of 'demand' in society, actually, *it did not*. People didn't feel a sudden need for all the new products like cars, cigarettes, boxed crackers and paper tissues being produced just because they were there. The fact of the matter is the rising class of new capitalists at the beginning of the 20th Century were actually able to supply *far more* than they could sell. How tantalising that must have been, to see what looked like unlimited resources combined with unlimited production. How could they turn that into unlimited growth when the public had never before experienced such luxuries?

If the public did not have a natural demand for products now made possible by dint of this new technological era, businesses would just have to *create* that demand so they could have a market in which to sell.

And so, modern marketing was born.

THE MYTH OF SUPPLY AND DEMAND

Although commerce has existed since Man first realised it was more efficient to collaborate in the exchange of goods and services than fend solely for himself for everything, it was technology and mass production that made it possible for us to create disproportionate imbalances between what we were able to produce, and what we reasonably could consume. In other words, technology gave us the ability to produce more than we could practically *use*...unless someone educated us in the reasons why we would want to consume more than we thought we needed. Essentially, marketing is that 'education.'

Let's return once again to the tobacco industry. The mass production of cigarettes began in the year 1882[6] and they were one of the first mass-produced and mass-marketed consumer items the world had ever seen. It's true that people had used tobacco for thousands of years, but prior to the mass production of cigarettes, it was used either as part of a ritual or a recreational pastime. People smoked tobacco in pipes or cigars, or used it as a chew. It took time to prepare and I imagine it was sort of messy. Because of both the practical aspects of tobacco consumption and the social conventions associated with it, we do not generally find widespread accounts of people becoming addicted to it prior to the end of the 19th Century.

But once cigarettes were mass produced, everything related to tobacco use changed. Tobacco was now available in neat, tidy little 'doses' called 'cigarettes.' No assembly or clean up (apart from disposing of the butts) was required. Your cigarettes were all uniform in size, and you didn't have to think about how much you needed. Just pop one in your mouth and light up. They also came in a convenient, little packet you could carry around in your back pocket or your handbag. Nothing could be easier. Millions and millions of people would be queuing up to buy them right off the assembly line, yes?

But actually, this was not the case. While manufacturers could now produce millions of packs of cigarettes a year, there was no proportionate body of tobacco users who could consume them as rapidly as they were produced. This meant if the cigarette industry wanted to *sell* what they were now able to produce, they had to *create the desire* in people to buy them. In other words, they had to identify potential new tobacco users and 'train' them in the many uses and advantages of cigarettes. This passage by Christine Wenc expresses this perfectly:

Mass production requires **convincing people to become mass consumers**. This required a shift in the way people thought about the objects and goods that made up everyday life. At the turn of the 20th Century, people were not accustomed to filling their homes with large quantities of consumer products. Modern advertising, also developed during this period, not only informed people of new products, it **also taught them how and why to use them.** Significantly, marketers quickly learned that **consumers responded much better to messages that relied on**

emotion and inference rather than facts, especially when **they wanted to get people to desire something they had never heard of before** [emphasis added].[7]

In other words, capitalists needed to 'invent' reasons why the public needed these new things they were producing; they had to create *false needs*. Furthermore, these false needs are created not so much by the actual merits or benefits of a product, but by 'messages that relied on emotion and inference.' The tobacco industry, and surely any new industry in those times and in the times ahead, succeeded not so much because it supplied a demand that already existed, but because it *invented* a demand through marketing. We have already seen how early cigarette advertising stirred up 'emotion and inference' by fabricating an emotional link between smoking cigarettes and sexual desirability or power. Bernays and other early influencers were not merely manipulating human behaviour—*they were consciously creating the perceived needs and wants of the times.*

Creating false needs, along with its insidious and multi-faceted partner 'creating false scarcity,' are cornerstones of old-school marketing, and play a huge part in what is making humanity and our planet ill. We will explore both of these in detail when we look at the 'Deadly Sin of Scarcity' later in the book.

THE MYTH OF CONTINUAL GROWTH

> *'Why should we be in such desperate haste to succeed,*
> *and in such desperate enterprises?*
> *If a man does not keep pace with his companions,*
> *perhaps it is because he hears a different drummer.'*
> **~Henry David Thoreau**[8]

While selling and trading is as old as the hills, marketing in its modern form really only started with the rise of technology. Advertising—in print, then radio, then television, then the Internet—became the vehicle for the ever-increasingly ubiquitous marketing message. Given how much we in Western society consume (and how much people in 'developing' nations seem to want what people in 'developed' nations have), marketing appears to have done its job—*to create a desire* in people to spend their money.

But towards the end of the 20th Century, and surely in the first decade of the 21st, it would appear we have reached something of a critical mass. The imbalance between what we can produce and what we can consume as a planet has grown to such proportions that the system is no longer healthy. In fact, it is out-and-out diseased. The reason why it has become diseased is simple: there is a natural rhythm to life on planet Earth and our economy has attempted to 'march' faster than that rhythm. At an environmental level, when you extract resources from the Earth faster than they can replenish themselves (if indeed they are renewable in the first place) or, at the other end of the production cycle, when you create a glut of products that are used and disposed of faster than the planet can absorb them back into its eco-system, *the system will collapse.* It's really a no-brainer. There is nothing radical or 'doomsday' about this statement. If you pour water into a rain barrel faster than you can siphon it off at the bottom, it will spill over. The principle is simple and you don't have to be an environmentalist to understand this.

Similarly, at an economic and sociological level, when you push human beings to *desire* to consume more than they can reasonably use at a cost that is faster than they are capable of earning, *you create a socioeconomic system that will collapse.* We can see the evidence all around us. From individuals to entire countries, we have become a society dependent upon credit. Our national economies are always in deficit (meaning we are not in good relationship with our money), and we find ourselves working under stress simply to keep up with our debts.

Over time, inflation sets in as a means to balance the imbalance. Salaries might rise, but so does buying, as people fear shortages and continual price increases. No matter how much we earn, we never feel satiated because there is always something 'more' we are being told we need. Eventually, the economic imbalance caused by overspending and debt catches up with businesses. The businesses close and people lose their jobs. Those who are still employed remain in jobs in which they may be unhappy, simply to hold on to some semblance of economic stability. And ironically, this creates even more stagnation in the economy because there is less focus on creativity and innovation, and more focus on basic survival. What was once a belief in unlimited economic growth devolves into economic stagnation, decay and dissolution. The toll this takes upon both the emotional and physical wellbeing of our societies, both in developed and developing nations, is immense.

We are caught in a proverbial hamster-wheel created by this delusion of never-ending economic growth. There IS no such thing. Nature has no such prototype. Whether we are talking about organic life forms or galaxies, growth is always part of a natural cycle that occurs between birth and death; it is never an end in and of itself. Continual economic growth is no more part of the natural order of the Universe than continual birth without death. Our bodies heal themselves. So does the Earth. The natural order of the Universe is to be self-sustaining. But self-sustaining is not the same thing as undying. Birth, death and change are all part of what you might call the 'permaculture' of life.

Just like our physical body, our social body is also an organism. The 'organs' of a society are things like political systems, belief systems (religions, philosophy, sciences, etc.), creative expression (language, arts, culture, social customs, etc), technologies (including communications) *and* its economy. And just like our bodies, each of these organs has an impact upon the others.

All life is holistic. If we make changes in one of these social organs without attention to the other, we cannot help but create a change, or even an imbalance, somewhere else in the system. In the latter half of the 20th Century, technology had a massive impact upon every facet of our social organism, especially upon our economy. But what we failed to see clearly was that, because our economic model of continuous growth was born well before these modern technologies existed, it was already an obsolete model when technology started to rise, especially in the post-World War II era. The fundamental principle of continuous growth in the capitalistic model was perfectly fine when it took two weeks for a letter to cross the Atlantic Ocean. But in an era when it takes two seconds for an instant message to travel around the planet and back again, the principle of continuous economic growth becomes like a Stage 4 cancer that has metastasised beyond our control.

Today, our money and our resources are moving faster than we are able to keep up. And just like a cancer, the more we surgically cut into the diseased cells, the more the disease will spread. The more we try to fix a flawed system, the more imbalanced we become. In short, our own commitment to growth has caught up with us. The Founding Fathers of the United States said they held it to be self-evident that all people had the right to 'life, liberty and the pursuit of happiness.' They never said, 'Life, liberty and the pursuit of continual economic growth to the point of planetary-wide self-destruction.'

The recent 'crisis' in our Western economy was no accident. It was not only inevitable, but an absolutely *essential* event if humanity is to survive as a race. Just as there are earthquakes when the pressure of the tectonic plates beneath the surface of the earth becomes too great, our economic 'earthquake' in the form of the credit crunch, failing property markets, bank closures, corporate bankruptcies and high unemployment rates were necessary and natural measures our social organism took in order to save itself from imploding (or exploding). While much was said in the media about the fall of communism in the late 20th Century and how it was a system doomed to fail, fewer in the West have articulated the fact that our current model of capitalism also appears to be on life support. Rather than continuing to attempt to resuscitate our economic system in the vain belief it will return to its former 'glory days,' it seems to me it is time we accepted the reality of the situation, and pulled the plug to let it die a natural death, as all social systems do over time.

When I say a 'natural death,' I mean just that. We can achieve nothing by an economic or political revolution, or by swinging 180 degrees in the opposite direction towards a socialist model. For within socialism lie many of the same economic dependency problems that have infected our current capitalistic system. No past theoretical model will serve us unless it integrates our economy not only with the sustainable needs of the entire global community, but also with the sustainable environmental needs of our planet Earth.

Only then can we even begin to entertain the idea of a *sustainable economy*, in which marketing stops creating false needs for the purpose of continual growth, and again takes up the function it is actually supposed to perform—communicate we have something of value to share.

THE TRUE COST OF CONVENIENCE

One afternoon in 2009, I stood in line behind a group of five teenage boys while shopping at our neighbourhood convenience store. As I stood there with my basketful of veggies and green tea, I noticed these boys had their shopping baskets full to the brim with items I would consider to be 'non-foods': candy, crisps, fizzy drinks, strawberry milk and so on. I was shocked to see how everything they had chosen was something manufactured and sold in a wrapper or a container, and that there wasn't a single item I would consider to be actual *food* like fruit, nuts or even real milk. They didn't even have a loaf of bread or a sandwich. It was all junk food—and a lot of it. There had to have been around £30 worth in total.

I started having an internal dialogue complaining to myself that these kids simply didn't care one bit about health, nutrition or indeed Nature. I found myself thinking things like, *No wonder they fall asleep at school all the time. No wonder there is so much ADHD. No wonder there is so much aggressive behaviour,* and so on. Then I got even more cynical, *Just look at all those candy wrappers. I wonder how many of them are going to end up on the ground instead of in the bin.* Basically my inner chatter was all your typical self-righteous 'grown up' grumbling about the 'misguided' younger generation.

After one of the boys paid for his share of the goodies, he went and sat down on the edge of an unused counter as he waited for his mates to check out. He dug into his stash and opened a bag of rather frightful-looking artificially coloured candies. As he bit into one of the candies, he grimaced and spoke rather loudly:

'Ewww!' he said, 'These are horrible!'

'Yeah, man,' one of his friends said, 'It's like I told you. You shouldn'ta got those. You shoulda bought Pop Rocks.'

'Na, man,' another friend said. 'Not Pop Rocks. Those'll give you migraines.'

'It's true, it's true,' another friend confirmed, 'Jake told me he got migraines from eatin' them.'

'Migraines!' exclaimed the first boy. 'Why would anyone want to do that to themselves?'

He continued to eat his candies.

'Ewww!' he said, 'These really are horrible!'

I looked at these young men—all of about 15 years old—and realised they were trapped. They didn't *want* to be ignorant; they actually wanted to know the truth about how to take care of themselves. They weren't buying this junk because they were reckless. It's simply all they knew from television, teen magazines, and 'word on the street.' And perhaps it's also all their parents knew. Even many of their schools served highly-processed foods at breakfast and lunchtime. These boys didn't actually know what *real* food meant, nor were they accustomed to eating it.

I viewed this chance encounter as a call to action from 'the Universe.' If I could see a problem here, whose responsibility was it to do something about it? Clearly it was mine, not these boys'. If I wanted to educate the next generation about how food comes from the Earth and not from convenience stores, it had to begin with me and my own family. Only when we make even the smallest of changes within our own lives does a butterfly effect of change begin to spread in the world around us.

I stopped buying packaged foods at the supermarket and arranged for a weekly delivery of organic fruit, vegetables and dairy from a local farm. My entire diet changed not only because of the organic, whole foods, but also because I began eating seasonally for the first time in my life. I stopped paying a gardener to mow my grass in my under-used backyard, and announced to my local friends that I would offer the use of my property to anyone who agreed to grow an organic vegetable garden on the land. A local music teacher took me up on the offer of this 'garden share' and she cultivated a lovely crop of vegetables. There was more than enough for both of us. Not only did this cut my grocery bill down yet another third of what it had been, but it also cut my carbon footprint as my 'food miles' had now become 'food steps.' My change of diet to seasonal, organic, local produce also improved my health. The winter following our first home-grown crop (and in spite of it being one of the coldest winters in recent times), I did not suffer from the predictable seasonal respiratory infections that had plagued me every winter for nearly 30 years.

The garden share created a small but significant ripple effect on our neighbourhood as well. One neighbour who had been a recluse contributed his plot of land and an additional pair of arms to work on our project along with us. Other neighbours gave tools, seeds, small plants and advice. I spoke about my experience with garden sharing at a local green fair, and our Transition Town group commissioned some media students to make a short documentary film about it for the purpose of inspiring others to utilise and share their gardens for food production.

But for me, the most wonderful moment of all was the first time I took my then-four-year-old grandson, Percy, out to the garden to pick some fresh vegetables for dinner. First, I asked him to choose what he thought were the best courgettes (zucchinis). The marrows were substantial, and the plants were still blooming with their beautiful characteristic yellow-orange flowers. Then, I stuck my arm elbow-deep into the black earth to pull out a few potatoes. I held one up and said, 'Look, Percy! It's magic!' His eyes went wide with wonder. Then, I stuck my hand down and pulled out a carrot.

'But—it's dirty!' Percy said.

'That's right!' I said enthusiastically. 'That's why we wash them first.'

That was the moment a child experientially (not just theoretically) learned food comes from the Earth and not from the supermarket. That evening, he ate his vegetables—all of them—without even demanding his mother put ketchup on them, as he usually did at home.

As a Baby Boomer, I was brought up on supermarkets and packaged foods. The majority of fruit or vegetables my mother cooked were bought either frozen or canned. When I thought of green beans as a child I was much more apt to know the words to the jingle for the 'Jolly Green Giant' than I was to know what a bean plant looked like, or when beans were in season. In fact, there was no concept of eating seasonally at all. We still had a local dairy, but our milk—already processed—came in bottles, not from cows. And while we did have local bakeries, most of our daily bread consumption was so-called 'enriched' white bread that came in wrappers and was already sliced. Breakfast came from packaged cereals that might have been 'fortified' with nutrients, but were also full of processed grains and sugars. Packaged, dried pastas replaced the home-made variety my grandmother used to make. 'Homemade' cake frequently meant you mixed eggs and water with the contents of a box labelled 'Betty Crocker.'

Today, the disconnection between farm and table is even more pronounced. Typically, the dairies, bakeries and farms from which we receive our food are bigger and more remote, sometimes many thousands of miles away from where we live, resulting in virtually no connection to either the seasons or the naturally occurring immune-boosting properties of locally produced crops. Our disconnection from the source of our food impacts us physically, environmentally, economically and also spiritually.

Yet, our modern lifestyle is only deepening the chasm between our activities and our own humanity. We get up and grab a quick bite to eat on the way to work. We nibble a mindless lunch over our desks or pick up something from a fast-food establishment. We come home from work, too tired and hungry to spend time cooking, so we eat another hastily prepared, mindless dinner as we sit in front of the television set.

Our lives are fast. Our food is fast. We have no time or inclination to think about our food, in spite of the fact that it is as fundamental to our existence as breathing.

We have become a fast-food culture. And both our bodies and our planet suffer as a result.

How did we get this way? How did our culture come to so passively accept our 'divorce' from Nature all for the sake of so-called convenience? What convinced us this was a better way of living?

YOU DESERVE A BREAK TODAY

The post-World War II era in America saw the rise of the suburbs, as millions of veterans and their spouses (including my own parents) took advantage of the G.I. Bill and left their urban backgrounds to buy homes in new family-oriented housing developments. But while the G.I. Bill was a great financial incentive for young couples to buy homes after the war was over, there was one thing that made the shift from urban to suburban life both possible and practical for them—the automobile. But when these young families moved to the suburbs in their new cars, it also paved the way for another industry to break onto the scene—fast food.

McDonald's Restaurant was established in 1940, but didn't really take off until people moved to the 'burbs' after the war, marking the start of the Baby Boomer generation. By 1959, McDonald's had blossomed to 102 locations, and after they became a public company in 1965 their growth exploded. And it continues to expand to this day. According to their website, they are 'the world's leading global foodservice retailer with more than 32,000 locations serving approximately 64 million customers in 117 countries each day.'[9] Their 2009 annual report claims revenue exceeding $22,000,000,000 that year[10] (I put in all the zeroes to help you get the full impact of the figure), and their entry on Wikipedia claims their revenue in 2010 increased to over $24 billion.[11]

While McDonald's is certainly not the only fast-food chain in the world, it is certainly the most enduringly successful, if not also the most iconic. In September 2000, a few years after the fall of the Soviet communist regime, I visited Moscow for a week. While walking through Red Square, I couldn't help but burst out laughing as I saw, hanging up for sale in the stall of a street vender, a black souvenir t-shirt with the famous McDonald's 'Golden Arches' emblazoned across the front—but with the word 'McLenin's' written sarcastically beneath them. Seeing me laughing, the pedlar, who spoke decent-enough English, said, 'Come see the back of the shirt.' He turned the shirt over to reveal, in typical sardonic Russian humour, a picture of a broken hammer and sickle with the words 'The party's over' written beneath. It seemed apparent that in the former Soviet Union the

McDonald's logo had won the somewhat dubious honour of being *the* symbol of Western capitalism.

And as a capitalist success story, McDonald's is certainly a force to be reckoned with. They reportedly sell approximately 4.2 million hamburgers *per day* in the United States alone. Or to put it into context:

> McDonald's serves more than 75 hamburgers per second for every hour of every day of the year *[my note: this figure reflects worldwide sales]*. These are served to almost 30 million customers daily in the United States alone, and they require more than a billion pounds of beef a year—that's almost 6 million cows, making the company the number one meat purchaser in the world.[12]

Hmm...That's a LOT of cows.

When I read these statistics, I started wondering two things: 1) were there any statistics of the world's meat consumption both before and since the rise of fast-food chains in the 1960s? and 2) what is the environmental impact of consuming 6 million cows a year (not forgetting that this figure represents only one of many fast-food chains in the world)?

According to an article in *The Journal of Farm Economics* in 1944, the per-capita annual consumption of beef and veal in the United States in 1943 was around 75 pounds, or about 34 kilograms.[13] This was an increase of nearly 20 pounds per year, after many lean years of economic depression. By 1960, before the big boom of rivalling fast-food chains McDonald's and Burger King, beef consumption had actually declined slightly in the US, with a per-capita consumption of only around 64.2 pounds per year (about 29 kilograms). But within 16 years in 1976, beef consumption in the United States skyrocketed to an all-time high of about 94.4 pounds per year per person.[14] And between the years of 1970 and 1975, few people in America would not have been able to sing McDonald's 'You Deserve a Break Today'[15] or Burger King's 'Have it Your Way' jingles[16] (embarrassingly, I can still sing them today), as they battled it out for first place in the fast-food world. As brand identity successes, both of these campaigns were nothing short of historic. Of course, there is no way to prove that the massive increase in beef consumption in the US was the direct result of the aggressive marketing wars between these two rival companies during those years, but it sure does make me think.

But *beef* consumption is not the whole story. In recent years, per-capita beef consumption has actually returned to levels similar to what it was in the mid 1960s (whether this is due to the economy or to people becoming more conscious of its link to colorectal cancer is unclear). However, per-capita *meat* consumption, not only in the US but throughout the world, has not merely increased, but more than doubled worldwide since 1961. Furthermore, owing to the population increase over the past 50 years, the total global meat supply has nearly *quadrupled* since the 1960s.[17] Christopher Matthews, of the Food and Agriculture Organisation of the United Nations, explains how this radical increase in meat production is impacting our natural environment:

> Livestock now use 30 percent of the earth's entire land surface, mostly permanent pasture but also including 33 percent of the global arable land used to produce feed for livestock...As forests are cleared to create new pastures, it is a major driver of deforestation, especially in Latin America where, for example, some 70 percent of former forests in the Amazon have been turned over to grazing.[18]

Very few people seem to be aware of the huge differences in the yield between land used to raise livestock and land used to raise crops for human consumption. For example: it is estimated a hectare of potatoes can feed about 22 people a year and a hectare of rice can feed about 19; but a hectare used for beef production can feed only *1 person per year*.[19] I tried Googling the question 'How much land does a cow need to graze?' and found it was sort of like asking 'How long is a piece of string?' It depends upon the cow, the breed and the land. Nonetheless, a safe estimate would be to say a cow needs to have between 2.5 and 5 acres of land to graze adequately. This translates roughly into 1 to 2 hectares. This would mean that McDonald's 6 million cows require somewhere between 6 and 12 million hectares of land on which to graze. While one hectare of beef grazing land can feed only one person per year, that very same hectare could feed around 20 people if we used that land to grow rice or another crop.

This means that while McDonald's are said to be feeding 30 million US customers daily, the same land used by their cows could actually feed as many as *240 million* people every day if used for crop production instead of cattle. In this figure, were we also to include the cows raised to provide meat for other global fast-food chains, the figure would be far higher. If we estimate Burger King's input based upon their stated revenue of $2.5 billion for 2010[20], their land usage would possibly add roughly another 1 million hectares of land, which would feed yet another 20 million people if used for crops. And these estimates do not even include the additional land being used to grow cattle feed for these cows, which, as Matthews cited above, constitutes one-third of our global arable land.

In other words, if everyone simply *stopped* eating fast-food hamburgers (and didn't replace them with an equivalent amount of other beef products), it would make available enough land to grow food for not just the 30 million Americans (or 64 million globally) who frequent McDonald's daily, but a figure closer to the *entire US population* of over 311 million people[21]. We are often told there is a population problem in the world, but when I look at these figures, it seems clear that the problem is not our population. The real problem is that we consumers are biting into our Big Macs, blissfully unaware of how much our passive and ever-increasing dependency upon convenience is depleting our natural resources and ultimately turning our true wealth upside down.

But inefficient food production is not the only imbalance created by our addiction to fast food. It also has a devastating impact upon our climate and the very air we breathe. Livestock production is considered to be responsible for about 18% of the world's greenhouse gasses. That is greater than all the CO_2 emissions produced by *all* our petroleum-fuelled modes of transportation combined.[22] Also, the ever-increasing amount of rainforests being cleared to grow cattle feed creates an even greater imbalance between oxygen and CO_2 in our atmosphere. It also seems quite likely to me that if we continue to feed our addiction to 'fast meat,' we run the risk of widening the gap between poorer and more 'developed' populations, and of causing widespread famine due to misuse of our precious, arable lands.

In all fairness, it should be stated that increased environmental awareness and public pressure has resulted in holding companies like McDonald's more accountable for their actions, and they are creating initiatives for what they call 'improving the sustainability of beef production.' But their public reports would indicate that while they have made significant changes to their packaging to be less environmentally damaging (again, these changes are 'less bad' but not necessarily 'good'), so far much of the work towards achieving true sustainability is still very much in the research and developmental stages.[23] Call me a cynic, but to me making a big deal about changing your packaging to materials that are less environmentally damaging, when your entire infrastructure is inherently damaging to both the environment and the global economy, seems more like a PR move than anything else.

The last imbalance our fast-food consumption creates, of course, is upon our health. The impact of higher proportions of red meat in our diet is a hotly contested issue so I'm not even going to cite the references. Suffice it to say that in one corner you will find many researchers firmly asserting it significantly increases the risk of colorectal cancer, while in the other corner, others (especially within the meat-producing industry) say the evidence is inconclusive.

Whether or not you believe in the link between beef and cancer, there is a myriad of other health issues that must be considered. Industry livestock tend to be fed corn rather than grass, which compromises their immune system. Thus, they are given antibiotics to combat disease, which only compromises it more. And then there is the controversial issue of hormones, which simply did not exist before the dawn of the fast-food restaurant. According to an article in *Science News*[24], as many as 80% of American cows today are injected with both naturally occurring and synthetic hormones to make them grow faster or to produce more milk (the exception, of course, are those farms that maintain a certified organic practice). These hormones include Oestradiol, Progesterone, Testosterone, Zeranol, Trenbolone, Melengestrol and a genetically-engineered hormone called rBGH, or 'Bovine Growth Hormone' developed by Monsanto. These hormones have an astonishing and unnatural impact on cows. One report says, 'While the average dairy cow produced almost 5,300 pounds of milk a year in 1950, today [in 2003] a typical cow produces more than 18,000 pounds.'[25] We humans talk about the stresses that arise from being overworked, but imagine how having to increase production by more than 300% impacts these poor cows. And while it is still a subject of hot debate amongst scientists as to whether or not these hormones have a negative impact on human health, growth, metabolism and reproduction (frankly I cannot see how they cannot), based upon the fact that many farmers report widespread cases of bovine mastitis, hoof diseases, open sores and death from internal bleeding as a result of these hormones[26], there can be no doubt they negatively impact the health and wellbeing of the cows.

And then there is the issue of obesity caused by our ever-increasing caloric intake. According to a report from the World Health Organisation (WHO), our caloric intake per capita from the mid-1960s to the late 1990s has 'increased globally by approximately 450 kcal per capita per day, and by over 600 kcal per capita per day in developing countries.'[27] Their statistics show that the typical food intake of developed nations around 1964 was just over 2,000 calories per day, whereas it was closer to 2,700 by the end of the millennium. They also project that by 2015 we will be ingesting as much as 2,850 calories per day.

Where does most of this extra calorie consumption come from? It's difficult to say, but some studies would indicate that increased meat consumption is a likely place to start looking, along with the increase of sugars, saturated fats and processed foods in general. In the 1960s, the average American consumed a bit over 60 kg of meat a year, but by 2007 the US ranked 2nd in the world with a per-capita meat consumption of around 123 kg per person per year (the UK came in at 23rd with a per-capita consumption of about 85.5 kg).[28] The difference in the US is roughly equivalent to eating 1.5 quarter-pound burgers every day. According to McDonald's, a 'Big Mac' on its own contains 490 calories[29] even before you add fries (about 370 calories)[30] and a Coke (140 calories per 12-ounce serving)[31], so it's pretty easy to see how developing a habit of grabbing a fast-food meal even just a few days a week can result in an increase in both meat consumption and calories that matches these figures pretty closely.

Given the fact that our 'developed' lifestyles tend to be more sedentary (in front of a desk, in front of a TV) and less physical, the health implications of the increased caloric intake seem pretty obvious. Add to that the deterioration of the product, occurring due to the distance required to transport the meat, the fats in which the meat is cooked, the microwaves or infrared heating under which they are kept warm, and really there is very little that can be said for the nutritional, economic or ethical value of what we are eating when we 'have it our way.'

While I'm not attempting to claim the rise of the fast-food industry is directly responsible for this rise in calories, I do believe a significant portion of this caloric increase is the result of our increasing tendency to grab fast, high-calorie, ready-made foods on a daily basis from whatever source, rather than choosing lower-calorie, whole foods that might take time to prepare.

For me, the proof of this is in what those boys carried in their shopping basket at the convenience store that day. That memory is a constant reminder to me.

MARKETING AND THE SELLING OF IDEAS

So how does marketing play a role in all this?

While it is not my intention to single out McDonald's or any other company as 'the' culprit for our environmental and health woes, the rise of fast-food franchises is one of the clearest examples I have found to demonstrate how our lifestyle has been significantly shaped and altered by marketing. When we were invited to 'See the USA in our Chevrolet' in the 1960s, America took to the road. The idea of grabbing something to eat on the way started to become a way of life. Later, we were told we 'deserved a break today' and that we could 'have it our way,' and as more and more women—many of them married with children—moved into the workplace in the 70s, being told they deserved a break (i.e., from cooking) sounded pretty good.

We were sold a promise of happiness: happy meals, happy place, happy, happy, happy. The underlying message we received from such marketing was that eating fast food would buy us freedom and thus happiness. It would give us more time and therefore allow us to enjoy life more. This is the real reason why we buy fast food. When we place our order at the drive-thru, *we are buying freedom*, not hamburgers. I seriously doubt most people go to any fast-food outlet primarily for the food itself.

Remember what I said before about 'collapsed beliefs'? Well, in this case, we as a culture have adopted a completely new pattern of behaviour as a result of a collapsed belief from the fusion of two disparate entities:

Hamburgers = Freedom

Through the marketing messages we have ingested, these two things have become fused (or confused?) in our minds, when in truth they have nothing whatsoever to do with each other. It is this belief, not the food, which has enabled us to accept fast food as a viable option in our diet. And clever marketing is 100% responsible for planting that subliminal belief in our brains.

I have already said this, and I will be saying this many times throughout this book. My point in discussing this topic is neither to demonise any industry, including the fast-food industry, nor to single out a particular company as 'the bad guys.' That would only be continuing to deepen the schism between big business and the rest of the world. The real reason why I have taken the time to examine the fast-food industry is to bring to light one thing—

We are not consumers of products.
We are consumers of *ideas*.

Marketers are not selling us products, but ideas.

When we start to 'consume' the import of that statement, business owners might start to 'do' marketing more responsibly. But even more importantly, consumers will also take responsibility for how they choose to respond to marketing. That's when we'll start to see some big changes in the world.

POWER, IDEAS AND RESPONSIBILITY

> *'All power tends to corrupt,*
> *and absolute power corrupts absolutely.'*
> **~ Lord John Dalberg-Acton**[32]

Being human is all about having ideas. Our ideas are what make us both different from other creatures and different from each other. Ideas are also what make one group of people gel into a community, and set them apart from other communities. Ideas can define us or dissolve us. They attract us and repel us. They bring us together and tear us apart. They can clarify or confuse. They can terrify or inspire.

Ideas are all-powerful.

Although at a superficial level it would appear to be the case, consumerism is not really about the selling of products to make a profit; it is about *the selling of ideas to make an impact.* People do not buy things unless they have first bought the idea behind the thing. When Bernays wanted to influence a generation of young women to smoke cigarettes, his marketing message had nothing to do with cigarettes. Instead, he sold the *idea* of a cigarette as something that would bring a feeling of empowerment to women. When McDonald's said 'You Deserve a Break Today,' they weren't marketing their hamburgers; they were marketing the idea of how it would *feel* to have the McDonald's experience.

Ideas create feelings. When we respond to a marketing message, we are really responding to the feeling it arouses within us. Marketers have known this for at least the past century, if not since the beginning of commerce. Because marketing is the selling of ideas, and ideas create feelings, and feelings impel people to take action, marketing is very powerful.

Before the dawn of modern technology, the power of marketing was limited to the sphere of influence any one marketer could create by means of direct contact with his customer base, and the word of mouth generated amongst them. When the printing press was invented, that power grew immensely. Through print, we were at last able to communicate across time and space to remote markets.

But with the dawn of telecommunications, from radio to television to the web to email to social networking, the power of marketing has become immense. Never before have we been more able to buy—and sell—so many ideas. The world is dancing with ideas in every direction, and we are hungry to test them out. Just log onto Twitter for a few minutes and see for yourself.

Modern marketing is immensely powerful. And with immense power comes immense responsibility. But because some people in the world are prone to practicing immense *irresponsibility*, marketing also has immense potential to go horribly wrong, leading the public down paths of deception that result in our own self-destruction. This is not a melodramatic exaggeration. Later when we explore 'The 7 Deadly Sins of Marketing,' we will look at many ways in which irresponsible marketing creates unnecessary suffering in our world.

But lest we blame our modern woes entirely on irresponsible marketers, let us remember that we as consumers must also be responsible. We are all acculturated by our own consumer lifestyle, so much so that many of us hardly recognise it within ourselves. In the course of writing this book, what I have found so striking—and alarming—is the frightening *dependency* we have developed upon our own consumer culture. We have lost the knowledge and interest to produce our own food and other needs for our very subsistence. If our local shopping district disappeared tomorrow, we'd be baffled as to how to acquire even the barest of necessities for life.

Furthermore, our towns and localities have lost the infrastructure to provide us with those needs. When you walk along your High Street, you're not very likely to bump into your local weaver or tailor or shoemaker who makes products and sells them directly to the public. Being so removed from the source of our sustenance makes us terribly vulnerable. As Charlie Chaplin said in *The Great Dictator*, 'Machinery that gives us abundance has left us in want.'

How much are we *really* thinking about this? How much are we *really* bothered? How much responsibility are we as consumers taking in this important matter? When we upgrade our mobile phone every two years, how much thought do we give to what happens to the old one after it leaves our home, never to be seen again? How willing are we to change our own buying habits for the sake of helping restore balance in the world?

As consumers, we actually have the ultimate power *and* responsibility in this situation. When we change our consumption habits, businesses will change. When we no longer respond to the false needs and collapsed beliefs conjured by marketing, marketers will change. We are not helpless victims of the system. We *are* the system.

SUMMARY: THE RISE AND FALL OF CONSUMER CULTURE

As we progress through these pages together, I hope to be able to convey my belief that marketing is a *relationship.* We all play a role in that relationship—whether as a marketer or as a consumer. Like any relationship, our relationship with marketing (and our economy) takes work and commitment to keep it healthy. If we as consumers remain passive reactionaries in that relationship, we are actually giving marketing the very power we hate most about it—the power to exploit. Making the move from being passive reactionaries means we must open our eyes and become conscious and responsive. Only then will our relationship with marketing be not only resilient, but also healthy and useful to society. Marketing can be one of the most useful creations of humanity if we get it right.

To have healthy relationships with our loved ones, our economy, our society, our planet and our marketing we require *interdependence.* Independence is a myth; dependence is a death-sentence. Interdependence is the only truly supportive and sustainable type of relationship there is. But our present society has become so utterly dependent upon a large, complex and ultimately fragile system that we feel insecure, alone and isolated in the face of it. We shudder at the mention of economic collapse, because we have lost our ability to survive and sustain life itself. We have come to believe we are dependent upon corporations and banks, and this leaves us in a terribly vulnerable state of mind.

But interdependence is an entirely different thing. It means we make decisions based upon thoughtful consideration for how it impacts the whole. It means we feel connected to the whole organism of society, and we understand the vital part we play in helping that whole thrive. The shift towards an interdependent consciousness is just starting to come to the surface in our world. It is neither a revolution nor a retro 'tune in and drop out' throwback from the 1960s; this shift is *integrative*. It is one in which we experience the meaning and depth of our sacred relationship with our society and our world. You might think of it as the ultimate 'permaculture.'

It's a beautiful vision.

And I firmly believe humanity can manifest this vision.

Part Two

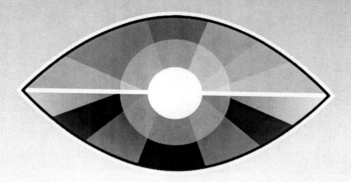

The 7 Key Relationships

Some Words on the
Nature of Relationships

> 'No man is an Island, entire of itself;
> every man is a piece of the Continent, a part of the main;
> if a clod be washed away by the sea,
> Europe is the less, as well as if a promontory were,
> as well as if a manor of thy friends or of thine own were;
> any man's death diminishes me,
> because I am involved in Mankind;
> And therefore never send to know for whom the bell tolls;
> It tolls for thee.'
> **~ John Donne**[1]

Our lives revolve around relationships. Just about every soap opera, drama series, sitcom or major film you can find revolves around the ups and downs of relationships. Pick up a weekly tabloid at the newsstand and see if you can find a page that does not have a story on the rocky state of someone's personal or professional relationship. We are obsessed with relationships, yet we are equally obsessed with the idea of independence. It's small wonder, then, why we see so much conflict in the world. We are continually seeking to connect, but pushing each other away just as strongly. This conflict is not so much due to our failings as human beings, but to our misunderstanding about the nature of relationships. Meaningful relationships cannot exist where there are two independent parties. Our very nature is to be *interdependent* beings in relationship with one another, from personal relationships to global economies to our relationship with the Natural World.

For some, the concept of interdependence might be a bit frightening, thinking it implies the sacrificing of our uniqueness, self-reliance and personal liberties. We have seen the atrocities and violence committed in the past by totalitarianism and extremism, and our value of 'independence' seems to be the only logical rebuttal. But seeing ourselves as islands in the vast ocean of Creation can only result in deepening the alienation, exploitation and marginalisation we already see and feel in our world today.

We do not really seek independence; we seek *belonging*. We do not want to be alone; we want to be valued. Our real challenge at this pivotal point in history is to re-examine our value system, and see that we are naturally interdependent beings. Not only is every other facet of Creation vital to our health, happiness and fulfilment, but we are equally vital to the health, happiness and fulfilment of the rest of Creation.

Interdependence is not at all the same as 'co-dependence.' Interdependence is when we consciously create healthy, sustainable relationships, in which all parties are dedicated to ensuring that everyone and everything within that relationship is thriving. Co-dependency is when the parties within the relationship have become emotionally incapable of living without the other, and are prepared to drain the 'juice' out of the other in order to survive. Interdependence is mutually beneficial and nourishing. Co-dependency is parasitic and unhealthy. Interdependence is sustainability. Co-dependence is self-destruction.

As we said in the previous section, our current global economy has become a co-dependent system. Consumers have become dependent upon big businesses and banks, and big businesses have become dependent upon the consumer and the flow of resources whether in natural, economic or human form. And if these resources are not within their immediate reach, historically both governments and businesses have sought them out at any cost, leading to the pillaging of land and water, the displacement of communities, the invasion of sovereign states and the cultural genocide of many peoples. All this has generated catastrophic imbalances both within our natural environment and global economies. We are stuck in a gridlock that will never take us forward, and can only worsen if not addressed immediately and radically.

Co-dependency is addiction. Like any addiction, the first step in overcoming it is to recognise and acknowledge it. It took me many years to recognise the depth of my own economic co-dependencies, but from the process of my own 'detox' I learned that nothing can control us without our first *believing* we need it (or need to avoid it). In our modern world, there are a great many things we have come to hold as necessary for love, safety, social desirability and happiness that are purely the result of our society developing beliefs around those things. We do not really become dependent upon those things themselves, but upon the *idea* of needing those things. Most of these ideas are intricately woven around what I call 'The 7 Key Relationships': our relationships with Self, Source, others, our businesses, our audience, money and marketing. These relationships impact all of us, both as business owners and consumers. The relative degree of interdependence versus co-dependence within these relationships influences how likely or not we are to 'play' the consumer game in response to marketing.

Because interdependence is the most important element in all these relationships, none of them can be understood in isolation. The state of any one of these relationships also influences the state of the other six. If we heal or harm one of these relationships, it is bound to have a ripple effect upon the others. Once we become aware of how these relationships play out in our individual lives, the addictive gridlock of our co-dependency might start to break down, as we open the doorway to co-creating a new system of interdependent relationships that will not only benefit us on a personal level, but also our communities, our economies and indeed our entire planet.

As we begin our examination of these 7 Key Relationships, I invite you to consider both the current state of your own relationships— whether personal, spiritual or professional—as well as how you would like to change them, and how this shift will impact not only your own life, but also the world around you. In doing so, I believe you will begin to see the power of interdependence, as well as the very important role you play in the healing process of humanity and the planet.

Key Relationship #1: Our Relationship with Self

'But you have hair that is the colour of gold...
The grain, which is also golden,
will bring me back the thought of you.
And I shall love to listen to the wind in the wheat...'
~ **Antoine de Saint-Exupéry**[1]

Our humanity is a miraculous thing, and our lives are intricately woven into the fabric of Creation. Each of us plays a vital role not only within our society, but also within the balance of Nature. Each of us is a unique configuration—a pattern of cells, desires, thoughts, ideas, talents, values, passions, idiosyncrasies and feelings that is singular in the Universe. Our true worth is inherent in the very fact that we exist at all. We are, quite simply, amazing.

But all too many of us today find it hard to tap into that wonderful essence of Self, and instead seek to define our worth by means of external validation. When we are not in good relationship with Self, that validation usually comes in the form of money or the things money can buy. We imbue cars, clothes, cosmetics and other consumer products with the power to make us feel more sexually desirable or socially valuable. And when we believe these things will bring us status and confirm our worth, we will go to extreme measures, spending beyond our means, to feel that worthiness we believe we lack.

Our never-ending quest for external validation can only ever result in debt, economic dependency and feelings of loss and emptiness. Conversely, when we find ourselves absorbed in debt, dependency, loss and emptiness we can almost always trace it back to feelings of personal worthlessness. And when such debt, dependency, loss and emptiness become rampant throughout society, as they are today, we become faced with a pandemic breakdown of our relationship with Self.

Our relationship with Self is pliable, especially when we are young. From 1999-2007, I taught music technology in the further education system here in the UK. The majority of my students were young men between the ages of 17 and 19. Nearly every one of them wanted to be the next big hip-hop producer like P. Diddy or Timbaland. Many of my female students aspired to be the next Beyoncé. These young people idolised these heroes not only for their talent, but also for their fame, glamour and influence. With rose-coloured glasses, they believed a big record label would 'discover' them, great fortune would descend upon them, and the fame they would receive from being a (hugely) successful recording artist or producer would finally make their lives worth something. They aspired to have big cars, big houses and big reputations. They saw success in the music industry as the means to finding a sense of self-worth and respect they felt was lacking in their day-to-day lives.

Sadly, natural talent aside, only a tiny percentage of these students had the long-term drive, self-discipline and self-belief to achieve what they desired. And amongst those who were motivated, rather than taking charge of their future by planning and building a proper music business for themselves, many of them fell into the musicians' trap of continually spending beyond their means and going into debt to obtain the latest equipment or software they had seen in industry magazines, believing these would give them 'the edge.' It was like an addiction with no end, arising from feelings of not being good enough, and from a desperate need to be recognised by others.

What so many of these students didn't realise was that self-worth doesn't come *from* achieving success; it is the only way *to achieve* success. Self-validation is an inner game, and it will never come to us from the outside. If they wanted to find happiness, they needed to be in good relationship with themselves first and foremost. They needed to value and respect themselves at a deep level. I tried my best to instil this message in my students, but with so many coming from broken homes and with the media telling them that fame and glamour made you 'someone,' it was sometimes difficult for them to hear this message above the constant din of consumerism. While several of my students indeed went on to achieve great things in the industry, I watched many others leave the system deeply disappointed and no better off than before.

And when people with little self-belief are continually disappointed in life, they can sometimes become angry and even aggressive. When I served as the head of a performing arts department, I frequently had to address many incidents of bullying, most of them between young women. Invariably the 'bullies' had pretty tough lives. Many were homeless, abused, broke, pregnant (or had had an abortion) and substance-dependent. Several had eating disorders and tended to self-harm. Nonetheless, they were usually adamant in refusing help from me or another adult. Accepting help would be an admission of their vulnerability; their tough appearance was their only protection, a defence learned early in life arising from feelings of being disconnected and helplessly on their own.

The more disconnected from humanity we feel, the more worthless we feel. We humans require a sense of self-value and belonging. And when we don't have it, we will go to any means to obtain it. Combine this disconnection with anger or frustration, and the results can be catastrophic. Back in 1989, people around the world were horrified to hear news reports about 15-year-old Michael Eugene Thomas being strangled to death by a 17-year-old peer for his Nike Air Jordan shoes.[2] Air Jordans, named after and promoted by basketball idol Michael Jordan of the Chicago Bulls, were some of the hottest-selling and most heavily advertised sports shoes on the market at the time. This tragedy started an ongoing media debate about the impact of marketing upon vulnerable youth who suffered from a poor self-image.

But while its connection to Michael Jordan made this the most high-profile case of its kind to that date, we soon found out it was not the first such incident, as we came to learn that urban youths had been killing each other for name-brand sports shoes and jackets since the early 1980s. In fact, we learned that many name brands had become emblems of various inner-city gangs and drug dealers.[3] At first, the public were outraged when they heard that teenagers were being murdered in cold blood for their sportswear, and that commercial brands were being used as 'uniforms' by criminal organisations. But soon, we found ourselves confused as to whom we should hold responsible. Whom could we blame for these atrocities? Sportswear manufacturers? Retail outlets? Drug dealers? Gangs? Parents? Michael Jordan? The whole of society?

Or what about the marketers?

It would indeed be very easy to point a big, self-righteous finger of blame at marketers for creating a glamorous image for sportswear that would attract vulnerable youth. But let's also bear in mind that if we reduce responsibility only to marketers, we're apt to find ourselves stuck in a 'chicken or egg' kind of dilemma. Which came first—the marketing or the mindset? In other words, did the marketing messages *cause* our feelings of unworthiness, or are we as a society capable of creating and reacting to such marketing messages because they are *a reflection of* our own feelings of unworthiness?

What we are facing here is a much bigger issue. The rise of gangs in our modern society came about because large factions of our urban youth felt marginalised and without personal identity. Adopting commercially branded sportswear to mark 'who' you are and who you 'belong to' makes sense in some sad way. When you are part of a broken culture without personal heroes, such as family elders, you adopt heroes from the most ubiquitous and glamorous source—advertising and media.

But while on the one hand marketers cannot control how youth decide to utilise their products, on the other hand it does fall upon the heads of marketers to be responsible not to create a glossy world 'out there' that is likely to trigger feelings of emptiness within our children. As adults, we can collectively start to change the world by shifting our focus away from seeking external validation in our own lives, and by making our relationship with Self our first priority. Our self-worth cannot help but impact our friends, family and all around us. We will inspire our children and students. When our youth learn by example how to be in good relationship with Self, they will not be susceptible to marketing messages that undermine their own self-worth. And when the public stops listening to marketing, marketers have no choice but to change their marketing strategies.

Key Relationship #2:
Our Relationship with Source

The word 'source' with a lowercase 's' has many shades of meaning. It is commonly defined as 'the point at which something springs into being or from which it derives or is obtained.'[2] Other meanings from the same dictionary include 'the point of origin' or 'one that causes, creates or initiates; a maker.' Still another definition describes 'source' as 'a generative force.'[3]

When I use the word 'Source' (with an uppercase 'S') in this text, I shall mean something similar to, but distinctly different from the definitions above:

'Source' is that energy which generates, sustains and regenerates all components of Creation.

Source is not just the initiator, but also the sustainer and the regenerator of existence. We cannot fully understand life without considering the complete cycle of creation, sustenance and dissolution (or regeneration). We can see this for ourselves even in the simple act of composting. By 'components of Creation' I include all things relating to mind, body or spirit, whether tangible or intangible, sentient or insentient. 'Imagination,' for example, is just as much a 'component of Creation' as is granite. Really, there is nothing we can cite that is not ultimately from Source.

I do not wish to complicate the term 'Source' by adding socially conditioned or religious shades of meaning. If you wish to include the concept of God, goddess or any entity whom you consider to be a personal Creator into this word, that is your prerogative of course. My reasons for keeping it simple are practical: regardless of what 'add-ons' we might choose to put on this term, and regardless of whether or not we embrace a spiritual path or practice, we are *all* in relationship with Source by dint of the very fact we exist. Personal belief has nothing to do with the reality of that connection, but it has everything to do with how we express it. When we begin to impose specific belief systems, we lose that all-embracing universality in which everyone is present. While religious differences have caused countless conflicts between us throughout history, our one commonality has been that we are all in relationship with Source, physically, mentally, spiritually and emotionally. Source has no exclusivity.

When we are in good relationship with Source, remarkable things happen to us. We feel loved, connected and supported because we feel the presence of Source everywhere we look. We live and eat according to the rhythms of our planet, resulting in better health and overall wellbeing. We feel a sense of gratitude, because we are aware of Source sending us our sustenance at every moment. We see loss as a natural part of the cycle and regeneration of life. We do not think to exploit Creation or any of its creations, whether sentient or not, because we know we would disturb the balance of life, which is sacred, precious and to be protected. We use only what we need, and do not waste lest we disrupt that delicate balance.

When we are in good relationship with Source, there is simply no marketing or media message on the face of the Earth that could compel us to harm the Planet, or utilise things that break the sanctity of the permaculture of all life. It would be like betraying our parents by robbing them, or betraying our beloved by having a meaningless affair.

But when we see ourselves as separate from Source, everything changes—our policies, our social organisation, our eating habits, our health and virtually every aspect of our lifestyle. And while it does not necessarily mean we become overtly cruel, it does mean we limit our capacity to feel empathy for the Natural World. When we feel separate from Source, we see Creation as an object rather than our beloved. It becomes an 'it' and we come to believe we can own it or dominate it in some way. We become indifferent to the balance of Nature and disconnected from the rhythm of Life. Because we do not step to that rhythm, we become physically and emotionally ill. When we cannot feel the rhythm inside us, we become fearful. When we become fearful, we feel needy and desperate. When we feel desperate, we become defensive. And when we are on the defence, we give ourselves full permission to exploit, use and waste whatever we find at our disposal. Life becomes an 'every man for himself' world. If, in this state, we become powerful in commerce or politics, our own lack of relationship with Source can reap disastrous results for other people and the planet. And if we market from this perspective, we can only exacerbate the problem.

Over the past few decades, big businesses got the message that our current practices are putting our entire planet at risk. Many large manufacturers are making the effort (or at least the show of it) to change. However, the sluggishness of our transition makes me wonder whether this is being done more from legal obligation, or to gain public support rather than from a genuine sense of love for Source. Back in 1977, in the midst of the infamous 70s 'oil crisis,' US President Jimmy Carter said, 'The diagnosis of the US energy crisis is quite simple. Demand for energy is increasing while supplies of oil and natural gas are diminishing.'[4]

In spite of this warning more than a generation ago, or the ever-increasing statistics showing how our petroleum consumption is impacting the environment, there seems to be little *urgency* to our commitment to change as a society. In fact, we are manufacturing and consuming more petroleum-fuelled vehicles than ever, and there are more motor vehicles per licensed driver than ever. According to one researcher, in the early 70s, there were only one million more motor vehicles than drivers in the United States, but by 2003 cars had outnumbered drivers by a whopping 35 million (17.85% more cars than drivers).[5] And although the number of licensed motor vehicles in the United States is reported to have dropped from 250 million in 2008 to 246 million in 2009,[6] this is still 15 million more cars than in 2003. Clearly, people don't really give a hoot. They just want their cars.

In the face of well-publicised environmental concerns and the rising price of oil, many of us will look at flashy car adverts for hybrid vehicles (those that use a combination of petrol and electricity) and we think they're great because they save money on fuel and placate our guilty conscience. Yes, it's true we are now starting to see hybrid and electric automobiles on the market. But today's electric vehicles can only run limited distances before needing to be recharged. They are impractical as there are no on-the-road charging points (although cities like Los Angeles are making plans to put this infrastructure in place by 2020). Of course, unless those electrical charging points are powered by non-petroleum-based energy, they are not truly 'carbon neutral.'

If we are making some progress, it's at a very slow rate and in very miniscule amounts. Hybrid vehicles, often falsely advertised as being 'green,' create the illusion that we are moving ahead, but such stop-gap solutions are only slowing down the degenerative impact we are having upon the environment, not stopping it. And besides, the consumer uptake has been definitely sluggish. In 2009, about 15,000 'alternatively fuelled' vehicles were sold in the UK; of these, a paltry *55 cars* were electric,[7] the other 14,950 or so being various kinds of hybrid cars. In the US, only 2.18 cars sold per 1,000 in 2008-2009 were hybrid cards.[8] My guess is that pure electric cars comprised just a tiny fraction of that.

But even if we completely turn around the automobile industry and manage to have a planet where every vehicle is running on 100% green energy, the very fact that cars are being 'consumed' at alarming rates worldwide is responsible for creating huge environmental imbalances at every step of the process—sourcing raw materials, manufacturing and the frequently overlooked issue of the *disposal* of our old vehicles.[9]

And economically, our addiction to cars doesn't really make much sense either. Over our lifetime, our motor vehicles and all the expenses related to them are probably the highest ongoing expense most of us will ever have. I haven't owned a car for the past twelve years, but between the ages of 21 and 44, I purchased ten used cars and vans. Between the cost of the cars, insurance, license and registration, inspection, repairs and the cost of petrol, my automotive expenses *far* surpassed by several tens of thousands what I paid to buy my current home. And my vehicles were just cheap used clunkers. What about new vehicles? Take a moment to calculate your own lifetime automotive expenses. You might be shocked.

But none of this seems to matter to us. We are hooked. We are hooked on cars. What was a luxury only 100 years ago is now a staple of our lives. We have created a world in which most of us cannot go to work, go shopping or visit friends without a car. Marketing has seduced us into seeing cars as things that are vital to our happiness, our freedom, our sense of status and even our sex appeal.

Back when I lived in Phoenix Arizona in the 80s and 90s, I would sometimes drive 100 miles a day, in 'gas guzzling' vans and other large passenger vehicles, just to 'make the rounds' for my business and my daughter's social life. I shudder to think how much I contributed to the brown haze that used to sit permanently on the horizon over the 14 years I lived there. Life without a car seemed unthinkable. But having now lived quite happily without a car for more than a decade here in England, I can assure you I haven't missed out on anything. In fact, life is happier. I love walking and I speak to more people during the day either when walking or on public transport. My spending habits have changed and my money goes a lot further than it used to. But most of all, my consciousness has changed. Feeling my feet upon the Earth every day has brought me closer to Source. My wants and needs are simpler. I am much more satisfied than I used to be. I cannot attribute all of this to not having a car, but certainly it must have contributed.

If we as a society were genuinely in good relationship with Source, both manufacturers and consumers would hurry up and make the commitment to change our consumer habits now and forever. Our dire situation brings to mind the poignant fairytale by Hans Christian Andersen called *The Nightingale,* in which a simple nightingale became favoured by the King, and came to sing to him every day. Everyone in the court would come to hear the beautiful songs of this plain, brown bird. The fame of this bird spread throughout the land. But then, one day, a smith presented the King with a gift—a golden, jewelled clockwork replica of the nightingale to delight the King and his court. Dazzled by the beauty and sparkle of the clockwork bird, the King wound it up and found it sang a whole repertoire of lovely melodies. The King and the court became so captivated by this mechanical bird, they quite forgot about the real nightingale. Ignored and forgotten, the nightingale flew away. But nobody noticed. They were too enchanted by the songs and sparkle of the golden nightingale.

But then one day, the clockwork bird broke and was suddenly silent. Only then did the King realise his beloved nightingale had flown away. Consumed with grief and remorse, he became ill and took to his bed. News of his illness spread throughout the kingdom, and people feared he would die. Finally, the nightingale heard the news of her King's illness. Full of love, she returned to the court and sang her sweet songs to him, healing him and making him well once again.

Each of us in our modern world is very much like this King. We have become so enchanted with the dazzling nature of our own inventions, that we have lost interest in Source and cannot feel the love it sends us at every moment. In fact, we scarcely notice Source at all. We drive to the supermarket and buy a plastic bag of nicely scrubbed carrots thinking we are buying healthy food, giving no mind to the greater impact of driving, plastic and of eating inorganically grown foods that are out of season. The average Western shopper rejects 'muddy' carrots (those with the dirt still on them) as aesthetically undesirable, having no idea that leaving the dirt on keeps them fresh and nutritious. Every aspect of our lifestyle reflects how very much we have become disconnected from Source.

Our environmental imbalances will never be corrected by government mandates or fear tactics. Nobody likes to be 'guilted' into changing their behaviour. The only true motivator in the world is love. Only when our love for Source is re-established will businesses, marketing and consumer habits change. Source is that energy which generates, sustains and regenerates all components of Creation. True awareness of Self includes Source. When we are in good relationship with Source, we are in good relationship with Self and everything else in Creation.

We live in an era where businesses are the real leaders in our world. To me, it seems clear that the decisions and actions made by big business impact the whole of our society even more than political policy. If this is the case, and if we are to survive as a race, a call to action must be made to businesses—from the sole proprietor to the multinational corporation—to redesign both their operations and their marketing so they are founded first and foremost upon the value of being in loving relationship with Source.

Imagine how much we would change the world for the better by this single, profound shift in perspective.

Key Relationship #3: Our Relationship with Others

Understanding our relationship with other human beings is at the foundation of every social science, whether practical or applied. Psychology, coaching, counselling, education, political science, criminology, anthropology and so many other disciplines that investigate human behaviour all focus on how people interact with one another. But what is most important to remember is that our interpersonal relationships cannot be divorced from an understanding of our relationships with Self and Source. Our opinions and beliefs about others are reflections of our opinions and beliefs about ourselves and the world around us. Just as we feel supported, loved and meaningful when we feel connected to Self and Source, when we feel connected to others, we feel not only these very same things, we also feel the ability to *give* support, love and meaning to others.

And just as when we feel separate and isolated from Source it opens the door to our exploiting it, when we feel ourselves to be separate and isolated from other human beings, we open the door to a whole range of exploitive behaviours. Exploitation and competition cannot exist unless we see ourselves as separate from others. Social values such as property ownership and independence are also by-products of feelings of separation from others. When feelings of separation are highly pronounced, all kinds of anti-social attitudes and behaviours can arise.

A tragic reality about separation is that we invariably come out the 'loser.' I mentioned in an earlier chapter how my grandfather, an immigrant from the Tyrol, went to work in the coal mines of Pennsylvania in the 1920s. My father grew up in deep poverty and, although he went to school, was teased by other children as being 'too black' (owing to his dark olive complexion and being a coal miner's child). The long-term effects of my father's feelings of being separate, different and inferior to others manifested as anger, aggression, violence, delusions and extreme racism. Needless to say, this had a big impact upon his family, friends and life in general.

When we feel separate from others, there is no possibility of being in good relationship with them; when we do not have healthy interpersonal relationships, it becomes a disease that gets passed down from one generation to the next. Separation from others in its most extreme form can result in dissociative disorders and other psychoses. Criminologists know that those who perform acts of extreme violence can only do so because they are incapable of empathising with their victims as fellow sentient beings.

Sometimes, whole societies can suffer from the disease of separation. It manifests in the form of radical nationalism, fanaticism, racism, imperialism or any other form of behaviour in which the notions of 'us' and 'them' have become the only means for them to feel safe from the 'outside world.' Seen from this perspective, at its roots, the terrorism we witnessed in the first decade of the 21st Century was very much the result of extreme feelings of disconnection one culture had towards another. Disconnection at that level causes societies to see each other as homogenous generalities, rather than rich, diverse collections of individual souls. 'The West' is seen as one big evil, and so is 'The Middle East,' depending upon on which side of the fence of separation you happen to be standing.

But because the ultimate problem is disconnection, no amount of warfare, economic sanctions or political posturing will solve the problem. While they may address our immediate need for safety and survival, in the long-term our attempts to fight aggression with aggression only serve to *feed* the original misconception that we are separate from one another. Thus fed, warfare reinforces the reasoning of both perpetrator and defender that the other party is the 'enemy,' and only helps us justify engaging in yet more violence.

You might not see the immediate connection between these examples and marketing, but a connection is indeed there. Whether we are marketers or consumers, each of us has a *fundamental relationship with others* that colours all our perspectives, decisions, values and actions. As marketers, when we see others as separate from ourselves, they become depersonalised and generalised. They cease being individuals and turn into numbers, demographics and statistics. When we communicate with people from this perspective, we cease speaking to people's hearts and minds, and instead choose words, images and messages for the purpose of inciting and normalising their reactions. And while on a 'scientific' level it definitely works (i.e., people do react; people do buy), if we are to begin the process of re-integration in our world, we have to ask whether or not this science is working for us as a race, and whether we wish to continue practicing it in our marketing.

When we see ourselves as separate from others, we are limiting both them and ourselves. We reduce our ability to see clearly the individuality of Self and Other without judgement, and thus we narrow the range of our vision overall. When we see ourselves as separate, we inevitably begin to compare ourselves. And when we compare, we begin to compete—not necessarily because we enjoy the competition, but more likely because we feel ourselves in need of external validation that comes by way of the experience of 'winning.' But winning comes at a great expense, for the end result is that both parties are measured solely by external properties that have nothing to do with their intrinsic worth. Our sense of self-worth becomes ephemeral, as does the worth we attribute to others. When we market from that perspective, we are not only undervaluing our customers and clients, but also our so-called competitors. But most of all, we are undervaluing ourselves.

As consumers, we often fall prey to myopic marketing messages that 'target' us as an audience with certain vulnerabilities rather than unique values. In fact, the messages themselves might not only be preying upon those vulnerabilities, but *creating* them through emotional manipulation. Many of the things we believe we need in order to be 'whole' in some way, are frequently the result of marketing telling us these things are a part of our value system. It stands to reason, however, that these messages can only impact us if we do not truly know ourselves or our place in the grander scheme of Life. If we are in good relationship with ourselves and Source, we are far less susceptible to such manipulation.

No matter at which end of the marketer-consumer continuum we are standing, the truth is this:

- Our treatment of others is always a reflection of our relationship with Self and Source
- Only when we are in good relationship with Self and Source can we also be in good relationship with others
- When we feel separate from Self and Source, we will also feel separate from others
- When we feel separate from others, we will tend to defend, exploit, manipulate or compete
- When we defend, exploit, manipulate or compete, we are projecting our own underlying feelings of worthlessness, isolation and lack of support

Therefore, if we wish to change the impact of marketing from exploitation to support, our first line of work—both for marketers and consumers—is to re-establish our relationship with Self and Source. Then, we may start the great work of loving others as ourselves, and we will work for the happiness of others; this is when the real changes begin.

We cannot continue to create a world in which any human being—or any living creature—is seen as a statistic or demographic to be influenced and bent to our advantage. You will hear me say this again and again: life is holistic. Our relationships are holistic.

Our relationships with Self, Source and others are not separate. Heal one and you will also feel the ripple effect in your other relationships.

Marketer, first heal thyself!

And then, proceed with the knowledge that if we wish to be happy in life, the most reliable course of action is to contribute to the genuine happiness (not profits) of others.

Key Relationship #4:
Our Relationship with our Businesses

Business owners—from sole proprietors eking out a living to those who head multinational corporations grossing billions a year—are no different from any other human being. They suffer the same pains and joys as any other person on the planet. They breathe the same air. And ultimately, they feel just as dependent upon the same economic system as everyone else in society.

But what makes business owners different from non-business owners is that they have another relationship in their lives that needs care and attention, and which greatly impacts both their lives and the lives of others—their relationship with their business. I had never really thought about this concept until I read Michael Gerber's classic guide for entrepreneurs *The E-Myth Revisited* some years ago.[2] In that book, Gerber explores not only the relationship between entrepreneurs and their businesses, but also the 'life purpose' of a business, although that phrase is my own interpolation of Gerber's intention. For something to have a 'life purpose' it stands to reason it has to be alive. We've already looked briefly at how our businesses are living entities, going through all the cycles of life—conception, birth, growth, propagation (i.e., generating products, ideas, sales, etc), decline and, ultimately, death. And in order to have meaning, every living entity, including our businesses, needs to have a 'life purpose,' a *raison d'être,* a reason to exist.

Many people who have studied Indian philosophy are familiar with the Sanskrit word *dharma.* I have seen it often translated as 'duty' but my own personal understanding of the word is different. The root of the word is *'dhri'* which means 'that which holds things together.' To perform one's *dharma* means to do that which holds life together. Water has a *dharma;* the Earth has a *dharma;* we humans have a *dharma.* While you might call this 'duty' I prefer to translate it as 'life purpose.' The *dharma* of water is not merely its 'duty'; it is what it does according to its Divine nature. Its *dharma* is to flow, to quench, to nourish, to cleanse, to freeze, to warm, to cool and to be one of the essential building blocks of life. The *dharma* of the Earth is to be the Source, the shelter, the sustenance and the point of dissolution and regeneration for all life forms within her proximity.

What then is the *dharma* of Man?

Probably every self-help book on the market has addressed this question, whether explicitly or implicitly. While it is not the aim of this discussion to define the *dharma* of mankind, I will say this much about it: we know we are living our *dharma* when we feel a powerful connection to ourselves, our work, other people and our world. When we are thusly connected, our *dharma* indeed becomes the force that holds things together. It becomes a thread in the fabric of Creation.

BUSINESS AS DHARMA

My personal belief is that our businesses exist to provide us with a vehicle for, and a mirror of, our *dharma.* You can notice this especially when business owners pass away. Take as an example The Walt Disney Company, which after the death of founder Walt Disney in 1966 (followed not long after by the death of his brother, Roy O. Disney, in 1971) went through decades of upheaval and identity crises to such a degree that, in 2003, Walt's nephew (Roy E. Disney, son of Roy O.) said it had become 'a rapacious, soul-less' company.[3]

While these are very strong words, few who watched the transition that took place in The Disney Company between the 1970s and the end of the 20th Century would disagree that it had changed radically in character. Surely, some of that change was due to the natural shifts in societal tastes and trends over time, but I do believe it was equally due to the absence of Walt's consciousness. The original company was the outward expression of one man's vision and life purpose. Remove the man with the purpose, and you remove the purpose for the business. When our businesses are aligned to our true purpose, they take on a life and identity of their own that reflect our own consciousness. When they are not, they become 'soul-less' profit-making machines that can be handed over to anyone else with business sense and enough capital. You might call this a kind of 'dharma franchise.' You can easily sense the difference between a 'dharma franchise' and a business that reflects a true dharma.

THE DOUBLE DHARMA OF BUSINESS

While a business might be a reflection of the personal dharma of a specific human being, there is also an overall dharma of businesses in general. The ultimate life purpose of any business is not to make a profit, but rather to *foster the flow of currency and goods throughout society*. Without the flow of money and goods, society will go as stagnant as a pond that has no rainwater to wash it clean. But profits are not enough to ensure flow. If our aim is solely profit-driven, we are not necessarily contributing to the greater flow of currency, as we may cause that money to become glutted in one corner of our world without much movement.

At the other extreme, if we take the high moral ground and are *not at all* concerned with money in our businesses, we are also contributing to economic stagnation. This is the mistake many 'spiritually' minded new business owners make. They intuitively sense there is something not quite right about profit-driven businesses, but they make the error in thinking that making a profit is the problem. It's not. Putting personal profit ahead of greater economic responsibility is the problem.

In either case, if business owners do not work with the aim of helping money flow easily and continually through our society, serious imbalances can occur resulting in poverty, widespread debt and false economies. If we view our businesses in isolation from the rest of society, we might be addressing our personal *dharma*, but we are not fulfilling the *dharma* of being a business owner. The ultimate purpose of a business is to *serve our economy*, not our customers, our shareholders or ourselves. Thus every business is alive, and has a dual life purpose—a *'double dharma'*—that of its creator/owner and that of society at large.

OUR RELATIONSHIP WITH THE DHARMA OF OUR BUSINESS

As our businesses are living entities, we have a relationship with them. And just like any other relationship, it can be healthy and life-giving, or dysfunctional and life-stealing. When we regard our business as a 'thing' that is separate from us, it is impossible for us to activate the *dharma* of that business. When we do not see it as a beautiful entity that has incarnated to co-create something with us, it becomes merely an object that serves the few and not the many. When a business creates products and services from this perspective, you can sense *dharma* is missing.

When external advertising companies are hired by such a company, capturing a genuine connection to the *dharma* of that company in their marketing campaigns can be challenging if not impossible. Thus, we have today a vast body of marketing that succeeds more by dint of the cleverness of the marketing itself, than from the essence of the company, products or services. When *dharma* is absent, advertising become an exercise in reinforcing brand identity rather than communicating intrinsic values. The fact that the majority of marketing messages we hear every day come from this place is a clear reflection of how disconnected we have become from our own businesses.

At the other end of the spectrum are the small-business owners, who can speak for hours about their values and life purpose, but somehow cannot convert these values into the exchange of currency. These 'nice people who hate marketing' often have a sense of altruism that blinds them to the *double dharma* of their business. They can see the 'life purpose' of their business inasmuch as the value their services will provide, but they cannot see the bigger picture of the value their *business* will provide. While they detest greed and materialism, they often fail to see that making their business profitable not only allows currency to flow, it also enables them to create jobs so others can thrive as a result of their success.

Because of this thinking, many small-business owners make the mistake of waiting too long to bring staff (whether outsourced or employees) into their company. Back in my 'starving artist' days, I also made this error. As a result, I was always in an economic rut, continually living from hand to mouth. But once I started hiring staff to help me run my business, money actually flowed in faster and came in larger quantities.

If you remember back when we talked about the *varnashrama* system, we said the mercantile class is the 'digestive system' of the social body. In order to function properly for society, business requires both regular feeding (income) and elimination (spending). If a business serves only our personal *dharma* but not its social function (its *double dharma*), it has failed in its purpose, as it is not contributing to the flow of wealth in society.

BEING IN GOOD RELATIONSHIP WITH OUR BUSINESSES

The health of business in our world depends not only upon business owners, but also upon every member of society. Not only must business owners be in good relationship with their own businesses, but everyone must also be in good relationship with business as an integral part of our social system.

We business owners must see and relate to our businesses as living entities, and treat them with all the care and respect due to another living being. We must not only see clearly our own life purpose or *dharma*, but we must also be able to express that *dharma* through our businesses. And then, we must also ensure our businesses serve the greater *dharma* of business by contributing positively to the economic flow of currency in society. Lastly, we must ensure that every aspect of our marketing is congruent with the *double dharma* of our businesses.

As consumers, we have an equally important role to play. We must first come to understand the nature of our relationship with business as a consumer. We must ask ourselves whether we ever feel resentful, disempowered, separate, victimised or cynical about business in our world. If so, we must then ask ourselves what impact this is making not only upon our own lives, but upon the rest of society. We must ask ourselves how much we believe in the greater *dharma* of business, and how we are helping to support the actualisation of that *dharma*. We must ask ourselves how actively we are setting boundaries for what we are willing to accept from businesses or not. We must ask ourselves how we as consumers can help influence businesses to be more *dharma-driven*.

If business is the 'digestive system' of society, fighting against it is self-destructive. It's like going on a starvation diet. The only way for that digestive system to be healthy is for life-giving substances to flow freely in and out. If we wish to have a truly enlightened world, it must include our businesses. We must come not only to love our own businesses, but the institution of business in general. We must care for it and protect it, and allow it to flourish and fulfil its greater purpose.

Business has a *dharma* to fulfil. We are not really business owners or consumers; we are the stewards of that *dharma*.

When business is what the world calls it to be,
it will set the world on fire!

Key Relationship #5:
Our Relationship with our Audience

> 'My conception of the audience is of a public each member of which is carrying about with him what he thinks is an anxiety, or a hope, or a preoccupation which is his alone and isolates him from mankind; ...I regard the theater as a serious business, one that makes or should make man more human, which is to say, less alone...
> the prime business of a play is to arouse the passions of its audience so that by the route of passion may be opened up new relationships between a man and men, and between men and Man.'
> **~ Arthur Miller**[1]

> 'The play was a great success but the audience was a disaster.'
> **~ Oscar Wilde**[2]

The language of marketing is a strange jungle of confusing and seemingly contradictory terms. On the one hand we speak about our 'audience,' referring to those people we believe will be interested in our products or services. The word 'audience' implies that these people are willing participants in the 'play' of our activities. They are watching us. They are paying attention to and are interested in what we do. It implies we have some sort of reciprocal relationship with them where we perform and they express their appreciation or displeasure.

But actually, in traditional marketing, that's not really the case. Most of the time people are NOT paying attention, and the whole challenge for us marketers is to find ways to get people to turn around and look at us. Therefore, the world is not our 'audience' at all. They haven't paid any money to come see us perform. When people sit down to watch TV it's highly unlikely they are thinking, *Oh boy, I'm really looking forward to watching the adverts tonight!* no matter how creative those adverts might be.

And so, because our audience is not paying attention to us, we invent the term 'target audience.' We aim at a particular audience as though with a weapon. We use the crosshairs of age, gender, location, economic status, educational status and so many other demographics to focus our aim. When we have our prey within our line of vision, we shoot them with Cupid's arrow of intoxication, triggering their emotions in such a way as to build desire—desire they might not otherwise have had without our intervention. If taken to extremes, the whole idea of a 'target audience' can turn into as much of an oxymoron as the term 'friendly fire.'

That the language and ethos of marketing seem to mimic that of warfare is not a new observation, and it has been the topic of many articles and books on the subject, including the iconic *Marketing Warfare* by Al Ries and Jack Trout.[3] Terms like 'target audience,' 'marketing campaign,' 'launch,' 'conversion' and even 'guerrilla marketing' are all subtle, but revealing, indications of the nature of our *relationship* with our customers. 'Marketing warfare' means our customers are not so much a willing audience as they are populations to be invaded and converted to our way of thinking. As Ries and Trout shared back in 1986:

> The true nature of marketing today is not serving the customer; it is outwitting, outflanking, outfighting your competitors. In short, marketing is war where the enemy is the competition and the customer is the ground to be won.[4]

As consumers, we frequently find ourselves stuck in the cross-fire of a psychological battle between warring 'nations' (i.e., competing companies) where our hard-earned cash and brand loyalty are the prizes up for grabs. Here's an analogy to illustrate how this happens: Imagine for a moment you are a child listening to your parents arguing every night. Day in and day out, they have the same argument over and over. You are small, but they are big and loud and you can't shut them up. All through the shouting match, you are taking it all in, but the messages seem to contradict one another, and you don't really know what to think or believe. You feel 'on edge,' confused and at a loss to know whose judgement to trust. As you grow up, you end up annoyed with both parents equally, and you don't feel inclined to side with either one. Nonetheless, consciously or not, you have mentally taken a position in the argument, even if you don't say it aloud. Depending upon which parent you 'sided' with, you might unconsciously adopt some of their values, opinions or behaviours as your own. Alternatively, you might become so fed up with both of them that you turn into a rebellious teenager embracing a completely different set of values to either parent.

Of course, there is always the possibility that you sit peacefully unperturbed amidst the battle, mentally sending love to both parents, transcending the entire situation. But in reality, such a thing is rarely seen. When children are exposed to continual aggression in the household, it almost always results in some sort of negative impact. They might grow up to have emotional issues around trust, abandonment or commitment. They might have nervous problems, anxieties or anger issues. But they are also most likely to find it challenging when called upon to exercise their powers of discernment when faced with important decisions, because throughout their lives they have constantly been told one thing whilst seeing another.

Now, let's apply this analogy to marketing.

Consider the position in which we find ourselves when we as consumers are caught in the 'battle' of some of the most famous 'wars' in marketing history, such as the great 'Cola Wars' between Coke and Pepsi, the 'Burger Wars' between McDonald's and Burger King and of course the 'Computer Wars' between Microsoft and Mac (all described by Ries and Trout across several chapters in *Marketing Wars*). Just like the child passively listening to the back-and-forth counterpoint of the parents' arguments, television viewers are also stuck in the cross-fire of the battles of competing companies. Like the child, we dislike hearing all the constant squabbling, but we have no power to shut them up completely because these ads are just so ubiquitous. At least a child can go to school or his friend's house for some relief; the consumer, on the other hand, has little respite, being subjected to the same battles on TV, radio, newspapers, magazines, billboards and, now, the Internet.

Like the child, we find ourselves reacting as we start to lean towards a particular brand over the other. But there is so much 'arguing' coming from both sides, we find it difficult to keep up or make an informed decision on which is truly the best brand to choose. Our powers of discernment become blurred, as we hear all kinds of mumbo-jumbo features, statistics and benefits of whatever product we are being fed to consider. The marketing triggers our emotions even without our being aware it is happening. Eventually, either we choose one brand over the other, or we become so fed up that we switch off and attempt to detach ourselves from it altogether.

But what is even more incredible, is that this battle is going on with multiple brands of multiple types of products, day in and day out. It's not just 'Burger Wars'; it's car wars, pet food wars, beer wars, toothpaste wars, shampoo wars, supermarket wars, music wars, home improvement wars, cosmetic wars, life insurance wars, airline wars, film wars, deodorant wars, breakfast cereal wars, candy bar wars and you-name-it wars. Nor is it just two battling 'armies' in each war, but dozens of different brands all aggressively competing for our loyalty. And on top of all that, the very media (radio, television, magazines, newspapers) sponsored by these brands are equally vying for our attention.

No wonder there's so much talk these days about attention deficit disorder.

For many years, that was the scenario of television marketing. But over the past two decades, the relationship between mainstream marketing and consumers has changed. Consumers are no longer a completely captive audience but more of a 'moving target'[5] by dint of the introduction of the remote control device and, more recently, digital television. We not only have the option to channel surf during ad breaks, we now have the option to record our programs without any advertising whatsoever.

As the relationship between marketers and their audience changed, marketing itself also changed. It had to. As technology provided consumers with more choice as to how and when they would 'consume' marketing, marketers had to become more creative, visually glossy and entertaining. They had to learn how to create advertising that would keep us watching and would stick in our brains long after we switched off. But this 'stickiness' meant we were now being increasingly influenced by how much we *enjoyed the marketing* itself and less and less by the merits of the product or service being advertised, only serving to blur our powers of discernment even further.

A perfect example of this is the recent 'Chrysler Eminem' advert used in the 2011 Super Bowl broadcast. The ad is a series of images of the 'Motor City' of Detroit, over music by native Detroiter, Eminem. As Eminem drives his sleek, new Chrysler through the city streets, a narrator talks nostalgically (and with attitude!) about Detroit. It is indeed a brilliant piece of cinematography. But it is also a brilliant piece of theatre, as it plucks the heartstrings of the audience via images and references to both the Great Depression and the recent recession, transparently aiming to stir up feelings of both national and local pride. One reporter described his own reaction to the advert:

> Overall, the ad is an astonishing work of art and one of the best television commercials ever made, a mini-documentary about the history and current personality of a region...This ad hit me like a poem and a prayer with perfect pitch. You know how some movies get rated with two thumbs up? This commercial gets two fists up for a city that can still pack a punch.[6]

It does beg the question, however, 'But is the *car* any good?'

Ok, you might ask, 'So what's so bad about that? What's the harm in making Americans feel proud of their country and Detroiters feel proud of their local industry?' This question can only really be answered by looking at the relationship between the advertisers and the audience. Playing to an audience's emotions is a vital part of theatre, as cited above by the late, great American playwright Arthur Miller. But Miller's view of the relationship between theatre and audience is that it should be mutually beneficial to both parties. The role of the playwright is to provide a mirror of emotions common to all human beings, for the purpose of feeling a greater connection to one another and the world in which we live. Reciprocally, the role of the audience is to feed back to the playwright as to how effectively he is communicating these emotions. The impact of art is dependent upon this mutual relationship between artist and audience.

But when theatrics are used in marketing, they cannot possibly create the same effect unless *the relationship* between marketer and audience is the same. But it's not. The intention of the marketing piece is not to create art for art's sake, but to influence people to buy a product. To that end, the audience is the intended 'target' and the 'weapon' is the manipulation of their vulnerabilities. When this is the case, theatrics become a mere smoke screen for the actual intention.

Manipulating public feelings of national or regional pride is called propaganda in politics. I'm not sure we have a word for it when it's used in marketing. I've interviewed several Americans about this particular advert, and most of them say watching it makes them 'feel good.' After all, the US automotive industry has been going through a lot of turmoil since the 2008 recession, and this advert evokes heroic feelings of national pride. But come on! Let's get real, Slim Shady. Buying a Chrysler might help the Chrysler Corporation but it is doubtful it will rescue the American economy. It will not make you a Detroiter or show you are patriotic. And it definitely will not make you tougher, cooler or a famous rap artist. Chrysler wants you to spend your money on their cars. End of story. I'm not saying that's a good or a bad thing. I am saying that's the *only* thing. And if we've bought into the 'feel good' factor of this advert, it only goes to show how effective the advert is. We've become, as they say, 'hooked.'

Bernays would have been impressed.

But times are changing. As we step more deeply into the era of social networking, the relationship between marketer and consumer is transforming. Customer feedback, interaction and 'multiple screens' of contact not only mean marketers need to be more transparent and direct, but also that consumers now play a bigger role in determining what they are willing or unwilling to accept. In other words, our audience is now becoming an actual 'audience' and not merely passive receptacles of our images and words. And that's a good thing. By opening up a dialogue, marketer and audience can become allies rather than predator and prey. Together they can direct the future of commerce so it gives society what it actually needs, instead of what marketers *tell* society it needs.

Every time technology becomes more complex, the impact of marketing significantly increases. Print was more impactful than word-of-mouth, radio more impactful than print, television more than radio, and the Internet more than television. But now, social media has reconfigured that impact yet again, offering both marketers and consumers the chance to take equal responsibility for the relationship between them. It takes two to have any relationship, and both marketers and consumers are equal players in the game of commerce. In today's world, our moral obligation as marketers can no longer be just about profits, but rather about the care, respect and nurturing of our relationship with the public on a global and holistic level. And as consumers, our role must be to provide the checks and balances in the system by letting marketers know how well they are doing, either in words or through our consumer habits.

No longer can marketing be seen in a vacuum, but rather as a vital element of our social experience. Making that experience something of value can only arise when the relationship between marketer and audience becomes actively co-creative. With that in mind, I would like to offer my reworking of Arthur Miller's eloquent quote above as it might apply to marketing, as we progress towards a better relationship between us:

I regard marketing as a serious business, one that should make us feel more human, which is to say, less alone, and which arouses the genuine passions of its audience in such a way that strong, new relationships are forged between each person and the rest of humanity, and between humanity and the Planet on which we live.

Key Relationship #6:
Our Relationship with Money

I n his book *Walden*, 19th Century American Transcendentalist Henry David Thoreau wrote an extensive chapter called 'Economy' in which he candidly shared his personal opinions on the economic state and attitudes of modern society, as well as a detailed account of how he made the shift from 'civilized' life to create a simpler life in the woods on Walden Pond. In that chapter, Thoreau skilfully demonstrated that by living simply and sustainably, he was able to produce not only the same income he had made in his former lifestyle, but also a house in which he could live without rent or debt for the rest of his days should he choose. To Thoreau, possessions were not the mark of a person's success, but a weight, a trap, a burden which take away our freedom. He pitied *both* those who were born into wealth, for the fact that they can never break free from the shackles of their property and possessions, as well as those who labour or are poor, because they suffer from the burden of their desires to attain these very same possessions.

I can only concur with Thoreau's sentiments about humanity. I have coached many people who had a lot of money and status, but who suffered from the greatest anxiety over losing it. They often hid their fears, emotional vulnerabilities and financial challenges from others, fearing other peoples' judgement or cut-throat competition.

Thus they were never able to tap into a support network when times got rough. They often felt trapped by their situation, and saw no clear path back to their own happiness.

At the opposite extreme, I have known people who lived in abject poverty throughout their entire lives, especially when I lived and travelled in India. My first extended stay in India was in Calcutta in 1980, during the days of Indira Gandhi. The level of poverty one sees in a city such as Calcutta is unfathomable to most Westerners, and it is often difficult to know how to respond to it. When Westerners walk through the city streets unescorted, they are approached almost continually by beggars. These beggars are born, grow up, breed, raise their children and die on the city streets. Most sleep out in the open; a few lucky ones make huts of straw behind the storefronts. Many are visibly diseased or deformed either from birth defects or accidents. Many of the beggars are children—scruffy, dirty, undernourished and pitiful.

When I first came to India, I noticed that most Calcuttans walked past the beggars without even noticing them. Very few stopped to give charity, and they would often get angry if accosted by a beggar. I wondered why this was the case. When beggars first approached me in Calcutta, it was very difficult to define my emotions. I had feelings of compassion, pity, fear, horror and guilt all rolled up into one. I would give my spare change to them, thinking they would say 'thank you' and that would be the end of it. But then, as I lived and walked on these streets over many months, many of the beggars to whom I had given money would seek me out every day, asking for more and more. If I didn't, they would get angry and start shouting at me. Over the months, I realised my charity had made no visible impact upon their situation and that their requests for money never ceased.

Over time, I began to feel anger, just like so many of the native Calcuttans felt. I felt exploited by beggars. I found these to be difficult emotions to resolve, considering their indisputably dire situation. Guilt and anger became fused into resentment and blame—at myself, at the beggars, at the Indian government, at the world. I didn't like feeling this way, and couldn't figure out how it had happened to me.

When I returned from India the first time, I stayed at my parents' home on Long Island for a few weeks. This house in which I had been raised, which had always been so familiar to me, now seemed like an alien planet. The wall-to-wall carpet, the massive colour TV, the tidiness, the neatly trimmed lawn, the refrigerator full of food all seemed surreal and beyond my understanding. I felt no more at home there than I had in India. I felt just as angry there around all that comfort as I had in Calcutta surrounded by poverty. I was confused. I felt alone. But at age 25, I was as incapable of expressing my culture shock as I was of understanding it.

It was the first time the world had challenged me to look at my relationship with money. And although I returned to India several times over the next 20 years, it would take me longer than that to step up to the plate to accept that challenge and finally understand why I felt what I felt.

MONEY CAN'T BUY YOU LOVE

In 2001, when I was still living in London, a female friend of the family came along with us on one of our trips to India. We had planned on a 6-week pilgrimage to different spiritual sites across the northern part of the subcontinent. Because so many of these sites were off the beaten path for Westerners, we asked a temple musician we knew from the Punjab to be our travel guide. Our friend was also Punjabi (although she had never before been to India as an adult, having lived most of her life in the UK), and enjoyed conversing with our guide in their mother tongue as we rumbled along the dusty roads in our rickety hired car. A week or so into our journey, our guide brought his three young children to travel along with us to see some of the holy sites, while their mother stayed at home back in their small village. His children were beautiful, and genuinely adorable, and they became close to all of us, especially to my then-17-year-old daughter and our Londoner friend.

Our friend had a very soft heart, and was prone to shower those she loved with gifts. Spending money on others was one way she showed her affection. After some weeks of travelling together, our friend began to see our travel guide as her big brother. She said she felt like an 'auntie' to the three children and said she wanted to help the family financially, as they were too poor to give the children a good education. The family all lived together in a tiny single room, which could hardly be called an 'apartment.' Our travel guide worked as a metal box maker, and his earnings were around a meagre £60 per year. Feeling a great sense of pity, after we returned to the UK, our friend arranged to send the family money to pay for tuition to send the son to a good school.

But over the coming months, the children's mother began to put pressure on her husband to ask for more and more money. Having opened the Pandora's Box, our friend found it difficult to refuse these requests. Over the span of a year, she maxed out her credit cards with cash advances to the tune of £32,000 (about $50,000). Having this amount of money in India is like being a millionaire. Eventually, we heard through the grapevine that the musician was building himself a house—more like a small mansion with expensive marble floors—with the money our friend had given him. In the meantime, our friend went broke and lost her own house in London as they had run out of money to make the mortgage payments. Worst of all she felt deeply betrayed, unloved and painfully foolish.

But the story doesn't end there. As the temple musician became wealthier and wealthier, his behaviour changed completely. His sweetness and approachability vanished and he became pompous and vain. He came to the UK in 2002 with a travelling *kirtan* party (religious congregational chanting), acting like a celebrity with no time for those who were originally his friends. Later that year, I returned to India and met him at a festival in Uttar Pradesh. I asked if we could have a private talk about his taking so much money from our mutual friend. I wanted to explain the depth of financial hardship this had caused her family.

At first he was adamant and defensive, saying, 'But she *wanted* to give me this money.' But after some time, he broke down in tears, as he could no longer maintain his hardened exterior. He wept, saying this money had become a curse. He said his whole town and temple community were gossiping about him. It had caused arguments between him and his wife. His children now expected things they had never wanted before. He said he wished he had never accepted the money. He said he wished he could sell his palatial house, give back all the money and go back to his simple way of living. But he gave the excuse that his wife wouldn't have it. He said he had come to realise she had secretly never respected him in the past, because he never made enough money to support his family above poverty level. She was impressed with his ingenuity for finding a willing patron who would take care of them, and now if he tossed it all away, he feared his wife would deride him and his children would hate him for putting them back into poverty. What's more, the whole town would then come to know the truth about how he got his unexplained riches, and he would be disgraced forever. He would have nowhere to go, and would lose everything and everyone in his life.

He cried bitterly, saying, 'I thought this money would bring us happiness, but it has ruined my life.'

Then, after several minutes, he seemed to have a change of heart. He became quiet, sat up straight, dried his tears and announced with conviction that he was going to sell the house and give all the money back. He was willing to face the ramifications of this decision, no matter what they might be. But although he sounded quite determined, I was unconvinced.

To my knowledge, this has still not happened.

THE MYTHS WE CREATE ABOUT MONEY

I'm telling these stories to demonstrate the many ways our relationship with money not only affects our behaviour, but also influences the way we see ourselves and the rest of the world. The key to understanding our relationship with money is that it has nothing to do with how much money we actually have. Rather, it is determined by our *beliefs about* money. Many of us carry around an unconscious belief that our financial wherewithal has some bearing upon our personal worth. When our relationship with money is tied to our personal worth, we will inevitably feel like a failure if we think we do not have 'enough' money, whatever 'enough' might mean to us.

To compensate for this horrible feeling of being a failure, many of us create yet another myth—the myth that there is a connection between poverty and spirituality. In other words, we make up the story that having money is antithetical to being spiritual, good or virtuous, etc. But this belief in 'spiritual poverty' creates a great irony, because it makes us feel like failures *whether we have money or not.*

At the end of his chapter on economics in *Walden,* Thoreau inserts the poem, 'The Pretensions of Poverty,' by 17th Century English poet Thomas Carew[2], which is a critique of the attitude that poverty gives us a 'moral and intellectual superiority'[3] over those who have money. Having been part of many spiritual communities in the past, I have seen this attitude many times; most people I have seen speaking from this perspective are invariably stuck and suffering in their poverty, and are frequently resentful and bitter towards the rest of the world.

Another group who commonly demonstrate this attitude are creative artists. The idea of the 'starving artist' is really just another type of 'spiritual poverty' and is an expression of this same paradoxical relationship with money. The exaltation of the starving artist, who never 'sells out' might on the one hand be an expression of artistic integrity, but it is also frequently a compensation for feelings of shame, failure and social alienation. Having romanticised my own starving artist status for many decades when I was a freelance musician, I speak from personal experience.

Conversely, when we feel we are spiritually or artistically unworthy *because* we have money, we are really just facing the other side of the same coin. The belief of 'spiritual poverty' drives us to feel guilty when we believe we have 'more than enough' money, whatever we believe 'more than enough' to mean. When you combine this 'I have more than enough' guilt with a poorer person's 'I don't have enough' shame, you have a recipe for exploitation and crime, where the less financially endowed in society feel entitled to get their share, whether by out-and-out theft, economic dependency or social welfare, which only reinforces the gap between the so-called haves and have nots, and leads to increased distortions in our relationships with money.

Our ideas of 'not enough money' and 'more than enough money' are defined by our personal and cultural relationships with money.

And these relationships are defined by two things: our beliefs about ourselves and our beliefs about what money represents. In the story of the temple musician, we see a complex web of different relationships with money coming into play—our friend, the temple musician, the musician's wife, the temple, the local community, all had different relationships with money that informed their opinions and their behaviours. But all of these relationships revolved around a connection between money and self-worth. This is another example of a 'collapsed belief.' And as we have seen, collapsed beliefs can be very damaging.

When we fuse 'money' and 'self-worth' together, whether we believe we have 'enough' money or 'more than enough' can influence how we feel about our own lovability, social status, respectability, competence, goodness, intelligence, integrity or spiritual advancement. When self-worth is tied to money, we might feel we need to give money to others in order to be 'good,' 'lovable' or 'virtuous'. Conversely, we might feel entitled to take money from others without earning it because we judge them to be 'spiritually inferior' for having money. Or, we might judge ourselves as worthless because we don't have money, and become depressed, unmotivated and resigned.

The bottom line is this: no one is happy—neither rich nor poor—when their sense of personal, social or spiritual self-worth is fused with money.

HOW WE INHERIT OUR MONEY GENES

Just like all relationships, our relationship with money starts in our parental home. My parents were teenagers during the Great Depression of the 1930s. Both grew up in relative poverty. My mother left school and went to work at age 14 to help support her single mother and younger brothers. My immigrant father grew up in the coal mines of Pennsylvania. The eldest son of five children, he took his first job at the young age of 8 making deliveries for a local vegetable vendor. He made 5 cents a day, and was allowed to take home whatever slightly wilted or over-ripe vegetables other people didn't buy, so his mother could make dinner for their family.

My parents frequently spoke about the coming of World War II with some degree of nostalgia, as the symbolic demarcation between their impoverished upbringing and a better life. Suddenly, there were jobs to be had and money to be earned. After the war, there was the G.I. Bill, which not only helped to finance ex-soldiers through their education, but also enabled them to obtain mortgages for homes at interest rates that were so low as to be nearly non-existent. But the memory of poverty in early life left an indelible imprint upon both my parents, for as I grew up in the Baby Boomer generation, the pursuit of financial security was drummed into me by both my parents as being of such great importance it eclipsed nearly everything else.

But the context of my upbringing was completely different. I grew up virtually without economic 'lack' in that my father made adequate money to support the whole family. We always had food, clothes, housing, education, recreation and holidays. My parents bought a new car (for cash, I might add) every four years like clockwork. I was 'programmed' by the age of 5 that I would be going to university to pursue at least a Bachelors degree.

Our family were not by any means wealthy, but our material quality of life was good. My parents were never in debt, but they also never had a real surplus of wealth. In spite of this, however, there was an undeniable underlying current of economic fear in my family. To talk about money was taboo in our household. It was almost as if talking about it would put a curse upon us. Whenever I innocently asked my mother how much our new car cost or how much my father made at his job, she would just say, 'Oh...enough.'

Over time, I came to recognise that my parents' early upbringing had established a relationship with money that was largely fear-based. Working at a job was not seen as the means to happiness and fulfilment, but to survival and financial stability. Thus, when I was in my teens and expressed the desire to pursue a career as a musician, I was told it was an irresponsible choice and that if I 'must' go into music I'd have to study to become a music teacher instead. Any kind of entrepreneurial pursuit was viewed as risky, and the only truly secure path in life was to find employment with a large company—one with a good pension plan. Working for a well-established company was seen as the only responsible economic choice.

We don't just inherit our eye and hair colour from our parents. We also inherit their belief systems around money. You might call these belief systems our 'money genes.' And if I analyse my own family history as a case study, it is quite clear that I (along with probably millions of other Baby Boomers) inherited some very striking money genes from my parents:

1. **That money was hard to get,** and if you pursued happiness instead of money, you were likely to be poor your whole life
2. **That money was hard to keep,** and if you took any financial risks in life, you were bound to lose money
3. **That without employment, you were economically vulnerable,** and the only 'safe' course of action was to be employed by a big company/corporation
4. **That without education you were not employable, and therefore economically worthless** because education and qualifications were the only way to attract big, rich companies to hire you
5. **That when you grew old, you would be helpless and poverty stricken** unless you had a pension from these big, rich companies

What is so shocking to me about my money genes is that in spite of the emphasis upon the acquisition of money in my parental home, these beliefs contain not one single positive message about our *relationship* with money. Every message says 'Caution!' 'Play it safe!' and 'Stay in the box.' They say, 'Don't be creative or independent. It's too risky.' They say, 'If you don't play by the rules, you will suffer.' They say, 'Loss is inevitable.' They say, 'Your worth is determined by how well you fit into the system.'

It's really small wonder why the hippy generation came about. It was merely as a rebellious response to this conditioning. The Baby Boomers rejected the values of the 'older generation' as being too materialistic and restrictive. The problem, of course, was that our generation was a ship without a rudder. We might have rebelled against our parents' anxiety-riddled relationship with money, but we didn't have a model with which to replace it. As a result, we were the generation that became dependent not so much upon big corporations, but upon big banks—in the form of credit.

My daughter's generation inherited their money genes from my generation. Taking on much of the financial 'lostness' of our generation, they were pretty much born into their parents' debt. It's really not all that different from patterns of familial abuse or addiction. Just as dysfunctional family relationships tend to get passed from one generation to the next, our ancestral relationships with money also get passed down through the generations, until someone finally wakes up and understands what's actually going on.

OUR DYSFUNCTIONAL RELATIONSHIP WITH MONEY

Imagine for a moment if money were a person with whom you had a romantic relationship. Imagine waking up every day fearing the loss of that love, and feeling their love was 'hard to get.' Imagine believing you need that hard-to-get love in order to be safe, thus becoming emotionally dependent upon it. Imagine your lover continually assessing your worth according to your achievements, which drives you to work harder and harder to gain their approval. Imagine becoming increasingly dependent and desperate to hold on to that relationship, fearing that without it you will find yourself old and helpless, ultimately to die a miserable, lonely death.

If this were a relationship with a human being we would call it 'dysfunctional' and possibly even 'abusive.' A healthy person would not hesitate either to improve or to end such a relationship. Why then do so many of us walk through life tolerating this abusive relationship with money? Why do we rarely, if ever, question it? Why do we not see the impact this relationship has not only on us, but also on our children? Why do we not notice how it impacts us collectively as a society? Why do we not think it is our relationship with money that is at the root of our global economic problems?

I think the answers to these questions must be given in two parts.

The first reason is because most of us are probably *unaware* of our relationship with money. We know how that relationship makes us feel, but we don't realise the extent to which we are giving it power and control over who we are, what we do and how we behave. The second reason is because we have let money dictate the course of our lives for so long (including when we are rebelling against it), we have begun to see it as 'bigger than we are.' We see it as an immense force beneath which we feel insignificant, powerless and without any real choice. When this happens, we become resigned and hopeless.

When we are both unaware of and resigned to our situation, we become exceptionally vulnerable to being controlled by others and programmed for failure. A dysfunctional relationship with money limits our choices and goals in life, and is the primary reason why so many creative, spiritually-minded and sensitive people have difficulty starting and succeeding in their own businesses. They might have many dreams and passions, but beneath it all they are still carrying around the 'money gene' that starting their own business is just about the most selfish, irresponsible and risky thing they could ever do. It is self-indulgent. Their families will starve and they will bear the brunt of the guilt for it when their venture goes belly up.

Even if they do start a business, these same people tend to quit early in the game as soon as the going gets rough, not so much because they are 'bad' at business, but because when they experience the inevitable start-up setbacks, they fear they have made a fundamental error in starting the business in the first place. Some fail because they worry that if they make money it will make them appear insincere. Subliminally, although probably not consciously, they believe society is not designed for people like them to succeed.

OUR RELATIONSHIPS WITH MONEY AND MARKETING: THE CONNECTION

As consumers, if money becomes our unconscious abuser, we become susceptible to being 'infected' by all kinds of marketing and media messages addressing our stability and safety. Insurance (home, car, life, health, pets), credit ratings, mortgages, banks, investments companies (the tax department!), etc., are all industries that flourish upon our fear of loss—especially loss of money. If our money gene ties money to our sense of social or sexual self-worth, we might feel the need to spend on more expensive 'luxury products' for the purpose of making us feel we are 'worth it' or to gain some sort of imagined credibility in other people's eyes.

As marketers, we face a tremendous challenge and responsibility, because we are *both* marketers as well as consumers. We are both vulnerable and powerful when it comes to money. This can be a deadly combination unless we evolve to a very high level of personal awareness and moral strength. Being in this position, we of all people must be especially aware of our relationship with money. If we enter the arena as marketers without that awareness, we become vulnerable to the temptations of our own powerful position, and are unlikely to be able to understand our own motivations. Furthermore, if we fail to take responsibility for the impact we create through our messages, we may become prone to exploit the vulnerability of others who are less aware, by preying upon their fears. However, when we become aware of not only the vulnerabilities of others, but also of ourselves, we might begin to develop a more holistic and compassionate approach to marketing, in which a keen sense of social and moral responsibility underpins our intentions.

MOVING TOWARDS A NEW RELATIONSHIP WITH MONEY

Of all our human creations, money is the one that often evokes more emotion than any other. A piece of music might move us to tears, but our emotional relationship with money can impact nearly every life decision we make. Our relationship with money can influence whom we choose to marry, where we choose to live, what we choose to do for a living, how we choose to dress and how we raise our children. It can be the fuel of many heated arguments between families, friends, businesses and governments. Our relationship with money can drive us to be the most obsessive of misers, or the most generous of philanthropists. Our relationship with money can create both peace and war. And our relationship with money also determines how we spend it, as well as how we obtain it from others.

It is not money itself that creates these things, but our relationship with it. Money has no magic powers other than those with which we endow it, both individually and collectively. Back in the early 16th Century, Sir Thomas More wrote about man's relationship with money (in this case, silver and gold) in his book *Utopia*. In his mythical society, silver and gold were used to forge chamber pots, shackles for prisoners and ornaments to identify criminals.[4] This, he thought, would change Man's desire for silver and gold, as they would come to be associated with shame and imprisonment rather than with glory and power. Of course, the logical argument I see to this is that if their relationship with the *idea* of wealth did not change, the Utopians would sooner or later replace silver and gold with something else that served the same purpose (just look at how much we value credit cards today).

It simply isn't enough to reprogram our associations with and beliefs about money—we have to change our emotional relationship with the idea of money, so we can begin to relate to it in a different way. Here's my idea for what that might look like:

Money is a convenience we created to make it easy to share things of value.

This new definition removes the negative emotive impact, opening up many possibilities for shifting our relationship with money:

- **If money is a convenience,** it is not a necessity. If we do not view it as a need, we cannot become co-dependent upon it
- **If we created money,** we are the masters of its destiny and not the other way around
- **If money makes things easy,** it shouldn't be hard to get or keep
- **If money is for sharing,** it is meant to move and flow. It is not the natural state of money to be hoarded or amassed
- **If the purpose of money is to share things of value,** our values must always be our most important focus

How different would both our marketing and our consumer habits become if we adopted this new relationship with money? How different would our lives and world in general become? Like Sir

Thomas More, I can only imagine such a world with great hope and faith.

But I do believe we humans can create such a world.

Key Relationship #7:
Our Relationship with Marketing

J ust like all of the Key Relationships mentioned thus far, we have a relationship with marketing whether we recognise it or not. Whether we are marketers, business owners or consumers, we all have a relationship with marketing. This relationship especially impacts the way we think about and respond to our economy. And just like any other relationship, our relationship with marketing can be healthy and life-giving, or dysfunctional and life-zapping. In my observation, there are basically three types of dysfunctional relationships we can have with marketing: passive, aggressive or resistant. Conversely, there really is only one kind of constructive relationship we can have with marketing: co-creative.

THE PASSIVE RELATIONSHIP WITH MARKETING

The passive relationship is where we 'just take it all in' without much conscious thought. The 'freezers' mentioned earlier in this book have a passive relationship with marketing. When we have such a passive relationship, we put up no effective resistance against the subliminal messages marketers want to plant in our minds. It doesn't necessarily mean we are attracted to everything we see advertised; nor does it mean we are even completely aware of the information we are downloading. In fact, if we were more aware, we'd probably not want it to take up so much space in our brains. We become tolerant of marketing to such a degree that we accept all kinds of hype, deception and annoyance we would probably never tolerate in our personal relationships with friends, family or colleagues. We become the compliant receptacles of information we don't really need or want. We might even say we become 'programmed' or 'brainwashed' to believe certain 'facts' that may or may not actually be true. Traditionally, this has been the position of the average consumer in our modern world, although with the dawn of social media this is beginning to change, but only just.

THE AGGRESSIVE RELATIONSHIP WITH MARKETING

For every passive relationship, there is a corresponding aggressive one. When marketers play the role of the aggressor, they see the consumer as 'the ground to be won'[2] and they utilise whatever tactics they need in order to win the consumer. When marketers have an aggressive relationship with marketing, marketing becomes economic warfare. It becomes a competition where everyone pulls out all the stops and the ends justify the means. While they may not out-and-out lie, their version of the 'truth' often becomes a bending of reality to suit their purposes.

Consumers can also have an aggressive relationship with marketing when they become activists who protest, and sometimes wage media 'warfare,' against specific marketing campaigns or products. While this might seem to be part of the necessary checks and balances to keep marketers on the straight and narrow, in terms of long-term effectiveness, it is not a whole lot different from a family row. It might result in winning legislative victories and putting new policies in place to bring more ethics into marketing and packaging, but it is simply treating the symptoms and not the actual cause of the problem. It does little if anything to help us create a healthier relationship with marketing.

THE RESISTANT RELATIONSHIP WITH MARKETING

The third 'dysfunctional' relationship we can have with marketing is 'resistant.' At a consumer level, a resistant relationship is when we are aware marketing messages are impacting us in a way we don't like, but we don't do much more than complain and avoid them. Although we resign ourselves to the presence of marketing in the world, we attempt to remove ourselves from being exposed to it as much as possible. The resistant consumer often has an emerging awareness that marketing is making him ill, but doesn't yet know how to utilise that information. To give an analogy, the 'resistant consumer' is the channel surfer during commercial breaks and the 'passive consumer' just leaves the adverts playing while waiting for their TV show to come back on the screen. Of course, the resistant consumer might also practice 'marketing abstinence,' which is not watching television or reading newspapers and magazines at all. But as marketing is simply so ubiquitous, short of moving completely off grid and into isolation, total marketing abstinence is hardly likely in the modern world.

Many small-business owners also find marketing to be abhorrent and therefore develop a 'resistant' relationship with it. I already spoke how creative artists, spiritually minded and holistic professionals often fall into this category, but these are by no means the only kinds of people who have a 'resistant' relationship with marketing. These people do all they can to avoid having to do marketing, even though they know it is necessary for their business to succeed. They feel powerless at the idea of marketing themselves, and justify all the reasons why they don't, won't or can't do it.

A resistant relationship with marketing doesn't do anything to make marketing any better, and it can destroy a small business. Let me give you an example of resistance in action. Back in 2007, when I was writing *The Garden of the Soul*, I received an email invitation to attend a weekend seminar in London on the topic of running a non-fiction book launch. The presenter was an American marketer who had created bestseller campaigns for some of the top-selling self-help books on the market. The lecture theatre was packed with over 200

British coaches and holistic therapists, all aspiring self-published authors.

While the first day was pretty much a rehashing of things I already knew, the second day was packed with new, useful information. I was excited by it. But the rest of the audience were not quite so smitten. During the Q&A sessions, the audience gave the presenter a lot of flack, claiming her marketing strategies were too 'aggressive' and too 'American.' During the breaks, I stood around sipping my herbal tea, listening to what other people were saying. The vast majority of them, mostly new coaches, resisted the marketer's presentation entirely, saying things like, '*I* can't do things like that. *I'm* not that kind of person. *I'm* not a salesperson. Well, if *I* did what she's saying to do, my clients wouldn't trust me anymore,' and so on. And then, I heard many of them say, 'It's because she's American. *We* don't do that sort of thing here in the UK.' Little did they know a Brit-American was standing right next to them (my British accent can be pretty authentic when I'm in the right environment).

While the content of the seminar was very useful, I found the banter between this highly experienced American marketer and the roomful of British coaches and holistic practitioners to be positively fascinating. The Brits surely *knew* marketing was essential to their businesses, or they wouldn't have come to the seminar. Nonetheless, most of them loudly pushed away the information during the seminar, and then colluded in the corridors during the breaks to reinforce their resistance.

I do not believe it was a simple case of American versus British sensibility. As I am both American and British, I think this was simply a rationalisation. Rationalising is typical when we are in a resistant relationship of any kind, including our relationship with marketing. It's tantamount to denial. I believe it was much less a cultural divide than one of mindset: the 'spiritual poverty' mindset discussed in the previous chapter. And as we said, 'spiritual poverty' is a collapsed belief wherein anything to do with money is seen as being antithetical to spirituality. This collapse can extend to marketing as well. When it does, we will have a resistant relationship with marketing, tending to push it away rather than work with it. Resistance can destroy a business.

I admit that the presenter at this seminar wasn't very 'Brit-centric;' nor was the way she expressed her ideas very 'coach-centric.' But unlike so many of my colleagues in the audience, I saw no need to throw the baby out with the bathwater. I could see through the limitations of the presentation, and recognise a science behind the presenter's methods that could be harnessed and reinvented to create marketing strategies that were congruent with my own style and personal values. Instead of pushing back, I simply reinvented it. I started to see marketing as a creative adventure rather than a necessary 'chore' in my business.

Looking back, that was the moment I moved from being in a resistant relationship with marketing to a co-creative one. And this shift in my relationship with marketing—from dysfunctional to functional—had a massive impact upon my business.

THE CO-CREATIVE RELATIONSHIP WITH MARKETING

A co-creative relationship is one in which all parties are actively aligning and inventing their relationship together. In coaching we use the concept of co-creation all the time. No two relationships with our clients are the same. If they were, we would not be infusing our clients with choice or allowing their brilliance to shine.

By nature, a co-creative relationship requires interaction. Passivity, aggression or resistance cannot produce co-creation. In marketing, one aspect of co-creation means there is a clear dialogue between a business and the consumer. As social media and blogging continue to grow and become a part of our daily lives, such dialogue is becoming increasingly possible. Consumers can feed back to businesses in ways they never could before. They can express their likes and dislikes, their approvals and objections, and generally help keep companies on their best behaviour. This alone is already changing the face of marketing, and if it continues to evolve, the passive-aggressive relationship of marketing will eventually become a thing of the past.

But if marketing is truly to evolve, co-creativity must extend even further. Resistance to marketing must change into empowered co-creation. Marketing can no longer be seen as a 'thing' or an 'action' in isolation, but as something that has a life of its own, which is woven into the fabric of our society. Marketing makes an impact, just as art makes an impact. If marketers and business owners approached marketing with the kind of relationship an artist has with his canvas, we might begin to feel differently about it.

When our relationship with marketing is co-creative, we will see that what we create is not merely an advert, but an experience and an expression of values.

We will understand the importance of taking responsibility for these experiences we create, and these values we express.

We will learn that marketing is a powerful creative force that cannot be disrespected or taken lightly, lest it go terribly wrong.

We will begin to see ourselves in a different way.

We are not just marketers; we are messengers. The substance of our message has the potential to change the world.

We will begin to see that marketing is not a job, but a sacred responsibility.

With this in mind, and much as we did when we spoke about money, let us now try on a new definition for marketing, stripping away the dysfunctional trappings of the past:

Marketing is the act of communicating we have something of value to share.

- **If marketing is an act,** we will understand that it begins and ends with us, and requires our full attention and conscience
- **If marketing is communication,** we will focus not only on what we are saying, but on what consumers are saying to us
- **If marketing is about value,** we would never consider marketing things people do not need or want
- **If marketing is about sharing,** our genuine aim would be to give, not gain

Imagine a world where this kind of marketing permeated our business ethics and practice. Such a world would have immense possibilities.

Of course, to find a path to any new destination, it's always useful to have a map, as well as information about detours and road works that might lie ahead. And with that in mind, we now enter the territory of 'The 7 Deadly Sins' and 'The 7 Graces' of marketing.

Part Three

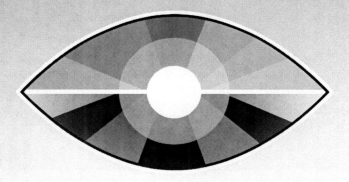

The 7 Deadly Sins of Marketing

Some Thoughts on the Use of the Word 'Sin'

'Define your terms...
or we shall never understand one another.'
~ Voltaire[1]

My first encounter with the word 'sin' was when I was transferred into a Catholic school at the age of seven. The first story I heard about it was, of course, the story of the Garden of Eden, which is said to be where 'sin' originated—the aptly named 'Original Sin.' To my seven-year-old mind, the whole notion of Original Sin seemed horribly unfair. I couldn't understand why I had to 'toil by the sweat of my brow' simply because Adam and Eve had taken a bite of an apple. But none of my teachers seemed to be able to tell me what the big deal was. Later, when we kids started to hit puberty, the word on the street was that 'Original Sin' was just a euphemism for Adam and Eve 'getting it on' back in the garden. But I still wasn't buying it. I couldn't understand what kind of intelligent God would put two people together, all alone and naked in paradise (with not a heck of a lot to do), and then get all bent out of shape because they had sex. To me, this explanation made God sound either naïve or sadistic. Why did He create two genders anyway? Was he intending to propagate the human race, or was that just a happy accident caused by Adam and Eve's 'oops' moment? No, nobody's explanations made sense to me, and by the time I was 12 years old I had rejected the entire concept. Since then, I've hardly ever used the word 'sin,' even when speaking about moral and ethical issues.

149

Nonetheless, I have chosen to use it as the springboard for the concepts we are about to explore; for it is the very fact that this word is so controversial, and that it seems to evoke such powerful emotional responses from so many people, that makes it such an appropriate term.

The word 'sin' infers a belief in the existence of good and evil, or right and wrong. It also requires the existence of 'judgement.' When we call something a 'sin,' we are judging the thoughts, words or deeds of others—or of ourselves—to be bad, wrong, destructive or evil. Judgement always requires us to become separate from the thing or person we are judging. There is no way to judge something if we do not place ourselves above, outside and away from it. Some people call this 'objectivity,' and most people seem to believe objectivity is a good and essential thing. Judgement is a *measurement* against a scale of value we have created in our own minds. When we judge something as sinful or not, we are measuring the relative worth or goodness of something or someone against that scale. And when we do this, we are also in effect measuring ourselves.

In ancient Sanskrit, the word for this measurement is *maya*. In common popular culture, the word *maya* is frequently translated as 'illusion,' 'delusion' or 'infatuation.' Etymologically, the word *maya* means 'not that' (*ma* + *ya*), and in practice *maya* means 'the act of measuring.' When we say something is 'not that,' we are measuring it against something else we are using as a point of reference. Even when we say something as basic as, 'I am a woman, and he's a man,' we are saying, 'He's not that thing I am using as a point of reference' (i.e., myself). We are making these kinds of instantaneous judgements every moment of our earthly existence. The next time you go into town to do your shopping, take note of how many measurements you make within a mere 60 seconds. How many times per minute (or even within a single second) do you assess someone to be the same or different from you in terms of gender, age, size, beauty, etc? How many more ways do you unconsciously assess as desirable or undesirable the clothes, bodily figure, face, hair, jewellery, etc., of other people when you pass them in a public place?

Author Malcolm Gladwell wrote about this very topic in his eye-opening book *Blink*.[2] His point in writing this book was to show how we humans do not always 'think through' our judgements of the world around us or even base them upon rational thinking. Rather, we quite often sum things up in our minds in a split second. Sometimes this can be a good thing because it allows us to tap into our intuitive powers, or respond quickly to a situation that requires us to do so. But other times it can lead to snap judgements that are not only based upon our preconceived assumptions of the world around us, but also upon our beliefs about *ourselves*. How many times a day do you find yourself assessing your own worth or lack of worth when making these snap-second measurements of other people? For example, when you pass someone on the street, you might unthinkingly say to yourself, 'I'm taller, shorter, thinner, fatter, prettier, not as pretty, richer, poorer, younger looking, older looking, etc.,' than that person. Then, if you happen to catch yourself making such judgements, you might criticise yourself for making these judgements in the first place. You might say things like, 'you're so insecure' or 'you're so critical of other people' or 'you're not a very nice person,' etc. Life becomes a mental ping-pong game where we are continually being bounced back and forth between judgements of others and ourselves.

If it seems like we are swirling in a seemingly relentless whirlpool of judgement, we sort of are. In Indian mysticism, the material world in which we live is considered to be the world of *maya*—the world of measurement. When we begin to measure things (i.e., judge them), we become plunged into the attitude of *maya*. When a living entity becomes enthralled by *maya*, it takes birth within the material world, not really as a punishment, but as a means to be able to carry out its *desire* to measure things. Our earthly experience can be said to be *maya* because everything we observe is based upon our own measurements.

But all these measurements are based upon two fundamental errors. The first error is the belief that we are separate from what we see around us. It is impossible to measure something unless we assume the perspective of being separate. The second error is that matter is seen as something 'concrete.' We can only measure something if we believe it has predictable, definable properties. To measure something, it has to have 'thingy-ness.' But both mysticism and modern quantum science tell us that both of these beliefs are flawed, and that when we make any kind of judgement from the perspective of these two erroneous beliefs, all of our subsequent conclusions will also be flawed.

Some spiritual teachers say this world of measurement is nothing but an illusion, and is hence ephemeral. And while that might be true, I believe this material world is *maya* not necessarily because it is actually an illusion, but because we in this material world have adopted the state of mind where we have embraced the *attitude* of measurement. In other words, WE are the ones who create an illusory world of relative truths as soon as we say, 'I am not that. That is not me.' We have created this world of *maya* through our judgements.

Quantum science would seem to support this idea. One thing that makes it so different from classical physics is its fundamental principle that the presence and influence of the observer must be considered in any observation. In other words, there simply is no way to 'measure' the world 'out there' because *we* are a part of the very thing we are trying to observe. The other principle of quantum science is that matter doesn't really 'exist' but it appears to do so as the result of the influence of Consciousness and Will. In other words, matter appears to exist because of our desire to observe it. Particles of matter become measurable only by dint of our desire to measure them.

In the same way, we feel ourselves to be separate from Source *only* by dint of our desire to *be* separate. The Absolute is immeasurable. It is beyond any measurements of time and space. It possesses no 'relative' qualities of big/small, old/young, black/white, etc., we might ascribe to it. The Absolute is all possibilities at all times and in all places. If it were not, it would not be Absolute. The moment we say 'I am not that,' we have placed ourselves outside the One, the Whole, the Absolute. We have rendered ourselves finite and temporary. The moment we say, 'I am not that,' we have begun to make judgements, comparing ourselves to everything around us, and have adopted the belief that we are observers on the outside looking in, or inside looking out. When we place ourselves outside the Whole, we feel lost, helpless, fearful, inadequate and alone. And when we feel lost, helpless, fearful, inadequate and alone, we lose our sense of direction, and believe it is 'fair game' to exploit the world around us, in order to protect ourselves. And when we give ourselves such permission, whether consciously or not, we have stepped into the arena of what might be called, for lack of a better word, 'sin.'

'Sin' then is the behaviour that manifests when we are disconnected from the Whole—from Source—and which fosters even greater disconnection. Sin is the *symptom* of our suffering, not the cause. Crime is not the cause of social discord. Greed is not the cause of corruption in business. Rather, they are the symptoms of a fundamental disconnection from Spirit. To say that 'greed' is the cause of corruption is simply to pass the blame upon those whom we perceive to be 'greedy;' but this, too, is also a judgement. And any judgement we make, even if it seems necessary at a practical level to maintain social order, only deepens the fundamental spiritual disconnection between Man and Man, and between Man and God.

The ultimate result of this attitude of separation is grief, fear and feelings of helplessness, individually and collectively. Our illusion of separation is woven into the very fabric of our manifested world. If there is such a thing as 'Original Sin,' I believe it refers to this fundamental error: that we believe we are separate from Creation and Creator, whoever or whatever that might be.

It is from this belief in our separateness that all suffering and conflicts arise. 'Sin,' 'evil' and 'greed' are not the real disease of existence. The real disease is Disconnection—the first of the 7 Deadly Sins we shall examine. We *all* suffer from this disease, to one degree or another. Manmade judicial systems and regulatory laws might put a bandage on the societal wounds we create, but they will never heal them. Only when we feel one with, and inseparable from, Source do we cease to exploit the world around us.

The only cure for Disconnection is Reconnection.

It isn't mandatory to believe in God or any kind of deity to come back to this state of Reconnection. The Universe is surrounding us at every moment and there is no dearth of pathways back to Source, all of them valid. While we may or may not believe it, we live in an impartial Universe that is equally compassionate to all.

If you think we've strayed way off-topic here, wondering how this could possibly have anything to do with business or marketing, I assure you it is at the very foundation of it. In fact, it is our tendency to measure and put everything into nice, neat categories that has most likely been preventing us from looking at business and marketing in this more holistic way.

As we begin our discussion of 'The 7 Deadly Sins of Marketing,' I invite you to read not only with an open mind, but also with a willingness to consider a different way of looking at marketing, and indeed the world around you. The purpose of exploring these 'sins' is never to point the finger of blame on anyone, but to illuminate how our pandemic feelings of Disconnection have resulted in many assaults against our planet and our own Divinity. Let us not use this paradigm as yet another tool to measure and judge, but rather as a map to lead us to discover the many layers of dust clouding our consciousness. And when we learn to clear that dust, we will at last see the world—and ourselves—more clearly.

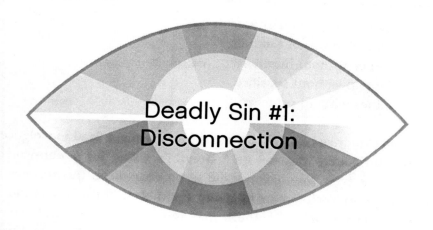

Deadly Sin #1: Disconnection

> *'A person cannot do right in one department whilst*
> *attempting to do wrong in another department.*
> *Life is one indivisible whole.'*
> **~ Mahatma Gandhi**[1]

One day in 1946, an eager, young 12-year-old boy came to live with his elderly grandfather.[2] He had moved in so he would be able to sit at his grandfather's feet every day, gathering all he could from his grandfather's wisdom before his elder departed from the world. Over the two years they spent together, the boy had learned many important things from these daily lessons. But during one particular lesson in 1948, his grandfather wrote down a list of seven short phrases on a piece of paper and handed it to him. As the boy read these bold and stirring phrases, he was probably too young to realise these words were meant not just for him, but for the entire World. And almost surely, neither of them would have suspected how soon their time together was to come to an abrupt end, thanks to the well-aimed bullet of a zealous assassin.

I am, of course, talking about the great, non-violent activist Mahatma Gandhi. Shortly before his assassination in 1948, Gandhi is said to have given his grandson, Arun Manilal Gandhi, a list he called 'The Seven Blunders of the World':

1. Wealth without work
2. Pleasure without conscience

3. Knowledge without character
4. Commerce without morality
5. Science without humanity
6. Worship without sacrifice
7. Politics without principle [3, 4]

It was Gandhi's belief that these seven blunders 'lead to violence'[5] and will ultimately 'destroy us'.[6] Gandhi's vision for a non-violent world was holistic. Non-violence did not merely mean the absence of wars, crime and political or religious squabbles, but a way of life in which we 'live simply so others may simply live.'[7] He understood there was no way to fix any of our social, economic or political problems without looking at the whole picture. Nothing could be viewed in isolation; every thing and every person on this planet is connected, and every action and decision we make has an impact upon the entire system. When we walk through life believing we are disconnected, there can be no stability in our economy and no peace in the world.

And for all these important reasons we start our discussion of 'The 7 Deadly Sins of Marketing' with 'Disconnection.' As we shall see as this book unfolds, Disconnection is at the root of all the subsequent 'Deadly Sins' we shall examine later.

While Disconnection is at the foundation of all of Gandhi's 'seven blunders,' with regards to the topic of this book, the ones of particular relevance are 'science without humanity' and 'commerce without morality' (or 'business without ethics' as Stephen R. Covey calls it in *Principle-Centred Leadership*[8]). And truly, in our technological era, you cannot really separate the two, because in many ways science and technology have pretty much created the state of present-day commerce.

EVIDENCE OF OUR DISCONNECTION

Sometimes we look at the world around us and just have to wonder how we allowed ourselves to get here.

We wonder how we have arrived at a tipping point in our history where our CO_2 emissions are in excess of 30 billion metric tonnes per year.[9] We wonder how our rainforests, which some say are responsible for generating anywhere between 20% and 40% of our planet's supply of fresh oxygen[10, 11] and which are virtual treasure troves of biodiversity and natural medicinal resources[12], are rapidly being wiped out by big industry. We wonder how we have come to accept the fact that our global military spending is an estimated $1.6 trillion per year[13], while millions of people around the globe have inadequate water, nutrition, housing and education. How did we create this place?

Our wonderment can be answered in a single word: Disconnection. While having become problems in and of themselves, these issues are actually the symptoms, not the cause, of an underlying social disease—the disease of Disconnection from both our Source and our humanity.

Disconnection is a worldview, a cosmology, in which we perceive ourselves and all the components of the Universe as separate entities. While we know we have an impact upon each other, we do not fully see the integrative and interdependent nature of our relationships with people, our economy and the planet. We imagine we can control our destiny by sheer will, and most of our actions are directed by our individual desires rather than by true awareness. The human will is a powerful and precious thing to be sure, but when our will is directed by such disconnected desires, that power can also be very destructive. They can lead to serious imbalances in both the natural order of life and the flow of currency, which can in turn create suffering, ill-health and hardship not only for human beings but for all Earth's inhabitants. Only when we suffer from Disconnection can a society possibly think to exploit and wreak havoc upon the balance of the precious resources of our world—whether animal, plant, mineral, water, soil, air or human being—for the purpose of scientific advancement, technological advantage or economic profit.

Disconnection is at the foundation of all our social conventions, including our economic systems, political systems, educational systems and, of course, our businesses. Climate change, air and water pollution, genetic modification, soil erosion, environmental toxicity, resource pillaging, consumer waste, widespread increases in cancers and metabolic diseases and other imbalances are all the result of our spiritual Disconnection in our business practices.

When businesses operate from Disconnection, their creations will always be unnatural and unhealthy for the public. One obvious example is children's breakfast cereals. Many modern breakfast cereals for children are comprised of up to 50% sugar (some even more than 50%),[14] which can lead to early tooth decay, hyperactivity, low energy, mood swings, addictive behaviour and overall poor health. Only a society suffering from Disconnection could invent (and willingly consume) 'food' that actually harms our children. Similarly, we can look at the oil industry. By now, most of us understand the harm that the consumption of oil has had upon our air and waters, but this seems to make very little difference to our consumer habits. Fewer people realise how our dependency upon petroleum-based products such as plastics in virtually everything we touch and consume fills our daily lives with ever-increasing carcinogenic chemicals.

Only a very disconnected society could create and become dependent upon industries that are harmful by their very nature. We cannot simply blame businesses for our consumption habits. On the Gandhi Institute website they say, 'Non-violence means to practice mindful consumption.'[15] While we might believe we are starting to rectify these imbalances through recycling and government regulations, our seeming resistance to *radical* change, both as business owners and consumers, can only be attributed to our own Disconnection at a societal level.

Because Disconnection is at the very foundation of how we see the world, it can also be the most difficult of all the 'Deadly Sins' to shift. It is not a simple matter of changing our behaviour or creating laws that will impose social responsibilities upon businesses and governments. Nor is it adequate that we understand the problem merely from an intellectual point of view. This is a *spiritual* issue. The mind is a wonderful thing, but the intelligence required to shift from Disconnection to Connection lies at a much higher level of awareness than mere intellect.

The good news, however, is that once it is shifted, all the other 'sins' are very likely to dissolve effortlessly of their own accord.

COMMERCE WITHOUT MORALITY: UNRAVELLING THE CAUSE

Disconnection not only influences the kinds of businesses we choose to create; it also influences the *attitude* with which we conduct our businesses. Disconnection opens the doorway to free exploitation of resources—people, animal, plant and elemental (earth, air, water, energy, space). Once we have opened the door to exploitation, our world begins to spin out of control. Because exploitation is the natural by-product of our Disconnection, our society has become caught in a spiral of cause and effect, wherein our Disconnection causes us to exploit more, and our exploitation causes still more Disconnection.

We might be tempted to 'blame' the 'greedy' or 'unethical' corporations or governments for this. But blame is also a symptom of our disconnected perspective. These establishments are comprised of people; 'they' are not separate from 'us.' We are one humanity. 'Greed' and 'lack of ethics' are not the cause of behaviour—our cosmology is. Greed is only ever present when we feel impoverished in some way, whether materially, emotionally or spiritually. At the root of our feelings of impoverishment is fear for our very survival. We can only ever feel impoverished and fearful for our survival when we feel disconnected from Source; the wealth of Source is unlimited.

If 'greedy' corporations are battling against each other for survival, it is because they are afraid. As we've seen, fear can incite us to fight, and cause us to react in ways that bypass both logic and values. Fear can lead us to find acceptable the practice of being secretive and deceptive. It can lead us to rationalise 'attacking' those whom we perceive to be a threat. In business, this means we allow ourselves to destroy the competition and be driven solely by goals of ever-increasing profits. These are the 'sins' we see right on the surface. But at the root of these is fear; and at the root of the fear is Disconnection.

When commerce is out of balance, so too are the citizens of the world—the consumers. When Disconnection is the underlying worldview, consumers who are less economically privileged are more likely to feel vulnerable and fearful, because they have become dependent upon a system that is itself full of fear. Fear, as we've seen, can be the catalyst for both aggressive and passive behaviour. When people feel powerless economically, they often become passively ensnared in a seemingly hopeless dependency upon welfare and credit. Other times, the truly desperate will become aggressive, seizing what they believe they are entitled to through crime or violence. These behaviours are no less exploitive in principle than the practices of big businesses. But because these people feel so vulnerable, many will justify their exploitation by blaming it on the 'system,' i.e., the government or the economy. Again, it is Disconnection alone that is the cause.

The working and middle classes, filled with capable and responsible people, are not immune to these fears. They fill their lives with hard work so they can pay for all the consumables they are convinced they need, in order to maintain a certain 'standard of living.' Ironically, this standard of living only increases their feelings of Disconnection, which in turn increases their anxiety, which in turn increases stress and feelings of helplessness, which in turn increases their addiction to over-consumption in order to feel 'safe.' Again, some will blame their stresses on inflation, governments, employers or the moral devolution of society. But they are merely highlighting the symptoms of the disease, and not the cause, which is again Disconnection.

If we wish to reverse 'commerce without morality' and reinstate ethics in our businesses, we must come back to the origin of the problem, instead of trying to patch up a broken system. Looking at the symptoms can only give us an indication of how far astray we've come, but it can never heal us of the disease.

DISCONNECTION AND MARKETING

So now we come to marketing. We've already talked about the ancient Sanskrit *varnashrama* system, where commerce and agriculture (the *Vaishya* class) are thought of as the 'digestive system' of society, because they provide the necessities for living a long and healthy life. If we take this analogy one step further, we might view marketing as the liver within that body. The liver is the organ that filters out impurities, and passes the remaining matter to be circulated to the rest of the body. Thus, the liver is ultimately responsible for what the rest of the body is 'fed.' It is the job of the liver to ensure the body receives only that which is pure, nutritious, supportive and life-sustaining.

Similarly, marketing is the carrier of what we 'feed' society (and under the word 'marketing' I include any media responsible for the dissemination of ideas). Through marketing, we are telling society about things and ideas we believe they should consume. These marketing messages themselves are 'consumed' by the masses from a very early age. We marketers are therefore responsible for ensuring those messages are 'pure, nutritious, supportive and life-sustaining' to the whole of society, and most especially to the vulnerable.

But if we marketers suffer from the disease of Disconnection, we will perceive ourselves as separate from the Whole. The more separated we feel from something, the less responsible we feel towards it. If we are very spiritually disconnected, we cannot help but also be very socially and environmentally irresponsible. Without a feeling of responsibility, our marketing messages cannot help but become misleading, deceptive, manipulative and even damaging to the whole of society.

As consumers, we might believe that creating regulations and guidelines for marketing ethics can help address the problem, but once again we are only treating the symptoms of a much greater illness. While these things may result in keeping the cancer from spreading, they can neither eradicate it nor restore our world to optimum health. Reconnection is the only way back to balance, and the only antidote for Disconnection.

SUMMARY: HOW DISCONNECTION IS MAKING US ILL

Disconnection is the primordial human illness. It separates us not only from each other, but from the Planet on which, and Universe in which, we live. Ultimately, it separates us from Source, Spirit, God or whatever word you wish to use. When we feel this separation, we suffer from an underlying feeling of lack of safety. Many spiritual practices say that the very fear of death itself is due only to this feeling of Disconnection, and when we feel connected to Source, there can be no fear.

When we feel fundamentally unsafe, our bodies become continually bombarded by stress hormones, tension and disease. When we are in 'survival mode,' we will do anything to alleviate our feelings of insecurity. This 'anything goes' permission opens up the doorway to exploitation. Slavery, sweat factories, environmental imbalances, stress-related and autoimmune illnesses, substance abuse, crime, welfare dependency, economic crises, high interest rates and virtually anything you can dub as an illness—whether of body, society or the planet—can be traced back to the Deadly Sin of Disconnection.

And because we have adopted this 'anything goes' attitude and given ourselves permission to exploit, it opens the door to the next of our 'Deadly Sins': Persuasion.

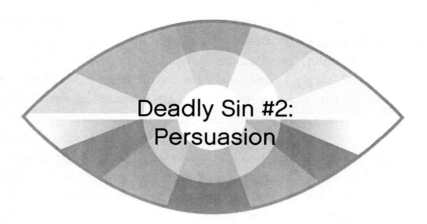

Deadly Sin #2: Persuasion

Recently a client told me about a teleseminar she had attended with a well-known business coach. The topic of the teleseminar was how coaches could get a higher conversion rate, by learning how to 'close the deal' during telephone consultations with prospective clients. The leader of the teleseminar advised the coaches to take payment immediately via credit or debit card over the telephone before the consultation was over, assuring them this was the fail-proof way to ensure a high conversion rate, and ultimately attain financial success.

I listened to this with some bemusement, as it brought to mind the time I had been given exactly the same advice by one of my business advisors, when I had first started my coaching practice. At that time, 'closing the deal' was a foreign concept to me, having come from a background as a 'starving artist' where many of my financial negotiations involved yielding to the demands of an event organiser or venue owner. This new, aggressive, 'close the deal' strategy felt unnatural to me. I initially told myself it was because I hadn't done such a thing before and that I would get better with practice. But after several months, my attempts at 'closing the deal' didn't seem to be working. Whenever I tried to secure payment over the phone, my prospective clients would get panicky. After hemming and hawing, they would verbally promise to send payment, but then write or call me later to say they had changed their minds. I simply wasn't mastering this 'close the deal' thing at all. I felt like a failure at business. Over time, I came to dread doing consultations. The closer I came to 'closing the deal' the tenser and more pessimistic I became. I believed in advance the deal was not going to close. And when you are in that state of mind, there really is no chance of closing a deal. Clients might not be able to articulate what they are sensing at the other end of the phone, but they certainly can pick up on it and intuitively don't want to get involved.

My business advisor and other 'close the deal gurus' offered many reasons why I (and others like me) couldn't seem to secure clients this way. Most of these reasons revolved around my relationship with money. They said I didn't value myself enough to ask for money. They said I was afraid that asking for money would make me appear to be disingenuous and greedy. They said I had made up stories in my mind about money being evil, and was thus pushing money away. And while these explanations undoubtedly held a grain of truth, these advisors seemed to infer that 'closing the deal' was the 'right' way of doing business, and my inability to do it would eventually prove to be my downfall as a business owner. Hearing their concerns, I began to doubt myself and start to wonder whether I was cut out to be a 'real' businessperson. In some twisted way I had bought into their 'close the deal' idea, even though I couldn't succeed at it.

But as the years progressed, my business improved radically. Why? Because I decided to throw out the 'close the deal' strategy altogether. I had come to see that the reason I had failed at closing the deal was because it was incongruent with my personal value system. The practice of 'closing the deal,' I felt, was disempowering those whom I sought to empower through my services. It was robbing my clients of their fundamental right to choose, by using the triggers of fear and urgency to influence their decision. It was coercing people into doing something they either didn't want to do, or they were not yet sure they wanted to do.

The practice of closing the deal can be summed up in a single word—*Persuasion*. Once I saw this, I also understood why I couldn't do it. Persuasion just plain felt 'wrong' to me, no matter how many business gurus were telling me it was 'right'. When I realised this had to do with values rather than business skills, I was able to change the way I did my consultations with clients. I made it a policy never, ever, to ask clients to make a decision at a first meeting. In fact, I told prospective clients clearly at the beginning of the call that I did *not* expect them to make a decision that day, and would not ask them to do so. This felt 'right' for me, as it was congruent with my personal values. This shifted the atmosphere completely, both for my clients and myself. Clients were put at ease and spoke more openly. I was able to concentrate more on what they were saying without an attachment to the result. Ironically, *more* prospective clients made the decision to work with me during our first meeting than when I had tried to 'close the deal' in the past.

Abandoning Persuasion as a practice was one of the most lucrative business decisions I ever made. It also taught me a valuable lesson about what makes a 'real' businessperson: to be a real businessperson, you've got to *be* real first.

UBIQUITY DOES NOT MEAN IMMUNITY

Persuasion in marketing is subtle and sometimes hard to recognise. There are two main reasons for this. First, it's because Persuasion is surrounding us at every moment. We've become so inundated with it, we don't notice it anymore. Persuasion is like telephone poles. Telephone poles are everywhere but how many of us even notice them? But if you were a time traveller from the 17th Century who suddenly dropped into our current era, you would see these strange-looking objects in every direction. You might think, *What are these weird things? Are they some sort of manmade tree?* The unnaturalness of their uniformity and the fact they were all strung together with millions of miles of wires might make you feel confused, angry or even afraid. You might be baffled as to why no one around you seemed to notice them, or why they tolerated their imposing presence. It would seem like a mad world.

Like telephone poles, persuasive marketing is barking in our faces at nearly every moment of our lives—on TV, on the Internet, on the radio, in the newspaper, driving on the highway, walking along the High Street, practically everywhere you look—but most of us have built up an unconscious filter, believing the messages have no impact upon us. After all, we are intelligent human beings; we are streetwise and are not so easily manipulated. We are 'used to it' and therefore immune to it. But that is a delusion on our part.

Recently, faulty plumbing caused some serious damage in my flat, and my insurance company arranged for a contractor to sort it out. The contractor sent a builder by the name of Michael to tear down my bathroom wall and replace the damaged plastering and tiles. As I work from home, I was two rooms away while Michael was doing his work. Within a short time, I started gagging from the fine particles of dust being spewed into the air from the plaster, grout and newly cut tiles. I was coughing, wheezing and my eyes were running. The air was positively caustic. Even though it was winter, I opened all the windows, and then went into the bathroom to see Michael. I noticed he was wheezing heavily as he worked, but he wore no protective face mask.

I asked, 'How can you stand all this dust? I can hardly breathe, and I'm at the other end of the flat. Why aren't you wearing a mask?'

'Really?' he replied, 'I don't even notice it, Miss.'

But the truth was his breathing was laborious. He was probably about 40 years old, but his constant, wheezy breathing made him sound like he was about 90.

'*You* might think you're immune, but I don't think your lungs would agree,' I said. 'I can hear you struggling to breathe. You might want to have your lungs checked by a doctor.'

'No, no, I'm all right, Miss. I do this kind of work every day. I'm immune to the dust. It doesn't bother me.'

Of course, this was sheer delusion on his part. The only thing that had become 'immune' to the dust was Michael's awareness of it.

He might have been able to switch off mentally, but his lungs didn't know for beans about being immune to the dust.

In much the same way, persuasive marketing has entered our societal 'lungs' without our being aware of it. We are breathing in persuasive messages so frequently we are no longer aware it is happening. We imagine we are filtering out the information, but the truth is we are not. These messages are entering our psyche regardless of our awareness of them, and are impacting our consciousness whether we choose to believe it or not. How many times have you found yourself humming a tune you don't really like, simply because you heard it so many times on the radio or TV and the 'hook' of the tune got stuck in your head? Similarly, all the persuasive messages of marketing are surrounding you and going into your brain. You'd have to be a hermit to avoid them. And if you think you are immune, you are mistaken. You might believe you are a person of high discrimination, immune to being 'persuaded' to buy something you do not wish to buy. And while I would hope this to be true, remember that 'marketing' is not just the selling of products and services; it is first and foremost the *selling of beliefs.*

THE SELLING OF BELIEFS

The practice of Persuasion in marketing is not simply a matter of marketers trying to convince you to buy their products and services; it is actually the practice of *selling you a set of values and beliefs.* We've seen this already when we talked about Bernays, but it plays a part in every single aspect of consumerism. For example, in order to persuade people to buy into a debt management program, it is first necessary to convince society they need to have credit. To persuade people to buy 'anti-aging' cosmetics, you first have to convince society that youth is better than maturity. To persuade people to buy the latest mobile phone gadget, you first have to convince society that mobile phones are an essential part of their lives.

This then is the second reason why Persuasion is sometimes hard to recognise: *it can often masquerade as social values, which may or may not be your own.* And because these social values often mask the marketing pitch that lies behind them, we unconsciously become predisposed to accept the product or service being marketed, well before we consciously decide whether or not to buy it. Thus, before Persuasion can work on a marketing level, a value system must be taught not only through marketing itself, but also through education, politics and journalism. These social institutions might rightfully be included under the umbrella of 'marketing' as they are in the business of 'selling' us ideas and ideologies. And like commercial marketing, they also use persuasive tactics.

Once we have bought into an idea, we can be persuaded to take action—whether that action is to buy a particular product, vote a certain way in an election, or accept our own economic dependency upon the 'system'. Persuasion does not begin with an advert; it begins with creating a web of social values we have unconsciously accepted (or not). If we find ourselves confused, overwhelmed or at a stalemate in our lives—as so many people do when they hit their 40s or 50s—it is often because we have finally had a head-on collision with the values we have been fed throughout our lives, and those which are genuinely our own.

THE SYSTEMATIC CREATION OF DISSATISFACTION

Early in my career, I took an eight-week course from a well-known business coach. A few years later, this same coach sent me an invitation to attend a free 15-minute strategy session, which she was offering to a limited number of her former students. She said it would be a brainstorming session to address my current business challenges. Having had a past association with her, I signed up for the brainstorming session in good faith.

When I got on the call, she started off the conversation by asking, 'What's the most challenging business issue you are currently facing?' I shared my challenges with her, assuming we would brainstorm a few ideas together as promised in the email I had received from her. But after I finished talking, instead of offering ideas, she said, 'Uh-huh. Well...let me ask you this, Lynn. Are you a six-figure coach yet?'

For a moment, I was rendered speechless by this unexpected non-sequitur. My brain started clicking so loudly you could probably have heard it down the street. *What's this about? Why isn't she addressing any of the things I just said? And what does she mean, 'yet'? Am I* **supposed** *to be a '6-figure coach'?*

But I answered simply, 'No, I'm not a six-figure coach. Not even close.'

'So how much *do* you make a year?' she asked. 'Like what—only about 60 or 70 grand?'

I could feel myself physically shrinking inside. It felt like an invasion of my privacy. Moreover, it was not at all relevant to the purpose of the call. And to make matters worse, at the time I was still just getting my business off the ground, and my income was around one-third of the figure she was calling 'only.' I started to feel small and inadequate. It was an uncomfortable experience.

'Yeah, somewhere around there,' I lied.

Seemingly oblivious to how I was feeling, she told me she had a solution to my business woes: a big whoop-dee-doo boot camp she was running on the other side of the planet from me that cost $12,500 for two days of training—not including travel and accommodation of course. It was very 'exclusive' and was limited to 20 people.

No shit it's exclusive I thought. *Does she think more than 20 people would shell out over 12 grand for this? And, hey, do the maths:* (my brain does a quick calculation) *that's a quarter of a million dollars for 12 hours of work. Do I really think this woman's training is worth over $20,000 an hour?*

Ha! So that's how people get to be six-figure coaches? I thought (with not a small amount of cynicism).

To say I was shocked at her proposal is a gross understatement.

I politely told her I wasn't interested, buffering the rejection with the excuse that it was too far to travel for a two-day course.

'But don't you *want* to be a six-figure coach?' she countered, with just a hint of taunt in her voice.

Do I? I asked myself.

There was no 'right' answer to this question. If I answered, 'No' I would look like I was not very business-minded. If I said, 'Yes' she would be able to dive in and say, 'Then you should come to boot camp!'

I didn't answer. Instead I said, 'Look. I've got the money, but there is no way on the face of the earth I am going to spend over 12 grand—plus travel and accommodation—to fly to the other side of the world for a two-day course, no matter what it is.'

Then she said (and here's where things *really* got interesting), 'Well, gee...if you're going to *limit yourself* like that, then...'

This put me over the edge. Outwardly I was calm; inwardly I was livid.

'I'm not *limiting* myself,' I interrupted, as politely as I could muster. 'I'm simply saying 'no' to you.'

My brain was rapidly calculating how many hours (or months!) of help I could get from my Virtual Assistant with that $12,500...*No contest,* I thought.

The woman made a few more attempts to sway me, using 'trigger' words like 'success,' 'self-sabotage,' 'limiting beliefs,' 'empowerment,' 'thinking big,' 'taking risks,' etc. Sometimes these words can empower a client; but clearly she was using them to try to manipulate me into feeling fearful, stupid and inadequate. Our horns were fully locked in this dance with the 'Deadly Sin of Persuasion.'

The more she tried to persuade me, the more irritated I became. In a last-ditch attempt to 'close the deal' she offered me a two-hour business planning session for $3,500.

I told her I'd think about it and hung up, as politely as I could.

Of course, I had already decided there was no way I would ever work with her again. I immediately unsubscribed from her mailing list and felt extremely disappointed about what had just happened. Not only did I feel I had been brought onto the call under false pretences, but I was deeply disappointed in her sales strategies. Every tactic she had implemented seemed to be designed to induce feelings of inadequacy and shame over money. Then, when I didn't respond to these tactics, she shifted strategies, and tried to incite shame by saying I was limiting myself. But in reality, I was *not* feeling inadequate due to my income, and I did *not* view my decision not to spend $12,500 as irresponsible or self-limiting. In fact, I felt quite the opposite. I had come onto the call believing in this person, but now her persuasive and manipulative sales tactics had damaged—if not destroyed—my faith in her integrity. It was a shame, really.

I tell this story to provide a blatant example of how marketers attempt to create feelings of inadequacy—whether to do with money, status, appearance or general desirability—in order to persuade their customers to buy. But most of the time this kind of manipulation is much less obvious. And because it is largely subliminal, it has far greater potential to influence us without us even realising it. Over 50 years ago, the late author and journalist Vance Packard published his superb book, *The Hidden Persuaders*. In his final chapter, entitled 'The Question of Morality,' Packard strongly questions the morality of the use of Persuasion in marketing, media and politics, frequently asking the question 'What is the morality' of manipulating the subconscious minds of the public, simply because we happen to be clever enough to do so?[2] In that chapter, one of the specific industries he cites as an example is the cosmetics industry. Packard says:

> An ad executive from Milwaukee related in *Printers Ink* that America was growing great by the **systematic creation of dissatisfaction**. He talked specifically of the triumph of the cosmetics industry in reaching the billion-dollar class by the sale of hope and **by making women more anxious and critical about their appearance.** Triumphantly he concluded: 'And everybody is happy'...But is 'everybody happy'? [emphasis added][3]

This 'systematic creation of dissatisfaction' is what I call 'creating false needs,' and is a topic we will examine in greater depth when we discuss the 'Deadly Sin of Scarcity' later in this book. But suffice it to say for now that one of the key characteristics of Persuasion in marketing is that it seeks to psychologically and emotionally disempower its customer, and then swoop in for the 'kill.'

Packard's question 'What is the morality?' is just as valid today as it was over 50 years ago. Real values have no 'sell by' date.

HITTING US OVER THE HEAD: THE PERSUASION FORMULA

One of the first things many Internet marketers learn from business gurus is how to craft an online sales letter. You probably know the ones I mean. Typically, they go something like this:

1. You start with a massive headline in red font
2. You talk about the pain or problem the reader is experiencing
3. You say the name of your product and list all the ways this product will address that pain or problem (the 'benefits')
4. You go on to explain all the specific features of your product
5. You provide 'social proof' by showing a bunch of testimonials from past customers
6. THEN, in case they weren't sold on the product yet, you have a list of about a gazillion bonuses with vastly over-inflated estimated values of hundreds or even thousands of dollars
7. You repeat the benefits, features, blah, blah, blah again, using slightly different wording each time
8. Only AFTER all this, you finally tell the price and say how it's radically reduced from its usual price
9. THEN you have the button that says 'buy now'
10. You show your 'money-back guarantee' with a nice, big, golden seal
11. You throw in a few more testimonials just for the heck of it
12. Another BIG 'buy now' button, possibly flashing
13. THEN, when the reader clicks away from the page without buying the product, a form pops up saying, 'Wait! Don't go! I'll give you this extra thingamabob if you buy today before midnight!' which takes them back to the 'buy now' button

In my own work, I write a lot of sales pages for clients. I'm not going to lie. When I put together a sales letter, I do follow some of the organisational logic of this formula. It's important to identify a problem before you show a solution, for instance. But while the logic behind the formula might make sense, in practice the vast majority of sales pages I see online have all the charm of a Chihuahua with an attitude problem. Bark, bark, bark, bark! That's what they sound like with all the big lettering and exclamation points. What must our customers think of us with all that barking going on? Testimonials? Money-back guarantee? While they are meant to inspire confidence, when the marketer is so busy yipping at me, it makes me wonder if these testimonials and guarantees are simply all hype. Do I feel respected? Do I feel known? Do I care? Nope.

Personally, I actually *hate* this formula and never use it as is. People don't need to be told the same thing 10 times in different ways to have all the information they need to make up their minds. And if they click away from the page, well they've clicked away. It's such an infringement on people's right to choose (not to speak of an insult to their intelligence) to use pop-up messages saying, 'Wait! Are you SURE you want to leave? You're going to miss out on all this very important stuff...are you really, really, *really* sure?' If I hate it as a consumer, why would I use it on my potential customers?

So why *do* Internet marketers use these horrible sales pages? Many proponents claim this formula is based upon scientifically tested principles of personality profiling, and that it is systematically designed to get a high amount of opt-ins. Because so many people believe this to be so, they follow this model in every Internet marketing piece they create. But does this formula actually *do* what they want it to do? In a conversation on the *Warrior Forum,* the question was asked, 'What is the average conversion rate for a good landing page?'[4] The wide array of answers varied from below 1% to 50%. The point is there *is* no set answer. A formula does not make a sale. There are simply too many variables, which are simply too numerous to list here. And besides, what about requests for refunds by people who experience 'buyer's remorse' after feeling like they had made too hasty a decision? One sale does not automatically ensure you have made a loyal, long-term customer.

In my experience, the relationship we have with our customers is the primary influencer in making sales. And when someone new comes our way, they're not always ready to buy something right away. Our aim should be to cultivate a close relationship (which doesn't just mean finding a way to get their email address). This relationship is precious and it must be built upon trust and mutual respect. Using heavy-handed persuasive sales letters that say the same thing over and over does little to develop a long-term relationship of trust and respect.

My policy in creating sales copy is this: give the customer the information they need to make the decision *they* want, not the decision *I* want. It is time to shift our focus away from conversion towards relationship-building.

SUMMARY: HOW PERSUASION IS MAKING US ILL

Persuasion is insidious. In order to persuade, you must first disempower. Disempowerment does not come in one fell swoop. It is slow and constant. Nor does it always hit us over the head. Rather, it works like a finely pointed chisel, chipping away one granule of our being at a time, until we crumble under its continual hammering at our integrity.

Persuasion is treacherous. It doesn't care who it hurts along the way to its end. When you use Persuasion as a marketing strategy, you might very well 'close the deal' in the short term, but in the long term, you are making the world a lonelier place, for you are increasing the rift between one human and another. You are eroding trust, shutting down doorways to innovation and feeding the disease of Disconnection.

Persuasion is manipulative. Manipulation cannot take place without the intention of disempowerment. When an advert says to buy a product 'because you're worth it,' the implication is that you are not worth much if you don't buy the product.

Persuasion is pervasive. It shows up in nearly all forms of marketing, whether of businesses or ideologies. And the tool that shapes that cornerstone is the manipulation of human emotions, especially fear, shame and overall feelings of inadequacy.

Persuasion arises from Disconnection. And the by-product of Persuasion is still more Disconnection. When we are persuaded, we feel resentful, angry, ashamed, bitter, embarrassed, blaming, unlucky and any other number of negative emotions. These are not expansive, inclusive and unifying feelings. They increase Disconnection and discord in the world. And the more Disconnection, the more permission and power we give to exploitation, dominance and control over our fellow human—and the planet. Persuasion, therefore, is both *caused by* and *the cause of* Disconnection.

Persuasion makes us ill both as the persuader and the persuaded. As the persuader, we are disconnecting ourselves ever-more from the rest of humanity, by making life all about who can best dominate the other person. The toll this takes upon us is physically, spiritually and emotionally toxic.

When we are the consumer on the receiving end of Persuasion, we are constantly on our guard. We have 'alarm bells' ready to go off at any moment, amplifying stress in our lives. We are likely to manifest a kind of passive-aggressive attitude, our moods oscillating back and forth between rage at the injustice of the attempted 'robbery' of our free will, or depressive feelings of loss of our ability to choose and direct our own lives.

At a societal level, Persuasion erodes our trust in others. People become sceptical of everything, continually looking for 'the catch' (oftentimes, justifiably so). And when trust at a societal level has eroded, the very fabric of that society starts to unravel.

There can be no real safety without community, no progress without connection. And when there is no trust, neither community nor connection can exist.

And when there is neither community nor connection, there are no boundaries.

And when there are no boundaries, it plants the seeds for the next Deadly Sin: Invasion.

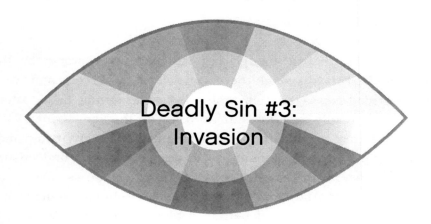

Deadly Sin #3:
Invasion

'Look, you fools, you're in danger! Can't you see?!
They're after you! They're after all of us!
Our wives, our children, everyone!
THEY'RE HERE, ALREADY! YOU'RE NEXT!'
*~ **Invasion of the Body Snatchers**[1]*

I am sure you hate it as much as I do. Three or four times every day, always at around the same time, the telephone would ring. I noticed it more when I started working from my home. I could almost predict, depending upon what time of day it was, which of a half-dozen or so sales calls it would be. It didn't matter how many times I hung up; they would only call back another day. It wasn't until I discovered there were services that could block unsolicited telemarketers from calling that the calls finally stopped.

Cold calling is perhaps the most obvious example of 'Invasion' marketing. Someone forces their way into your life, uninvited, into the sacred space of your home. You are in the middle of doing something else and this call takes you completely off track. Not only do you have to waste time telling the caller you are not interested, but after you hang up you also have to shift gears and refocus on whatever it was you were doing before the telephone rang. Even if you hang up the phone right away, it is still time stolen you can never get back. Really, cold calling is a kind of theft. But for some strange reason, while we would never tolerate theft under any other circumstances, cold calling is not illegal. It's bizarre.

THE SCRIPTED COLD CALL

Cold calling is bad enough but it's made even worse by the depersonalised way in which they are delivered. Most calls start with a pre-recorded message rather than a live caller saying 'hello.' Then, when you do finally get a live human being on the line, about 99.9% of the time they are reading from a script. While many companies believe scripts help to standardise customer relations and ensure consistency across the board, I do not believe they are as effective as employers believe. And frankly they drive me absolutely up the wall.

Here's a story to demonstrate why scripts don't work: My daughter (now grown with a family of her own) is a very high-functioning autistic. Although she was diagnosed with Tourette Syndrome and Obsessive Compulsive Disorder (OCD) when she was a young girl, her autism was not diagnosed until she was in her 20s. Back when she was getting ready to celebrate her ninth birthday we planned a party for her at our house so her school friends could come over for party games, cake and ice cream. In preparing for the party, my daughter invented a special game for her friends to play together. I don't remember what the game was, but I knew she had gone to a great deal of effort to prepare every last detail. On the day of the party, everything seemed to be going quite well. But when it was over, my daughter told me she was disappointed because, 'Nobody said their lines like they were supposed to when we were playing the game.'

I probed a little further and found out she had created an entire script in her mind about how the game would go. Friend A would sit in this cushion and say this line; Friend B would sit on another cushion and answer with another line, and so on. But the problem was, this wasn't a play on a stage—it was real life. When they went to play the game, her friends sat where they wanted to sit. They said what they wanted to say. Nothing was quite the way my daughter had envisioned. As a result, she was sad because she felt the party had not been completely successful.

I learned years later that this kind of behaviour is typical of autism. Creating a mental script is one way to feel safe when you do not have the neurological wiring to respond spontaneously to a social environment. Of course, the problem is that these scripts never play out according to plan. People are unpredictable. The ability to respond to such unpredictability is essential to being able to connect and relate to other human beings. Without this, we are likely to feel dissociated, confused and unable to see our own impact. As a child, my daughter often worried she was 'boring' because she couldn't see or appreciate how lively and creative she naturally was. Her script was a way to ensure she had something interesting to say.

I cite this example as an analogy for why the scripted cold call is *not* as effective as companies might believe. In fact, I think they do much more harm than good. When telemarketers use a script, not only have they disconnected from the person at the other end of the line, but they have also removed *themselves* from the conversation. What is so fascinating about scripted calls is that many telemarketers do not seem able to 'improvise' when the call does not go according to plan. I've experienced this numerous times. Here is a nearly verbatim dialogue of a call I received in 2010:

Telemarketer: 'Hello, is this the business owner?'
Me: 'Umm...Who's calling please?'
Telemarketer: 'This is the National Business Service.'
Me: 'I've never heard of the National Business Service. Who are you?'
Telemarketer: 'Am I speaking to the business owner?'
Me: 'Um...Yesssss...And who are YOU?'
Telemarketer: 'I'm calling from the National Business Service to make sure we have your details correct in our system.'
Me: 'What do you mean 'details'? I've never heard of you before and I've never given you any details. Who are you?'
Telemarketer: 'I'm afraid I need your details before I can give you any further information.'
Me: 'Excuse me? Why should I tell you anything until you tell me who you are?'
Telemarketer hangs up.

The telemarketer had no idea how to respond to me. Furthermore, he was undoubtedly instructed *not* to use his brain or resourcefulness. My non-compliance resulted in him ending the call without even saying, 'I'm sorry' or 'Goodbye.' But this didn't seem to deter the company. Another representative called me back with the same script a few weeks later. This time, I didn't let them get further than 'This is the National Business Service' before I hung up.

Here's another call I received when I was a new life coach, fresh out of training:

> *Telemarketer: 'Hello, is this Lynn?'*
> Me: 'Yes.' (I was wondering how she knew my first name)
> *Telemarketer: 'Hi, Lynn, I'm from XYZ Company. Now the reason why I'm calling you today, Lynn, is that I'm looking for one more life coach in Bedford. But I have to ask you first, Lynn, would you like to have more clients?'*

Hearing my name over and over as an attempt to connect with me was starting to grate on my nerves. I didn't know what she was after and I resented being asked such a leading question. She knew damn well that most people were likely to say 'yes' to this question. I was already feeling manipulated.

> Me: 'Umm…Well, yes…but…'
> *Telemarketer: 'That's great! We've got something just for you, Lynn, that can dramatically improve your business by blah, blah, blah…'*
> Me: 'But what exactly is the service? I never buy adverts.'
> *Telemarketer: 'Oh, it's not like anything else you've seen. Our service has been proven to improve business by sending traffic to you, blah, blah, blah, blah.'*
> Me: 'Can you please stop reading me the 'pitch' and TALK to me? What exactly IS the service? Is it a web listing? Because if it is…'
> *Telemarketer: 'No, we're nothing like that. Our service can guarantee you will be recognised as the leading expert in your geographic area.'*
> Me: 'But most of my clients are in other countries. I'm not interested in something aimed at my geographic area…and I don't advertise.'

Telemarketer: 'Well, Lynn, I do need to let you know that I have a limited special offer for this service today because I can only take on one more life coach in Bedford...'

Me: 'Are you even *listening* to me? When will you stop reading your script and speak to me?'

Telemarketer hangs up.

Strangely enough, the very same woman called me up again about three months later, with exactly the same opening line. I said to her, 'I remember you. You called here a few months ago. I recognise your voice.'

Sounding surprised, she said, 'You recognise my voice?' *(nervous laugh)* 'Is that a good thing?'

'Well...' I started.

She hung up.

In my opinion, scripted pitches—whether for a cold call or a 60-second elevator pitch—are the very bane of marketing. While widely regarded as neat and concise, they are by nature full of Disconnection and almost always Persuasion. Sprinkle in some Invasion and you basically have your typically scripted cold call. They are an Invasion not only of our precious time, but also in how they attempt to direct our responses through the lack of flexibility of the script itself. In this way, they become an Invasion of our freedom to be who we are and to choose whether or not we wish to hear specific information.

A CULTURE OF INVASION

While cold calling might be the most *obvious* form of invasive marketing, it is neither the only form nor even the most pervasive. Every unsolicited email we receive, even if we do nothing more than delete it, robs us of another minute of our precious life on Earth. And email is not the only Invasion. Every piece of printed junk mail we receive in the post that (hopefully) finds its way into our recycling bin is not only a waste of our valuable time, but also a waste of precious natural resources. We might well create better spam filters and other protective measures against them, but the real issue is that we have created a *culture* in our society that has rendered Invasion acceptable. We allow ourselves to be invaded by advertising several times an hour at regular intervals whenever we watch TV or listen to the radio, and somehow accept it as part of daily life without resistance. Why we have come to accept adverts as the norm is really only a matter of conditioning. Just like the presence of telephone poles, we have stopped noticing the presence of advertising in our everyday experience. Marketing is so ubiquitous, if we removed it we might suddenly realise how very tolerant of it we are.

In his book *Permission Marketing*, Seth Godin pretty much sums up all traditional forms of marketing as being 'interruption' marketing. That is to say, they are 'optimized to interrupt what you're doing'[2] and get you to look at what they are selling. Whether you are watching a television program, driving down a motorway or sitting at home and the phone rings unexpectedly, whenever advertising breaks your concentration and sends your attention in a completely different direction it is 'interruption marketing.'

As a culture, we have been so tolerant of these interruptions that we actually have a whole subculture based around them. I remember as a child how we used to parody commercials saying things like, 'I can't believe I ate the whole thing' (Alka-Seltzer) or 'Mother, please, I'd rather do it myself' (Anacin). I seem to recall this last line being turned into a very cheesy country song played on top-40 radio in the 60s. I even remember how my cousins from rural New Jersey cousins used to tease me by singing, 'You can take Lynn out of the city but you can't take the city out of Lynn' (an 'homage' to the jingle for Salem cigarettes). The catchphrases of our lives are comprised of a never-ending kaleidoscope of commercial branding messages, so seamlessly woven into our popular culture we scarcely notice them. And rarely do we even think to challenge their right to be there.

And if you add to this, the stealth, if not insidiousness, of product placement on television shows and films, Invasion is simply everywhere. Our brand awareness is practically hard-wired into our psyche. Our children can recognise packaging of products long before they are even able to read what the packages say. Invasion starts at such an early age it is difficult to imagine our lives without it. Sort of like *Invasion of the Body Snatchers,* we look and sound perfectly normal but we have been invaded by something that alters our perception and behaviour at a fundamental level. It's creepy.

PASS THE GARLIC, PLEASE

Invasion is far deeper and subtler than mere 'interruption.' Yes, we might have signed up to a particular mailing list and yes, we might have come to accept television advertising as 'normal,' but that does not mean it is not an 'invader.' Just because Count Dracula cannot enter his victims' homes without being 'invited' does not mean he is not invading their space. He dupes his unsuspecting victims through his hypnotic charm, enticing them to open the window. Entranced, they undo the shutters and let him in, seemingly by their own will, unaware of the harm he will inflict upon them.

Invasive marketing is every bit as much a vampire—a *social* vampire—as Count Dracula. We let it in, lured by the sexiness, humour or 'hook' of the advert. And just like Dracula's victims, we allow the vampire to come into our consciousness, allowing the sensuality of its kiss to linger within our memory and permeate our value system. We come to accept it as a part of our reality. We make it part of our culture. Eventually, we no longer question its presence in our lives. We become tolerant of, and desensitised to, its influence. We lose our ability to discriminate between what we hold as truly valuable and what we are told to value. We remember name brands and catchphrases without even being aware they are setting up shop in our cerebral cortex.

But as I experienced when my television broke, when we cease to feed our consciousness a daily diet of marketing and media messages, the stealthy invader begins to lose its influence over us. It's like living every day next to a construction site and getting used to the sound of heavy machines drilling into the street. Then one day the construction is finished and you suddenly realise how much noise had been in your brain. I'm not suggesting the only antidote for invasive marketing is to get rid of your television set. A slow return to sanity begins when we awaken our awareness of how we are being invaded, and what is being stolen. When this awareness is finely honed, we find we can walk into the most invasive of environments, and not feel its effects. Living in such awareness is like having your own endless supply of vampire-repelling garlic.

HAS THE INTERNET CHANGED THINGS ALL THAT MUCH?

Seth Godin uses the term 'permission marketing' to refer to the practice of having to give your consent to a marketer before they can contact you. I'm sure most of you have joined a mailing list to receive information at one time or another and received newsletters and other pieces of information from the sender. While Godin rightly shows that 'permission marketing' is a radical shift in paradigm from 'interruption marketing,' it is my experience that simply opting into someone's mailing list or agreeing they can call you as a result of meeting them at a business network meeting, hardly exempts us from Invasion. I can't tell you how many times I met someone casually at a network meeting, or even signed up to their list, and found myself unsubscribing within a few days after being bombarded with one, two or even three emails a day from them. Even if I invited them in at the onset, exploiting my invitation and hospitality is still Invasion.

If anything, the increasingly sophisticated technology on the Internet has made Invasion marketing even more prevalent. When we surf the Net looking for something specific, we frequently find ourselves so inundated with pop-up forms, sponsored links, affiliate banners and Google ads it's hard to find the actual content we're looking for. Things that make marketing easier for business owners frequently have the inverse effect upon the consumer. I've lost count how many times I mindlessly clicked away from a page to check out another link on the page, and then forgot to find my way back to where I started. I've even gone to turn off my PC at the end of the day and realised an email I had started composing that morning never got sent, because I had gone off to look up some information, and subsequently got distracted by other 'Invasions' that popped up along the way. At first, I blamed my diminishing attention span on age, but now I believe it is due to the ever-increasing amount of Invasions coming at us on an almost moment-to-moment basis.

Has the Internet changed things all that much? I would have to say yes and no. Yes, in that it has made marketing even MORE predominant in our world. In the Golden Age of television advertising, we saw adverts only from either the big international corporations or our local shops and service providers. Nowadays, we see them from everyone. Furthermore, the search engines and shopping sites all know our preferences, and they target their adverts according to our past browsing and shopping habits. Yes, it's smart, but it's still invasive. I am not a 'demographic'; I'm a complex human being with complex desires and interests. Just because I'm over 50 and single, don't assume I want to see adverts of dating sites for over 50s (!). The Internet hasn't fully succeeded in creating a revolution of 'permission' just because we subscribe to mailing lists. The issue is much deeper than that, and the real solutions are far more complex.

SUMMARY: HOW INVASION IS MAKING US ILL

Invasion is making us ill—as individuals, as a society and even economically. Cold calling and unsolicited emails interrupt our work efficiency by disturbing the flow of what we are doing. The time that is wasted in taking such calls or dealing with these emails is not limited to the call or email itself. After we hang up on an uninvited caller, or delete unwanted messages, it can often be difficult to shift our brains back into gear. Our creative flow has been disturbed and our concentration disrupted. This can cost us not only time but also money. It can also make us frustrated and angry, which only makes it even more difficult to connect with ourselves, our work and our colleagues. Scripted calls have an even worse impact, as they increase our feelings of separation from others, as we are not co-creators of the conversation. They can leave us feeling manipulated and not seen as a whole human being.

Invasion is one step further than Persuasion. If Persuasion puts us on our guard, Invasion makes us ready to attack. Energetically, it increases negativity and distance between people, and erodes trust more than Persuasion alone. It makes us suspicious of anyone who comes wishing to share what they have with us. Our culture begins to 'bite the hand that feeds it' by regarding all businesses as shifty and shady. It creates a schism in our relationships with Self, others, our businesses, our audience and marketing, even though we are responsible for tolerating, if not inviting, this Invasion into our world.

Because Invasion puts people on their guard, it is necessary for marketers to 'hook' the consumer quickly before they move away. And the best way to do that is to create a smokescreen that puts the customer at ease so they don't realise what is happening, something that will encourage the unwitting customer to open the window and let the vampire in.

This smokescreen is at the foundation of Deadly Sin #4: Distraction.

Deadly Sin #4:
Distraction

'Old George Orwell got it backward.
Big Brother isn't watching.
He's singing and dancing. He's pulling rabbits out of a hat.
Big Brother's holding your attention
every moment you're awake.
He's making sure you're always distracted.
He's making sure you're fully absorbed.
He's making sure your imagination withers.
Until it's as useful as your appendix.
He's making sure your attention is always filled.
And this being fed, it's worse than being watched.
With the world always filling you,
no one has to worry about what's in your mind.
With everyone's imagination atrophied,
no one will ever be a threat to the world.'

~ Chuck Palahniuk[1]

I n music they call it 'the hook.' A 'hook' is that part of the song that just plain makes you remember it. It's not always the chorus. It's not always even the words. Sometimes it's something quirky. But it's always something easy to remember. The opening guitar riffs in Led Zeppelin's *Whole Lotta Love*, The Smiths' *How Soon is Now?* or Michael Jackson's *Beat It* are the hooks to those songs. The 'da-da-da-duuuuuuuum' of *Beethoven's Fifth* is the hook to that symphony. We recognise these compositions the instant we hear their hooks. They bring us instant recall of the entire piece. It's also what 'hooks' us into familiarity with that song, and makes us want to run out and buy it when we hear it a bunch of times on the radio. We can't get the hook out of our heads.

Marketing has a similar concept. It's called 'brand identity.' Jingles and catchphrases are all 'hooks' marketers use for the purpose of creating brand identity. They help keep the name of the brand in the front of our minds instead of buried in the archives of our memory. And anything that keeps a brand in our consciousness is generally considered to be good marketing. When we buy something because we can't get that hook out of our heads, marketers are happy.

So what's wrong with that? Isn't one of the goals of good marketing to establish a strong brand identity? Well yes, but if consumers buy products on the strength of the merits of the *marketing hook* and not necessarily the product itself, there's plenty wrong with it. When this happens, what might be seen as good branding can actually be guilty of what I call the 'Deadly Sin of Distraction.'

Think of a magician on stage. He is a master of Distraction. Distraction is used to focus your attention away from something in order for something else to happen, unseen. Pickpockets utilise Distraction in the same way, but to a different end. And marketers use Distraction all the time, for the purpose of directing your attention towards the advert, rather than allowing you to think too much about the product. It's just like a magician's sleight of hand.

Distraction is the practice by marketers of directing our attention *away* from the product towards something else, which is generally irrelevant. When you break it down, there are basically two types of Distraction in marketing:

1. Establishing a random brand identity that has nothing to do with the product
2. Making you want to buy a product just so you can get something else

TYPE 1: ESTABLISHING A RANDOM BRAND IDENTITY

Right now in Britain there is a popular ad campaign featuring a cast of fuzzy animated meerkat puppets. This campaign, for the company 'Compare the Market dot com,' exploits a play on the words 'market' and 'meerkats.' The running joke is that people keep typing in 'Compare the Meerkat dot com' on the Internet, trying to find 'cheap car insurance.' This campaign has evolved over the months, as people have gotten to know the meerkats now by name. Compare the Market dot com now offers 'claw stitched' cuddly meerkat toys when people buy car insurance through them, and now have full-blown websites at BOTH the 'market' and the 'meerkat' Web domains.[2] In fact, on the meerkat site, you can 'compare the meerkats' in a variety of poses, from yoga to body slamming. When you finish 'comparing' your meerkats, a pop-up window appears saying, 'Warning! This site is for people who are serious about meerkats, not time-wasters looking for cheap car insurance' with buttons that take you either back to the 'meerkat' site or the 'market' site. The amount of effort and creativity that has gone into this cute and cuddly parallel universe is astonishing.

So what's wrong with a bit of fun? How can this possibly be a 'Deadly Sin'? While I agree this is a brilliant marketing hook, it has nothing whatsoever to do with the services being offered, and isn't designed to help people make any kind of *intelligent* choice. In fact, they aren't supposed to think, just remember the name. Ironically, we are quite likely to go to 'Compare the Market (or Meerkat) dot com' when we are looking for car insurance without even *comparing* other websites who offer this type of service, simply because the marketing campaign has 'hooked' us.

Another classic example is the series of Budweiser commercials in the early 2000s that featured a line-up of animated frogs 'croaking' the name of the beer: 'Bud...wei...ser.' People (well, some people) thought it was funny but it was simply another random exercise in brand recall. Nothing in the advertising had anything to do with beer at all. Viewers had no real reason to buy beer, or indeed this particular brand of beer, from the merits of the ad.

When we are hooked by funny adverts and cuddly toys rather than the quality of the company, we're basically being played by marketers. They know talking about car insurance or beer is boring and it's tough to stand out in the crowd with all the competition. So let's not talk about car insurance or beer at all. Let's talk about meerkats and frogs. That's not boring; that's funny. People will keep watching and in the meantime we're pulling the rabbit out of the hat—planting the name of the company in people's brains.

Again, this is all Distraction. It distracts us from the fact that these adverts are trying to *sell* us something, and focuses our attention on entertainment. It dulls our senses and derails our powers of discrimination. It prompts us to act simply because the advertising is 'sticky,' not necessarily because the products or services have anything much to offer over their competitors. And while, just like a master magician, Distraction in marketing is often masterfully done, it is nonetheless as 'deadly' a sin as any of those that have come before.

TYPE 2: BUY THIS TO GET SOMETHING ELSE

One of the memories I have of being a little girl was Cracker Jack. Cracker Jack was molasses-flavoured candy-coated popcorn and peanuts. Popular at baseball games, Cracker Jack tasted pretty sickly and its primary ingredients were sugar and corn syrup.[3] I associate Cracker Jack with summertime. It's something we would always buy on summer holiday, especially at the beach and at the fireworks display on the 4th of July. We'd eat our Cracker Jack and bits of the very sticky popcorn stubbornly stayed on our teeth. Needless to say, as we children were hardly in the habit of stopping playing to go brush our teeth after eating a box of Cracker Jack, I had a lot of cavities as a child. But we were all too happy to put up with rotting teeth and the sickly taste of Cracker Jack for one thing— the toy surprise that came in every box. The cheap plastic toys were admittedly pretty useless. Sometimes we were able to play with them for a little while before they broke or got lost. Nonetheless, we kept on spending our allowance money on Cracker Jack, because we enjoyed the feeling of anticipation as we dug down to the bottom of the box to get our toy surprise.

This is a classic example of Distraction Marketing Type 2: when our focus is taken away from the product on the promise of getting something entirely different. These days we see even more examples of this kind of Distraction marketing, especially targeted at children. In the summer of 2006, McDonald's launched a campaign cashing in on the popularity of (although they used the words 'inspired by') the Disney film and theme park attraction *Pirates of the Caribbean.*[4] Dubbed McDonald's 'Summer of Happy Meal Fun,' every purchase of a Happy Meal or Mighty Kids Meal would come with 'one of eight adventurous toys for perfect pirate make-believe...while supplies last.' Admittedly the toys were a cut above the toys in Cracker Jack boxes, ranging from a pirate bandana, to an inflatable pirate sword, plush toys and other goodies. In addition, to 'hook' the parents as well as the kids, McDonald's added another feature to this campaign called 'Search for the Golden Treasure Happy Meal Game' wherein 25 'lucky buccaneers' got a chance to win a trip for four to either Walt Disney World or Disneyland.

Ok, now I have to say I'm a fan of collaborative marketing and I do utilise it in my own work, but this is slightly different from what I would consider to be a legitimate collaboration. When I do collaborations, my promotional partners are all offering something relevant to the product or service on offer to my customers. If I'm promoting a book on health and healing, for example, my collaborators would offer gifts in that same niche. Also, the primary focus of the promotion is the book itself, and customers are given plenty of incentives to buy the book regardless of the nature of the collaborations. While I imagine some people might buy the book to get the bonuses, most buy the book to get the book.

But *Pirates of the Caribbean* has nothing whatsoever to do with hamburgers, nor does a fast-food restaurant have anything really to do with children and happy families (although the public image created by McDonald's would lead you to believe otherwise). There is absolutely no link between these two products. Nor is there any reason why a child who wants a pirate toy should need to eat a hamburger (not to speak of eating many, many hamburgers) so he can collect all eight toys or try to find the winning ticket to Disneyworld. The marketers of this campaign diverted the focus away from the 'thing' being sold, and redirected our attention to something completely unrelated. Never mind the food, let's just focus on the 'good times' you're going to have when you buy Happy Meals for the kids. When the promotion itself overrides any talk or focus on the product itself, encouraging people to buy simply for the promotion on offer (and sometime to buy multiples so they can 'collect all eight,' win a contest, etc.) it opens the door to exploitation. And by far, the most vulnerable people to that exploitation are our children.

While adults might respond to things that trigger fear, sex or humour in marketing, kids tend to respond to things that are either fun or make them feel 'cool' in their social environment. Using 'fun' to get kids to ask for name brands is something marketers have always done, and are doing even more with the rise of the Internet. An independent study revealed that 43% of primary school children surveyed said 'they would buy or eat more of a food brand' because they saw it online or *played a game* about that product.[5] I'm not sure about you, but the idea of influencing children's eating habits through online games and other lures sort of leaves an icky sticky feeling in my teeth.

What we as a society allow to enter the consciousness of our children today will have profound effects upon the future of the planet tomorrow. Think back to how much Distraction marketing has influenced your own tastes and desires from childhood to adolescence to adulthood. How did it establish your eating habits, your taste in fashion and your spending habits? How does your childhood conditioning continue to influence them? How does it impact your current economic situation? How does it influence how you have raised your own children?

It's a bit spooky to think about.

SUMMARY: HOW DISTRACTION IS MAKING US ILL

Distraction is an interesting 'sin' because in some ways it's the most difficult one to recognise. It isn't exactly 'lying' but it's not exactly truthful, either. It is subtle and often comes across as 'charming.' It exploits things we enjoy—like humour and fun—to refocus our attention onto what it wants us to see. It dulls our senses with entertainment and derails our powers of discrimination. It smilingly lures us into buying things simply because the advertising makes us feel a certain way. It pretends to be our friend, but is more like a 'Pied Piper' leading us away from home.

All in all, Distraction is a bit like the sociopathic narcissist who can charm others into believing he only has their best interests at heart, but really has no concern whatsoever for anyone but himself. This 'almost a lie' puts Distraction somewhere in the cracks, but only a tiny step away from the out-and-out untruthfulness of the next Deadly Sin: Deception.

Deadly Sin #5: Deception

When I was five or six years old (1960-61), I saw an advert on television for a fabulous-looking dollhouse called the 'Marx-a-Mansion Dream House.' One of the many advertised features of this 'mansion' was a 'real working doorbell.' On the television advert the bell went 'ding-dong' just like the doorbell at the front door of my house. It also showed lamps that lit up when you flicked the switch. Every time I saw the advert I got excited. I begged my parents to get me this fabulous dollhouse for Christmas. My parents did indeed buy me the dollhouse and 'Santa' (aka my Dad) assembled it on Christmas Eve while I slept. I woke in the morning to see this wonderful new 'mansion' sitting under the tree. Bubbling with excitement, the very first thing I wanted to do was ring the famous 'real working doorbell.' But to my disappointment, this 'doorbell' was just a little spring mechanism with a tiny tin bell attached. When I pulled it to 'ring' the bell, it made an irritating clacking noise as it snapped against the tin body of the dollhouse. No pretty ding-dong sound. Not even a 'zzzz' like a buzzer. In fact, you couldn't even hear the bell. Perhaps Louis Marx and Company had thought the 'ding-dong' sound on the advert was the sound of a child's imagination, but at age five, I took the advert literally and expected the bell to go 'ding-dong'. Then, I went to light the lamp, and found I had to pick it up and twist the lampshade to turn it on. There was no electric wall switch. And all the plastic accessories that looked so glamorous on my black-and-white TV didn't look the same either. I was disappointed, and I am sure my parents weren't too happy either, because while it was a perfectly good dollhouse it certainly wasn't all the company had claimed it to be. I did play with my new dollhouse until I grew out of it a few years later. But I never bothered to ring the doorbell.

This is my first memory of deceptive advertising. There were many such ads like that when I was a young child, and I remember being disappointment many times when a toy simply wasn't all it said it was on the advert. Surely over the past half-century both the UK and US have made great strides in purging these more obvious 'lies,' not just in children's ads but across the board. Over the decades, tougher trading and standards regulations have been placed on the packaging, labelling and marketing of all consumer goods to ensure all of us, including our vulnerable children, are protected from deceptive marketing claims.

But here's the irony of the situation: because we now have laws in place to protect us from blatant lies, we consumers seem to have adopted a false sense of security about our freedom from Deception. For while advertisers might no longer be allowed to make adverts that show a ringing doorbell that will never ring, marketing companies are still manipulating their *language* to make deceptive claims about their products, in ways that are frequently so subtle, most people don't even notice. Enter the 'Deadly Sin' of Deception.

WHEN IS THE TRUTH ACTUALLY A LIE?

When we think of 'Deception' we might be inclined to think of full blown-scams, such as 'get-rich-quick' schemes and bogus property investments. But scams are hardly the most widespread form of Deception, nor are they the most damaging to us as a society. Real

Deception is right under our noses in nearly every advert we see, posing as the voice of truth. But it's anything but.

For example, how many times have you seen an advert for mouthwash or deodorant and the announcer says, *'nothing lasts longer'*? Similarly, you might see an advert for a headache medicine that says, *'nothing works faster.'* The words 'nothing lasts longer' do NOT mean it's the longest-lasting; the words 'nothing works faster' do NOT mean it's the fastest. What they *do* mean is that this product is pretty much the same as some (or all) of the other competing brands. Think of how many toothpaste adverts you've seen where they say, *'nothing is more effective in preventing tooth decay.'* Again, it doesn't mean it's the *best*. It only means it's pretty much the same as its competitors. It might even mean that NO toothpaste is any more effective in preventing tooth decay than, say, rinsing your mouth out with water after meals. The point is, you cannot say anything definitive about the product based on a statement like 'nothing is more effective.' Legally, the company might be telling the 'truth,' but psychologically, we are hearing something else from what they are saying—which happens to be false. What we are actually *hearing* is 'this product is the best.'

Why?

Back when I did my MA, I took a course on statistics where we were required to create several different surveys to understand the principles of accurate research. One of the things we learned was the correct and incorrect use of *negatives* in survey questions. If you wish to use a mix of affirmative and negative statements in your survey, it is essential to make this very clear to the reader, or the data you gather from the survey is very likely to be inaccurate. Here's a brief example of what I mean:

Rate these statements on a scale of 1-5, with 5 indicating it is the most true, and 1 being the least true:

1. I tend to feel at ease at parties.
2. I feel confident at work most of the time.
3. I'm usually comfortable in social settings.
4. I don't tend to make new friends easily.
5. I enjoy meeting new people.

Notice how all five sentences are making a statement about social skills. When you give people a survey or test on a particular subject, they tend to quantify things in a consistent fashion. In this case, once they started answering the questions they would unconsciously *expect* to rate better social skills with higher numbers and lower social skills with lower numbers. But this list of questions has a problem. All of the statements are positive except number 4. In all of the questions, a higher value answer would indicate a higher degree of positive social skills—except in statement number 4. If you give statement 4 a higher number, it indicates a greater degree of *negative* social skills (or, put another way, a lesser degree of positive social skills).

In any survey, using a higher number to indicate a higher degree of negativity can often confuse survey takers, but it is even worse when you create a test or survey with *mixed* positive and negative statements like this example. In a survey or test like this, people are quite likely to answer the negative questions inaccurately, rendering your data basically useless.

One of the reasons for this lies in how we humans process information. In one study conducted by cognitive scientists Wason and Johnson-Laird back in the 1970s, it was shown that human beings tend to be slower in evaluating the truth of a negative statement than the falsity of an affirmative one.[2] In other words, if I were to make an affirmative statement like, 'this is the most effective toothpaste on the market in preventing cavities,' you would easily be able to evaluate its truthfulness. You would either accept my word for it or you might say, 'I'll believe it when you show me the evidence.' *Either* way—even if you doubted the truthfulness of my claim—you would easily be able to *understand* the meaning of the statement and evaluate its veracity for yourself.

However, if I were to say 'No toothpaste is more effective in preventing cavities,' your brain finds it more challenging to process the actual meaning of the statement. Marketers *hope* you interpret the meaning to be 'This is the most effective toothpaste on the market,' but actually that is *not* what they are saying. They are only saying this toothpaste is not any worse than other toothpaste, which tells you nothing factual about the effectiveness of any of these toothpastes.

Experienced marketers are experts in both psychology and legality. While saying 'nothing works faster' is legally 'true,' it's also designed to deceive the listener into hearing a positive statement (i.e., 'this is the fastest-working') which is *not* true. But if you took the marketer to court for fraud, you would lose. 'Technically' they are telling the 'truth,' even though the intention is to prey upon the brain's natural sluggishness in processing negative statements, and to deceive you into believing something they are *not* actually saying.

And when such statements fly by us in a matter of seconds within the context of a 30-second advert, these untrue truths enter our brains like a quick hit of caffeine from a triple shot of espresso. We don't even have *time* to process them logically, and we *infer* a truth from them that is not really what is being said.

Once you start looking out for these false positive messages in marketing, you'll see them everywhere. It's like a light switch that goes on in your awareness when you suddenly realise you know nothing about anything you've been buying.

QUANTITY VERSUS QUALITY = LEGAL VERSUS HONEST

Some of the most striking examples of deceptive marketing can be found in the food industry. Here, we are not merely talking about the advertising, but the packaging as well. Here in Britain, there is an independent group of parents aiming to improve the quality of children's foods and drinks in the UK who call themselves 'The Parents Jury.' The Parents Jury have done some remarkable studies on deceptive marketing in foods aimed at children, especially in the areas of breakfast cereals and fruit drinks.

A few years ago, the Parents Jury published something called 'Food Label Fibs,' wherein they gave an award for 'the most misleading but healthy-sounding description used on children's food labels.'[3] The fruit drink industry won the dubious honour of being the most misleading because so many leading products aimed specifically at children contained as little as *5-10% juice*. The other 90-95% was comprised of water, sugar, flavourings, artificial colours, artificial sweeteners (such as aspartame) and preservatives (such as sodium benzoate). Aspartame is an insidious chemical, which has been shown to break down in the body into formaldehyde and methanol, and can cause neurological dysfunction, fibromyalgia, cancer and many other serious diseases.[4] Sodium benzoate is another potentially harmful ingredient, as some claim it can increase hyperactivity in children or even convert into carcinogens.[5]

But beyond all this controversy, the one indisputable and utterly astonishing fact is that the companies who manufacture these products are perfectly within 'legal' bounds to use the word 'fruit' in their names, and to have pictures of luscious-looking, juicy fruit on their packaging, even though these drinks offer little (if any) of the nutritional benefits of eating fruit. Far from being healthy, if we are to believe the reports about aspartame, artificial colours and preservatives, the truth is these products are actually *unhealthy* to consume, and especially so for children.

And as if this weren't deceptive enough, I was truly shocked to read in the same 'Food Label Fibs' report that one leading 'fruit drink' brand here in the UK (with images of brightly coloured cartoon characters nearly bursting off the face of the carton) actually listed its sugars as 'carbohydrates' on the packaging. The word 'carbohydrates' doesn't sound nearly as off-putting as the word 'sugar' to a health-conscious parent. Again, it's technically 'true' and therefore legal—but is it *honest?*

To me, the bigger questions around such practices are these:

- Do such products, packaging and marketing practices provide our children the best possible start in life?'
- Does this practice of finding legal loopholes so you can 'lie' without technically 'lying' set a moral example for future generations?
- Does this practice build trust and confidence between our children and our businesses?

Tighter legislation will never create permanent solutions, until business owners realise their role as the 'torso' of society means they have a moral responsibility to *feed* our population, not *feed upon* them.

DECEPTION VIA ASSOCIATION

Another form of Deception is what I call 'Deception via Association.' This is the practice of creating a *false relationship* (and hence a collapsed belief) between a product and a completely disparate idea. Earlier in this book, we saw many examples of Deception via Association when we looked at early cigarette advertising, where the advertisers created an association between cigarettes and sexual identity. But Deception via Association can also arise when marketers use celebrities or other media personalities (such as cartoon characters or actors playing the role of a well-known television or movie character) as the 'image' of the product. The purpose of this association is to establish a psychological connection between the product and the qualities of the person or character representing that product. Sometimes these associations *seem* to make perfect sense, as when sports figures become the spokesperson for sportswear, or when glamorous actors and actresses become the spokespeople for so-called luxury items like perfume, cosmetics, hair products, etc.

But while these seemingly logical associations are sometimes tenuous at best, quite often advertising creates associations that are utterly random, and collapsed beliefs that are potentially damaging. For instance, in 2003 here in the UK, the cast of characters from the BBC children's show *The Tweenies* were pictured on packaging of food from companies like MacDonald's, Marks and Spencer and many others. While there is no qualitative link between The Tweenies and any of these products, by using The Tweenies image as their 'brand,' these products unconsciously became more desirable to children, creating the collapsed belief that 'The Tweenies are good; therefore these products are also good.' Strong protests came from parents around the country who questioned why the BBC (supposedly non-commercial) would encourage young children to consume foods proven to be 'either high in salt, sugar, fat and/or saturated fat, according to government guidelines.'[6] One parent from

Newcastle wrote to the BBC saying, 'Whilst shopping recently, the boys were pestering me for Tweenies yogurts. They could not understand why they weren't good for them if Milo *[one of The Tweenies characters]* could eat them, but at over 16% sugar, it is not a product I would buy.'[7]

Licensing The Tweenies image to third parties proved to be a real cash cow for the BBC. In the five years leading up to 2004, the BBC had reportedly raked in £350 million on Tweenies products, whereupon they eventually sold the children's characters to a private company. This new company reportedly projected their acquisition of The Tweenies would increase their profits by as much as £1 billion per year.[8]

That's a LOT of yogurt...and who knows what else.

Children emulate their favourite television characters; they believe these characters are their friends and heroes, who have their best interests at heart. When they see a product—from food products to pencils—with pictures of their friends and heroes on them, they feel emotionally drawn to them and want to own them. Choosing heroes and role models is an important part of children's self-expression. It fires their imagination and helps them identify their interests, dreams and personal values. For all these reasons, media companies, such as television, film and music producers, have a tremendous responsibility when it comes to communicating to children. Creating random, false relationships between commercial products and cartoon characters, film heroes or other pop icons can be terribly damaging to our impressionable youth, and is only sabotaging the future of our world.

EAT JUNK. BE AN ATHLETE

As of this writing, the 2012 Olympic Games are rapidly approaching, and the entire city of London is gearing up for what is likely to be one of the biggest (if not *the* biggest) public events the city has ever seen. The site of the Games is in a part of the East End of the city widely regarded as somewhat derelict. Winning the bid to host the Olympics in East London was seen as a great opportunity to give a life-restoring facelift to that part of the city, both economically and cosmetically. But since London won the bid, how the preparations for the Games are being handled has been the subject of many heated debates, including the dubious choices for some of the key sponsors. As one journalist noted:

> The Games will bring urgently needed regeneration to parts of East London, and bring great opportunities for promoting many positive things such as inspiring children and young Londoners to take up sport and other physical activity. However, healthy physical activity can only be achieved if it is fuelled by healthy, nutritious food. Here lies the appalling mismatch between the top 2012 sponsors **McDonald's** and **Coca-Cola** *[emphasis in original text]* and other fast-food and drink companies who have successfully secured exclusive marketing rights with the Games and at other major sporting events, or secured sponsorship deals with top athletes, which then continues to perpetuate the perverse link between fast-food and drink and sporting achievement.[9]

This is again another vivid example of Deception via Association, wherein advertising is creating a subliminal connection between junk food and being physically fit and healthy. Now, you might think to yourself, *I'm much too smart to be suckered into thinking that high-sugar, high-acid, high-additive junk food products make you healthy.* Ok, if you're an intelligent person, that's probably the case. However, while you might know these foods are not going to make you healthy, the very act of linking *harmful* products to what are otherwise considered to be *wholesome* cornerstones of our culture, is sending a subtle message that these harmful products are somehow 'ok.' And when people think things are 'ok,' they'll buy them.

It becomes 'ok' to pump caffeine, sugar, phosphates and aspartame into our bodies instead of water when we're thirsty.

It becomes 'ok' to eat high-calorie, high-fat junk food for convenience or a treat.

Companies who produce these products are also 'ok'; after all, they're sponsoring the Olympics, so they must be 'ok,' even if they are creating harm elsewhere.

Deception via Association makes us unwittingly tolerant (if not forgiving) of a multitude of 'sins.'

GREENWASH: DECEPTION VIA GUILTY CONSCIENCE

Recently, I was travelling on the London Underground and noticed several adverts for a new company called Streetcar, which is part of a new wave of 'car clubs' cropping up around Britain. As of this writing, Streetcar claim to have a fleet of over 1,000 cars and vans parked at designated locations in different cities and counties around the UK, including London, Cambridge, Bristol, Brighton, Oxford, Edinburgh and Glasgow. Members pay an annual fee, which entitles them to hire local cars for short- or long-distance travel at hourly rates. Fuel and basic insurance are included in the fee. When finished with the car, the member returns it to its designated parking bay so another member can use it.[10]

While the idea of a car club sounded like a terrific idea at a glance, I was not so comfortable with how it was being marketed. The advert I saw had an alleged testimonial by a customer which said something to the effect of, *'Now I'm going green.'* There was something not quite right about this statement for me. In my experience, the average Londoner drives far less than he travels by public transport. In fact, when I first moved to London I bought a car but soon realised I didn't need it. Eventually I got rid of it. In my experience, a lot of Londoners don't have or use cars. Between the congestion charge, the traffic and the nightmare of trying to park, it really wasn't worth driving in London, especially when the public transport system in the UK is so extensive. Even when I left London I didn't replace my car and I haven't owned one for more than a decade now.

Knowing this, it seemed to me that 'going green' would only be applicable if the majority of Streetcar members were changing their lifestyle as a result of being in the car club. What we would have to see is both a reduction in new car purchases, as well as a reduction in car usage overall. But is that happening? The evidence from Cambridge seems not to support this idea. Deputy Leader of Cambridge City Council, Catherine Smart condoned the expansion of the company in her city, commenting that, '...for many families, belonging to the car club means they can completely avoid the need for a *second* car' *[emphasis added]*.[11]

A *second* car? Am I understanding correctly that families have been managing somehow without a second car, and now they will be *using* a second car through Streetcar? How is this a reduction in car usage? Now if significant amounts of people were opting not to replace their *first* car when it wore out, and switched to public transport, cycling or walking for most travel, using car club cars only for journeys that would be impossible or impractical via public transport, *maybe* we'd be able to say car clubs were helping us 'go green.'

But is that the case? It doesn't look like it. Nor does it even seem to be part of the plan. In an article entitled 'Making Cash While Going Green,' a radio station in Glasgow says of Streetcar, 'The worldwide car club hires out vehicles on a pay-as-you-go basis, *so city-dwellers who don't want to own a car can still get the use of one [emphasis added].*'[12] This doesn't say these people are going to *give up* their cars. In fact, if you read the comments on the previous article from Cambridge, you would clearly see the consensus is just the opposite. In the words of one Cambridge resident, 'Cambridge is, basically, giving in to car-centrism by making it easier to drive even if you don't own a car.' And still another reader cynically remarks, 'Are the city councillors going to use this service?'[13]

One of the big problems for drivers in British cities is limited parking space. Our city streets were built long before the age of motor vehicles, and many of the older Victorian houses, once homes for single families, have been converted into multi-family dwellings. This means our narrow streets are crammed with cars and parking is a nightmare. If car clubs could reduce the number of cars on our streets, this would relieve congestion not only on the roads but in our neighbourhoods. But in spite of the claims by Streetcar proponents, it doesn't sound like that's happening either. In Glasgow, Streetcar has been asking residents who *don't use* their parking spaces or driveways to rent them out, so they can park their own vehicles on residential streets. One Glaswegian who accepted their offer said, '*Not only am I doing my bit for the environment* by taking part in *a scheme which helps reduce cars* on the road, but I am also able to generate extra income' [emphasis added].[14]

Deception? Good grief, yes! First off, this isn't a 'scheme'; it's a privately owned *business*. Secondly, if the only way Streetcar can find parking spaces for the *two new vehicles* it places on UK streets every single day[15] is by renting space from residents who do not even *use* their spaces because they do not own a car, how in the world can we surmise they helping reduce the amount of cars on the road? Something doesn't add up.

But on top of everything else, the kicker is this: not a single one of Streetcar's advertised vehicles is 'green.' While advertised as 'fuel efficient,' Streetcar's fleet is comprised of Volkswagens and BMWs, all with standard petrol motors.[16] There's not even a hybrid car amongst them, let alone an electric vehicle.

I cannot see the marketing angle Streetcar has chosen to be anything more than pure 'greenwash'—the practice of trying to look 'green' to curry favour with the public. These marketing campaigns are simply exploiting environmental issues to niggle the guilty consciences of both consumers and (apparently) our city councillors. They have somehow convinced some people that using a car club is 'doing our bit for the environment' when in fact it is doing little if anything but turning a profit for the company. While I have no real objection to the idea of car clubs, what I do seriously object to is the exploitation of the very serious issue of carbon emissions through fluffy 'feel-good' marketing pieces that delude the public into thinking they are in any way helping our environment by joining or supporting a car club. We are not.

Streetcar is not the only car club in the world taking this angle; nor are car clubs the only companies on the planet guilty of greenwash. In his excellent book *Ethical Marketing and the New Consumer*[17] Chris Arnold cites dozens of 'greenwash' companies in every imaginable industry. It's a practice that is widespread and ultimately damaging for two very important reasons: 1) it deludes us into thinking we are addressing important environmental issues that are not being addressed, quite possibly making the situation worse as a result of our complacency and 2) it simply increases the culture of Deception in marketing, creating less trust, less transparency and less confidence between business owners and consumers.

TECHNOLOGY AND DECEPTION

There is an old adage that says 'seeing is believing.' But in this age of digital photography and CGI effects, seeing is more commonly grounds for disbelieving. We've even created a verb from the name of the graphic editing software Adobe Photoshop; when we 'Photoshop' someone's image, we mean we're blurring or removing unwanted elements, such as wrinkles or dark circles beneath the eyes (in a photo someone took of me on the beach, I even 'Photoshopped' out the very large *derriere* of a sunbather in a red bathing suit who was lying a few feet behind me).

I love technology and I see it as a wonderful tool for communication and creative expression. But like anything truly powerful, technology can also be used for not-so-ethical purposes. I'm sure it comes as no surprise to anyone today that digital technology is often used as a tool to create deceptive marketing. In the well-known advertising campaign started by Dove in 2005 called 'The Campaign for Real Beauty,' marketers ostensibly wanted to demonstrate how extreme this digital Deception can become, and how destructive it can be. The advert that kicked it all off was called 'Dove Evolution'—a one-minute video of time-lapsed photography of a natural-looking young girl who, at the hands of a make-up artist, hairstylist, lighting crew and digital image editor, became transformed into a glamorous creature bearing little resemblance to the original person. The video ends with the words, 'No wonder our perception of beauty is distorted.'[18] To further the campaign, Dove subsequently started a fund called 'The Self-Esteem Fund,' the stated purpose of which was 'to make real change in the way women and young girls perceive and embrace beauty' and to 'help free ourselves and the next generation from beauty stereotypes.'[19]

Dove's 'Campaign for Real Beauty' was controversial to say the least. While on the one hand it received the praise of many women (and mothers of girls) who were supportive of and grateful for this positive message, it also invoked an onslaught of tasteless YouTube parodies and accusations of hypocrisy. These accusations were spawned by the fact that Dove's parent company (Unilever here in the UK) also owns AXE cosmetics, whose sexually explicit adverts were sending exactly the *opposite* message to their audience. This unfortunate connection seriously undermined Dove's sincerity to say the least.

I have no desire to enter into a debate as to whether or not Dove's intentions were genuine. Assuming they were, if we take the message of the 'Dove Evolution' advert at face value, the statement it makes about how our perception of ourselves and the world has been distorted by the technology of marketing is certainly valid. We often say 'a picture is worth a thousand words' but this is actually an understatement. Visual imagery is far more impactful than words, especially in advertising.

Most modern adults are intellectually aware of this, but how confidently can we assert that we are unaffected by the regular bombardment of false images about beauty (or any other subject)? We might think we're not paying attention and are therefore not affected, but are we? Scientists have ascertained that the brain has the power to prioritise the visual images it receives. In other words, it receives the visual messages, processes them, and only brings things into our conscious awareness when it deems them to be necessary.[20] This does not, however, mean that the brain has ignored or deleted the information it has received. *All* the visual images we see enter our neural pathways and are stored in our brains, even if we have yet to bring them into our conscious awareness.

Whenever we find ourselves expressing negative beliefs about our physical appearance, or anything else for that matter, it's worth taking a moment to consider where these beliefs come from. What visual images of 'beauty' have we stored away in our unconscious memory over the years? How many of these images came from intentionally deceptive distortions of the truth from marketing? How tightly do we hold on to these beliefs in spite of *knowing* they have come from marketing and media? Which beliefs about beauty and personal self-worth are truly our own?

It's pretty mind-blowing when we finally come face-to-face with all the distortions about Self we have ingested via Deception in marketing. But it's even more mind-blowing when we realise how stubbornly we hold on to these distortions, insisting we do not measure up to them. The world of *maya* is the playground for Deception. The more we are conditioned to compare and measure ourselves, the more we are likely to be affected by the Deadly Sin of Deception.

SUMMARY: HOW DECEPTION IS MAKING US ILL

If the first four Deadly Sins began the process of unravelling the fabric of society, The Deadly Sin of Deception in marketing (or Deception in anything) is that which starts to reweave that fabric into something so unrecognisable we start to feel alien even within our own world.

Deceptive marketing makes our bodies and minds ill—especially in the case of food products marketed to vulnerable children who cannot yet discriminate, and are still developing both physically and socially. They respond to cravings without thought and are dependent upon the 'mass' food culture, such as school lunches and vending machines.

But on a much subtler level, Deception creates false ideologies which can lead us to accept things in our world as 'ok' that are actually not at all ok. It can make us complacent about important environmental issues, thus taking our attention away from the need to look for genuine solutions to these problems. It can create false associations between consumer products and our own self-worth, causing us to become increasingly ravenous and empty at the same time.

As we come to realise that nothing can satisfy this insatiable hunger and emptiness we feel, we begin to lose trust in commerce in general. We begin to blame big business for our problems and become suspicious of the intentions of companies, even if they happen to be good. We begin to create a world in which no one is to be trusted.

But it doesn't end there.

Eventually, after allowing ourselves to be deceived again and again, we start to mistrust our own senses and our own powers of discernment. We have believed other people's lies so many times that we begin to call ourselves stupid, helpless and naïve. We cease to trust our own intelligence and self-worth, but we hide our 'failures' from others lest they discover what a 'loser' we believe we are.[21]

We feel more disconnected, alone and powerless than ever.

We become cynical. We give up on our dreams because we cannot believe in anything anymore. Dreams are for the vulnerable; and the vulnerable are doomed to being cheated.

And when we watch a documentary that talks about how the rainforests are vanishing, we get angry. But little else happens. We shrug our shoulders, feeling disempowered.

We say, *'What can I do? That's just the way the world is—corrupt. It's too big for me to do anything about it.'*

And so we don't do anything about it, because for us, Deception has become the Truth.

No wonder our perception of beauty is distorted.

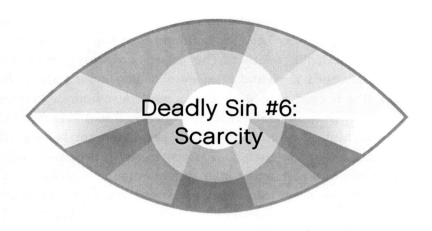

Deadly Sin #6:
Scarcity

'You can't always get what you want...'
~ The Rolling Stones[1]

One of the biggest beauty icons of the 20th Century was the late actress Audrey Hepburn. Her fine facial features, genteel demeanour and slender figure made her a favourite with men and women alike. Apart from her versatile acting talent, Hepburn was also widely renowned for her extensive charitable work for vulnerable children around the world during her time as UNICEF Goodwill Ambassador from 1989 until her death in 1993. When we think of Audrey, we think of an elegant woman who seemed to exude beauty without any effort whatsoever. But what few people know is that her slim physique was not some luck bestowed upon her by the beauty goddesses, but the result of hardship she endured early in life, which was more than likely partially responsible for her death from inoperable colon cancer at age 63.[2]

Audrey grew up in the Netherlands and was a teenager during World War II. During the German occupation of Holland in the 1940s, millions suffered and 18,000 died from starvation during the infamous *Hongerwinter* or 'Hunger Winter' that took place towards the end of the war. Amongst those suffering during those traumatic months were Audrey and her family. Her prolonged hunger made a permanent impact upon her relationship with food that was to continue throughout her life. In many published interviews, Audrey Hepburn spoke about how she had actually been 'chubby' as a child, but during the *Hongerwinter* she and her family were so hungry she started resenting the very *need* for food, and even began to feel angry towards food itself. To deal with her anger and resentment (and pain), she developed a mental strategy of telling herself she *didn't need* food. She is even quoted as having made a vow never to weigh more than 103 pounds (and standing at nearly 5 foot 7 inches tall, that is *very* thin). This in turn started her long-term behavioural pattern of not eating adequately to support good nutrition. In other words, she was in a permanent state of starvation and malnutrition, and although she never came out and used the word 'anorexia,' many of her biographers interpret her behaviour as being that of a serious eating disorder.[3] The fact that she eventually succumbed to colon cancer is thus no surprise as, according to some researchers, chronic malnutrition may account for up to 80% of all cases of colon cancer.[4] Having watched my own waif-like mother dwindle away to little more than bones until she died from colon cancer at age 69 just a few short months before Audrey's demise, after a lifetime of her smoking and eating like a bird, I can say I would have to agree.

HOW WE ARE HARD-WIRED TO RESPOND TO SCARCITY

I'd like to use the example of starvation as an analogy for how we human beings respond to Scarcity at an emotional and psychological level. Starvation is a kind of Scarcity—Scarcity of food and nourishment. When our bodies experience a prolonged Scarcity of food, they become undernourished and diseased. Eventually, they die.

And tragically, what often kills starving people is that their bodies become incapable of *absorbing* the very things that nourish them. The body of someone who is starving (and this includes anorexics) has difficulty absorbing nutrients. This can make a person seriously ill if food is reintroduced into the body too suddenly. In Ayurvedic medicine, if you go into a period of fasting as the result of an illness or as part of a personal discipline, you need to reintroduce food very gradually when the fast is over. Back in 2000, I had pancreatitis in India. During that time, my bodily functions shut down for nearly two weeks, and I was neither able to eat nor pass food at all. When I started to recover and my hunger started to return, apart from water the only thing doctors permitted me to ingest on the first day was a two-ounce glass of pineapple juice. The second day, I was given pineapple juice along with a tiny cup of very watery lentil broth with no salt or spice. Even after only two weeks of starvation, it took nearly a week before I could eat a complete meal. Scarcity is serious stuff.

At a more holistic level, if the *body* stops absorbing biological nutrients when it is exposed to Scarcity, what about the mind or emotions? In my experience, both personally and professionally, I have come to see that every aspect of us is hard-wired to respond to Scarcity. If we are starved of intellectual stimulation, we become less able to absorb new information. If we are starved of acknowledgement and encouragement, we become unable to accept praise or have self-belief. If we are starved of love and support, we become less able to receive love and support, and so on. Whatever it is that we are most deficient in, we become the most resistant to absorbing. And when many, many people become unable to absorb things like love, support, acknowledgement, praise, self-belief and intellectual stimulation, we as a society become very ill indeed.

In this light, Audrey's emotional response to Scarcity is not particularly odd. We see this kind of adaptive behaviour in people all the time, whether it has to do with lack of food or lack of love. It's ironic that our typical coping mechanism for Scarcity is to push away the very thing we most need and want, but it seems to be a part of how we are made. Scarcity—both physical and emotional— shuts us down. In fact, we'd be hard-pressed to find examples of one type of Scarcity not manifesting in the other.

Shutting down is almost autonomic. It is an unconscious, preventative measure that helps us cope with our feelings of lack. I call this condition 'the poverty of spirit.' When we are afflicted with this poverty of spirit, we walk through life feeling there is nothing or very little supporting us. We might feel the world is against us, God has forsaken us or we are alone. And just like malnutrition, living within this poverty of spirit becomes a self-fulfilling prophecy: the less love, wealth, joy, health and fulfilment we allow into us, the less comes to us over time.

In short:

Scarcity always creates more Scarcity.

THE GENETICS OF SCARCITY

There is a branch of biology called epigenetics, which has to do with the study of the alteration of the genetic code in living things as a result of external, environmental factors, especially during gestation. In other words, environmental factors surrounding a mother while she is pregnant can actually alter the genes of her unborn child, and impact that child's health for perhaps his or her entire life.

One of the most famous epigenetic studies was conducted with the victims of the Dutch *Hongerwinter*. In that study, it was shown that people who were fully developed reacted to the famine as you might expect—by becoming very thin. Because Audrey was already in her teens in 1944 when the famine began, her body (and mind) reacted this way. However, had Audrey been *pregnant* at the time, epigenetic studies suggest the famine would have likely produced the exact *opposite* effect on her child. The majority of the people studied who were conceived during the famine, while born underweight, had tended to be *overweight* their whole lives. Furthermore, they had a tendency towards diabetes, high blood pressure and a range of other metabolic and cardiovascular problems. Their explanation for this is admittedly speculative, but it certainly is thought-provoking:

> [We] think it's because your body tries to become as efficient as possible at storing calories, since there isn't much food around during your development. That works well, until suddenly you have all the food you need and more. Once you have too many calories, or even simply enough calories, your body can't stop storing calories. This causes you to have metabolic and cardiovascular problems associated with being overweight.[5]

To me, this is extremely compelling information on both a physical and metaphysical level. Using myself as an example, I have struggled through decades of metabolic and weight issues, and never really understood why when my own mother was a tiny figure of a woman. But understanding her lifelong pattern of malnutrition (including oxygen deprivation due to years of smoking, resulting in emphysema), it suddenly makes sense.

But the metaphysical implications are even more compelling, and we must ask ourselves: If human beings have a *holistic* response to Scarcity (i.e., we respond to it with our minds, bodies and emotions), then is it not logical that there is some sort of 'epigenetics' to our psychological and emotional responses to Scarcity? In other words, do our thoughts and feelings arising from trauma and lack get passed on to future generations?

I believe this is absolutely the case. We can see evidence of it every day. The poverty of spirit within families gets passed from generation to generation, whether in the form of economic hardship, abuse or other dysfunctional lifestyle patterns. These relentless psychological and emotional epigenetic patterns of Scarcity cause suffering not only for those who carry these patterns with them, but also for families, teachers, communities, employers, governments and anyone who interacts with them.

Seeing all of this, we simply must now ask ourselves three more important questions:

1. How is Scarcity at the foundation of economic theory?
2. How is Scarcity used in marketing?
3. Why in the world would people use Scarcity at all?

SCARCITY AND ECONOMICS

I was never a student of economics, so when I first started exploring the connection between Scarcity and economic theory, I was fascinated to find that Scarcity is at the very foundation of how many scholars define economics. Here are some definitions I found:

Scarcity is the fundamental economic problem of having **seemingly unlimited human needs and wants, in a world of limited resources.** It states that society has insufficient productive resources to fulfil all human wants and needs *[emphasis added]*.[6]

Scarcity is the condition where **human wants are forever greater** than the available supply of time, goods and resources...[it] is the **fundamental economic problem** that human wants exceed the availability of time, goods and resources. **Individuals and society therefore can never have everything they desire** *[emphasis added]*.[7]

Economics is the study of how best to **allocate scarce resources among competing uses**...Economic resources are limited in supply...Scarcity thus is the result of the **imbalance between our desires and available resources**...Thus it is **the foundation of economics** *[emphasis added]*.[8]

Wow. These are pretty powerful beliefs. Scarcity is 'the foundation of economics.' We live in a 'world of Scarcity.' We can 'never have everything we desire.' There is an inherent 'imbalance' in our world. If we take these and whittle them down, they can be reduced to two fundamental assumptions:

1. That human needs and wants are inherently *unlimited*
2. That the resources to satisfy those needs and wants are inherently *limited*

Our economic system is based upon an underlying belief that it cannot possibly bring fulfilment to all—*ever*. But if an entire economic system is based upon the assumption that it will never work, how can it possibly succeed?

Well...it isn't succeeding. Many economists today feel the paradigm of 'neoclassical economics' is starting to crumble.[9, 10, 11] Global economies are struggling, people in the West are surviving on the false-economy of credit, and our planet is in serious chaos both socially and environmentally.

But why?

To my non-economist mind, the problem seems to lie in the very assumption that Scarcity is the 'fundamental problem.' If whole nations of people live according to the belief that there simply isn't enough on this planet to go around, they will of course create imbalances attempting to ensure they have 'enough' for themselves. And the ironic result of this, of course, is that when people do this, they actually *create* the very Scarcity they fear.

But what is even more profound is that these Scarcity assumptions shape our *entire worldview*, not just our economy. They transform into a core belief system that leaves us in a very vulnerable place, where we are open to all the fears that arise from the 'inevitability' of Scarcity. As we have already seen, we human beings react to Scarcity at a physical, mental and emotional level, both as individuals and as whole societies. What impact does it make upon us at a global level when our Key Relationships with commerce, money and Source are driven by the assumption that Scarcity is inevitable?

But there is a catch: Scarcity cannot arise unless there is a 'human need or want' driving it. In other words, Scarcity is not so much a 'thing' as it is the ephemeral result of our own desires. There can be no Scarcity unless we have *the belief that we need something.* And getting to the root of these beliefs is the real key to understanding—and overcoming—Scarcity. Once we see how these beliefs arise, the entire issue of Scarcity begins to shift.

WE CANNOT LACK WHAT WE DO NOT BELIEVE WE NEED

> *'What is this you call property?*
> *It cannot be the earth, for the land is our mother,*
> *nourishing all her children, beasts, birds, fish and all men.*
> *The woods, the streams, everything on it belongs*
> *to everybody and is for the use of all.*
> *How can one man say it belongs only to him?'*
> **~ Massasoit**[12]

The one thing economists are right about is that Scarcity is *not* an absolute. It is proportionate to our needs and wants. So the question we really need to ask is this: Is our assumption that we human beings have unlimited desires that can never be satisfied fundamentally true?

I don't believe it is. In my reckoning, Scarcity is a *feeling* arising when we *believe* something is important for our happiness, while also believing it is difficult or impossible to attain. This is not just limited to 'things,' but also to intangibles—love, connection, beauty, self-worth and so on.

Consider the period in history when the Europeans began to settle in North and Central America. The Native Americans whom they met had no notion of the ownership of land. Apart from the practice of agreeing to hunting rights on specific territory, the idea of *ownership* of land was as foreign to them as the idea of owning the air. The land was the Earth, and the Earth could not be claimed by any human. This fundamental difference in the belief systems between these two cultures was quite possibly the most influential factor in the clash that would arise between them. One group had a 'need and want' that the other simply didn't perceive. One felt lack, and the other did not. Why the Europeans felt the way they did was surely, in part, a cultural residue of their long battle to rise above the remnants of their own feudal system from past centuries, but as the Native peoples of America had no such cultural conditioning, their needs and wants were markedly different.

Our modern world would undoubtedly look very different had the early European settlers come to the Americas with a different worldview. The expanse of land that was actually available to them when they came to the New World was probably mind-boggling, compared to the geographic parameters of the European nations from which they had come. Imagine if they had adopted the practice of living *with* the land, rather than owning it, as the Native peoples were demonstrating. What would the Americas have looked like by the time we came to the 21st Century? This single change in perspective would have created a *completely* different future. It would have changed the shape of governments, land use, technology, education and, of course, the economy.

But the fact that Europeans came from comparatively tiny countries in a post-feudal society. They had experienced Scarcity of resources partially due to famine and disease, and partially due to ongoing political squabbles both within and between their nations. These experiences eventually fostered the idea of property ownership; when we believe there is not enough to go around, we inevitably seek to protect ourselves by creating the idea of ownership. And if everyone behaves this way, we become vulnerable if we do not follow suit. Once again, Scarcity always creates more Scarcity.

We cannot judge in hindsight and say this behaviour was 'right' or 'wrong.' As we've seen, our economic belief systems are inherited and often difficult to recognise, and fear is often the gatekeeper of that belief system. Unless the European settlers had somehow been able to see through the filter of their own fundamental belief system, overcoming economic fears that had been passed down through their culture for centuries, there is very little possibility they would have behaved otherwise.

SCARCITY AND MARKETING

Understanding how we create and respond to our belief systems is the key to understanding how Scarcity works in marketing. As we have seen, Scarcity is one of the most fundamental triggers of human behaviour, both physical and emotional, both conscious and unconscious. And because it is so powerful, the potential for exploiting Scarcity for selfish, if not malicious, ends is immense. This passage from a blogger on marketing just about sums it up:

> Competition for scarce resources serves as an extremely powerful motivator, because it causes us to react with primitive and emotional responses rather than with logic and reasoning...The effect of this can encourage people to buy things they would normally not buy, and pay more than they would normally pay. Simply because they feel they are competing against someone else to obtain it [sic].[13]

What I find so astonishing about this blog post is that the author talks as if using Scarcity to evoke 'primitive and emotional responses' rather than 'logic and reasoning' in order to 'encourage people to buy things they would normally not buy, and pay more than they would normally pay' is actually a pretty smart thing to do. And the truth is, most old-school marketers would not only be likely to agree, but they also use this knowledge to their advantage *all* the time in their marketing by *creating the illusion* of Scarcity in the public eye. They do this primarily via three strategies:

1. Creating false needs
2. Creating false shortages
3. Creating perceived and planned obsolescence

But wait a minute. Didn't the earlier economists say that our capitalist economic system was founded upon *solving* the problem of supplying 'unlimited' human needs and wants with 'scarce' resources? Then how is it possible that capitalists themselves might be responsible for *creating* these unlimited human needs and wants in the first place? Does our 'relentless quest for more and better' really arise from 'necessity, increased income, development and growth'[14] or are we largely being programmed to *believe* we need things we do not? In other words, is Scarcity just as manufactured as our supposed needs?

CREATING FALSE NEEDS

The difference in perspective towards land ownership between the European settlers and the Native American people is a good example of how human needs and wants are not always based upon what we *actually* need, but frequently upon what we *believe* we need. We saw this also in the case of the cigarette industry and many others we have examined thus far. If we do not believe we need something, as long as it is not actually vital to our survival, we cannot feel the 'insatiable wants and desires' arising from feelings of Scarcity if it is absent. Conversely, if we *believe* we need something, even if it is not essential to our survival, we develop the *belief* of Scarcity if we cannot have it. And because the belief in Scarcity motivates us at a cellular level, marketers know that *creating false needs* can help them motivate consumers to buy what they simply do not need, and which might actually be harmful.

Annie Leonard, founder of 'The Story of Stuff' and author of the book of the same name, uses the term 'manufactured demand' to express this practice of creating false needs. In her excellent video 'The Story of Bottled Water'[15] she shows how the bottled water industry became successful using three strategies to 'manufacture' the demand for bottled water: scaring, seducing and misleading. Initially, they scared the public into believing tap water was unsafe. Next, they 'seduced' the public into buying into the idea that bottled water was fresher, cleaner and healthier, by using images of natural settings on the packaging and adverts. Finally, they grossly misled consumers about the health benefits of bottled water. Far from being a healthier alternative, recent laboratory studies in Germany have demonstrated that water in plastic bottles actually leaches oestrogen-mimicking chemicals[16] that some claim are carcinogenic (although the claim is still highly controversial, I myself believe it is true). Thus, the entire bottled water industry is founded upon a fabricated need.

Unfortunately, creating false needs does not create imaginary effects. In her book *The Overspent America,* and cited by Annie Leonard in *The Story of Stuff,* Juliet B. Schor draws a link between television viewing and consumer spending and debt, estimating that 'each additional five hours of television watched per week led to an additional thousand dollars of spending per year.'[17, 18] Nor are the *emotional* needs we imagine we will fill by overspending truly imaginary. In order for marketers to create false needs, they first have to create feelings of fear, disconnection or inadequacy. Once we are convinced of these feelings, we will do anything to fill the emptiness they bring. When it is not filled, we continue to search for it, having become addicted to the seduction of consumerism.

And that is when the vicious cycle of economic Scarcity actually begins in the form of debt, waste and imbalance—both ecological and economic. Soon we begin to justify our consumer behaviour, *believing we live in a world of lack.* But the root of our fears is actually a phantom of our own creation.

CREATING FALSE SHORTAGES

If human beings can be motivated to act by the fabrication of false needs, it stands to reason they can also be motivated by the fabrication of the *shortage* of those false needs. In other words, people can be stirred into action not only if there is an actual shortage of a perceived need, but if they are simply *led to believe* there is a shortage. A 'false shortage' is exactly that: being led to believe something we think we need is not readily available. Like false needs, false shortages (or false Scarcity) are illusory. They can be created by making people believe there is a limited quantity of something they want, a limited timeframe of availability, a limited timeframe at a particular price, or a combination of all of these. In the world of business and marketing, false shortages are known to 'elevate consumer demand above levels that may otherwise be achieved in the absence of such scarcity' when in fact the product or service is 'neither precious, nor difficult to produce.'[19]

We see examples of this nearly every day, some more extreme than others. Marketers are continually using Scarcity to 'motivate' and manipulate people into action. John Quelch of Harvard Business School says that 'creating the illusion of scarcity can be a smart marketing strategy' because marketers 'understand that, by using the illusion of scarcity, they can accelerate demand. This false scarcity encourages us to buy sooner and perhaps to buy more than normal.'[20] Quelch offers the pre-launches of the iPhone and the seventh Harry Potter book as examples of marketing campaigns that gave the public the impression that supplies would run out before demand was met. This not only resulted in massive sales of both products but also, Quelch adds, 'The heavy crowds drove sales of related products in Apple stores and bookstores during a relatively slow sales month.' False shortages help to 'hype up' the perceived value, often resulting in a temporary increase in retail price of a particular product and a quick increase in short-term profit.

False shortages are all around us and they come in many shapes and sizes. They can be so subtle, we scarcely notice them. Some are seemingly innocuous, such as a limited-time offer of something at a special price. This kind of 'Scarcity of opportunity' is so common we have come to accept it as normal.

The flipside of a 'limited-time special offer' is the *planned price increase*. A recent example occurred here in the UK when our VAT (value added tax, which is the equivalent to sales tax in the US) increased from 17.5% to 20% on 1 January 2011. There was not a shop on the High Street that did not take advantage of this planned price increase by having massive post-Christmas sales saying, 'Buy now and save before the VAT increase.' In truth, they would have had big post-Christmas sales anyway, just as they have every year between Boxing Day and New Year's Eve. But by filling the public with fear of this 2.5% increase, they were also able to fill their shops with customers frantically trying to pick up everything they could lay their hands on. I only know this because I went shopping to pick up a few household items on New Year's Eve afternoon, and found myself amongst throngs of people loading up so many bagsful of goods you'd have thought it was Christmas Eve rather than New Year's Eve.

What I found so bizarre about all this was that, when it boils right down to it, a 2.5% increase is about the price of a large cappuccino on every £100 purchase. To me, it's not *really* a big motivator to get me to spend more when I don't need to. But having had to wait in some pretty long queues to pay for my shower curtain hooks and purple bed cushions, I'd have to say this Scarcity strategy clearly worked for the retailers.

Planned price increases are just as powerful a 'motivator' as false shortages, because they send the same message: 'You can't always get what you want.' Mortgage brokers use planned rises in interest rates to their advantage in the property market. Oil companies use planned increases in the cost of oil to their advantage at the pumps. False Scarcity is used by corporations, small businesses, Internet marketers, journalists and even governments. Keep your eyes open, and you'll see it nearly every day. The next time you feel motivated to make a purchase simply because it is on sale, or to buy two of something instead of one because of a limited-time special offer, take a moment to ask yourself why you're *really* buying it.

CREATING PERCEIVED OBSOLESCENCE

Throughout the 1990s, I co-owned a small electronic recording studio and dance record label with my then-husband. We produced some pretty nice records there and recorded some albums for independent artists. To stay competitive in the electronic dance market, we felt some pressure to upgrade our equipment on a continual basis. It's not that the equipment broke. It's that it was 'out of date.' Synthesisers and electronic effects do not all sound the same. A good producer can tell exactly what year a recording was made just from the sound of the synths and reverbs used. No sooner had we purchased the latest toy, we would find ourselves 'needing' another—and then another. Scarcely a month went by without feeling the urge to make another major purchase. And if we couldn't buy it, we felt anxiety over how it would impact both our business and our creativity. After years of being 'starving artists,' we had truly become hardware junkies.

Then, as the 21st Century loomed on the horizon and technology got smaller, faster and more amazing than ever, we also became software junkies. Slowly all of our very expensive hardware became utterly obsolete. A decade of building our studio had run us into serious debt. At the end of the day, what our studio earned for us was never nearly as much as we spent.

The continual, nagging urge to buy the latest piece of kit is actually quite common amongst musicians of all genres. Back when I taught music technology, I warned students about the dangers of becoming hardware and software junkies, but all too many of them became addicts nonetheless. What drove all of us into a mad spiral of debt all in the name of music?

The answer: 'perceived obsolescence.'

Perceived obsolescence is when a consumable you have is still perfectly good, but it is *perceived* as being no longer valuable. For example, in the early 80s analogue musical equipment was rendered obsolete by the rise of digital equipment. This early digital equipment used '8-bit' technology. Then, towards the late 80s, this 8-bit digital equipment was rendered obsolete by the appearance of 12-bit and then 16-bit technology. Later, 16-bit was replaced with 24-bit, 32-bit, 64-bit, 96-bit...I've lost count.

You don't need to understand what any of those numbers mean to understand the point. As technology 'improves' we find ourselves seduced into buying the latest gear. Things are not really obsolete; it is only our perception that has rendered them as such. They still work just as well (or poorly) as they ever did, but we have become convinced we *need* them to do more, so we reject them in favour of the latest model.

Ironically, the music industry expressed an unpredicted reaction to this perceived obsolescence in the early 90s. Many musicians, both in Europe and the US, rejected the 'cold' sound of digital equipment and were hoarding older analogue synthesisers from the 70s and early 80s (I know, because I owned many of them myself!). Personally, I believe this was partially because so many musicians were broke, and couldn't afford the newer technologies, so they were grabbing up keyboards that had been discarded by those who could afford to buy the new digital kit. However, the marriage between these older synths with digital technologies produced sounds that were unprecedented, and thus began the age of hip hop, house, acid, trance and rave music.

What is interesting about this phenomenon is that it created an increase in perceived value of the old 'obsolete' instruments, and drove the price of these 'vintage' instruments sky-high. Of course, a mass rush to buy up used, vintage instruments is not particularly good for business if you happen to be a manufacturer selling brand new products. A classic example of an instrument that 'should have' become obsolete but underwent a resurrection is the Roland TB-303 (originally produced in 1982-84), which had become the unexpected cornerstone of underground dance music in the early and mid 90s. Roland Corporation and other electronic instrument manufacturers realised they needed to do something radical to take back the market. In short, they had to devise a way to stop people from buying used equipment, even if it was their own brand. In 1996, they released their MC-303, the first in a series of models to emulate their own 'vintage' TB-303, but with the latest digital technology, at last *rendering their own product obsolete!* I find this to be a remarkable example of how companies depend upon perceived obsolescence, and how far they will go to ensure the balance between old and new is maintained.

We'd be hard-pressed to find anyone in the 'developed' world who has not fallen prey to perceived obsolescence. Every time we feel the urge to upgrade our operating system, buy the latest style shoe, replace our wardrobe because the height of our hemlines or the flare of our trousers are just too 'last season,' we are the victims of perceived obsolescence. It causes us to overspend, over-consume and dispose of things that are not actually ready to be discarded. We are once again propelled by the unconscious reaction to a feeling of Scarcity, by being led to believe if we don't have the latest thing, the best thing, the fastest thing, etc., we will lose out in some way.

When I referred to myself earlier as a 'hardware junkie,' I wasn't being cute or colourful. I meant it. When we are hooked by the insidious allure of perceived obsolescence, *we are addicts.* An addict cannot live without his next 'fix.' He is dependent upon and controlled by his addiction. He will drive himself to the point of destruction in pursuit of what he believes will feed his addiction. He never feels like he has enough. He is in a state of continual 'need'— continual Scarcity.

Consumerism is a drug.

Perceived obsolescence is the syringe.

Scarcity marketers are the pushers.

It's up to us to stop using.

CREATING PLANNED OBSOLESCENCE

I am pretty eco-conscious in my personal and professional life. I have a printer at home but I don't use it (or even turn it on) unless it is absolutely vital for me to have something in hard copy. And over the past few years, I have become increasingly eco-conscious and have been printing less and less. So why is it that my printers don't seem to last any longer than they did when I used them all the time? It seems after I've owned my printer for a certain period of time, it simply stops working and tells me 'Your printer's parts are at the end of their service life,' even though a few minutes ago it was printing just fine. What gives? Is it my imagination or do my printers have a self-destruct mechanism built into them that goes off at a set interval after they leave the factory, regardless of the amount of use they have had? Am I the only person experiencing this?

Apparently I am not. When investigating consumer forums for Epson printers (the brand I always end up buying, for some reason), it seems a heck of a lot of people are talking about the 'self-destruct' features in Epson printers. I say 'self-destruct features' (plural) because it covers *many* components of the printer:

First of all, there's the ink cartridge. The word in the forums is that Epson puts a chip in their ink cartridges so they stop the printer from working either when they go below a certain level or when they are tampered with. This chip makes it virtually impossible to refill cartridges (which would be more 'environmentally friendly,' as it would create less waste) because the cartridges won't work anyway after the chip has gone off. True, there are many helpful techies on the Internet who will give you solutions such as how to reset this chip,[21] but how many people amongst the millions who are buying these printers are going to do that?

Next, there are the ink pads. These are the spongy things inside the printer that absorb the excess ink. At some point they become saturated and need to be replaced. You would think the manufacturer would make this easy to do (like the way you clean out the overflow in your washing machine every month or so), but they don't. Instead, this particular manufacturer offers no solution to the problem. They simply say your unit needs servicing. Of course, if your low-end printer only cost you between £30 and £50 and service charges run about £30 or £40 an hour, what are you likely to do? Of course, you run out and buy a new printer. Again, I found instructions on the Internet for how to replace the ink pads[22] but not only is it a messy task, the parts are frequently not easily available, and not a whole lot cheaper in comparison to the cost of a new printer. So how many people bother to find out how to fix the problem and go to the effort of actually doing it? My guess is not many.

And then there is the whole printer in general. Many people on consumer forums I have visited seem to believe there is actually a self-destruct mechanism built in to certain printers, wherein they simply 'shut off' and refuse to work shortly after the warranty runs out! While this may or may not be the result of the afore-mentioned flooded ink pads (my printer said nothing about the ink pads needing replacing; it simply said my 'parts' are no longer serviceable!), and I have found no concrete evidence that Epson has an intentional 'time bomb' built into their units, the fact remains that these kinds of brick walls, more often than not, result in the consumer going out and buying another printer.

I am sure you recognise this scenario, whether we are talking about printers, mobile phones, car parts, canned food or other consumables. And I'm sure we have all gone out and bought ourselves a new printer (or whatever) simply because it seemed like the easiest solution. But while it might look like the *easiest* solution, have we considered the bigger impact this makes upon our society, planet, health and economic wellbeing?

HOW OBSOLESCENCE HITS US IN THE WALLET

Most of us buy a low-end printer to save money, but if it suddenly shuts down after less than two years of use without any means to make it work again, we're stuck with having to make the choice of servicing it or buying a new one. If there's no economical way to get it serviced, in all likelihood we will simply get a new one. We might choose to buy a new printer every two years or so because it seems like the most economical option, but it's quite likely we'll end up spending more in the long-term on cheap printers than we might have spent had we bought a more expensive one in the first place. After getting tired of having to replace our printer so frequently, we finally might be tempted to spend a little more on a more expensive model; but in all likelihood this new, more expensive one will become technologically 'obsolete' by the time the cheap printer would have worn out anyway. Really, between perceived obsolescence and planned obsolescence, we're caught between a rock and a hard place.

Take a moment to consider how much money you have spent on printers in the past 10 years, or any other modern commodity that simply *wore out*. You might also ask yourself this same question with regards to clothing. When I was a child, my mother's wardrobe from the 1940s and 1950s was almost indestructible. The quality of the dyes, the tailoring and the weave of the fabrics were always superb. I remember when I was a teenager, I used to take the beautifully woven fabric from my mother's old woollen skirts and turn them into 60s fashions with my sewing machine. Some of my trendiest 'mod' outfits were made from recycled fabrics from the late 1940s.

But these days, most clothing I buy tends to look sad and old within a few washings. Our Walmart and Primark consumer culture has trained us to be happy with things that are 'cheap and cheerful,' but in reality we are caught continually in the cycle of needing to replace everything we own within a relatively short span of time. Between the planned obsolescence of cheaply made clothing and the perceived obsolescence of an ever-changing fashion industry, we are compelled to buy clothing more frequently than would otherwise be necessary. 'Cheap and cheerful' is sheer delusion.

NOT A CONSPIRACY THEORY

Planned obsolescence is neither paranoia nor a figment of our imagination. It is a consciously executed practice within our modern business culture. What might (or might not) surprise you to learn is that planned obsolescence is actually a key component of the modern capitalistic model. Without it, so-called 'unlimited growth' is impossible. Activist and writer Micah White explains how planned obsolescence was proposed as a possible solution to rectify the economic challenges during the Great Depression of the 1930s:

'Planned obsolescence' may sound like a conspiracy theory but it was once openly discussed as a solution to the Great Depression. In fact, most scholars trace the origin of the term to Bernard London's 1932 pamphlet, 'Ending the Depression Through Planned Obsolescence,' in which London blames the global economic Depression on consumers who disobey 'the law of obsolescence' by 'using their old cars, their old tires, their old radios and their old clothing much longer than statisticians had expected.' London's sinister solution was to propose a government agency that would determine the lifespan of each manufactured object whether it is a building, a ship, a comb or a shoe. Those frugal consumers who insisted on using their products past the expiration date would be penalized. London explained his plan simply: 'I propose that when a person continues to possess and use old clothing, automobiles and buildings, after they have passed their obsolescence date, as determined at the time they were created, he should be taxed for such continued use of what is legally 'dead.'[23]

Consumer watch-dog Annie Leonard says, 'planned obsolescence is another word for "designed for the dump."'[24] The objective of planned obsolescence (or 'death dating') is to control and limit the lifespan of products, so consumers must purchase new products at more or less *predictable* intervals of time. Having 'self-destruct' chips in our electronic devices is one way to ensure this. Having a 'sell by' or expiry date on food, drugs or cosmetics is another. Even when our Brita water pitchers flash after so many days it increases the likelihood we will replace our water filter cartridge whether it is used up or not. The theory is that if companies can predict the intervals at which people will buy their products, they can also predict their profits and ensure business growth.

But surely this is a delusion.

What if consumers simply move towards a different brand?

What if advancements in technology render their products completely obsolete or sudden changes in economic trends or social values shift the way people spend?

In spite of these 'what ifs,' planned obsolescence is a major part of modern business. In *Made to Break* author Giles Slade gives many examples of how planned obsolescence has been used in business since at least the 1930s, in the manufacture of everything from automobiles to lightbulbs.[25] It is, frankly, everywhere.

THE ECOLOGICAL EFFECTS OF OBSOLESCENCE

It's easy to see how buying more products than we actually need impacts our bank accounts. But our over-consumption is also responsible for serious ramifications at an environmental level. Apart from the devastating effects of over-exhaustion of our natural resources, or the pollutants and toxins generated in the process of manufacturing, what about all those things we *throw away?* Annie Leonard says our linear system of production is a 'system in crisis' because 'you cannot run a linear system on a finite planet indefinitely.'[26] She gives the shocking statistic that 'the average US person consumes twice as much as they did 50 years ago,' and that 99% of everything we purchase is 'trashed within six months.'

While more and more of us are becoming conscientious about recycling plastic bags and glass bottles, very few of us give much thought to the even bigger environmental hazard of the rapid consumption of electronic goods. Think back to the last time you disposed that broken printer, TV, mobile phone or computer when it became 'obsolete,' either by death dating or because it couldn't do what the latest gadget could do.

Leonard says our 'designed for the dump' culture is causing us to generate 25 million tonnes of e-waste per year,[27] and that even those electronics that are said to be 'recycled' are not truly. In fact, she says most recycling of e-waste is 'anything but green.' While reusable metals might be salvaged, the remainder of the materials are either put into landfills or incinerated, releasing toxins like PVC, mercury, solvents and flame retardants into our soil and atmosphere. Heck, that old TV I tossed out when it blew up in 2008 probably had as much as five pounds of poisonous lead inside of it. According to Leonard, 'IBM's own data revealed that its workers had 40% more miscarriages and were significantly more likely to die from blood, brain and kidney cancer,' owing to exposure to toxins emitted from electronic goods.

At a practical level, the only solution to these issues is to undo the unholy marriage between perceived obsolescence (via marketing) and planned obsolescence (via manufacturers), and rethink our economic model. Leonard says that 'product take-back laws,' wherein manufacturers become legally bound to deal with the waste generated from the products their customers discard, are certainly one way forward, as they would compel manufacturers to make things that were longer-lasting, less toxic and more recyclable.[28] But such change is unlikely to happen unless manufacturers have an incentive; this incentive can only happen if consumers come together and insist such changes are initiated and enforced, for the sake of everyone on the planet.

All this brings us back around to consider the root cause of all of these forms of Scarcity—Disconnection. Laws might be necessary when ethics and values have become distorted, but as we've seen throughout the six 'Deadly Sins' examined so far, laws are easily twisted to serve selfish ends. The only true, permanent solution is a radical shift in value system wherein we come back to living in tune and in rhythm with our planet, our home. If we as a culture were connected to Source, not only would we never dream of polluting the planet with toxic e-waste, we would never have thought to invent products containing environmental toxins in the first place. We would never be susceptible to planned or perceived obsolescence, because it would simply be against our core values and worldview.

Then, the only thing that would become obsolete would be obsolescence itself.

SUMMARY: HOW SCARCITY IS MAKING US ILL

We started this chapter by discussing how Scarcity is built into our modern economic model, and is even taught in universities as one of the fundamental elements of economics. The underlying belief of Scarcity is that there is a fundamental imbalance between human wants and our ability to fulfil them. Scarcity is seen as one of the most compelling motivators in marketing and spin doctors of Scarcity appear not just in advertising, but also in journalism, media, politics and any occupation involved in the business of 'selling' ideas and beliefs.

But Scarcity messages can only impact us when two things are present: 1) you must have a genuine belief you need something and 2) you must feel uncomfortable by the idea that you cannot have it.

The Deadly Sin of Scarcity in marketing is the practice of creating false needs and wants, and then creating various means by which people will feel anxious about ownership of these things. Strategies such as planned and perceived obsolescence are ways of manipulating these anxieties. Mostly, these false needs are created upon the message that we are already in some way lacking—that there is Scarcity and lack of wholeness in our own being. We are told we need to be sexier, thinner, richer, more attractive, more sophisticated, more prestigious, more advanced, more, more, more...But the truth is, not only do we not need these things, the things themselves are illusory. They are simply ideas we have been conditioned to believe. But all the products in the world cannot convince us we are enough, we are loved, we have value or we are important. And because these things never bring us what they say they will, we are left feeling ever-desirous of more. Thus we get caught in a whirlwind of Scarcity...or at least we believe we are. In truth, there is no such thing. Scarcity is just a belief—an illusion created from the feeling of lack arising when we are not satisfied by our 'false' needs.

And by false needs I am not just talking about our addiction to the latest gadgets. I am talking even deeper than that. On a visit to the United States in January 2011, I was shocked at how many people told me they were staying in jobs they hated, often putting aside their true dreams and aspirations, because they were terrified of losing their health insurance. The irony, of course, is that the stress of their jobs and the unhappiness they feel are far more likely to *make* them ill than if they lived happy, fulfilled lives.

Economic dependency is integral to this Scarcity model. We convince ourselves we need pension plans, life insurance, health insurance, indemnity insurance and, above all, good credit ratings. We convince ourselves we do not have enough money to attain our (false) needs, so we become dependent upon credit to attain a standard of living we are told we 'should' have. But the web of debt in which many of us find ourselves is, more often than not, due to the fact that we as a culture do not recognise the difference between what we actually need and what we have been convinced we need— through marketing.

Human beings existed for thousands of years without the majority of modern commodities we now consider essential. Why are we willing to put ourselves through so much agony, anxiety and stress working to attain needs that have been fabricated, and are not really fundamental to our physical, spiritual, social or emotional wellbeing? It seems to me this is the real reason why many of us feel so trapped and so economically challenged.

Our natural world is organised in such a way that our genuine needs for life replace and replenish themselves. Food grows. Water flows. Our bodies heal. People die. The next generation is born. Life is amazingly intelligent. And while, in the name of 'civilisation' we have created many needs for ourselves which we now find difficult to do without, so much of what we feel we lack is due to our belief that we need more than we actually do.

If such needs are actually false, they are also ephemeral; there is no possibility of attaining what they promise to give us. If we continue to run after that which cannot be attained, we will drown in our own poverty of spirit. Scarcity only ever creates more Scarcity. It will create more wars, more lies, more deception, more separation, more suffering, more stress, more illness and ultimately more hopelessness. And then we will indeed find ourselves in lack of thing that *do* make us wealthy—clean water, fresh air, nutritious food, fertile soil, connected communities, self-worth and so many other *genuine* human needs.

If marketers stopped creating false needs, the public would stop over-consuming.

If we stopped over-consuming, we would stop exploiting the Earth and each other.

If we stopped exploiting, we might re-establish our ability to validate both ourselves and others, so everyone would feel a sense of self-worth.

If we had self-worth, we would stop feeling helpless and emotionally impoverished.

If we stopped feeling emotionally impoverished, we would stop going into debt, because we would stop seeking external gratification as a means to fill whatever it is we feel we lack.

If we were not so much in debt, we wouldn't need to work so hard at jobs we didn't like.

If we stopped doing what we didn't like, we'd have time to do things we liked, and would feel richer, fuller, happier and healthier...

The list goes on.

The onus of eradicating Scarcity is on manufacturers, marketers *and* consumers. While manufacturers and marketers must take responsibility for the impact they create when utilising Scarcity to manipulate public spending habits, consumers also need to step back from Scarcity marketing and refuse to allow it to control their destiny. But these behavioural changes will only occur if we as a society commit to re-establishing our lost connection to the Whole— the Whole of our society, our economy and our natural world. As long as we regard ourselves as separate and disconnected, no lasting shift of behaviour can possibly occur.

Edward Bernays had it right about one thing—people behave in response to what they believe is true, and this truth may or may not have much to do with what is *actually* true.

The Truth is we live in an abundant Universe, when we live in Connection with it.

Scarcity is the great lie.

And it is this lie that drives us to compete for space, which brings us to the last of our Deadly Sins: Competition.

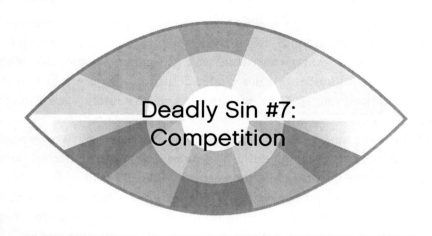

Deadly Sin #7: Competition

'There can be only one.'

~ The Highlander[1]

ack in 1965 when I was in 5th grade, our school held a
spelling bee in which two students from each class, from
grades 5 through 8, would be selected to compete for the
chance to go on to the regional spelling bee competition. I was
selected as one of the two representatives from my class. My co-
contender was a girl named Kathy. Kathy was a good friend who had
always been a very close 'number-2' to my 'number-1' position in the
class. Being the perennial number-1 was not always a happy role for
me. While it might have pleased my parents and teachers, it did little
for my social life at Catholic school. Most teachers in those days were
not inclined to treat students equally or even with respect. Slower
students were frequently verbally humiliated, and misbehavers were
commonly beaten with a yardstick in front of their peers.

While most of us today would find such practices to be
unthinkably cruel, what might not be so obvious is the impact such
inequity had upon the students who were *excelling* in the system.
Because my grades were good, teachers always gave me extra
responsibilities (whether I wanted them or not), setting me apart
from the other students. Some of my classmates viewed me with
resentment, and cooked up many schemes to get me worked up or to
get the 'privileged girl' into trouble. Two of them—one boy and one

girl—seemed devoted to the task of being my personal tormentors, especially around grade 5, when their bullying grew to a fever pitch.

All this set the stage for what was to happen on the day of the spelling bee. All students from grades 5 through 8 were taken to the school auditorium. The hall was packed. Kathy and I were brought onto the stage along with the other spelling bee contenders. She and I felt dwarfed amongst the older children on the stage. It was scary standing next to these gigantic 8th graders, who, at nearly 14 years old, looked like adults, while we were only little 10-year-olds.

Then the spelling bee began. The words were fairly easy at first, and both Kathy and I sailed through the first couple of rounds. Then, as the competition progressed, kids started to get eliminated. The other 5th graders were the first to go. Then the 6th graders went. Even one or two 7th graders choked and were knocked out of the contest. Soon Kathy and I were left on the stage with just a handful of 7th and 8th graders towering over us. I started to get nervous and could feel myself getting very hot under the lights of the stage.

Then my turn came again and I walked up to the microphone in front of the audience of my peers and teachers to spell my next word. I can still remember what it was: 'sheriff.' I heard the word and repeated it and...hesitated. I knew there were double letters in it, but under all the pressure I simply couldn't see the word in my mind. Did it have two r's? Two f's? Both? Needing to make a decision, I plunged ahead and spelled the word, not at all sure of myself. After I finished spelling the word, there was a weighty, pregnant pause. The hot stage lights seemed blinding as I stood there waiting for the verdict from the judges. My glasses fogged up as I could feel the salty sweat ready to drip into my eyes, but I didn't dare move. It lasted probably for all of about three seconds, but it seemed more like five minutes.

Then I heard the fateful 'ding' of the bell on the judges' desk—I had misspelled the word. I was out of the competition. While I was disappointed, I also was sort of relieved to be able to get off that stage and take a seat in the audience.

As I sat down amongst my classmates, almost as if orchestrated, my two personal 'bullies' turned around and started chiming, 'You *lost?* You lost! Bet you're not used to losing, huh? Nya-nya! You're a loser! *Loooo-ser!'*

'Hey, loser, Kathy's beating you. Betcha you're jealous, huh? You must be jealous. You *must* be. You're jealous, Lynn. You are. You're jealous. *Jea-lous! Jeeeeea-lous!'*

Kathy got up to spell her next word and made it through to the next round. Soon she was standing up there with only three other students, all 8th graders. Now the bullies had gotten a few sympathetic followers to join them in their chanting, *'Jea-lous! Jea-lous!'* I could feel myself getting even hotter than when I had been up on stage. I felt embarrassed and angry but could not speak up, especially with our teacher, Sister Mary What's-her-name, shooting us the evil eye every few moments.

But more than that, I was confused. *Jealous?* It hadn't even occurred to me to be jealous. Kathy was my friend.

Was I jealous?

I didn't know what jealousy felt like. I knew I was feeling hot and angry at my 'tormentors.' I knew I felt humiliation. But was it because I had lost, or because I was being teased? Was I really a loser? Was it important to win? Was I *supposed* to want to win? Was I *supposed* to feel bad that I hadn't won?

I wanted to run. I wanted to scream.

Is this jealousy? If it is, I don't want it, I thought. *It feels horrible. This is the worst feeling I've ever had in my life.*

I shut my eyes and focussed on the horrible feeling I was feeling in my body and my mind and—I prayed.

Dear God, please take away my jealousy. I don't want it. Take it away from me, please. It's horrible. Never let me feel jealous. Never, ever, ever! Please, please, please. I want to feel happy for Kathy. She's my friend. Make me happy for Kathy. Please, please...

I could feel the heat and discomfort of my emotions mounting like an inferno inside me. It was the first genuine moral crisis I had ever experienced in my life.

Then, something truly remarkable happened. I began to feel the heat leave my body. I became filled with a peacefulness and serenity I had never before known. I felt a lightness of being. If there was ever an example of a prayer being answered, this was it.

I opened my eyes and saw that Kathy was now alone on the stage next to a single 8th grader. She was in the final two contenders! Wow! What an amazing feat!

My classmates turned to me and said, 'Betcha you're REALLY jealous now. Kathy's gonna win.'

I looked straight at them and said calmly, 'What are you *talking* about? I WANT her to win.'

And I meant it.

Suddenly the bullies were utterly speechless. And like magic, all eyes turned away from me and back to the stage, as if nothing had happened.

The tenacity between Kathy and her 8th-grade rival was remarkable. The words got increasingly difficult, but it seemed neither could make a mistake. They battled it out for what seemed to be a very long time. The gridlock was so tight I started to wonder if the teachers would call it a draw at some point.

Eventually Kathy misspelled a word and ended up in second place. But it didn't really matter because every teacher in the school gushed over her as if she had actually won. What a fantastic achievement for a little 10-year-old girl to take on all these teenagers and come in second place. It was a really big deal. Flashbulbs were going off in all directions as photos were taken for the local newspaper.

I looked over and saw Kathy smiling shyly, if not a bit uncomfortably, at all the praise being showered upon her. And amidst the hubbub, what I was most pleased with was the fact I was genuinely happy for Kathy. I could feel a physical rush of delight inside me.

As things started to quiet down, Kathy slipped away from all the photo-taking and gushing, and went off to look for me. I'm not sure, but I think she wanted to make sure I was ok about 'losing' to her. When she found me full of smiles and excitement for her victory, she looked visibly relieved and started babbling a blue streak about how nervous she had been, and how hot it was under the lights, etc., etc. In me, she found an understanding comrade. We sat together, rolling our eyes as we replayed some of the day's events, sharing our thoughts and feelings in a way only we could have possibly understood. I was happy to be there for her; I was also happy she was there for *me*. Had I allowed competitiveness to shut my heart to her, both of us would have been completely alone.

It was then I understood the full gift of the blessing I had received that afternoon. I had not merely been graced with freedom from jealousy; I had been given a feeling of wholeness as a human being. I felt no need to measure any portion of my self-worth against that of another human being—who is equally whole and equally worthy. And although I was only 10 years old at the time, that incident changed me for the rest of my life. I can honestly say that, although there have been times in my life when I would get upset when I felt 'rejected,' the one thing I have never felt is jealousy.

And for that, I am eternally grateful to my childhood bullies.

THE INNER GAME OF COMPETITION

Jealousy burns us from the inside out. It is like a fire that gets into the blood and destroys our joy. But jealousy is merely the symptom of a much deeper inner game of *competitiveness,* and cannot arise unless this inner game is present. Competition is not a game between two people or two teams. It is a game we play within ourselves, and has nothing whatsoever to do with other people. That being said, although competitiveness is a solo game, it still has a tremendously powerful impact upon those who are the objects of our competitiveness, even if they are not playing our game. Even when the inner game of Competition is played within the mind and heart of one party in a relationship, whether between individuals, businesses or nations, we have fertile ground for abuse, bullying, exploitation and even terrorism.

And when it is played by both parties, we have war.

Our happiness in life has nothing whatsoever to do with the seeming successes or failures of others. When we believe the opposite, we have Competition. Competition can only occur when beliefs and feelings of Scarcity are present. There must be an unconscious belief that, *If another person has what I want, it means I cannot have it.* When we (knowingly or not) believe there is only a finite amount of joy, riches, success, praise, fulfilment and happiness in the world, we adopt a win-lose mentality, in which the only way to get what we want is to make sure others don't. The flaw in this line of reasoning, of course, is that if we see through the filter of Scarcity as our worldview, no amount of 'winning' will ever make us feel full.

The ways we compete against others and ourselves are often so subtle we might not even notice them. Trying to undermine another's validity through criticism and comparison is one form of Competition that tends to go under the radar. Few of us will actually plot to sabotage another person's success, but nearly all of us have competed at one time or another by criticising others or finding fault with them for no particular reason, whether privately in our own minds or socially in conversations with others. Habitual and unconstructive fault-finding of others (which is not the same thing as pointing out harmful or aggressive behaviour) is a characteristic of Competition, and always a symptom of an underlying Scarcity mentality. We feel the need to assert our own value at the expense of another because we feel *we* are lacking in some way, whether financially, mentally, physically or socially.

THE TRIPLE-EDGED SWORD OF COMPETITION

Competition is so ubiquitous in our daily lives we scarcely notice it. We learn it at school and carry it on when we grow up in the world of politics, sports and, of course, business and marketing. Some people even bring it into their marriage or other family relationships. But the fact that it is all around us doesn't make it 'ok.' Competition is actually a weapon with a vicious triple-edged blade:

1. It hurts the person who embraces it
2. It can hurt the person(s) on the receiving end
3. It hurts, if not destroys, the *relationship* between the parties involved

But wait a minute—Competition is a weapon? Isn't it a part of the natural way of life? Isn't it the thing that makes us all work harder? Isn't it the thing that helps us improve and grow as a race? Isn't it a necessary component of our economic security? Without it, don't we all become lazy, complacent blobs?

These are some of the common misconceptions many of us in Western society have been taught to believe, especially in the half-century following the World War II. In many ways, the argument in favour of Competition has been at the foundation of the argument between capitalism and other economic models, especially socialism and communism. However, in more recent times, many studies suggest Competition is *not* vital to a thriving capitalistic model. One of the most comprehensive monographs on the subject is the book *No Contest: The Case Against Competition* by Alfie Kohn.[2] Throughout that book, Kohn shares evidence from a wide range of resources that demonstrate that—far from being a positive element in efficiency, productivity or creativity—Competition is generally *detrimental* in everything from education, to sports, to the arts, to business, to journalism, to you name it.

Amongst Kohn's dozens of examples was a study of how journalists who feel compelled to 'compete' for space will frequently 'hype up' and distort their stories, leading to reporting that is not only 'inaccurate but even irresponsible as a result of competition.'[3] In other studies, it was shown that children who were asked to compete against others tended to produce less creative and less imaginative artwork than those who worked collaboratively.[4] In all areas of life, the overwhelming evidence is that Competition actually takes us further away from our own excellence rather than closer.

The takeaway from all these studies is that there is a world of difference between being motivated by 'Competition,' versus being motivated by our own integrity. As Kohn puts it, 'excellence and victory are conceptually distinct...[and] the two are *experienced* as different. One can attend either to the task at hand or to the enterprise of triumphing over someone else—and the latter often is at the expense of the former' (emphasis in the original text).[5] In other words, our belief that Competition is necessary for personal, economic and societal growth is simply a myth, and is actually detrimental to our creativity, productivity, integrity and our ability to work together and form strong interpersonal relationships.

For those who prefer more scientific evidence, in his book *One Small Step Can Change Your Life,* Dr Robert Maurer discusses how our brains react to thoughts we find overwhelming. For example, if an overweight man were told he needed to lose 100 pounds right away, the immensity of the task would be likely to trigger fear and anxiety, sending him into 'survival mode.' According to Maurer, this fear activates the amygdala in the middle part of our brain, which is responsible for our 'fight or flight' responses to stressful situations. He says, 'One way it accomplishes this is to slow down or stop other functions such as rational and creative thinking that could interfere with the physical ability to run or fight.'[6]

What does this have to do with Competition? Something I know from both my professional experience in the arts as well as a coach for other creative individuals is how easily we can go into anxiety when faced with the need to produce, perform and, yes, compete, in front of others. It's amazing how quickly and completely our creative and resourceful minds can shut down when faced with these scary challenges. If Maurer is correct in his theory of the links between fear, the amygdala and our ability to respond creatively, it is certainly easy to see how Competition simply cannot bring us to a higher level of excellence as individuals, nor to a more connected and open way of being with each other.

Competition hurts. It hurts us not only emotionally, but also as a society because it drives us further away from each other and restricts the potential of what we can create together. For these reasons, when we build and operate our businesses upon a foundation of competitiveness, we cannot help but fail in the long term.

THE ECONOMIC MYTH OF SURVIVAL OF THE FITTEST

> *'Growth of a large business is merely a survival of the fittest...the working out of a law of nature.'*
> **~ John D. Rockefeller[7]**

As a child growing up in the 1950s and 60s, I was taught by my parents and teachers that Competition was a good thing. It was believed to strengthen character, society and, most of all, the economy. Competition was seen as part of the natural order and was considered the means to ensure 'survival of the fittest,' associated with the evolutionary work of Charles Darwin. A competitive world meant we would always have only the best-of-the-best. Our very future was dependent upon having 'winners' and 'losers'.

But the connection between the term 'survival of the fittest' and evolutionist Charles Darwin is, in fact, a bit of urban mythology. The term was not coined by Darwin at all, nor did it have anything directly to do with Darwin's idea of 'natural selection.' The term 'survival of the fittest' was first used in 1864 in the book *The Principles of Biology* by sociologist and economist Herbert Spencer[8], who creatively adapted Darwin's ideas to fit his own socioeconomic theories. Spencer's highly influential status amongst 19th Century thought-leaders was no doubt responsible for the term catching on in nearly every area of 'educated' Western culture at the time, and became the underpinning belief of the rise of what many began to refer to as 'Social Darwinism' in economics. Within this context, we see the start of the age of rugged individualism and capitalism in the US, and the height of imperialism in the British Empire. 'Social Darwinism' is a term generally used in a derogatory fashion to describe an economic system based upon an 'anything goes' or 'laissez-faire' policy in which businesses were justified, by natural law, to do anything and everything they could to knock out competitors and 'win' whatever prize to which they aspired. After all, if scientific evidence suggests that all life is based upon a law of 'eat or be eaten,' it stands to reason that the advancement of the human race *depends* upon our eating up the competition. But is this true?

WHY COMPETITION IS AN OBSOLETE MODEL

> *'The law of competition, be it benign or not, is here; we cannot evade it; no substitutes for it have been found; and while the law may be sometimes hard for the individual, it is best for the race, because it ensures the survival of the fittest in every department.'*
> **~Andrew Carnegie[9]**

Capitalism was a great idea when it was originally conceived. But so were socialism and communism. Democracy was a great idea when it was created. But so was monarchy. All ideas are great when they speak to the times and the needs of the people contemporary to their creation. Ideas become not so great when they cease to do so.

Ideas are theoretical, and theory is never the same thing in practice. All great ideas when put into practice, and most especially political and economic models, will have their challenges. Over the past century, capitalism, socialism and communism have all had to stand up to the litmus test of economic depressions and recessions, world wars and political upheavals. And some of these economic ideas have stood the test of time more effectively than others.

Ultimately, the success of any idea in practice is completely dependent upon how congruent it is with the social and historic context in which it operates. The rise of marketing in our culture was simultaneous to the rise of big capitalism—really the rise of the corporation—at the turn of the 20th Century. As we said earlier, these times ran parallel to the rise of the evolutionary theories of Charles Darwin, as well as the psychological theories of Sigmund Freud, both of which made their impact upon the socioeconomic thought of the day.

Within the context of those times, both capitalism and marketing made sense. America was an evolving economy (I cite America only because it is where the capitalist movement first took off at that time in history). Competition was seen as a natural element in the process of cultural evolution. Within the context of the times, the ends (i.e., economic growth) justified the means (Competition).

An economic model based upon Competition can only arise when we feel ourselves—whether as individuals or nations—to be separate from others. While the sovereignty of nations, races, political systems and religions might create solidarity within their boundaries, they ultimately create separation from everything and everyone else. Nationalism might create a stronger country, ethnic pride might help integrate minority groups, and religious piety might uplift and bring order to its adherents, but taken on a wider scale, these things can also separate and disconnect these social institutions from the rest of the world. And when that happens, Competition for land and other resources, economic exploitation, political domination and even warfare become imminent.

The same can be said for how we conduct our businesses. When we view our businesses as separate and in Competition with 'others' in the market, we have taken ourselves out of the bigger picture, when we are in fact part of the same landscape, the same eco-system. Our notions of individualism obscure our ability to see our impact upon the whole. When we see ourselves as separate, it leads to a feeling of isolation, which in turn leads to our own beliefs in Scarcity. When we reach this point, the 'survival mode' is triggered within us, wherein we give ourselves permission to exploit both the planet and other living beings in whatever way aids us in meeting our desired end. And thus begins our dance with competitiveness in our business and marketing practices.

Competition can only arise from Scarcity: when there is an underlying belief that there isn't enough in the world for everyone to have what they need or want. It can only occur when we believe there can be only one winner, and that winning is all that matters. In the case of marketing, our Scarcity belief drives us to compete for what we believe is a pool of 'limited customers.' When we have this outlook, we are most likely to do one of two things: 1) we will try to corner the market (i.e., make sure we get the existing customers at the expense of our competition), or 2) we will attempt to create *new* markets, using Persuasion, Invasion, Scarcity and whatever other 'Deadly Sins' we consider necessary. Historically, 'cornering the market' might have meant the formation of mega-corporations and monopolies, until governments had to intervene. With regards to creating new markets, it meant creating false needs for our existing market or expanding into the fertile territory of developing nations, to convince people to adopt new behavioural patterns and consume products they never before thought they needed.

But times have changed. Most of us have learned that trying to corner the market only creates economic imbalances that threaten the flow of the whole system. Some of us are learning that continually creating new markets creates both economic and ecological imbalances. But few of us have yet caught onto the fact that, since the rise of the Golden Age of capitalism, two important shifts in our world have rendered our former economic model utterly obsolete:

1. Manufacturing technology has turned us into over-efficient producers
2. Communications and transportation technologies have fundamentally transformed our relationships at a global scale

Unless we become flexible enough to adapt and modify our existing economic models—whatever they might be—to this new context, we will find ourselves continually trying to patch up what really can no longer be maintained. It's like trying to keep the floodgates of a dam from bursting by plugging it with chewing gum. The time has come for us either to build a different dam, or to let go and allow the waters to flood where they will, so we can see the new terrain for what it actually is.

THE PROBLEM WITH OUR OWN EFFICIENCY

Before the rise of mass-production, we humans pretty much produced materials in rhythm with our rate of consumption. Maintaining this natural rhythm between production and consumption ensured we did not extract resources from the Earth more quickly than they were able to be replaced by the natural pace of our planet. Furthermore, what we consumed was pretty much bio-degradable, which meant our supply of resources was relatively sustainable.

In a culture where this kind of natural rhythm is maintained, Competition in business has a limited negative impact upon the world at large. There is only so much damage you can do when the pace of society is generally in step with the rhythm of the planet. However, as technology entered into industry, that rhythm was lost. We began to produce at a far greater rate than what we could consume, and the things we began to produce were not so easily recyclable. Earthenware was replaced with plastic containers. Wooden carts were replaced with steel vehicles. If you combine rapid production, rapid consumption and disposal, and non-biodegradable products with a belief in perpetual growth, what you end up with is too many goods on the planet, with nowhere for them to go.

So what happens when Competition drives us to produce at a rate that is out of step with the world? Well, we've already looked a bit at how it can impact our environment, but what about our health? When food growers, for instance, are competing to have the biggest, shiniest and largest yield of vegetables they can, while ensuring they can sell them at the lowest prices, what do they do? They use chemical pesticides and fertilisers. Of course these are highly effective in killing insects and increasing food crop yield. And they might even decide to use genetically modified (GM) seed in order to grow bigger, tougher crops. Because they have less loss to natural pests, they can offer their products at more competitive prices than traditional, organic farmers. Because their vegetables have thick, tough skin, they can store them longer and ship them over longer distances.

People go to grocery shops and see nice shiny, uniformly-sized vegetables on the shelves and compare their prices to the possibly less shiny, less uniformly-sized organic vegetables, and decide to go for the cheaper option. The problem is, it doesn't really end up 'cheaper' at all. Not only is the nutritional content much lower owing to its having travelled a longer distance and being stored for longer periods of time, but exposure to chemical pesticides and fertilisers has been proven to create immune system deficiencies that can lead to all kinds of disease, including brain cancer[10], stomach cancer[11] and testicular cancer[12]. And again, we're not even talking about the damage it does to our soil, air and water supply. The next time we succumb to Competition by counting our pennies when we choose which vegetables to buy at the grocery store, it might be better to start counting all the ways we are *really* paying for our food.

It doesn't take an economist or an environmentalist to understand that we simply cannot continue to embrace a competitive business culture in which 1) we produce more than our planet can sustain naturally, or 2) we compromise health and environmental stability in the name of producing that 'more.' We are not living in the same world in which Dale Carnegie flourished at the turn of the 20th Century. We are not living in the same world as Edward Bernays when he staged his 'Torches of Freedom' campaign. We can no longer see economic growth as the justifiable end to whatever competitive means we use to reach that end. If we don't adapt as business owners and marketers, we will not be the 'torso' that feeds the world, but the disease that eventually kills it.

HOW COMPETITION CHANGES

As a Baby Boomer, my parents were in their early 20s during the World War II. Like so many other children in my generation, my parents' civic values were extremely audible in our household when I was growing up. Coming on the heels of Franklin D. Roosevelt's many civic projects aimed at helping to resuscitate the flagging American economy during the Great Depression, the perspective of this era of reconstruction was a curious fusion of commerce and nationalism—what was good for the American corporation was seen as good for America. To me, it felt as though most American adults at that time felt 'big business' was almost synonymous with *democracy*. Consumerism was inextricably entangled with the idea of political freedom, when in fact they are two entirely separate ideas.

While authors Strauss and Howe believe this 'civic' era was part of the natural cycle of human social behaviour,[13] I believe this peculiar collapse of beliefs could only have come at a time directly following the great capitalist era of Carnegie, Ford and Rockefeller. On the one hand, my parents' generation were the inheritors of the worldview of 'Social Darwinism' where Competition and unlimited economic growth were seen as part of the natural order. On the other hand, the hardships of the Great Depression and the ensuing World War compelled them to become civic-minded for the sake of their nation. When you fuse these two ideologies into one collapsed belief, you basically have the ethos of the 1950s and early 1960s.

The anti-establishment attitudes that subsequently arose in the youth movement of the late 1960s were the symptoms that we had swung into a new, more idealistic era, where conformity and nationalism were loudly shunned.

Today, a generation later, that 'pendulum' (as author Michael Drew calls it[14]) has swung back towards the start of another so-called 'civic' era, but with a marked difference from that of the post-war times. Our current civic era began at the dawn of social media, which is responsible for creating a fundamental shift in our communications—possibly the biggest since the dawn of civilisation. With social media, we have not only become more community-driven, we also have become less insular and less protective of our *ideas*. The concepts of copyright and intellectual property have become malleable, if not ambiguous. As social media becomes increasingly central to our daily lives, boundaries defining personal and professional privacy, once so very important to us, now seem to be dissolving.

When possession itself is so difficult to define, how can Competition really flourish?

Socialnomics author Erik Qualman remarks that social media has already taken us from a business-driven economy to a 'people-driven economy.'[15] This shift away from individualism towards community changes not only the way we do business, but the way we communicate *about* our businesses—i.e., our marketing. Social media has made it possible for the consumer to have as much (if not more) influence upon public opinion as those who had traditionally controlled media and marketing in the past. It has also levelled the playing field between marketers, making it possible for small, independent businesses to market themselves cheaply (or for free) without needing to 'compete' against large corporations for advertising space. These two factors alone cannot fail to change the face of capitalism over the next decade.

Another thing that makes this civic era markedly different from the previous one is our rising awareness about ecology. Community no longer simply means people; it means animals, plants, soil, water, air and everything else on the planet. In such an era, Competition becomes an obsolete ideology, because we realise we can no longer afford to think we are independent, but rather *interdependent*.

While some people will inevitably hold onto Competition with an iron fist, it is rapidly losing its status in our socioeconomic model. And, not surprisingly, as Competition loosens its grip on our economy, there seems so far to be no negative impact upon our political freedoms.

COMPETITION VERSUS SPIRITUAL GROWTH

One of my favourite authors, M. Scott Peck, describes the shift away from competitive individualism towards community as part of the process of spiritual evolution. In his superb book *The Different Drum*[16], Peck describes what he calls the four stages of spiritual development, which I paraphrase here as:

1. Chaos/Disorder
2. Organisation/Regulation/Blind Faith
3. Scepticism/Rationalism
4. Unity/Mysticism

Interestingly, Peck advises us to be mindful of the fact that Stage 3 (Scepticism) can look very much like Stage 1 (Chaos) to someone in Stage 2. A Stage 2 person adheres to a particular ideology, such as a religious or political belief system. To them, someone questioning the status quo (Stage 3) might seem to have gone 'astray' and be in danger of falling back into Chaos. Peck explains this is why some Stage 2 people try to bring Stage 3 people back to the 'flock,' so to speak. They cannot recognise that the other person is actually moving forward on their spiritual journey. Basically, a lower-stage person cannot recognise or understand someone at a higher stage, but a person truly in Stage 4 (Unity) should be able to understand and communicate with people in all stages.

If we apply Peck's model to the rise of the American economy over the past 100 years or so, we might compare the early days of 'laissez-faire' capitalism in the late 19th and early 20th Century, leading up to the Great Depression as Stage 1 (Chaos). This was followed by Stage 2 (Organisation/Regulation), marked by an era of increased nationalism and organisation during the years of F. D. Roosevelt's presidency, World War II and the decade to follow. Stage 3 (Scepticism) has been pretty much increasing since the middle of the 1960s. We can see that the rise of conservatism in the late 20th and early 21st Century seemed to be an attempt of old 'Stage 2' folks to draw in the reins on the sceptical 'Stage 3' society, which was moving further and further away from institutional norms.

So as we are swinging towards a community mindset, does this mean we are now at the threshold of Peck's 'Stage 4'? Are we standing at the entryway into what he calls 'Unity' consciousness, where we as a society become accepting of and open towards all others, ceasing to impose our will upon others through ego and exploitation? Are we standing on the precipice of a more equitable, less competitive and globally-focussed awareness, both socially and environmentally? Or are we just swinging into a cycle that will inevitably swing back the other way over time?

Regardless of which, if either, is true, one thing is unquestionable: society in our current era is different in every possible way from what it was at the dawn of Social Darwinism. Competition in commerce cannot possibly hold the same place in our economy as it did 100 years ago. Even if all the serious ecological concerns we have discussed were no longer relevant, it would not change the fact that technology has fundamentally altered the way marketers communicate with consumers. Communication is no longer linear, but circular. Social media has made it impossible to follow the old competitive model. Competition no longer works in a world where customers speak to each other, and marketers must speak at eye-level with their customers. No longer can marketing come from an ivory tower high above us, in which we feel like helpless pawns trapped inside a propaganda machine.

Businesses and marketers are part of 'us,' whatever 'us' is. And if that 'us' includes our planet as well, we know our very survival depends upon our interdependence.

The glory days of Competition are over.

SUMMARY: HOW COMPETITION IS MAKING US ILL

Just as each of the other 7 Deadly Sins was built upon the former, Competition only arises when Scarcity is present. As we have seen, Scarcity is a belief, not a 'thing.' When someone has a fundamental belief there isn't enough to go around, we develop the belief that 'If so-and-so gets want I want, then I cannot have it.' We develop a win-lose mentality where there can be 'only one' winner in any given situation. This tears away at the fabric of society, as it ruins our ability to collaborate and co-create. It creates feelings of isolation, fear and vulnerability. It makes us defensive. It drives us into loneliness, desperation, depression and despair. It leaves us fearing we can trust no one, and that there is no one to call upon for help when we need it.

When we are locked in the grips of Competition, we feel the stress and continual pressure to go higher and higher. The higher we rise, the more we fear the loss of what we imagine we've gained. We become secretive and protective of what we believe we own. And because we feel so utterly alone, we lose any sense of accountability for our actions. We come to feel we can do whatever we want because we do not share or depend upon anyone but ourselves. And even that relationship is tenuous because we can no longer trust ourselves, as we have lost our connection to our core values.

When we compete against others, we are cutting off our own life-blood. We cannot be there for others when compete against them, nor can they be there for us. Competition for economic or political dominance fragments and destroys the harmony of our world. It opens the doorway to total disintegration of our Key Relationships. When we are no longer in relationship with each other, we see each other as competitors. We become a world of me's and you's who are inescapably separate.

When that separation is very pronounced, the burning fire of jealousy can enter us and make us feel even more desperate.

From desperation comes violence, exploitation, resentment, fear, terrorism, theft, rape, pillaging—all the things some people might use the word 'evil' to describe.

But, if you look at the core of the issue—the root cause—it all comes back to the same thing: a feeling of Disconnection.

It is time to find the pathway back to that Connection we have lost.

Clearly, it's time for a new paradigm.

Part Four

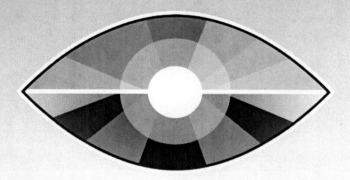

The 7 Graces of Marketing

Some Thoughts on the Use of the Word 'Grace'

'...the heart giveth grace unto every Art.'
~ **Henry Wadsworth Longfellow**[1]

When I wrote the previous section of the book, I looked up the etymological origins of the word 'sin,' and I was surprised to find no cognate link to Latin words. I had rather assumed that it had something to do with the Latinate word 'sin' meaning 'without,' but I was mistaken. The only etymological origins I found were to the Anglo-Saxon word 'synn' (noun) or 'syn' (verb), the actual meaning of which is said to be 'with reference to human law or obligation, misdeed, fault, crime, wrong.'[2] I found this interesting, as it made me think that, while the word 'sin' is widely associated with Christian theology, perhaps the semantic meaning behind the word is something we as a culture developed much later, as its original meaning had to do with social ethics rather than 'absolute universal law.'

In contrast, my research for the word 'grace' yielded much more varied results. Its origins are indeed Latin (*gratia*), with links to ancient Greek *(kharites)*, and the word has various shades of meaning in both classical Greek and pre-Christian Roman secular culture. Some theological and some aesthetic, these meanings are simultaneously similar to and different from each other, and express six primary threads of meaning.[3] Here's my own summary of what they are:

1. **Grace can refer to a gift from the Divine,** such as being forgiven or helped in some way
2. **Grace can refer to the quality of being filled with the Divine,** such as when a person has virtuous qualities and character
3. **Grace can refer to the quality of someone who is aesthetically pleasing,** such as when someone is beautiful in form, movement, charm and personality
4. **Grace can refer to the act of giving thanks,** such as the practice of saying sayin 'grace' before a meal; this usage of the word is also cognate with the English word 'gratitude,' Spanish *gracias,* and the Italian *grazie,* etc.
5. **Grace, as a verb, can refer to the act of showing favour to another person,** such as when we 'grace' someone with our presence, or God 'graces' us with a special favour
6. **'The Graces' can also refer to goddesses in Greek and Roman culture** (also known as 'The Charities' from the Greek word *kharites*), who are said to preside over various qualities of beauty, aesthetics and refinement[4]

I quite like all of these meanings and would like to include a little bit of each into the spirit of our discussion of The 7 Graces in the following pages. The 7 Graces are indeed a 'gift' in that our understanding of them comes from an inspired wisdom with origins in the Divine, whatever that might mean to us. When we live and breathe these Graces as a way of life, we become filled with our own Divinity. When we are filled with our own Divinity, we become aesthetically pleasing to others, and make the world a more beautiful place. When we are practicing these Graces, we are in a continual flow of giving to others, and when we are in that flow of giving to others, we are also continually receiving, and hence living in a state of gratitude. We ourselves become walking representatives of the Graces we embrace, making it easier for others to see how to apply them in their own lives.

The 7 Graces, therefore, are not so much codes of conduct as they are shifts in our 7 Key Relationships with Self, Source, others, our businesses, our audience, money and marketing. These shifts in turn give us great potential to create powerful and purposeful expressions of who we are and what we value most, and provide a conduit for our economy to flow and our society to benefit.

Whenever I have spoken in public on the subject of *The 7 Graces of Marketing*, I could feel a tangible weightiness in the air as the topic descended through the '7 Deadly Sins.' Conversely, as soon as 'The 7 Graces' entered the room, the atmosphere became alive almost instantly. So, as I begin to write the following chapters, let me hold the intention to uplift, brighten and electrify whatever words choose to appear on these pages, so you may feel the presence of The 7 Graces as tangible energies—if not entities—filling you with ideas, inspiration and hope.

Even without yet putting these Graces into practice in your business or your personal life, the moment you allow their energy to fill your heart and mind, you will have already begun to change the world.

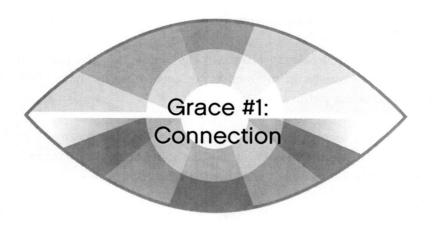

Grace #1:
Connection

> *'If I were to boil down into one simple definition*
> *the philosophy of so many of the world's primary cultures,*
> *I would say that they know the world that knows them.'*
> **~ HRH The Prince of Wales**[1]

In Classical Greek cosmology, there were three types of 'music,' generally translated into Latin as *Musica Instrumentalis, Musica Mundana* and *Musica Humana. Musica Instrumentalis* is what we typically think of as 'music'; it is that which is produced by some sort of physical sound vibration, whether from the voice or an instrument, and is audible to ordinary human hearing. At a higher level is *Musica Mundana,* generally translated in English as 'Music of the Spheres.' *Musica Mundana* is that music, inaudible via ordinary physical hearing, produced by the movement of the planets, stars and entire cosmic creation. The astronomer Kepler was particularly interested in *Musica Mundana,* and he devised an entire system of astrology around the vibrational ratios between the planets. Lastly, there is *Musica Humana.* This is the most subtle form of music, and is that which is sung by the human soul. It is the music of spirit that resonates via the hearts of all sentient beings, and from the Heart of the Creator and Creation Itself. I like to call this kind of music 'Music of the Heart.'

Being able to 'hear' these three types of music is what brings joy, meaning and Connection to all living creatures.

THREE PATHWAYS OF CONNECTION

While I don't know how the Greeks really thought about these three types of music, in my own experience, each of them is 'heard' via three distinct pathways:

- *Musica Instrumentalis* is heard via the body or matter
- *Musica Mundana* is heard via the mind or consciousness
- *Musica Humana* is heard via the heart or spirit

In our modern society, very few people can articulate the existence of these three types of music, although I believe they are undoubtedly known to all of us at an intuitive, unconscious level, as part of the experience of being alive. And even after being aware of their existence, we do not necessarily have the sensitivity and awareness to 'hear' them fully. I remember when I first listened to a Brahms symphony as a young child, it sounded like a 'wall of noise' to me and I could make no sense of it whatsoever. Later, when I was a music student, I was taught how to hear music at a deep level in order to understand its subtlety and appreciate its aesthetic beauty. As a music teacher I passed on this ability to hear *Musica Instrumentalis* to my students. It was always fascinating to see how they reacted when their ears first 'opened up' so they could actually *hear* the music, as they realised how much delight they had been missing in the past.

The more subtle forms of music, *Musica Mundana* and *Musica Humana*, are no different. While we are born with the innate ability to hear these musics, it does not mean we *will* hear them. Just as I was listening to the Brahms symphony but could not 'hear' it, we are walking through life continually immersed in both the Music of the Spheres and the Music of the Heart, without necessarily hearing them. On a daily basis, we walk, breathe and function to the pulse of the Music of the Spheres, and we feel, express and know both ourselves and others through the melody of the Music of the Heart. Yet we may be so out of touch with our ability to 'hear' these musics that we are unaware of their presence.

The first time I unknowingly 'heard' *Musica Mundana*, I was at the Grand Canyon, where I came face-to-face with the Milky Way at 2 A.M.; later that morning I heard it again when I saw the sunrise racing across the Canyon as if a blanket were being lifted from the surface of the Earth. These experiences plunged me into a deep awareness of where I was in the Universe, and how the Earth on which I stood was spinning at a rate of 1,000 miles an hour as it whirled through space. I knew these experiences were significant, but I didn't know precisely why. Then, about 15 years later, I sat atop a hill in a rural part of northern Spain on a silent retreat. I observed the world around me, simply witnessing whatever appeared without thought or attachment. After about two hours, I began to feel shivers up my spine as I 'heard' what I later described as 'The Song of the Earth.' It wasn't sound on a physical level as we think of it. Rather, it was an acute awareness of the continual flow of time, space, light, shadow, warm, cold, and all energies passing through Her. In that moment, I felt connected to the Earth—and to the greater Source—in a way I had never felt before.

The third kind of music, *Musica Humana,* 'The Music of the Heart,' is not contingent upon time, place or circumstance. It is the deep, immutable vibration of the Essence of who we are that cannot be destroyed or silenced. When we feel fully aware of, connected to and expressive of our true Self, we are hearing that Music of the Heart. When we see past the distorted reflections of who we project ourselves to be and see both ourselves and others as we truly are, we are hearing that subtlest of all music—*Musica Humana.*

It is the ultimate music of Connection.

CONNECTION AND CONSCIOUS CREATION

While these three musical terms might have been coined by the Greeks, their meaning is by no means unique to them. So many ancient cultures viewed reality as one in which we are intrinsically connected both to the world in which we live and to all other living beings. Only in the past half-millennium or so have we gradually adopted a worldview in which we are separate, and in some cases superior to, our environment. As technology has given mankind increasing power and control over the material world, the delusion of separation and domination has become stronger and stronger. And as that belief in our separation has become increasingly accepted as reality, we have created a serious imbalance in our experience of life that has impacted our physical and emotional health, our communities, our economy and, most of all, our natural world.

Just as Creation is a reflection of the consciousness of a Creator or collective creative energy, all of our human creations are reflections of our collective consciousness as a people. And amongst our creations is our economic system, which includes all aspects of money, business, trade and, finally, marketing. Because our creations are reflections of our consciousness, if our worldview is one of Connection, by nature our businesses and marketing practices will express and increase Connection. But if our cosmology is one of separation, every aspect of our businesses and marketing practices will express and increase that separation.

Understandably, to many of us, the idea that marketing could possibly be a connective, or even spiritual, activity seems pretty outlandish. In fact, marketing often seems to be the very antithesis of spirituality. But this is only because most marketing we see has been created from a place of Disconnection—from Self, others, our businesses and the world around us. But when Connection is established in all our Key Relationships, marketing can become a Divine activity through which we are able to actualise our *dharma* and communicate our core values.

CONNECTION TO SELF

Like all the '7 Graces' we will be examining in this section, the amount of Connection we create and bring into our marketing is directly proportionate to the amount of Connection we have in our '7 Key Relationships'. First and foremost is Connection to Self, for without it, Connection in any of the other relationships is simply not possible. When we are disconnected from Self, we walk through life as if in a dream, donning the cloak of an illusory perception of who we are. In this state of mind, we cannot possibly create Connection in anything we do, least of all in business and marketing.

When we are disconnected from Self, we make choices in life that reflect the illusory being we believe ourselves to be. We adopt behaviours we believe will protect that illusion, as our illusory self is all we know. When we feel disconnected from Self, we tend to believe we are inadequate. The more inadequate we feel, the more effort we will exert to prevent others from seeing our imagined inadequacies. This will inevitably manifest in our marketing.

When a business owner has a distorted idea of who he is, it will be visible in his marketing whether or not he writes the copy himself. He might use a bunch of glossy, overblown hype, with lots of slangy lingo, trying to look 'cool,' confident and successful. In Internet marketing, he might follow 'cookie-cutter models' of marketing set by others or use generic sales letters that go on and on. Both of these marketing strategies can be off-putting to potential customers (I know they are to me), and they don't necessarily show the essence of either the business owner or the company. At the opposite extreme, he might 'play it safe' by choosing marketing that is flat, lifeless and generic, thus attracting little attention. Or, his marketing might be evasive and 'fluffy,' using lots of pretty words with little substance, leaving the potential customer in doubt as to what the product or service is, or what makes it special or desirable.

Here's an example of how 'fluffiness' can appear even without a marketer being aware of it: A while ago, a client came to me to promote a book about how to find your true life path. She was a very attractive woman in her 40s, who looked many years younger than her age. In spite of being widely known in social media, she expressed disappointment and bewilderment that her past marketing efforts hadn't led to many customers, in spite of having many excellent products. By the time she came to me, she had come to believe the world must not be taking her seriously because she looked too young and 'blonde'. I doubted this was the case, so I took a good look at the copy she had been using, which she had written herself. I noticed there were lots of flowery words, and I couldn't see much substance that told me about the products. But most of all, I had no real sense of who *she* was from the materials.

Wanting to get to the bottom of why she seemed to be so absent from the marketing copy, we chatted for about 30 minutes. I asked her about her past, and remarkably I discovered she had previously written *dozens* of self-help books and had been a successful career advisor some years earlier. None of this important information was in her copy, not even in her bio. Why? Because she had developed some negative self-judgements about the quality of her past work and was trying to bury them. She felt these achievements were either 'too ordinary' or 'not good enough' to be mentioned. But in my eyes they represented some of the most credible testimonials of her lifelong professional focus. Because she had so much self-judgement about these parts of her life, she had failed to see how valuable they were, and had neglected to leverage them in her marketing copy.

Self-judgement is invariably the most common symptom that we are not fully connected to Self. Whether our marketing is fluffy, hyped-up or bland, if we are not 'in' our marketing, it's simply not going to work for us. In this particular case, my client was self-aware enough to revamp her marketing once she saw what was going on. But unfortunately many business owners might not be as self-aware or as willing to listen. They are too wrapped up in creating an image to see that it is clouding the soul of their business. They continue to 'push back' by finding all kinds of external reasons why their marketing isn't working. They'll blame the economy, their competition or even the consumers. But the person who blames the most is typically the one who feels they have the most to lose; when someone feels they have much to lose it is because they are not connected to Self. When we have our Selves, there is really not much we can lose.

Connection to Self is essential in marketing for three very important reasons:

1. Without it, we are likely to alienate our audience
2. Without it, we are likely to give a false impression of who we are and what we stand for
3. Without it, we are unlikely to attract loyal customers, as we are not allowing our customers to know us

True Self, being Divine, is the ultimate 'sales converter.' Self is the only real 'irresistible force.' When we are truly connected to Self in our marketing, it attracts those who are innately connected to us at the most fundamental level. Putting our whole Self into our marketing not only has a more favourable impact upon our customers, but it ultimately helps make our businesses more profitable.

WHEN 'SELF' MEANS 'SELVES'

The challenge of Connection is of course bigger when we have bigger businesses. How do we maintain Connection to Self and our business when we are part of (or head of) a large corporation with possibly tens of thousand of employees? It starts first and foremost with the owner or CEO, who must be highly self-aware and whose values must be in alignment with the business. Without this congruity, the rest of the 'Self' will lack cohesiveness. Next, the company ethos and purpose must be clearly communicated to everyone within the system, including suppliers and customers, who must also share these values. And lastly, of course, this ethos and purpose has to be expressed genuinely and transparently through any and all marketing.

At this point, we might find ourselves asking, 'And just how is all that supposed to happen in a big corporation? There's simply no way to ensure everyone is on the same page.' First of all, we need to remember that the 'Self' in a big business is actually the 'Third Entity' (a topic we will discuss later when we examine the Grace of Collaboration). The 'Self' *is* the company or corporation. It is no one in particular AND everyone collectively at the same time. While all these separate elements comprise the Whole, the 'Self' of a company is actually greater than the sum of its parts. Connection to 'Self' in the case of a large company means the key players in that company are in good relationship with that Third Entity—the 'Self' that is the business itself.

CONNECTION TO OUR BUSINESS

The degree to which we are connected to our businesses impacts both our business success as well as the world around us. Being connected to our businesses does NOT simply mean loving our jobs or the work we do. While loving our work is a natural by-product of Connection, it is not necessarily an indicator that we are connected to it. We might love our work because it's easy, fun or makes us lots of money. We might love the people with whom we work. We might get a feeling of self-satisfaction that we are doing our jobs well. While all of this is wonderful, real Connection to our businesses is dependent upon two things:

1. How well in alignment our business is with our true calling in life—our *dharma*
2. How much our business is 'in synch' with where we are on our life journey

Whether you are a sole proprietor, an employee or the CEO of a multinational corporation, there can be no real Connection to your business without connection to your *dharma*. But knowing what that *dharma* is, and hence how your occupation can serve it, can be challenging if you have no tools by which to discover it. In coaching, some of the most powerful tools of exploration are 'powerful questions.' Here's a list of what you might call '*dharma*-discovery enquiries.' Read them slowly, one at a time, and pause for a few moments before going on to read the next question:

Why were you born at this time in history?

What is it you are being called to create?

What impact will this have upon the world?

Why THIS? Why NOW? Why YOU?

And finally...

What role does your business play in this?

If you cannot answer these questions immediately, don't worry. Powerful questions have powerful answers, and they can take quite some time to appear. If you write these questions down and ask them several times over the course of the next few months (or as long as you need), you will hear the answers in due course. Don't 'try' to find the answers. In our modern lives, we tend to try to fill all the seemingly empty space in our lives. When we're on hold on the phone we have to listen to music we'd never choose for ourselves. When travelling, we're constantly plugged into iPods or reading the tabloids. We seem to have lost the ability to hear the sound of silence or recognise form within the emptiness. But there is no emptiness, only subtlety. This subtlety is *Musica Humana.* That is where the answers lie.

TEMPORAL CONNECTION—BEING IN SYNCH

While *dharma* is eternal, the actions by which we facilitate our *dharma* are temporal. Our occupations and activities over time are continually changing, depending upon where we are on our journey of life. Sometimes we become attached to an out-of-date self-image of the person we once believed ourselves to be, and we end up carrying on activities that were central to our *dharma* in the past, but are no longer relevant in the present. This can impact our businesses heavily if we are unaware or resistant to what is actually going on.

I have seen this many times with new clients. They say something along the lines of, 'I don't understand why my marketing isn't working. This product always used to sell before. I keep trying different tactics and nothing is happening.' What they may not be seeing is that both they and the world around them are in a continual state of flux and evolution. If your marketing used to work and it doesn't anymore, it's more than likely because both you and the rest of the world have travelled and transformed. It doesn't necessarily mean your business is failing, but it almost definitely does mean you are not 'in synch' with your business.

Say for example you have a product you've been offering successfully for years, and suddenly no one wants to buy it. Most business analysts will determine a number of possible reasons for this. Perhaps the product is old-fashioned and either needs a face-lift or to be retired altogether. Perhaps other businesses in your niche are now offering similar products and the market is saturated. Or, perhaps your product is fine, but you haven't made enough effort to expand your audience, and you have 'milked' your current audience dry. Any or all of these things might be true from a strategic level, but what many fail to consider is the possibility that you've actually outgrown the product *yourself*, and the Universe is telling you that you need to change something in order to progress along your path. Ask yourself the 'powerful questions' above and if the answers you're hearing tell you you're out of synch, it's time to stop putting so much energy into your old strategies, and time to start listening to what you are being called to do next.

I have seen many new clients get panicky when they find themselves in this kind of scenario. Admittedly, it's tough to let go of things to which we are emotionally attached, and sometimes we might be afraid of taking the financial risk of giving up something that had always been so dependable in the past. But panic never leads us to solutions. Panic precludes creativity. When business owners start to panic, they often start to spend money unwisely on advertising that ends up losing them yet more money. But no marketing strategy, no matter how glossy, can magically create sales for you if you and your business are out of synch. At times like this, the most useful thing to do is ask what it is you are holding onto, or what it is you are most afraid of. That does not mean you have to abandon all you did in the past; it means it's time to make space for something bigger. While your *dharma* is unchanged, you have inevitably changed. How can your business reflect YOU in the here-and-now?

This applies equally across the board to all businesses, big and small. When decision-makers in large businesses panic, they fail. And the bigger and more complex they are, the harder they fall. At the end of the day, each of us is a single human being, no matter how big our businesses might be. And as humans, we are subject to the same fears as anyone else. But when we are connected to the life, soul and flow of our businesses, panic is far less likely to overcome us and cloud our discernment. When we have a Connection with our business, it becomes a channel for clear communication with the public. It becomes a high-horsepower vehicle for the creative expression of our values. Such a vehicle is tremendously powerful, and tremendously attractive to those who resonate with those values—our audience.

CONNECTION TO OUR AUDIENCE—A HOLISTIC VIEW

Before the industrial revolution, a business owner was limited by the parameters of their locality. Once mass-production and mass-transport entered the scene towards the end of the 19th Century, everything changed. Companies were bigger, and so were their audiences. In the early days of capitalism and at least up to the 1970s, most big businesses designed their marketing aimed at reaching a 'mass market.' They cast a wide net, hoping to catch as many undifferentiated 'fish' as possible.

But now in the 21st Century, in spite of the fact that the rise of the Internet has enabled more people to start businesses and reach potentially billions of people, most small businesses are focusing almost exclusively on niche markets, rather than trying to be all things to all people as they had in the past. On a practical level, it makes perfect sense for at least two reasons: 1) the world is simply too big for us to try to reach everyone and 2) if we don't make ourselves look different from everyone else, we simply won't get noticed at all. But beyond the practical logic of niche marketing, the rise of the niche is actually swinging us back to a part of our culture we had gradually misplaced over the past half-century or so—community.

Community has become a bit of a 'buzz word' over recent years. People tend to toss the word around to mean a group of people who all know and like each other, but real community is much deeper and functional. Best known for his book *The Little Prince,* French author Antoine de Saint-Exupéry penned a poignant scene in his lesser-known book *Flight to Arras*, wherein he describes the 'river' of humanity as thousands of people fled their towns and villages in war-torn France during World War II. A reconnaissance pilot for the French military, Saint-Exupéry saw communities ripped apart when key business owners left their villages in search of safety. In the book, he tries to convince people to stay in their homes, but he is told, 'It's no good. We'll have to go.'

'Why?' he asks.

'The baker's gone. Who'll bake our bread?' is the reply.[2]

Apart from being one of the most moving journals on the topic of war, Saint-Exupéry's observations also give us a glimpse into the intimate connection between businesses and communities. Local businesses have always been part of the very fabric of community life, since the dawn of civilisation. Local businesses not only provide the public with services and products that meet their unique needs, they also provide *business owners* with a sense of *purpose and belonging*. In Abraham Maslow's famous 'Hierarchy of Needs,' having a sense of belonging is one of our primary social needs; without it we cannot develop self-esteem or ascend to self-actualisation and fulfilment in life.[3] In other words, for a human being to be happy and healthy, having a place and purpose in one's community is absolutely essential.

Although many (if not most) of us were raised in a world of shopping malls and chain stores, a community that includes local businesses is actually a vital part of our human experience. When local business owners are part of the community, they also know what the community wants and needs. They understand their 'audience' because they are connected to them as part of the same socioeconomic system. And because they are *part* of the system and not outside of it, they also find their own needs are met by other business owners in turn.

It is really only since the post-war era of the 1950s and 60s that this critical molecule in the chemistry of our society has been mutated. When I was a child, my local shopkeeper used to know I collected a particular brand of children's 'punch-out books.' Hence, every week, when I got my allowance, I knew there would be one copy of the latest edition waiting for me at the shop, without having to ask for it. But then, in the mid-60s, our first 7-Eleven store opened near the railroad station, and within a year or two, the local family-run convenience shop that had been there for decades shut down, being unable to compete with the extended hours, wider selection and cheaper prices offered by the 7-Eleven. Everyone in my neighbourhood was walking around drinking bright blue Slurpees, but I never saw my beloved punch-out books again.

In the 1990s, a similar phenomenon happened when Blockbuster started opening up stores all over Phoenix, Arizona, where I was living at the time. One by one, all the local 'mom-and-pop' video rental stores shut down within less than a year. The owners at the mom-and-pop shops always knew a lot about just about every film they had on the shelves. They also knew their customers' taste in films and could make recommendations quickly (and usually got it right). But at our local Blockbuster, the only person to speak with was an apathetic 18-year-old kid working part-time who had no clue about anything except what 18-year-olds like to watch. I'd end up spending hours reading the back covers of the videos, trying to decide whether or not to rent them. Often, I walked out of the store empty-handed, feeling too overwhelmed and bored by the whole experience.

While punch-out books and video rentals may seem like trivial things that cannot make much difference in life, the truth is that pretty much all our present-day interactions with commerce is with big businesses rather than with local ones. This has created a Disconnection between businesses and communities. In fact, it destroys communities. Connection between local businesses and the consumer is one of the key ingredients in the creation of any sustainable and thriving community life.

BUSINESS AND THE DELICATE BALANCE OF COMMUNITY

When local businesses go out of business because 'outside' businesses come in, it has a devastating impact upon the community. People get excited and hopeful when big chain stores come to town because they believe they will create more jobs and bring more money into the community. But in reality they are making the community less self-reliant, less enterprising and ultimately more dependent. The money coming into the community in the form of salaries can never bring true economic freedom. Employees make enough to survive and spend on what they are influenced to buy from advertising, but they will never make enough to thrive or be free from their employer. It's really like a modern-day version of serfdom where the worker is paid, but is ultimately dependent upon the landowner. When a corporation falls, everyone working for the corporation falls with it. The failure of a single corporation can affect tens of thousands of employees and their families, not to speak of their shareholders and consumers who depend upon them for their supplies. We have only to look at the recent crisis in the Detroit automotive industry to see an example of this.

But the holistic economic implications of our dependence upon corporate culture are even more far-reaching and compelling. Because employees within a corporate society are never truly financially independent, they are incapable of providing for their own security. That is why we need things like pension plans and social security, which are continually draining the economic resources of our governments, and ultimately the people. And because people are so dependent, when they lose their jobs for whatever reason, they do not have the financial or intellectual resources to start their own enterprises, which means they have no alternative but to find yet another 'job.' This, then, creates ongoing dependency upon a welfare system supplied by the state, which in turn drains our overall economic system even further.

But when local communities have strong *local* businesses, owned and operated by local businesspeople (not franchisees), if one business fails or a business owner dies, the community is woven in such a way that it is more resilient, and can adapt much more easily when situations change. The need to be dependent upon the state is lessened as more people within the community are self-reliant. The community as a whole is more adaptable to change because it is not dependent upon a single industry or company, but is comprised of a web of enterprises that support each other rather than compete with one another.

Here's an example of just how vulnerable we have become because businesses have lost their Connection to their audience: In the past, the majority of our food was produced locally, either on our own land or on the land of local farmers. Today, most of us in the 'developed' world are dependent upon getting our food from large supermarkets. These supermarkets ship food from great distances— frequently thousands of miles—to hundreds or thousands of outlets. We call this 'food miles.' Many of us would be astonished to find out just how many thousands of food miles are in our shopping carts every week. A single banana may have travelled over 10,000 miles to get to your basket if you live in the northern hemisphere. As every food mile represents so much oil that has been used to ship it to us, our taste for non-local food has created a dependency upon the oil industry. Without fuel, we have no food. This was *never* the case until recent years. Even if we buy 'Fair Trade' or 'organic' produce, it means very little if we are buying foods from the big chain stores in the first place. This increasing distance between business and the consumer is wreaking havoc on:

- **Our environment,** due to fuel emissions of air-freight, as well as packaging (plastic, polystyrene, cardboard, metal, etc.) used to transport and store the food
- **Our nutrition,** due to eating foods either out of season or which have been chilled, frozen or otherwise stored for months before consumption, thus significantly reducing their nutritional properties
- **Our health,** due to eating foods that are likely to have been produced with the aid of chemical fertilisers, pesticides, preservatives or artificial colouring
- **Our economy,** due to the combination of resultant over-inflated prices on food, and lack of money going back into the local economy (especially local farms)
- **Our community,** due to increasing economic dependency upon external entities, and increasing lack of local enterprise and self-reliance

It is absolutely vital we re-establish the lost Connection between business owners, their businesses and the public. It's not simply an economic issue, but a matter of human survival. We NEED communities in order to be human; Connection to local businesses is a crucial part of what makes up a community.

CONNECTION AND THE CONSUMER

We consumers are fairly complacent about our dependency upon big businesses. We are accustomed to them supplying us with all the things we would have produced for ourselves in the past. Somehow we believe we are advancing as a culture, but very few of us even have the basic knowledge of producing our own food and clothing. We have lost the natural rhythm of night and day because technology illuminates our world 24/7. We are rapidly losing Connection to all the things that make us human.

In spite of this, the sheer thought of withdrawing from this co-dependent system leaves many of us terrified and overwhelmed. How could we possibly go 'cold turkey' and live without the conveniences we have created over the past century? How could we possibly lose our addictions to television, global travel, automobiles, and so many other things? The turmoil of such a withdrawal seems far greater than the addiction. We have lived like this our whole lives, so we tell ourselves we can probably survive just a little longer until clever technocrats create an easy way out for us. Thus, we shirk our responsibility in the situation, imagining ourselves powerless to change it.

Our lack of Connection to our socioeconomic system has put us in a terribly vulnerable place. If a major war were to break out suddenly causing oil to be in short supply for an extended duration, how long would our 'educated' society survive, considering we have pretty much no survival skills and no infrastructure in place for food production? What would happen in urban centres? How long would it take before riots, looting and widespread crime broke out? And even if we finally got our act together and replaced all petroleum-based fuel sources with bio-fuels or other solutions, we might succeed in diverting a global war, but we still will not have addressed the other issues arising from our social and economic dependency upon big business.

If, however, communities contained all the resources for their inhabitants to survive, they would quite likely be able to ride out the storm of any conflict that might arise. By 'resources' I don't just mean food and clothes; I mean knowledge, health, economic stability and, most of all, *people*. Real community is a collective of local service providers, craftsmen, retailers and consumers, whose ethos would be to work collaboratively together in support of the whole entity—the community—of which they were a vital part. They would know each other and be able to come to each other for help and partnership. This kind of coalition not only creates a strong economy, but a resilient society in the face of calamities that may and will arise over time. In short, *community is the immune system of a society, protecting it from social 'disease' and demise.*

TRIBES AND INDUSTRIALISATION

When we think of the word 'tribe,' we commonly think of a group or clan of people joined by ancestral blood lines, who identify with each other at a cultural level. But a real tribe is a micro-society, meant to be self-sustaining. It includes a system of hierarchies and roles, all of which serve the collective values of the greater tribe itself. In order to be self-sustaining, the diversity of roles must cover a wide spectrum—from administrators to spiritual teachers, from warriors to healers, from labourers to artisans. Within that spectrum, not only are the needs of the group met, but also the needs of the *individual*. It is a social system in which everyone's personality and talent is regarded as a valued asset to the whole.

A smaller version of the 'tribe' is the extended family, which we still see in many cultures today, especially in the East. An extended family refers to several generations of relatives either living under one roof, or in close proximity to one another. My paternal grandparents' living arrangement mimicked some of the extended family life they had back in the 'old country' of the Tyrol. While they lived in their own house, three of their adult children resided within a few miles of them, along with their spouses and children (and later, grandchildren). My grandparents' house was rarely empty, with relatives dropping in randomly every day of the week. Like the tribe, the extended family provides support, safety and a sense of identity. Unlike the tribe, it is neither broad nor diverse enough to guarantee everyone a 'role' that both serves the whole and satisfies the individual. Like the tribe, everyone is linked by ancestry and a common culture. Unlike a tribe, an extended family is not a self-sustaining unit, and is dependent upon a bigger community for its sustenance. Extended families, therefore, need villages, towns or urban centres to survive, whereas a true tribe may not.

Then we have the 'nuclear family.' This is the arrangement whereby a set of parents and their children live in a dwelling separate from other relatives. While the majority of people alive in the Western world today were probably raised in some form of nuclear family, the nuclear family as a social structure only started to emerge in Western Europe in the 17th and 18th Centuries—at the dawn of industrialisation and early capitalism.[4] At that time, governments were also changing, turning from small regional states into larger sovereign nations. A new era of nationalism began, gradually replacing older allegiances to the tribe.

Notionally, the nuclear family brings mobility and choice to its members, as they are no longer geographically tied to live near their extended families or tribes. Being such a small collective, the ability to express one's talent and ideals are far less likely to come from within the family unit, meaning the individual is almost always *required* to go outside the family to find personal or economic fulfilment. This often means children will move away from their parents when they mature. However, while there might be more freedom of movement and choice,[5] there is inversely *less* safety, support and sustenance in the nuclear family, as there are fewer people to provide the needs for the individuals within it. Thus, a society comprised primarily of nuclear families is dependent upon not only urbanisation, but also upon *industrialisation*. It simply does not have the means to survive without it.

Because the nuclear family is so dependent upon external support, it also contains within it the seeds of its own demise. This is undoubtedly why the classic nuclear family model of 'husband-wife-kids' has mutated into many variations over the past half-century, including single-parent households, and unmarried and/or same-sex couples with *or* without children. All of these are justifiably called 'nuclear families' in that they are the key unit with which we identify. I believe this trend is also visible in the increased amount of middle-aged women living on their own (I'm one of them). I cannot think of any woman in my parents' generation living without family, yet I know dozens of them today.

The more fragmented and isolated our 'nuclear' units become, the less self-reliant they become; and the less self-reliant they become, the more dependent they become upon both industrialisation and the state for economic support and subsistence.

But big governments and big businesses are far from being satisfactory replacements for a tribe. They offer no real emotional, cosmological or genetic connection between the members of the system and the system itself, which means we fail to find a sense of 'belonging' within them. While 'the system' can hopefully provide us with the basic necessities of life, when people feel dependent upon a system rather than being a vital and integral part *of* it, they will inevitably experience a lack of self-worth and purpose in life.

It is not so difficult to see how such feelings of pointlessness and dependency fostered a rise in an existentialist view of life in the 20th Century. Futuristic authors George Orwell (in his book *1984*) and H.G. Wells (in his book *The Time Machine*) beautifully expressed their opinions about the dangers of our becoming dependent upon the state, decades before most of the world was even aware of what was happening. By creating a world in which we have become dependent upon industrialisation and big governments, we have robbed ourselves of the most fundamental social unit of humanity—the tribe. Surely this is the reason why so many of us today find ourselves craving Connection, belonging and self-purpose.

But if community is the immune system of humanity, it seems to be trying to bring our society back to health in spite of ourselves. How so? Social media. Through social media, millions of people are now re-creating a technological alternative to the tribes of the past, where we might again finally find a sense of belonging.

TRIBES, NICHES AND MARKETING

'Who ARE all these people following me?'

That's what one client asked me a week or so after I started working to build her Twitter account. A week before she had never used Twitter. Now, she had 250 followers but had no clue who they were or why they were following her.

The simple answer was this: these people (or at least some of them) were her tribe.

Back in the beginning of this book I talked about how I didn't feel like I 'fit' in my business networks. The simple explanation for this is that these people were not my 'tribe.' While most were very nice folks, they embraced a worldview significantly different from mine, which caused me to feel like the odd person out. My Global Wellness Circle project gave me a greater feeling of belonging, but wasn't expansive enough to impact my business. Ultimately, social media was the platform that provided me the space in which I could define my social circles by my own criteria, and also have a wide-enough audience upon which to build a business without having to depend upon *any* external networks, advertising or other forms of business support.

In other words, it was sustainable. It was a tribe.

In his book *Tribes,* marketing expert Seth Godin says it takes two things to turn a group of people into a tribe: 1) a shared interest and 2) a way to communicate.[6] Social media provide us with both. Rather than being united by blood, geography or common history, cyber-tribes are united via shared interests and experiences. Social media gives people multiple avenues by which they can communicate. But I believe these two components alone are not enough to make a true tribe. Shared interests and a mode of communication provide business owners with a 'niche' or target audience for sure. But the most important ingredient to turn a niche into an actual tribe is a *shared value system*. In other words:

> *While common interests define a niche,*
> *common value systems define a tribe.*

WHO YOU ARE IN YOUR TRIBE

The thing that makes us 'somebody' in a tribe is the role we play within it. Whether we are the local weaver, green grocer or shaman, our role brings meaning to our lives by enabling us to serve our community in a way only we are able to provide. In much the same way, we also play a role in our 'tribes,' whether in cyberspace or in our localities. Who we choose to be in our tribes will define not only our business success, but also our relationship with the tribe as a whole. Business owners who enter the social media world regarding it as a numbers game are seriously missing the boat. Numbers are great, but they mean nothing without substance. I'll take 2,000 (or even 200) loyal followers over 20,000 random 'connections' any day. Casting a wide net may have worked in the days of passive television advertising, but not in this era of social media. If you are a business owner or a marketer wishing to gather *both* quantity and quality in your tribe, you only need to do two things:

1. Be you
2. Be a leader

'Being you' is all about being authentic, natural and human. To me, the biggest turnoff is when a marketer or business bombards me with a bunch of overblown hype. Please don't tell me your products or services are 'life changing.' Let *other* people tell me how you have changed their lives. Connect with me. Speak *with* me, not *at* me. We are all people. It doesn't matter how famous, rich or gorgeous you might be. It doesn't matter if you are a mega business. Playing the celebrity card might build you a fan club, but it doesn't build a tribe.

'Being a leader,' whether in social media or in life in general, does not mean you are the most known, the most powerful or the one with the most money or followers. Being a leader does, however, mean you are one of the most *influential.* Influence has to be earned. It comes only when we have four very important ingredients:

1. a vision
2. a voice
3. connections
4. values

Before anything else, a leader needs **a vision** and **a voice.** If you have a vision, but you dare not speak it, you are not a leader. If you talk a lot (or loudly!) and you have no vision, you are not a leader.

After that, you need **connections.** You don't just need to know a lot of people; you need to know a lot *about* a lot of people. You need to know where you can go for help when you need it, and where to send other people if they come to you for help. When you meet new people, think who you might connect them with, or how you might connect with each other, collaboratively.

Vision, voice and connections mean very little unless they are underpinned by the fourth ingredient—**your values**. Without values, leadership becomes tyranny. Your values are the thread that weaves your vision, your voice and your connections together into something that serves the tribe, rather than just your own desires. Values are what bring meaning to your vision and passion to your voice. Values are what make people want to connect with you and stay with you.

Remember: *common value systems define a tribe.*

To be true business leaders, we cannot regard ourselves as being outside the tribe. Leaders are a part of the tribe. Indeed, they are the essence of it. When business owners understand this fully, we will at last be able to restore this lost Connection between businesses and their audience, and begin the rebuilding of communities, both virtually and in our towns and villages.

WHAT QUANTUM SCIENCE CAN TEACH US ABOUT MARKETING

Quantum physics has taught us that there is no such thing as objectivity in the physical world. All things are part of the same stuff. The scientist cannot observe reality without taking into consideration his own presence within that reality. The impact we create upon the world around us will inevitably impact us as well, because we are part of the whole, and not separate from it.

These same scientific principles can teach us a great deal about old-school marketing versus this new paradigm I call the '7 Graces' model. When we look at these two approaches to marketing, we can see they each parallel the cosmological view of their respective eras. Old-school marketing comes from an age where most people had a mechanistic view of science, where objectivity was at the foundation of their belief system, and the world was a place of measurement, linear sequences, logic and observable cause and effect. The 7 Graces model is born of an era in which the cause and effect of science has yielded to a holistic view of systems and inter-relations, where linearity is blurred (if it exists at all), and both the observer and the observed must be taken into the equation of one's results.

To put it more simply:

- **In old-school marketing,** the marketer believes he is standing 'outside' his audience, and views that audience as 'the target.' As such, the relationship between marketer and audience cannot help but create imbalance and Disconnection.
- **In the 7 Graces paradigm,** the marketer now views himself to be part and parcel of the very audience he is addressing. The audience are 'his people' and he is related to them via common values and mutual respect. As such, their relationship cannot help but create (or restore) balance and Connection.

Back when I worked as a college director, I couldn't count how many times I heard teachers complain 'the system' was a mess. They would always say, 'the college thinks this,' and 'the college thinks that.' What they failed to see was that they *were* the college. They *were* the system. We are always part of and connected to the system.

When we influence another entity, for ill or for good, we are not only influencing that entity, but the entire system. And when we inflict harm upon any part of the system, we are also harming ourselves because we are inseparable from that system. It stands to reason then—if we approach marketing from the perspective that we are separate, and our aim is to exploit another being for our own gain—we are damaging the entire system including *ourselves.* Marketers simply have no more excuses for regarding the public as separate, exploitable entities, falsely believing they will escape from the impact they themselves are creating.

It's not a threat. It's not dogma.

It's not 'woo-woo' or even *karma*.

It's simply science.

SUMMARY: HOW CONNECTION CAN HEAL HUMANITY AND THE PLANET

The age-old 'Golden Rule' says, 'Love others as you love yourself.' But unless we see we ARE the other, this can at best be lip service. To love others as ourselves, we need to be able to hear the *Musica Humana* emanating from their hearts and minds, and recognise that tune as the very same one that vibrates within our own being.

We business owners are a part of 'the system' called humanity. What we do as individuals may impact our immediate circles, but what we do as business owners creates a much wider impact. Unless we see both our importance and our responsibility within this tribe of humanity we serve, we can never hope to prosper, for without that awareness we will only continue to generate increasing imbalances in society, the economy and the natural world. We might mistakenly believe we are increasing our wealth, without seeing how we, as one humanity, are losing wealth in so many other ways. We might delude ourselves into believing we are successful, without seeing how the imbalances we create will ultimately result in a breakdown of the entire system.

It is only through Connection to Self, our businesses, our audience, the planet and everything else within this system we call Creation, that businesses and marketers can begin to render true service to the world, and hopefully begin to restore the balance that has been so deeply disturbed as a result of worldwide industrialisation over the past two centuries. Connection is not only the means by which we can 'love our neighbour as ourselves' but, indeed, by which we can love ourselves. We are not separate, you are I; business owners and consumers are not separate; people and planet are not separate. We are all part of this mysterious, interdependent system called Life on Earth. Everything we do, think, feel and say has an impact upon the rest.

And for that reason, regardless of whether you are a small-business owner, a corporate mogul or a consumer, performing just one small act of Connection cannot help but have an impact upon the Whole. We are not powerless. We are not helpless. Being part of the Whole, we are never helpless. All great change starts with one small change.

Step outside into the wide world.

Connect.

Listen to the song of humanity.

If your heart does not melt for it, at least allow it to melt with compassion for you who cannot yet hear that music.

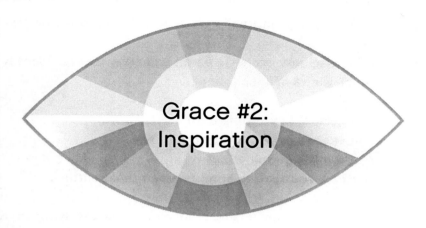

Grace #2: Inspiration

> *'The glory of friendship is not the outstretched hand,*
> *nor the kindly smile, nor the joy of companionship;*
> *it's the spiritual inspiration that comes to one*
> *when he discovers that someone else believes in him*
> *and is willing to trust him with his friend.'*
> **~ Ralph Waldo Emerson**[1]

W e think of inspiration as a 'thing' but it is actually an act, an exchange, between sentient beings. At least one etymological scholar says the word originates in the Late Latin *ispiratio* perhaps around the 3rd Century, and is derived from a verb that means 'to breathe into.'[2] The modern word 'spirit' in English is actually from the Latin word *spiritus* for breath (or *spirare*, the verb 'to breathe').[3] Thus, in its truest sense, inspiration means something that is life-giving. When we are inspired, we feel alive, as if something wonderful had been breathed into us. Conversely, when we inspire others, we breathe life into them.

Imagine a person on the street has collapsed from a cardiac arrest. He is unconscious and has stopped breathing. Someone, a complete stranger, comes along and gives the victim 'the breath of life.' Within a few minutes, the victim has recovered and is breathing again, even before the ambulance arrives. A few days later, the victim and the rescuer meet face to face in the hospital. Imagine how the person who was rescued feels towards the person who 'inspired' him to live. Imagine also how the person who performed the act of 'inspiration' feels. It's a mutually shared exchange bringing joy to both parties.

Using this imaginary scenario as an example, we can identify a few key characteristics of 'Inspiration':

1. It is an **action**, not a thing unto itself
2. It is an **exchange** between living entities
3. It creates a **life-giving effect**
4. It **creates a connective bond** between those entities

Now imagine that same person in cardiac arrest lying in the street, but this time the 'rescuer' decides to pump the victim's lungs full of carbon monoxide from the exhaust of his car. Of course, the victim would die very quickly (and the so-called rescuer would hopefully get arrested!). When a person dies, we say they have 'expired,' meaning they have breathed *out* their last breath. The fact that the word 'expiration' is the literal opposite of inspiration helps us to understand the purport of the word 'inspiration' even more: inspiration is that which gives life. That which takes life away is not inspiration.

In marketing, we are also given the same choice: shall we be inspiring or expiring? When we pollute the mental, emotional or spiritual 'breath' of others with life-stealing words, we create fear, anxiety and diminished feelings of self-worth. These are toxic messages; they are 'expiration,' not 'inspiration.' Expiration is the natural end-result of Persuasion marketing, as its ultimate aim is to disempower the consumer. Whether in marketing or any other kind of communication, whenever our aim is to disable, discourage or disempower others, the psychological and biological stresses we incite literally rob them of life.

In this era when marketing is so pervasive, we marketers have both an immense opportunity and an immense responsibility. Every single word we send out into the world has the potential to deliver either a life-giving message or a life-robbing one. At every moment, we are then being asked to make a choice: Persuasion or Inspiration? Which will it be for me? Whenever I start working with a new client, one of my mantras for them is, *'Your job is never to persuade, only to inspire.'* But is it possible to sell products and services without using old-school 'land the deal' strategies? Will people respond to marketing if they have no sense of urgency or fear? Is it possible to abandon Persuasion as a motivator and still motivate our customers enough so we can stay in business?

INSPIRATION THROUGH GIVING

We have said that Inspiration is both an *action* and an *exchange*. Thus, if we are to 'sell' using Inspiration, our marketing (the action) must be an *exchange* between us and our audience. It cannot be a one-way communication. This exchange must be life-giving, and create a connective bond with our customers. How can we achieve that? We do it by turning the tables and going against all logic of business: Instead of trying to 'get' from our customers, we *give* to them.

What kinds of things can we give? Reliable information is one thing. When we give good, honest, information and advice to our audience, they not only regard us as credible leaders in our field, they come to trust us and see us as generous. Back in the 'old days' when we had tribes and extended families, we didn't have mass educational systems; we had elders. The elders always passed on their wisdom. Apprenticeship was also a fundamental part of our educational system, in which a senior craftsman passed on his knowledge and wisdom of the trade. But as industrialisation took over, we became increasingly disconnected from this practice.

The giving of knowledge is a life-giving exchange that creates a connective bond of trust and communication between marketer and customer. True giving is not just 'giving' information about your product. While giving accurate information about your product is an important part of Transparency, it is not actual 'giving.' An example of such 'pseudo-giving' would be those toothpaste commercials where some supposed market researcher stops some supposed unsuspecting passerby and asks them to test their toothpaste for sensitive teeth. They show the customers a drawing of a tooth and tell them that it's the miraculous 'Pro-Mumbo-Jumbo' formula (patented of course) that makes the toothpaste work. What is worse is that it is presented in such a way that it seduces the viewer into believing this is some sort of actual clinical survey, or that they are learning something scientific. This is not only deceptive, it is also life-robbing because it *wastes our time* by telling us nothing really useful at all. This, like the vast majority of adverts on television, billboards or in magazines, is all 'take' and no 'give.' If we want to inspire through giving, it has to be something actually helpful to the consumer.

With the rise of blogging and social media, business owners now have an unprecedented opportunity to *give* to their customers. Experienced bloggers and Internet-based business owners know the best way to keep an audience is to demonstrate you are consistently willing to share your knowledge and expertise with them. On-the-ground businesses are gradually catching on to this concept too. One of my less typical clients was a company providing property services to homeowners and apartment complexes in Northern California. Owned by a husband and wife, they had been running the business for over 20 years but had just hit a brick wall financially, so they came to me to see if social media could help them get their feet back on the ground. I built a modest WordPress blog for them and helped them get started in social media; we spent a few months working together as I showed them how to utilise and benefit from these resources. When they first started to blog, they wrote a couple of articles that were basically brochure pieces, talking about how good their company was. I told them that even if people somehow found their blog, articles like these would pretty much ensure they would click away and never come back again.

'So what do we say?' they asked.

'You've been in business over 20 years. What do you know about property services?' I asked them.

'Well...lots of stuff,' they said.

'Great,' I said. 'Start talking and I'll type. Let's make a list of all the services you do.'

Without hesitation they started rattling off all their services, from carpet installation to crime scene clean-up. Within two minutes we had a list of at least ten different services.

'Excellent,' I said. 'Now let's go down the list. For each item, think of maybe two or three questions people have asked you about these topics over the years.'

Being the experienced professionals they were, they very quickly came up with a substantial list of tips that could only have been learned from years in the trade. They covered everything from how to get rid of mould, to eco-flooring to the legal requirements for cleaning up bio-hazards. I found it surprisingly interesting.

'Great,' I said, handing them the list we had assembled. 'Here are the topics of your first 25 blog posts. If you write one a week, you'll have material for the next six months.'

Over the next few weeks, they very quickly assembled an impressive collection of informative blogs on a wide range of industry-specific topics, which any property manager would be delighted to find as a resource. We then made sure their search engine optimisation (SEO) was solid, and that their telephone number and other contact info was at the bottom of every post. We created five or six tweets for each post, and set them up to recur on a regular basis. Then, we started searching Twitter for potential property managers in the San Francisco Bay Area.

Within a few months, their great info-blog had attracted over 2,000 followers via Twitter, and the wife was also starting to connect directly with others she was meeting on LinkedIn and Facebook. She then started to attend local network meetings she had found via her new connections. She continued to offer generous information at the live meetings, and intuitively started sharing contacts and connections with others. Very soon, others were sharing back with them, sending referrals their way. By giving what they had plenty of—specialist knowledge—they had sprouted a whole new side to their business, opening up new connections and possibilities for growth.

Now you might not think a bunch of articles on mould prevention and the like are particularly 'inspirational,' but what *is* inspiring is the *act of giving and exchanging* itself. When business owners demonstrate genuine generosity of either their time or their wisdom, it is inspiring. Furthermore, when they show they have enough character, experience and self-confidence to share what they know with others, they send the unspoken message to their audience that *they know still more, and therefore have a lot more still to give.*

I've heard a number of clients worry they might be giving away 'too much' when they provide information on their websites and blogs. I believe that's underestimating the breadth of your professional expertise. You can write all the blog posts you want on how to clean your carpet and the like, but it will never be a replacement for 20 years of practical experience. We should never worry about giving away 'too much.' It is impossible. If you want to inspire, give, give, give.

While giving information is one of the easiest ways to give, giving can come in many other forms as well. You can give good value for money. You can give fun. You can give gifts. I always get my clients to build a selection of free gifts to give their customers. You can also give *community.* Using social media, you can create a space for shared values, where people feel a sense of belonging. You can use any number of ways—from creating an actual membership community site, to having a Facebook fan page where people can interact.

And last of all, you can give *yourself.* Show up personally online and be authentic, honest, available, approachable and, most of all, friendly. I don't care how big a business is; in this era of social media, if you do not show up as the face of the company online, you are missing a golden opportunity to create Connection and provide Inspiration to your customers.

INSPIRATION AS EMPOWERMENT

> *'You are already the hero of your own life.*
> *You did not earn this title. You did not have to.*
> *You were born the hero. It is your birthright.'*
> **~ Lynn Serafinn, *The Garden of the Soul*[4]**

The recent recession first hit Britain in 2008 when I was still doing personal life coaching. For many months that year, I would receive calls from desperate clients who were going through difficult times. Much of them had anxieties revolving around money, which is why they called a coach to help. But ironically, when it came to the part in our initial meeting where we inevitably had to discuss the cost of services, they would start to hem and haw, expressing doubt that they could afford me. When this would happen, I would ask them whether or not they would hire me if money weren't an issue. If they said yes, I told them to go away for a week and use their natural sense of innovation to create a solution. I told them, however, in order for me to agree to their proposed solution, it had to adhere to these conditions: 1) it would not involve barter, 2) it would not cause them to go into debt or put them into financial hardship, and 3) it would not involve bargaining me down on my price. Once they had come up with a solution, they could come back to me.

This in itself was a very interesting exercise, and what people didn't realise was that it was their first opportunity to experience empowerment in our work together. Invariably, the people who really wanted my services came up with extremely creative solutions. Some devised monthly payment plans. One gave up her housecleaner for six months. Others miraculously found additional sources of income they hadn't thought about until they needed it for this purpose. Once they had created the solution, these clients became some of my most committed and focussed.

If you recall my earlier story about the 'land the deal' coach who had used exactly the opposite strategy with me, you will remember how it backfired. I am sure she had managed to persuade quite a few people using her strategy, but the question is, 'Are we serving our clients by disempowering them?' As a holistic marketer, I know if I procure money by trying to disempower my clients through fear or self-doubt, I am also hurting myself. Conversely, by creating an opportunity to allow my clients to choose their own solutions, I am not only helping them, I am helping the world in general.

The whole world benefits from the gift of empowerment. It is quite possibly the most inspiring gift we could offer any human being. Consider how it feels to show a child how to do something for herself. Think of the look on her face—the smile, the confidence, the joy, the self-worth. Imagine a world filled with children who feel like that, growing up into empowered adults. The world would be filled with less stress, less crime and less economic hardship, as people will be empowered to make conscious, informed spending choices rather than reactive, addictive ones that come from feelings of fear and unworthiness. When Dr Martin Luther King Jr. said, 'I have a dream,' he was empowering his listeners. Any truly inspirational message is empowering. When we inspire, we empower, because we are breathing life into our audience.

THE THREE CORNERSTONES OF EMPOWERMENT

As holistic marketers we are committed to the empowerment of all human beings. If our practice is in any way disempowering, we have failed both ourselves and our customers. The cornerstones of empowerment are marked by three essential elements: *truth, time* and *space*.

Truthfulness empowers. Deception disempowers. When we marketers give our customers the facts, rather than our version of the facts, we empower them to choose. Of course we can express our opinions or give our perspective on things, as this is one important way to bring our own humanity back into our marketing. But if our perspective is presented in such a way that it infers it is THE truth as opposed to *our* truth—as in the case of so much marketing—we will find ourselves slipping backwards into Persuasion.

Time empowers. Lack of time disempowers. When we create anxiety and impose pressure on our customers to make decisions faster than they are able to process the 'truth,' we are disempowering them. I never insist my clients make a decision to work with me on the first telephone conversation (although many do). When adverts scream at us to 'Hurry now before you lose out!' they are disempowering. While we all have to set time parameters for our promotions, if our deadlines are set with the sole intention of creating anxiety, we are disempowering our customers and again resorting to Persuasion.

Space empowers. Lack of space disempowers. Crowding our customers with too many confusing choices, too much hyped-up balderdash, or screaming at them with blaring sales letters or loud adverts is disempowering. The aesthetics of our marketing has a huge impact upon how it is received. Space in marketing can be achieved through clarity, respect and directness. Imagine your marketing piece is like a living room: Would you want to sit inside it for an evening, or would you be climbing the walls trying to get out because it's so crowded and uncomfortable? If you ask yourself that question every single time you put together a marketing piece, you will start to get a good idea of whether or not you are creating or taking away space in your marketing. If your marketing makes you feel claustrophobic, it's pretty fair to say you need to start performing a little marketing feng shui.

SUMMARY: HOW INSPIRATION CAN HEAL HUMANITY AND THE PLANET

We started out this chapter by saying that Inspiration is to 'breathe life into' another being. What greater duty could we possibly have, therefore, than to be inspiring to our customers?

When we inspire others by freely giving our knowledge, we also begin to create a huge body of resources, which can inspire and empower many generations to come.

When we inspire by giving good value, we not only improve the quality of life, but help to restore trust between businesses and customers.

When we inspire through fun, we show our lighter side and remind people we are not just about making money.

When we inspire by creating community and friendship, we help to heal and restore Connection in the world.

When we inspire by giving the gift of empowerment, we help people to believe in their own ideas, opinions and choices.

All these types of Inspiration create trust, support, safety and belonging in the world. We breathe life into society when we inspire.

One word of caution:

> *The real bottom-line to any business is not profit;*
> *it is **intention**.*

If we create pseudo-inspirational marketing for the sole purpose of trying to look like the nice guy, we're not really giving anything at all. Profits are of course important, but there is a difference between 'receiving' and 'taking.' One is Divine, the other destructive.

We know we are successful at Inspiration when what we give outweighs whatever we have gained, and what we have received from our business—and I don't just mean money—has breathed life back into *us*.

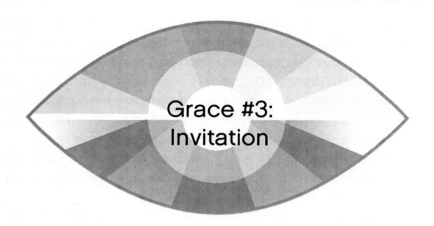

Grace #3:
Invitation

Back in 1984, I was living in the Alamo Heights area in San Antonio, Texas, along with my then-husband and our young daughter. In those days, we were musicians playing world music, including music from India and the Middle East. Through our music, we had come to befriend a very nice man named Abdulla from Afghanistan who played *dirbeki*, the traditional Middle Eastern clay drum often seen accompanying belly dance music. Some years before, when they were still living in Tabul, Soviet military had invaded Abdulla's family home in the middle of the night while everyone was asleep. Soldiers hauled off both Abdulla's father and eldest brother, and seized their family properties and possessions. Abdulla and his extended family, including his wife, mother and siblings had no choice but to flee to India lest they suffer a similar fate. Losing virtually every possession they had, they spent some months in New Delhi gathering what money and business resources they could salvage, and eventually moved to the United States. The father and brother were never heard from again, and although no one voiced this openly, everyone assumed they had been executed. The wife of the brother was pregnant at the time, and gave birth to a son long after they had left their native land.

Despite all the hardship and violence they had endured, Abdulla's family were resilient and remarkably positive and gentle. They were very close-knit, but also extremely open and inviting to anyone who came into their home. The most impressive display of their exceptional hospitality came one weekday evening when my husband and I dropped by their house. We hadn't called in advance, but that wasn't particularly unusual as we often came knocking on each other's doors without needing an invitation. But this evening, when Abdulla's sister answered the door, we heard a lot of music and voices coming from inside.

For a split second, the sister looked a little surprised, but then almost immediately said, 'Come in. Come in. We're having a family party.' She opened the door to let us in.

'No, no,' we said. 'We don't want to intrude. Just tell Abdulla we dropped by. We'll come back another day.'

The sister opened the door even wider, and said, 'No, no, no. I insist. You must come in. Please.'

By now Abdulla had spotted us and he said, 'Come! Come!' as the rest of the family also waved to us to enter. Feeling a little embarrassed for intruding, we came in. There was a massive spread of food and sweets on the dining room table and lively Afghani music playing over the stereo. Being strict Muslims, there was not a drop of alcohol to be seen, but there was plenty of aromatic coffee brewing.

Abdulla's mother, wife and sister came to me and gave me their usual greeting of kissing me on both cheeks. Then suddenly, they disappeared into the kitchen. When I asked Abdulla where they had gone, he said they were cooking dinner for us. The family knew we were vegetarians (they were not) and the women had gone off to make us a special meal.

We said, 'Oh, no, Abdulla, please tell them not to go to so much trouble. It wasn't polite of us to barge in unannounced like this...'

'No, no, no,' Abdulla said. 'You are our guests!'

Within what seemed like less than five minutes, the ladies produced a huge tray of beautifully spiced spinach and rice prepared in a pan that had been scrubbed to ensure there were no traces of meat in it. They presented this to us along with lovely flatbreads, salads, spiced lentils and homemade sweets.

The meal was genuinely delicious, but the flavour of the food was made even more delectable by the extra care and intention that had been put into its preparation.

After our magnificent meal, the family gathered chairs around in a circle. They handed my husband a drum, and me some finger cymbals. We started to play to the music, and everyone began to take turns dancing, singing and playing the drums. The men danced one at a time, waving handkerchiefs as they danced. The women danced together, in their glamorous Los Angeles-style party frocks, looking both demure and slightly seductive. It was a splendid evening and I left in very high spirits.

Obviously this incident made an impression on me, or I wouldn't be relating this story nearly 30 years afterwards. Some of us modern Westerners might read this story and say that Abdulla's family went 'above and beyond the call of duty.' But actually their behaviour was typical of the moral code of conduct within their family tradition. For them, the care of guests within the home is viewed as a sacred duty, and it is the responsibility of the host to ensure the guest is made to feel like they are part of the household, and that they are respected and cared for—even if they have dropped in unannounced.

I call this the Grace of Invitation.

'Invitation' as a social practice has been all but forgotten in much of our modern world. In most cultures, up until recent times, the code of conduct for a host was considered a sacred duty. When we say, 'Please come in,' to someone and invite them into our home, it means we promise to take responsibility for the care they will receive within our four walls.

True 'Invitation' is not simply an act of courtesy or politeness; it is a Divine service wherein we are seeing to the welfare of another human being.

MARKETING AND THE LOST ART OF INVITATION

Earlier in the book, we mentioned the term 'permission marketing' first popularised by Seth Godin in his book of the same name. 'Permission marketing' refers to our giving 'permission' to marketers by signing up to a mailing list. But 'permission' is not at all the same thing as 'Invitation,' and I really believe that without understanding the distinction between the two, marketers will continue to get it wrong.

When a customer lands randomly on our website via a Google search, it is very similar to them knocking on our door unannounced, as I did at Abdulla's party. If I click a link on Google and subsequently land on a website that screams at me with gigantic red headlines and schmoozy web copy, it's just as if Abdulla had greeted me at the door and shouted at me with widened eyes, saying, 'Ah ha! You're just the people I wanted to see! You've gotta get this widget. Your life won't be worth anything without it...' Instantly, I'd feel uneasy and try to find a way to escape. If I'm on a website and I'm made to feel this way, I'll probably click the 'back' button to get away. But no! I can't escape! A pop-up window asking for my email address appears and says, 'Don't go! If you stay, I'll give you this, that and the other thing. If you leave, you'll miss out!' Now, it's just as if Abdulla has grabbed my arms and is trying to pull me into his house against my will.

If you land on a website that makes you think, *Get me out of here!* it's reasonably fair to say it failed the 'Invitation' test. And still, marketers and software developers everywhere are creating (and teaching others to create) 'squeeze pages' that scream at the customer just like this. Yes, we're back to using 'Persuasion' and 'Scarcity' to create urgency and discomfort, because we've been taught these strategies result in greater sales conversion. And they might well do, at least in the short-term. But if we continually try to make our customers feel anxious, it is highly unlikely they will stay subscribed to our lists for very long or buy anything else from us, even if we somehow wangled them into making a purchase the first time around.

Invitation is the missing ingredient in these types of websites, as well as in so much of our marketing today. Abdulla's story can teach us a lot about this lost art of Invitation. To master this art, we need to embrace three essential components:

hospitality, respect and engagement.

HOSPITALITY, RESPECT AND ENGAGEMENT

When someone lands on our website, walks into our shop or comes into our 'space' in any way, it is the equivalent of them being guests within our home. While we cannot physically offer our Internet visitors the water, food, a comfy chair and cosy conversation during their stay, we can, however, offer them the virtual equivalent. All these components of hospitality make guests within our homes feel comfortable, relaxed and satiated. When a guest feels like this, they are happy to stay in our company, and when they do leave to go home, they carry with them the memory of how you made them feel.

In much the same way, when someone comes to our website, our aim should be to make them feel comfortable, relaxed and fully satisfied. If someone has come to your website, they are *hungry*—for information, for a solution to a need, for advice, for assurance, for fun—for *something*. Just as the best hosts will feed their guests with delicious food, the best sales pages are those that feed your visitors' hunger for information. If the site is for a piece of software, give your visitors lots of videos showing them exactly how it works. If it's for an event or a course, give them a taster and a concrete breakdown of what they'll gain.

What we shouldn't do is use lofty, overblown or ambiguous language telling our customers if they buy our product we'll tell them secrets no one else knows, or they will gain something they cannot gain any other way. Imagine coming into someone's home and being told such things by your host. You'd think you'd stepped right into the parlour of Mr Spider. Nonetheless, this is the kind of marketing messages we are subjected to every day, both on the Internet and on television. When we taunt customers with hype, distractions, ambiguity or delayed promises, we make them feel anxious, confused and eventually mistrustful. What is ironic, of course, is that all this lack of hospitality makes people less likely to buy from you at all, even if your product is the very thing that would answer their needs.

If people become mistrustful of us, it is more than likely because we are not showing them the *respect* they deserve. There are an awful lot of Internet marketers who make a formulaic show of their trustworthiness by integrating customer testimonials and money-back guarantees into their sales pages. But neither of these strategies is effective if a sales page shows little respect for the customer. Besides, most consumers nowadays are pretty savvy. They know testimonials could be faked and promises of money-back guarantees could be just words. And if someone comes to a website and gets that impression, it's more than likely because the marketing is not demonstrating respect for the customer's intelligence, values, health, happiness and freedom of choice. If marketers focus solely on conversion in creating marketing pieces, this will be the result.

Respect can only be present when marketers remember it is a privilege for people to give them their time and attention, and to consider using their products or services. The actual exchange of currency is not the result of a sales page. It is the result of a *relationship* between customer and merchant—between guest and host. Customers are the guests who knock on our door and we business owners, as their hosts, must create the quality of that relationship.

And finally, no relationship can be built without *engagement*. Old-school marketing was always a one-way street with no engagement between marketer and consumer whatsoever. The consumer simply absorbed the programming and was expected to buy. But as the world has changed, and is continuing to change, lack of engagement or interaction will probably turn out to be the fastest track to business failure in the coming generation. Just as when we visited Abdulla's home and his entire family engaged with us, to survive in the modern business world, we marketers must be engaging. We must listen and respond to our customers demonstrating *genuine* (not feigned) interest in them. We must make them feel valued, and invite their input and ideas. We must convey to them that they are a valuable part of our 'circle', our tribe, and that their voice is being heard in how we do business.

When all three of these components—hospitality, respect and engagement—are genuinely and authentically present in our marketing, we have a foundation for the Grace of Invitation to flourish.

HOUSEGUEST FROM HELL

Let's take a look at the flipside, where marketers are not the hosts into whose space the consumer has entered, but are now guests within the *consumer's* space. Again, I'll use a story to illustrate this scenario.

One day back when I lived in Phoenix, Arizona, our family received a phone call from someone in need. The man (I'll call him 'Sam') was about 40 years old and was a travelling 'monk' (although I use the term loosely), assisting his guru on a preaching tour around the western half of the US. Suddenly, on their way back from Arizona to Chicago, Sam's car broke down somewhere off Interstate-17 about three hours' drive north of us. His guru, who had already embarked in his own vehicle some hours before, carried on to his destination unaware Sam's car had broken down. The long journey would take three days and, as he was planning to camp under the stars at night, Sam's guru was basically out of contact until he reached Chicago later that week. This being the days before most of us had mobile phones, and being out in the middle of nowhere, Sam had no choice but to hitch a ride to the nearest payphone and call someone he knew in Arizona for help. So, he called us.

We had only met Sam once before, but we were friends with his guru, so we felt some moral obligation to help out. My husband drove up to northern Arizona to rescue Sam. Together, they located a service station who towed Sam's car to their shop, but they said they would not be able to assess the damage for a few days. As Sam was stranded, and our family embraced the value of extending courtesy to houseguests, my husband brought him back to our home until Sam could sort out his vehicle problems. We assumed it would all be taken care of within three or four days. At first, it was nice having Sam around as a guest. He had a great sense of humour and we enjoyed his company. He joined us for meals and it made for lively conversation. But unfortunately, all this was to be very short-lived.

After a few days, the service station called and said the car was kaput and would require a whole new engine, but they were not equipped to do such extensive repairs. Again, my husband made the long trek back to northern Arizona, this time to tow the broken car back down to Phoenix, where Sam could get it fixed.

At first we thought nothing about feeding Sam and driving him where he needed to go while he got his car repaired. He was our guest, after all. But as time progressed, nothing seemed to change in Sam's situation. Days turned into weeks, and Sam had done nothing to get the car fixed. We soon became aware that Sam had neither any money nor any urge to find any. After a few attempts at selling spiritual books at the local shopping mall, he quit, and started spending 100% of his time hanging around our home. He seemed to have stopped thinking altogether about getting back to Chicago. It was weird.

After a few weeks, our food, water and gasoline bills had more than doubled (and considering we were a family of three, that's saying a lot), but Sam offered no remuneration. It was clear he felt quite comfortable in our home and felt no shame in depending upon us for his every need. Of course, we had no such ability (or desire) to provide a full-grown man with this kind of financial and emotional dependency. But we saw no visible signs of him intending to move out of our house—ever!

Weeks turned into months, and our friendly relationship devolved into resentment and tension. A big, muscular mid-western lad who stood about 6 foot 5 inches in height, Sam said he had a back condition, for which he practiced yoga—shirtless, and wearing only a thin saffron-coloured loin cloth—for at least three hours every afternoon between 2 and 5 P.M. Some days he practiced in our living room. Our young daughter would feel embarrassed if she brought her pre-adolescent friends home after school, as they would have to scurry around his sweaty, half-naked body just to get into her room. Other days he practiced out in the garden, which we shared with three other families. If our neighbours had ever thought we were a wee bit mad, the sight of a gigantic, nearly nude, farm-boy yogi contorting for hours every day in front of the whole neighbourhood surely must have removed all doubt.

But for me the final straw was when Sam requested I make pancakes for dinner one day, and I obliged. I spent a good long time preparing a huge stack of homemade pancakes for both him and my family, but before anyone else came to sit down at the table, Sam grabbed the entire platter of pancakes, spread a whole quarter-pound stick of butter on them, dowsed them in half a bottle of syrup and ate them ALL, requiring me to spend another 30 minutes mixing another batch of batter and making yet another platter of pancakes for my family. As he sat there eating, blissfully unaware of what he had just done, I stared in disbelief not only at his rudeness, and not only at the fact that he was single-handedly consuming what I had prepared for four people to share, but also that he was devouring an entire stick of butter in one sitting.

I wanted to hurl him out the door, but looking at his bliss-filled face and lumbering form, I muttered sarcastically, 'Cholesterol? Me?'

After nearly three months, and without being offered a dime in return, we were finally able to extricate this houseguest from hell by calling his guru in Chicago. Aghast at what had happened, his guru made the 1,500-mile drive down to Phoenix, and took Sam back north. I still find it hard to believe Sam was 40 years old, but I fully understand why he had already been divorced twice.

WHEN MARKETERS BECOME TAKERS

The story of Sam has more useful lessons for marketers. Let's first look at online marketing. When someone comes to our website and signs up to our mailing list, they are no longer our guests as in Abdulla's story—we have now become *their* guests and are in *their* space. When a consumer supplies us with their email address, that person is, in effect, opening their door to us and saying, 'Yes, you can come in and stay here,' just as our family had opened our door to Sam. Unlike when they are coming into our space, we are now in their space.

And just as there is a moral code for hosts, there is also one for guests. However, I see few online marketers acting as if they truly understand this. While most of us would never dream of treating a host the way Sam did, when it comes to marketing, we feel justified in coming into people's homes, either through their Inbox or the media, and bleeding them dry with relentless advertising. When marketers operate on the assumption that it takes repeated exposure for subscribers or viewers to become customers, they find it necessary to saturate the consumers' consciousness with their message, without giving them much of anything in return. This is no different from Sam taking advantage of our hospitality, without offering any compensation for all he consumed at our expense. We marketers simply must start realising that coming into people's homes is a privilege, and cannot ever allow ourselves to become the proverbial houseguests from hell.

PUT A LITTLE EFFORT INTO IT

To be a good 'guest' in our customers' space is not just about being sensitive to the quantity of communications we send them, but also the quality of those communications. In the case of Internet marketing, while much of the quality of our communications lies in the copy we write, I believe a good deal of it also lies in our visual presentation. Presentation can make communication either inviting or invasive. I cannot count how many Internet marketers have sent me daily email messages in plain text format, with no colours, no images, no font formatting. There are two practical reasons why they do this. First of all, it's a heck of a lot easier and faster to shoot out a text-only email than to take the time to format it nicely in html. The second reason is because it supposedly minimises the likelihood of it being flagged as spam, as spambots are said to see html messages as more suspicious than plain text messages. I have to admit I find this to be bewildering, as most spam *is* sent as plain text, not html. After all, spammers don't take the time to format their email blasts (duh!).

In spite of what might seem like perfectly good, practical reasons, I think sending bland, text-only emails can actually backfire on marketers. When I did my M.A. in distance education, one of the primary rules we learned for creating online learning content was ease of readability. Layout, colours and font styles are crucial to a learner's ability to consume and understand the content. Good formatting brought clarity to anything from online courses to printed notes and assignment briefs. Using this knowledge, I helped standardise instructional materials for many college departments, helping them go from repeatedly failing their educational audits to passing easily year after year. So if formatting can make such a difference in how students perform, I can only assume it also makes a difference in how consumers understand and absorb email marketing.

When you get right down to it, marketing isn't really that different from education. Both are in the business of communicating information, and ensuring that information 'sticks' in the minds of those hearing it. When marketers put their ease of content creation over the ease of their customers' ability to digest that content, it can only be counter-productive. So I want to go on record here and challenge the pseudo-logic behind sending out plain text email blasts.

If we want to be 'inviting' to our potential customers and clients, we need to make an effort. Aesthetics are just as important as words—possibly more. There's a little Lebanese restaurant nearby where I live in Bedford. I like to pop in there every now and then just to get a cup of fresh mint tea. The tea is nice, but it's not necessarily any better tasting than tea you'd get at other Middle Eastern restaurants. What I enjoy is the fact that they bring it over in a cute little pot and serve it in a beautiful cut glass cup and saucer, gilded with gold trim. There's something about the care they give to the presentation that makes me want to spend two quid for a cup of tea and leave a pound tip after I've spent a lovely 20 minutes savouring the experience.

To me, both marketing and education are art. Good marketers and good teachers understand that people respond when their senses are engaged at all levels—mind, heart and body. Aesthetics are a tremendously important part of marketing. If we put no effort into making our marketing a pleasant experience, we are simply 'taking' and not 'giving.' When we send an email to someone, it's no different from knocking on their door and asking to come in. If you want them to welcome you, you can't just barge in and say, 'Buy my stuff!' Give your readers a reason to open your email in the first place. Give them great information. Give them nice colours. Give them videos to watch and audio to hear. Give them free stuff. Be *nice* to them for heaven's sake. They have invited you in. Don't take advantage of their hospitality and don't overstay your welcome.

For Internet marketing to shift from Invasion to Invitation, both marketers and consumers must become aware on which end of the host-guest spectrum they sit, and learn how to interact with each other from that awareness. When we marketers are the 'host' (as when people visit our website), it is our responsibility to treat our guests with hospitality, respect and sincere engagement. When we are the 'guest' (as when we send emails to people on our list) we must be sensitive, grateful and mindful of giving more than we expect to receive. But consumers can also help by ceasing to tolerate any kind of invasive behaviour from Internet marketers. If both marketers and consumers work together on this, Internet marketing would gradually transform into something much friendlier and more useful for all.

Knock, Knock. Who's There?

While any new invention starts with the vision of its creator, its actual form is created by the masses who adopt it into their daily lifestyle. Henry Ford, Thomas Edison, Alexander Graham Bell, Steve Jobs and Bill Gates all had visions for their innovations, but they hardly anticipated the breadth of change that would occur in the world as a result of their initial ideas. So too in the case of social media. Mark Zuckerberg and Jack Dorsey may have been the visionaries behind Facebook and Twitter, respectively, but just like the automobile, electric lighting, the telephone and the personal computer, the true power of these inventions owes less to their inventors than to the *public*, who reinvented them to suit their own needs and desires.

What the public reinvented with social media was the 'open door.' Suddenly, the world was knocking on our door and everyone was a potential friend. For many people, this shook up social codes around the need for personal privacy. But for many more it shifted the way they interacted with each other, paving the way for the resurgence of the lost art of 'Invitation.'

To get a better idea of just how significantly social media has already impacted the world, let's look at some statistics you might find surprising. The battle to obtain the patent for a brand-new invention we now know as 'the telephone' was fierce towards the end of the 19th Century, and it was only with a great deal of controversy that Alexander Graham Bell was awarded the patent in 1876. Thereafter, it took Bell a further two years to construct a model that was deemed suitable to be sold to the public, and the telephone hit the commercial market in 1878. Three years after that, in 1881, there were an estimated 49,000 telephones in use. Later, there were 600,000 telephones in use by 1900, 2.2 million by 1905, and by 1910—a whole generation after the first phone was put on the market—there were an estimated 5.8 million telephones in use worldwide.[2] Given that the world population was estimated to be around 1.75 billion in 1910[3], this means that about 0.33% (one-third of 1%) of the world's population had adopted this new the invention over a 32-year period, meaning an average uptake of about 181,250 new users per year.

Now let's take a look at the rise of social media in the early 21st Century. Facebook, which first came onto our radar in February 2004, was estimated to have had more than 500 million users by July 2010.[4] With an estimated 6.9 billion people on the planet in 2010[5] this means Facebook had been embraced by an astonishing 7.2% of the global population in less than one-fifth of the time it took the telephone to reach only 0.33% adoption. Even if we quadruple the figure of 49,000 users Bell had achieved in three years' time to about 200,000, to estimate how many phones might have been in use six years after it was introduced to the public, Bell would have been reaching only about 0.02% of the world's population (which was a little over 1 billion in 1886) compared to Facebook's 7.2%. In other words, the growth of Facebook during the first six years of its existence has been about *360 times greater* than the telephone!

And Twitter's growth is not to be taken lightly either. The very first 'Tweet' on Twitter was sent by Jack Dorsey in March 2006, and by its fifth anniversary in March 2011, it was estimated to have grown to 200 million users.[6] Using the same population statistics as above, this means Twitter reached 2.9% of the world's population in its first five years of its operation. Not only that, but Twitter claim to process over 200 million Tweets and handle over 1.6 billion search queries *per day*.[7] To give you a scale of what that means, it's equivalent to 23% of the world's population performing a Twitter search every single day of the year. It's astonishing, really, especially considering people are communicating in micro-bytes of fewer than 140 characters at a time.

If any of us doubted that the very foundation of how we communicate is changing as a result of social media, these statistics alone should give us pause to reconsider. Yet still, the topic of social media platforms such as Facebook and Twitter often become the butt of jokes and bring up many fears and misconceptions, as many people do not yet realise just what powerful communication systems they actually are—possibly even more powerful than the telephone— and how they are already changing the way we relate to one another (my late father, a former Bell Telephone engineer, is probably shouting at me from the grave right now).

The rise of social media has made our world both smaller and larger. It is smaller because it takes only a second for our news to be broadcast all around the world to thousands, or even millions, of people. The limitations of time and space seem to collapse, and we have now become used to sending and receiving information at lightning speeds. But it has also made the world much larger because our social circle has now become endowed with an unprecedented potential for growth. It has allowed more people to 'knock on our door' in a single week, than most people would have known in their entire lifetime only a hundred years ago.

And as more and more people knock on our door, and we in turn knock on theirs, a new era of social interaction has, by necessity, arisen. We have had to create new customs and conventions, and they are not so much driven by cultural preferences as by the nature of the technologies we are using. For example, it's generally considered fine to post updates many times an hour on Twitter, but not so fine to do the same on Facebook. Given the fact that hundreds of millions of people use *both* programs, it seems pretty clear that these social codes of conduct are due far more to the way these respective programs deliver data, rather than the personal preferences of Twitter versus Facebook users. I find this to be a fascinating thought—that technology is not only compelling people to create new social codes of interaction, it is also influencing what those new social codes will look like. And in turn, as new social codes are developed, still more new technologies will continue to arise to meet the challenges of the new ways we choose to communicate. Our social relationships and our relationship with communication technologies are in a continual feedback loop, each influencing the other.

Rather than seeing these changes as threatening, we can embrace the communication afforded to us via social media, as a golden opportunity to learn what it means to have an open door to all who come our way, and to begin a new relationship with an unknown person with trust rather than suspicion. We can use these technologies to re-learn and re-instate the lost art of Invitation, once at the foundation of our social interactions. And when we start to reacquaint ourselves with this lost art, we will soon understand how very important it is in both our personal and professional relationships.

SUMMARY: HOW INVITATION CAN HEAL HUMANITY AND THE PLANET

Invitation is a true 'Grace' because it expresses our 'graciousness.' Graciousness is a quality we admire in individuals, but how often do we think of it as a criterion for our professional practice? Admittedly, this shift from Invasion to Invitation is going to be one of the most challenging for marketers to make. We need to communicate with our customers, but because there is simply so much 'noise' out there, we have adopted the belief that if we are the loudest and most aggressive, people will hear us above the din.

But this is simply not true. Just as we said earlier that 'Scarcity creates more Scarcity,' similarly 'Invasion creates more Invasion.' The more we inundate our customers with noise, the louder others will become. And the faster and less caring we are in our communications, the faster and less caring our customers will be when they click 'delete' on our email, or flick away from our advert with their remote control.

The Grace of Invitation is all about *communication*. The first syllable of the word 'communication' means 'with.' We cannot communicate *to* our customers; we have to communicate *with* them.

Unless we are talking *with* each other, no one is really listening. And that leaves us in a loud, aggressive world where no one is really communicating.

We are all people, first and foremost. We want to connect. We need each other. We want to have the kind of relationships where we can knock on each other's door and feel welcome. We want to be invited in for a nice cup of tea. We want the kind of relationships where friends do not exploit each other's good nature, and where they treat each other with respect and gratitude.

If these are common values amongst us in our social life, why have we forsaken them in marketing? How incredibly could the world change if we simply reintroduced the Divine responsibility between host and guest, and applied this in all our business dealings?

How do we do that? We start simply by asking ourselves a question: *What one tiny thing can I do to bring this golden Grace of Invitation into my personal and business communications?* Then, shut your eyes and imagine how this one tiny thing could start a ripple of change. If Invasion creates more Invasion, surely Invitation will create more Invitation.

Then hold onto that thought and see if it makes you feel as warm and welcome as I did when I stepped into Abdulla's home over 25 years ago.

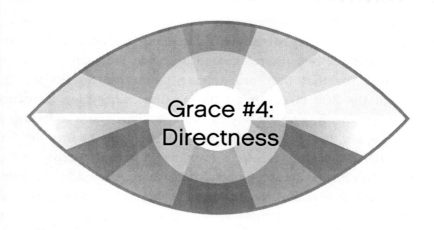

Grace #4:
Directness

> *'Give it to ya straight, no chase*
> *I'ma tell it like it is*
> *Look you straight in yo face*
> *And I'ma tell it like it is'*
> **~ Ludacris**[1]

I do most of my coaching over the phone or Skype. As my clients rarely turn their webcams on, there are no 'body language' cues to inform me, so I've learned to use my ears and my intuition to hear the real truth of what a client is saying to me. I have found that one of the most consistently accurate measurements of what clients are *really* feeling can be found in their grammar, especially in their choices of when to use first, second or third person when telling me a story about something that happened to them. When clients are talking about a very painful or even shameful trauma (which could be anything from childhood abuse to getting fired from a job), it is extremely common for them to deflect their feelings of shame and pain by saying things like, 'When that happens *you* feel like *you're* not worth anything,' rather than saying, 'When that happened, *I* felt like *I* wasn't worth anything.' Very often, when someone relates a personal experience in the second person 'you' rather than the first person 'I,' they are trying to distance themselves from the experience and the emotion (although they are usually unaware they are doing it).

There can be many reasons for this. One is that the emotion is still very painful. They're verbally distancing themselves from the pain by putting it 'over there' instead of inside themselves. Another reason could be that they are judging themselves for having the emotion in the first place (or for having done something for which they feel ashamed), and by saying 'you' it gives them a feeling of social proof, i.e., that other people also feel the same as they do. And lastly—especially if they rarely, if ever, use the first person—it can also reflect a chronic dissociation to their feelings, usually stemming from a deep lack of self-worth that goes far beyond a specific incident or memory. For such clients, saying 'I' can be one of the most uncomfortable things they've ever done, because they have lived for so very long not being able to acknowledge their own opinions, feelings or ideas. For them, the biggest shift they often experience comes simply from my pointing out every time they don't 'own' their emotions, until they develop their own awareness and begin to be able to express themselves without shame or fear. It's amazing how a simple change from 'you' to 'I' can do so much to heal a wounded soul.

But what is more interesting about this shift is that when we begin to 'own' our experiences through our language, we also become more 'direct' in how we express ourselves. This doesn't mean we suddenly become rude or show fits of anger with our family or in public. In fact, it usually means we are much less prone to do so because we cease putting up protective barriers around our feelings, making us more able to deal with conflict. Directness makes our relationships 'clean' and straight-forward, enabling us to have a deeper and more intimate connection with others.

WHAT IS DIRECTNESS IN MARKETING?

In marketing, Directness is the antidote for its 'evil twin,' Distraction. Earlier, I defined Distraction as 'the practice of using elements in your marketing that are either covering up or avoiding any real connection with the product or service being marketed.' Conversely, Directness in marketing is the practice of using elements that provide plain, unambiguous and relevant information about the product or service being marketed, AND express the genuine thoughts, opinions and values of the company or business owner. Directness does not depend upon gimmicks to communicate its message. It does not intentionally divert attention via the manipulation of irrelevant emotions or feelings, for the purpose of influencing the customer. Nor does it exploit public opinion, the latest craze or a political correctness that may not actually be a part of the company ethos.

In other words, Directness tells it like it is.

While on a theoretical level, Directness is probably the easiest thing in the world to practice, on a practical level—due to our social conditioning, personal fears and general lack of experience—it's actually one of the most difficult things for many of us to master. So let me tell it like it is and give some reasons why this might be so, and also some pointers on how we might all begin to move towards more Directness, both in our personal lives and in our marketing.

WHEN DIRECTNESS IS MISSING IN MARKETING

The practice of Directness in marketing has two channels: 1) being direct about the thing being promoted, and 2) being direct about who you are as a person and/or a company. For Directness to be truly present in our marketing, it must be expressed in both of these channels. Similarly, the Deadly Sin of Distraction has two channels, both of which have to do with intention: 1) when we consciously redirect someone's attention because we don't want to tell the whole truth about the product, or 2) when we either consciously or unconsciously redirect someone's attention because we are insecure or unsure of *ourselves*. Just as both of these types of Distraction would be equally damaging to a personal relationship, both are also equally damaging in marketing.

Let's imagine a marketing message is a suitor, and the consumer is a young girl being wooed. At first, the girl is charmed by the suitor's sense of humour, his charismatic ways and his suave and sexy words. She feels good when she's around him and finds herself desiring to spend time with him. But the other boys look at the suitor and shake their heads. 'How come all the girls are attracted to *him?* He's totally fake,' they mutter amongst themselves. They don't understand why this guy seems to get all the girls. But after a while, the girl tires of how much the suitor dances around the truth, and she realises she doesn't really know him at all. His humour, charm or sexiness only makes her irritable, because she knows there is no real connection between them. She comes to the conclusion he's all fluff and little substance, and she ends the relationship. He cannot understand how it happened, as he's been ever so sweet, charming and entertaining. She cannot quite put her finger on what went wrong either, but the experience has left her disappointed, and perhaps a bit cynical and mistrustful about relationships in general.

This story is quite likely to have come to the same end regardless of whether the suitor's behaviour was intentionally devious or totally unconscious. Perhaps his charms had been a deliberate cover-up for something dishonest; perhaps they were a façade because he lacked confidence. Either way, his persistent lack of Directness would eventually have driven the girl away.

When a marketer uses Distraction to attract and redirect the attention of the consumer, it's very much the same scenario. It might work well at first, but in the long-term, most people are going to tire of it unless they find some substance within their relationship with the company. What's worse, once consumers have been seduced by contests, quirky or provocative ad campaigns and other gimmicks that have little or nothing to do with the product or service involved, they are far less apt to trust that company later on down the line. Using charm without substance will only increase the need to find more and more new customers, and offer less opportunity to build upon the relationships already established. But when marketers practice Directness from the onset, they are laying the foundation for an open and honest long-term relationship with the consumer.

DIRECTNESS AND SELF-BELIEF

As mentioned above, sometimes marketers struggle with Directness due to a lack of self-confidence. I've seen this many times with small-business owners (especially new ones). This lack of confidence shows up in their marketing as ambiguity and lack of clarity. This is no less true for the owner of a large business. Although it is easy to slip into the belief system that our businesses are 'things' unto themselves, nothing Man creates can be separate from the human beings who created it. Regardless of how big or impersonal a business might appear to be, every syllable of the language we use to represent it is a reflection of the relationship we have with ourselves.

If you own a large company and it has gotten so big that 'you' are no longer present in your marketing, perhaps it's time to stop and pause to see how this happened and *why*. In much the same way as the story of the suitor and the girl above, if we do not allow our businesses to speak clearly as direct representations of our personal values, ideas and passions, the marketing that speaks for our companies will never be direct, and our relationship with our customers will never be truly intimate. For business owners—large or small—to create truly impactful marketing, they first need to get really clear about how they feel about *themselves*.

Like it or not, the world of consumerism is changing on the heels of social media. Marketers can no longer hide behind the distractive marketing tactics of the past. If you are a marketer, you've got to be present in your marketing. Because at the end of the day, people are not buying your products, they are buying *you*.

SUMMARY: HOW DIRECTNESS CAN HEAL HUMANITY AND THE PLANET

Directness is one of the most positive attributes of any interpersonal relationship, including the relationships between business owner, marketer and consumer.

Because Directness 'tells it like it is' and not how it isn't, it fosters one of the most important things in any relationship—trust. When we are consistently direct, people know they can trust what we say.

Directness brings our businesses down to earth rather than making them iconic 'things' that overwhelm not only the consumer but also the business owner.

Directness is about being real—real people with real thoughts and feelings. Our modern corporate world has depersonalised our relationship with our businesses. Directness brings that personal connection back.

Directness builds congruence. There's no such thing as 'public image' because our public image is congruent with the person we are at all times and in all situations.

Directness has no agenda. Rather than trying to seduce the public, it empowers them to make informed choices and practice the art of discernment.

All in all, Directness just makes things simple: no stress, no games, no pretence, no shame, no guilt, no hiding. I can think of few things more vital to the health of our relationships than these precious attributes.

And upon that simplicity, the practice of Directness lays the fertile ground for the development of Grace # 5—the lovely Grace of Transparency.

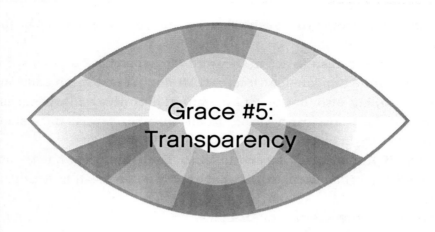

Grace #5:
Transparency

You might have thought the antidote to the 'Deadly Sin of Deception' would have been 'Honesty.' It's true that many people use the word 'transparent' to mean something along the lines of 'honesty without deception.' If a company has all their accounts in order and they are available to view by their stakeholders, they might be said to be 'transparent.' But true Transparency (with an upper case 'T') is something that goes far beyond mere honesty or lack of deception. The Grace of Transparency is something much more spectacular.

Coming from Latin roots and first appearing in the English language in the 15th Century, the literal meaning of the word 'transparent' is 'showing light through'; however it has come to take on a figurative meaning of 'easily seen through'[2] that many of us use to describe human behaviour. When we use it to mean 'easily seen through,' it also implies the possibility of its opposite, where something or someone is not so easily seen through. In this sense of the word, when someone is not being 'transparent' they are not merely being dishonest; they are being deceptive. Sometimes we might refer to such a person as being 'shady,' meaning they are preventing us from seeing something, and not showing us the 'light' of the whole story. You might also say they are 'keeping us in the dark.'

From this semantic use of the word 'Transparency,' we can see it is an accurate antidote for 'Deception.' It doesn't just mean someone doesn't lie, but also that they have natural openness and willingness to make the whole truth visible to all. In other words, they 'show light through' in all circumstances.

But if Transparency means to 'show light through' what *is* that light? If 'the light' means truth, what exactly do we mean by 'truth'?

NOT MERELY THE ABSENCE OF DARKNESS

If we use the word 'truth' with a lowercase 't,' we're referring to the act of speaking without falsehood. In the case of marketing, 'truth' in this sense would refer to our giving accurate and thorough information about our products and services. But while this kind of 'truth' is absolutely essential if we are to have honest businesses, it is still only what I would call 'relative truth.' There is another kind of 'Truth' (with an upper case T) that I shall call 'Absolute Truth.'

Absolute Truth is not, and can never arise from, the mere absence of a negative. When we add +5 to -5, we are left with zero. If a man is $1,000 in debt and you give him $1,000, he is still penniless. In the same way, if we simply stop our negative behaviours, we are not automatically creating something positive. Not lying is not at all the same thing as standing in Truth. When governments impose regulations upon companies to label harmful products as harmful, and to state these harmful effects in their marketing (such as health warnings on cigarettes or drugs), it results in only a relative truth. Certainly these regulations are imposed to protect the public, but if businesses operated from a platform of *Absolute Truth,* they would neither need regulations, nor would they be selling harmful products in the first place.

Relative truth at best brings our world to a place of 'zero'; but more often than not it doesn't even achieve that much. Making it mandatory to put health warnings on cigarette packaging might have stopped some people from smoking, but it has not succeeded in eliminating cigarette-related cancers. Putting criminals in prison might protect society from specific offenders, but it has never succeeded in bringing us to a point of 'zero crime.' And while relative truth struggles at best to bring us to a state of equilibrium, a true positive state cannot start from the outside; it must start from within. For this reason, no amount of activism or government regulations, no matter how righteous or necessary they might seem to be, will ever bring society into a genuine state of Truth—to Transparency.

The real light of Transparency is not the truthfulness of relative truths, but something that emanates from Absolute Truth. Absolute Truth is that which cannot be changed, mutated or destroyed, as it is the foundation of existence itself. Transparency, therefore, is not so much an action as a state of being whereby we walk through life brightly shining the light of Absolute Truth through our thoughts, words and deeds.

Tapping into Absolute Truth might sound pretty lofty, but it can be as simple as looking in the mirror.

THROUGH A GLASS DARKLY

> *'For now we see as through a glass darkly;*
> *but later, face to face.*
> *Now I know in part;*
> *but later I shall know even as also I am known.'*
> **~ Corinthians I, 13:12**[3]

A few years ago a woman in her 50s came to me for coaching. I'll call her Mel. Mel was a senior-level executive in a very large multinational corporation. She was widely respected by her colleagues, and by all accounts was an extremely successful businesswoman. She was genteel, articulate and always spoke in a musical, pleasant voice. But beneath her refined and amicable demeanour, she was sad, lonely and felt terribly isolated from those around her. After working with her for some time, it became obvious that over the years she had built up a myriad of emotional barriers that made it very difficult for her to get close to people. Most of these barriers originated from a deep fear of being seen for the person she believed she was. While outwardly an exceptionally accomplished woman, inwardly she deemed herself not nearly as 'big' or powerful as others perceived her to be. She feared if people got to know the 'real' Mel, she would lose all the respect and success she had amassed throughout her career. Thus, while Mel always showed a positive face in public, she never dared disclose any of her anxieties or personal challenges to anyone. Even with me, it took quite some time to get her to open up in our sessions (although in my opinion she never got really 'raw'), but after a couple of months she finally confessed her fears to me, saying she continually felt as if she were standing atop a narrow, giant pedestal, teetering precariously above everyone else, with absolutely no support. She was terrified.

I could see how alone and vulnerable Mel felt, and it was probably a huge breakthrough that she had been able to admit these feelings to me. I had hoped our work together would help her peel away some of these layers of fear and self-doubt, but I found it very difficult to get 'inside' or close to her, as her armour of distant civility was polished to a very high lustre. Then suddenly, after nearly six months of working together, just as we had finally found a chink in that armour and began to penetrate her fortress of self-beliefs, she called me up to say she wanted to stop the coaching. She said, 'Our sessions are starting to make me question every decision I've ever made, and I'm not sure I'm ready to do that.'

While on the one hand I was pleased something had finally shifted, I was also sorry to see her leave just as we had begun to clear the dust from the mirror in which she saw herself. But, *c'est la vie*. That's the way the coaching cookie crumbles. Ever respectable, Mel very graciously thanked me for our work together and hung up the phone with many kind words. I never heard from her again.

Mel's story is not at all unusual. Any coach can tell you how each of us has a personal library of 'stories' we tell ourselves that can sabotage our confidence, joy and sense of inner congruence. But in these modern times, especially since we have misplaced so many of the family and community structures of the past that used to bring us support and comfort—replacing them with an unstable dependency upon banks, employers and big businesses—so many of us are feeling more vulnerable than ever. Then, add to this the fact marketing is continually bombarding us with messages that cause us to question our worthiness on an almost minute-to-minute basis, it is easy to see how so many people in the modern world suffer from the 'I'm not good enough syndrome.'

Becoming aware that our 'I'm not good enough' thoughts are coming from stories we have unconsciously created is only the first step in our recovery. It brings us closer to a state of relative truth where we are no longer 'telling lies' to ourselves. But as we know, relative truth can at best bring us to a state of zero. To bring us upwards to a state of Joy, we require a positive shift to Absolute Truth. The journey to that Truth first entails untangling and lifting the veils of false-self we have both believed about ourselves as well as projected to the rest of the world, until we reach the luminosity of our true, naked Selves.

In 16th Century Bengal, Chaitanya Mahaprabhu described this process of unveiling as *'ceto-darpana-marjanam'*, which is sometimes poetically translated as 'cleansing the dust from the mirror of the heart.'[4] Anger, greed, avarice, blame and other such emotions are some of the things comprising this 'dust of the heart.' But the Sanskrit language is very deep and complex, and the word *'cetas'* (altered to *ceto* in the above text, according to Sanskrit grammatical rules) does not just mean 'heart,' but can also mean 'intellect,' 'consciousness' or 'life-force.'[5] This translation gives a slightly different spin on the phrase, as it tells us that the journey to Truth also requires the clearing away of all the mental misconceptions about who we are.

For many of us this 'clearing away' can be both an exciting and a terrifying process. Sometimes we backslide to seek the protection of our relative truths—our old and familiar stories—for fear of what we might find in the Light of our own Being-ness. Sometimes we might become overwhelmed by the intensity of the journey itself. Or, we might doubt the existence of true Self at all, or worry we won't recognise it even if it appears before us. In any case, there is no possibility of seeing ourselves clearly, when the mirror in which we are gazing is covered with the dust of falsehoods or relative truths about who we are. To come face-to-face with Self, we must first clear away the darkness of our distorted beliefs. This clearing out doesn't necessarily show us the Truth, but it does at least bring us to a state of 'zero.' Medieval Spanish mystic San Juan de la Cruz (St John of the Cross) refers to this state as 'the dark night of the soul'[6]—that state of seeming emptiness and 'lostness' that is pregnant with unlimited possibilities for being filled—with the Light of Truth, the Light of God, the Light of the Universe, the Light of Self.

'Emptiness' of emotional, mental and spiritual clutter is the first prerequisite for being filled.

RECLAIMING OUR LUMINESCENCE

Beneath the many layers of false 'self' we have come to accept as true is the essence of who we truly are. In Sanskrit, this essence is called *atma*. Possibly cognate with the Latinate word *alma,* the word *atma* is sometimes translated as 'soul,' but its true meaning goes further than what many of us mean when we use the word 'soul.' In the ancient Sanskrit scripture *Katha Upanishad, atma* is described as *na jayate mriyate va vipascin*[7], which means that which is 'never born and never dies' and is 'full of knowledge.' The word *cit* (pronounced *chit* and written as *-cin* in the compound word *vapascin*) is also sometimes translated as 'consciousness' or 'awareness.' This means that true knowledge is not comprised of relative truths we may have learned through mundane learning or achievement, but rather of the knowledge of Self that comes from being conscious and aware of Absolute Truth. Thus, *atma* is not merely the spiritual attribute that exists before birth and continues after death. It is pure consciousness and part and parcel of the Absolute. Furthermore, being Absolute, *atma* is by nature from suffering or *karma*.

Karma is an interesting concept, and whether or not people use the word, they tend to believe in it in some form or other. Most Westerners think of *karma* as the 'law of cause and effect.' This sometimes conjures up the notion of *karma* being some sort of cosmic mechanism that doles out rewards and punishments as the result of personal history or past deeds. Others cite the Biblical phrase, 'As ye sow, so shall ye reap' while still others express their understanding of *karma* by citing Newton's Third Law of Motion, 'To every action there is always an equal and opposite reaction.' Bu what is implicit in all of these explanations is the belief that *karma* is some sort of relentless and unchallengeable 'law' of the Universe, in which we have no choice. But over the years I have come to understand *karma* as something entirely different—as something *we* create as a result of our choice to stand in the shadows of our self-invented, relative truths rather than in the Light of *atma.*

Here's an example of what I mean: Some years back, a friend of mine had been suffering with both financial and relationship woes for a very long time. When I had first met her about 8 years before, I had also been in a very similar place; but since that time I had moved past my troubles and had become a very happy and satisfied person. Because she cared for me, she was happy for me, but at the same time she was morose and depressed over her own situation. She said she believed she was hopelessly trapped by some sort of bad *karma*, and that it seemed I had finally paid back all my *karmic* 'debts.' Seemingly resigned to her 'fate,' she sighed, 'I guess I'm just destined to be poor and unhappy. It must be something I did in a past life.'

I told her I didn't agree with that explanation. I had come to believe *karma* is not some sort of cosmic 'debt collection' service, with the Universe continually charging us interest, lifetime after lifetime. It is not something from which we will never be free until we've 'paid' it off with our suffering. *Karma* is not a 'thing' at all, but a perspective. It is the suffering we impose upon ourselves due to our insistence upon believing the false stories we make up about ourselves and the world. If we believe the 'story' that we are doomed and ill-fated, what we are really saying is that we believe we are unworthy of happiness. These stories have nothing to do with past deeds (although they are always the result of past conditioning). They are not even the result of deeds at all, but of the many 'monsters under the bed' we continually try to hide from others, but have privately come to believe as real. In the past, people might have called them 'demons.' Life coaches often call them 'gremlins,' 'inner critics' or 'saboteurs.' But all these monsters are nothing but the messages we have continued to tell ourselves about ourselves, often at the expense of our own happiness.

Even the most hardened and violent criminal, whose actions might be unconscionable to us, is simply the product of his false beliefs about himself and the world around him. And the more a person is convinced he is this false-self, the more harmful his actions against both himself and the rest of the world will be. This state of being is the true meaning of the word 'ignorance': being bereft of knowledge—Self-knowledge. Within the darkness of self-ignorance, there is very little opportunity for Light to shine. And without Light, there can be no Transparency.

But that which is Absolute is not subject to physical laws. There is no such thing as 'cause and effect' except within the world of relative truths. *Atma* is Absolute. It is only the false-self that carries the weight of our actions; *atma* carries no such weight. It carries no baggage, nor does it require any 'payback' in order to be.

There is such a thing as Free Will: the choice of whether or not to drag *karma* around with us. Creating suffering for ourselves and others is a choice. So is creating joy. I'm not saying it's easy; I'm saying it's simple. We simply can 'unchoose' *karma*, 'fate,' 'bad luck,' or whatever you choose to call it, anytime we wish.

The moment we choose to be real—to be *atma*—rather than to cling to the falseness of who we are not, not only does our own suffering cease, but our tendency to *create* suffering for others also ceases. And the tendency to create happiness soon fills up the emptiness, just like a ditch fills with water from a gushing stream. When this happens, we have moved not merely to the point of 'zero,' but to a place where unlimited joy and wellbeing is possible not only for ourselves, but also for all around us. And then, everything changes. We experience a great lightness of being. There is no question of our self-worth. How can any living creature, whose Essence is that of Truth itself, ever be unworthy?

Embracing our luminosity, however scary the journey might seem to us, is the first true step towards creating Transparency in the world. We will never be able to 'allow light to show' if we continue to stand in the shadows. Transparency means to walk in the light of our own luminescence and allow that light to be seen by all. Or, more simply put:

*Transparency means to KNOW who we really are
And SHOW who we really are.*

That's a far, far cry from merely being 'not dishonest.'

WALKING IN TRANSPARENCY

Transparency is not so much a kind of behaviour as it is a perspective and a way of being. Of course as our perspectives change our behaviours will also naturally change. If we artificially try to change our behaviour in order to seem more transparent without the underlying perspective shift, it will only serve to make us seem disingenuous—fake. This is most especially true in the world of business and marketing. Trying to win public favour through false Transparency is no better than not being transparent at all.

In practice, though, there are some behaviours that go along with genuine Transparency. Allowing our true personality and light to shine in the public eye is the most important. Whenever I host a radio show, webinar or other online event, my ultimate aim is for the audience to connect with my guests and get to know them as human beings rather than just experts in their field. Some guests feel uncomfortable with this and tend to hide behind their work and intelligence, while others are quite comfortable with being 'seen' as they truly are. These guests come across as genuine, likeable and approachable human beings, who aren't afraid to share their deepest thoughts, feelings and values. Of course, this doesn't mean they have to reveal every part of their private lives. In fact, Transparency could also mean they are open about saying what they do not wish to discuss and why. In this way, even refusing to answer a question can be a transparent expression.

Walking in Transparency can be a scary thing for those who have been conditioned to believe there is such a thing as perfection, and they fall short of it. What is important is to understand that these are just conditioned beliefs, blurring our ability to see ourselves as we really are. And what is even more important is to recognise the environmental influences—such as marketing—that contribute to this. The other day I saw an advert for a face wash and the very first word was, 'Imperfection!' With so many messages continually telling us we are imperfect, there's small wonder Transparency is so challenging for so many. And when marketers have depended upon such manipulation for so long, it's small wonder why they find Transparency challenging as well.

THE CHALLENGE OF TRANSPARENCY IN MARKETING

Transparency in marketing might seem diametrically opposed to what marketers traditionally have been taught. A well-structured marketing piece is always supposed to start with 'the pain' and then give 'the promise' of a solution to the pain. Unfortunately, what that sometimes means is that marketers create the *consciousness* of that very pain, as in the case of the advert above that screamed the word, 'Imperfection!' when showing a girl looking into a mirror. It's meant to portray the product or service being offered as some sort of altruistic gift from heaven to cure whatever 'pain' we happen to be suffering from. But the truth of the matter is this—the only purpose to the advert is to sell the product. If we marketers were truly transparent, we would state our true intentions rather than manipulate the emotions of the public.

Being self-help and mind-body-spirit authors, most of my clients tend to be genuinely altruistic. Most of them actually have written their books with the intention of changing people's lives. But while that might be the case, the point of running a book *launch* is to *sell books*. When I do a promotion for an author I do indeed tell our audience all about the great things they will find in the book, but I also tell them the truth—that I want the author to become a number-1 bestseller.

You might find this a pretty odd thing for a marketer to admit to their audience. You might think, *Won't that work against us? Dare we actually tell our audience that we want to sell a lot of books?* Sure, why not? The word 'sell' isn't a dirty word when we are being transparent in our marketing. I have found that when people have had a chance to really get to know the person behind the book (and aren't just given a pitch about the book itself), they genuinely *want* that author to succeed. So many readers have sent me emails telling me how delighted they were to be able to help such-and-such author become a bestseller. They love being a part of the author's success because they like *who* they are, and not just their book. Transparency strips away all pretence and unites people in purpose. And the bonus is that it's also good for business.

THE BIGGER WE ARE, THE MORE DISTANT WE BECOME

Transparency has a lot to do with congruency. I don't take on a new client unless I feel congruent with both their message and their values. I know I won't be able to be transparent in my marketing if I don't feel such congruence. Of course, if you happen to be an independent marketer who creates campaigns for large companies, you might argue that you don't have the luxury of being so choosey. And if you happen to be an in-house marketer employed by the company for whom you create promotional campaigns, you would probably find it even more difficult. 'A job is a job,' you might say. 'Sometimes we have to do things we don't like to do. It's all part of being professional. That's just the way the world is.' Well maybe that is just the way the world is now, but it surely wasn't always this way, nor do we have to lie down and take it passively.

How is it that we have created a business world wherein 'being professional' means accepting and doing things we not only hate, but also feel are in conflict with our personal values? I believe all this is an unfortunate side-effect of our own efficiency. While admittedly there are many large corporations who demonstrate their commitment to values by switching to green energies, using only ethically sourced and fair trade resources, or donating a portion of their profits to charities, generally speaking, our businesses have grown so large it has become difficult to align them to the values of anyone in particular.

It stands to reason that the larger the company, the bigger the bureaucracy, and the more removed different people are from the 'bigger picture.' To get an idea of just how removed people can get, let's use the example of an imaginary automobile manufacturer. While I admit I have no first-hand knowledge of what's really involved in such a scenario, I imagine it starts with a Board of Directors and

Chief Financial Officer who jointly decide what kinds of new cars they wish to manufacture that year, and how many they will produce. They commission a team of experts to design a new model that will appeal to the market they are trying to reach. Based upon their blueprint, another team create an estimate of the materials needed to reach the manufacturing targets the Board has set. Other people, possibly on another continent, extract the raw materials from the Earth. Then, other people refine those raw materials. Then, other people arrange the purchasing and logistics for the transport of all the materials to the factories.

Back at the main plant, a technical team design the prototypes of all the parts. Others create the machines that will cut the parts. Then, others make the actual parts and still others assemble them into a finished vehicle. Once manufactured, a team of people test the vehicle for safety, and make revisions until the final model is approved.

Then somewhere in the world, it doesn't really matter where, a team of marketers are engaged in creating the concepts for how to promote this new car. They may be part of the company itself, or they may be part of a large advertising firm that has landed the contract to promote this particular company or car. They come together and start to brainstorm ideas. They could go for the sexy, the high-tech, the comfort, the luxury, the practical, the economical, the safe, the professional, the family-oriented or the ecological angle, depending upon who they are trying to 'woo.' They know context is everything, and that they can create whatever image they want with the right marketing campaign.

Simultaneously, and probably someplace else, many others are negotiating advertising space on television, radio, magazine, Internet sites, billboards, etc. Still others are working out the details for the distribution and transport of the brand-new cars to retailers.

And then, finally, a customer walks up to a salesperson in a showroom and requests to take the new car for a test-drive. Depending upon how well it succeeds in making them feel sexy, high-tech, comfortable, luxurious, practical, economical, safe, professional, family-oriented or ecological, they make their decision to buy or not buy.

While that's a pretty long list of people involved in the process, it's my guess that in a real automotive company it's even more complex. But even with my simplistic rendering, it does take your breath away to think of how many hundreds of people are involved in the manufacture and sale of a single car. I don't think it's unreasonable to imagine it takes at least 500 people to bring a car from concept to consumer. And buried amidst this long list of people are the marketers. If a team of say 10 experienced marketers had been hired to create the campaign for this particular car, they would have comprised no more than 2% of the actual production process. It does beg the question: Where is the direct relationship between the actual product and the marketer? For that matter, where is the direct relationship between the business owner and the product?

Short answer: There probably isn't one.

In fact, it's nearly impossible for there to be one. Mass production and global distribution have created chains of operation in which business owners, resource providers, manufacturers, marketers and salespeople have become utterly disparate entities, who may never even know or speak to one another.

The bigger our businesses have become, the more diluted our personal impact upon them becomes, and the more likely our relationship with our businesses is to be estranged. The more estranged the relationship, the more difficult it is for a business to serve as a reflection of anyone's authentic values. Instead, our businesses mutate into impersonal entities unto themselves, which are more likely to become a charade of cookie-cutter values with the aim of appealing to what they believe is the current public sentiment. And when there are no authentic values underpinning a company, or they have become so diluted by the sheer size of that company that they don't have much potency, there can be no Transparency, because there is no 'light' to shine through.

Then, when a marketer—possibly from an outside source—steps into such a scenario, the chances of being able to create a marketing piece that is genuinely Transparent are virtually nil.

And ultimately, this entire process creates a gulf of distance in the relationship between the business and the consumer.

DISTANCE + DEPENDENCY = DISINTEGRATION

Where there is distance, there is Disconnection. But where there is Disconnection *and* dependence, it becomes the tipping point for social disintegration. Our modern society has become dependent upon an impersonal, megalithic economic system in which none of us have a face. As a planet, we are quickly losing our knowledge of what it means to be a human being. How many of us know how to grow our own food, weave our own cloth, make our own medicines or build our own houses? How many of us could adapt if the international structures to deliver petroleum products collapsed or, even worse, the reserves of oil vanished altogether? How many towns and villages have the economic infrastructure that could truly be called self-subsistent? Our ancestors did. We call ourselves 'advanced' but we are actually regressing. The harsh reality is this: consumerism is rapidly causing a cultural and intellectual genocide of human survival skills once known to our great-grandparents, which might never be known to our great-grandchildren. An economic system based upon dependency can never serve the needs of humanity.

Because of this, I believe our dependency upon big business will inevitably break down over the course of the next generation or so. But the good news is that this breakdown is not the signal of doom or even a 'bad' thing. Just as our bodies have immune systems that protect us against disease, I believe the 'social body' has an 'immune system' that protects humanity from destroying itself, and will bring us back to a more balanced, self-sustaining state.

I also believe we are already seeing the beginnings of this process of reform. The global recession that started in 2008 was only the beginning. What is even more significant is the fact that more and more people I know are leaving the corporate world, which was once deemed to be the 'safety net' by those in my parents' generation, and are starting businesses for themselves. More and more people are expressing the need to feel self-reliant, and to create businesses that are congruent with their values and passions.

It is my personal belief that living in self-sufficient communities supported by local businesses is the natural state of human society.

If we see so little Transparency in business today it is because our corporate world has shifted us so far away from that natural state. If it took us a couple hundred years to reach this point of Disconnection, it will probably take us a couple hundred more to return to balance. But that should not dishearten us. I believe every person who severs their dependency upon big business by starting their own small business, growing their own food or supporting their community in some way, is helping to restore us back to that natural state. Every single decision a person makes to come back to a state of congruence, brings us closer to the Divine Grace of Transparency.

SUMMARY: HOW TRANSPARENCY CAN HEAL HUMANITY AND THE PLANET

One of the favourite sayings at the Coaches Training Institute, where I did my coach training and certification, is 'Fulfilment is a radical act.' It's a terrific concept, and I would also add to this that Transparency is an even *more* radical act, that can only be attained when fulfilment becomes the focus of your life. Fulfilment is the place where we live and breathe our values. Transparency is the place where we express those values, and where these values are congruent in every aspect of our lives and our work. Transparency is the place where we take off our masks and stop pretending we're invincible. It's the place where we admit we need each other, and are not afraid to ask for help. And it's also the place where we don't speak to our customers as if they need our services more than we need them.

The ability to define and express our true values can take some time to master, especially when we have lived under the influence of conditioning that has dictated our beliefs and social responsibilities for most of our lives. How do we dare step against that grain of what we've been taught, and learn to march to the rhythm of these values once we've found them? And how can we tell them apart from all we've been taught in life?

Well, let me be transparent with you and share a personal journey I had in the course of writing this book. While I was very passionate about this project, when I first started writing I struggled to make much progress. I knew there was some kind of fear blocking me, but I couldn't quite put my finger on it. After some reflection, I realised I was afraid I would not be taken seriously because I was not a 'big' marketer with a 'big' company. I worried that 'real' marketers would say my ideas were naïve. But then, I woke up one day and realised all these fears were from past conditioning. I was still hooked by the belief system in which I had been raised, where big business meant success, prestige and credibility. Deep inside I knew these beliefs were not mine and were fundamentally against my core values. Yet, I couldn't identify precisely what these values were.

Then, while preparing for a talk on the subject of 'spiritual marketing' I was to deliver in Worcester, I was organising my scattered notes and realised I didn't have a real grip on what I wanted to say. How could I communicate my values to others if I could not yet define them to myself? I put down my pen and shut my eyes, spending a few moments in silence, finally opening myself to receive the wisdom that had been obscured by my fears and self-judgement. And in an instant, faster than I could even write them down, my values descended upon me like angels: Connection, Inspiration, Invitation, Directness, Transparency, Abundance and Collaboration—the 7 Graces.

It is the presence of these Graces that gave me the ability to write this book. Without them, I would have no direction, and even less courage. And surely, without them, I could never have found the wherewithal to be Transparent about my thoughts, feelings, fears or beliefs. At the end of the day, some readers might well call me naïve or disagree with what I have written, but the presence of my values helps me remember that it really doesn't matter. Our values are indeed like angels. They bring us back, again and again, to the person we really are.

In the 19th Century, Henry David Thoreau dared us to march to the beat of a different drummer. That beat is the rhythm of our personal values. The path to fulfilment is paved with these values. To find them, we must first quiet the mind so we can hear the music of our own hearts. Then, and only then, can we dance to that music and express those values through our every word and action. When we achieve this, we have become Transparent.

As more and more business owners embark on this march and begin to operate their enterprises from a place of Transparency, we will indeed see the world begin the vital transformation back to a state of balance.

And as we become increasingly Transparent and fulfilled, we will find we have unlocked the door to Grace #6: Abundance.

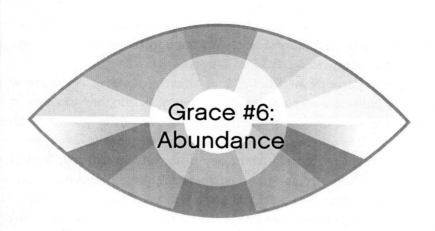

Grace #6:
Abundance

> *'Abundance binds us to the cycle of the seasons;*
> *it slows us down to the ripening moment of each fruit.*
> *Each tree was born from the water running through the soil,*
> *a tossed apple pip, a carefully tended sapling,*
> *the slant of the sun, a bird shitting,*
> *a foot falling in the right place—the elements, creatures*
> *and humans coexisting in the city.'*
> **~ The Abundance Handbook**[1]

With a population of about half a million, the city of Sheffield in England's northwest county of Yorkshire is something of a paradox. Steeped in history dating back thousands of years, this small market town experienced significant growth during the industrial revolution, and became world-renowned for its steel manufacturing, and especially for the innovation of stainless steel. Due to heavy air pollution and rapid low-income housing growth in the area, Sheffield's reputation by the early 20th Century was not particularly glamorous, and in 1937 was even dubbed 'the ugliest town in the Old World' by British author and journalist George Orwell.[2] Being the site of military ammunitions manufacturing during World War II, Sheffield was also a target for German bombing raids in 1940. The city struggled to rebuild during the coming decades, later to experience still more economic set-backs during the notoriously difficult 1980s.[3] Given its history of industry, working-class citizens and economic hardship, it is understandable why screenwriter Barry Hines chose Sheffield as the iconic setting for a fictitious nuclear attack in his brilliantly gripping, if not distressing, 1984 BBC film *Threads*.[4]

But the paradox of Sheffield is that in spite of its history of industry, pollution and economic hardship, in the 21st Century it is rapidly gaining a new reputation for being one of the 'greenest' cities in the UK. The official Sheffield City Council website says the city 'has more trees per person than any other city in Europe,' and that over 60% of the city is 'green space' including woodlands, public parks and gardens and national park space.[5] Thus arising from the ashes of its former negative image, in 2007 a remarkable new project was born in Sheffield.

Its name: 'Abundance.'

THE ABUNDANCE PROJECT

I first became acquainted with Sheffield Abundance when one of its founders came to speak to a tiny gathering of people, comprised of zero-carbon advocates and Transition Town volunteers here in Bedford in 2009. While the concept of the project is simple, its actualisation is both complex and impressive. The project began as an answer to a problem few had identified and no one had yet addressed: there are hundreds of perfectly good fruit-bearing trees in Sheffield that go unpicked, resulting in literally tonnes of local (and usually organic) apples, pears, plums, damson and other fruits going to waste year after year. Astonishingly, this was happening because many people didn't even notice these trees were there. In other cases, tree owners might not be physically able to harvest the fruit, or there are just too many fruits for the owners to use or store by themselves.[6] As one of my Transition Town colleagues cleverly put it, we find ourselves in a situation where people can be seen every day driving over fallen fruit while on their way to Tesco's to buy a plastic bag of shiny, but tasteless, apples. It is both tragic and absurd.

In Sheffield, a small group of volunteers, who were passionate not only about the environment but also about spreading the message that the world is abundantly bountiful, formed a team to address this problem. Over time, they mapped the trees that bore fruit within

Sheffield that were not being harvested. They approached tree owners and offered to harvest these trees for them. In the case of trees that were not on private property, they liaised with the local Council instead. The fruit would be harvested and then divided: the tree owners would take whatever share they wished for themselves, and the rest of the fruit would be redistributed on a non-profit basis to various community cafes, nurseries, Sure Start centres (educational, care and play centres for underprivileged families) and individuals. If there was more than could be eaten fresh, some of the fruit would be juiced or made into jams, chutneys and preserves and either given away or sold to support the project. Fully knowledgeable in the subject of permaculture, the volunteers also ensured that adequate amounts of fruit were left on the ground either to rot or to go to seed, as they would naturally have done without human intervention.

Since its inception, The Abundance Project has been an unquestionable success. Sheffield is no longer wasting its precious bounty, and many urban children and adults who might otherwise live on a diet of high-calorie, low-nutrition junk food are now eating daily servings of fresh, local, organic fruit at no cost. Winner of the 2010 Ethical Awards by *The Observer,* Sheffield Abundance soon became the inspiration for other Abundance Projects to start in Leeds, Manchester and Edinburgh.[7] But best of all, the people in our British urban centres are now beginning to notice, taste and appreciate the generous bounty of the Earth.

I am very impressed with the simplicity—and the understated spirituality—of The Abundance Project, and have hopes our Transition Bedford group will follow in the footsteps of Sheffield in the very near future. But regardless of whether or not this happens, my own life has become much richer simply as a result of hearing about Sheffield Abundance. Everywhere I stroll in our town of Bedford, I notice fruit-bearing trees laden with apples, pears, cherries, plums and damson. I walk along the wooden area on the eastern part of town and find an almost endless supply of Hawthorne trees, full of ripe red berries every autumn. Twenty years ago I spent a heck of a lot of money on Hawthorne berry capsules for a mitral valve problem I was experiencing (the remedy worked astonishingly well). Bedford could probably make an entire cottage industry from its wild Hawthorne trees.

Similarly, I look in my back garden and I see masses of relentlessly growing mint, lemon balm and nettles, and I wonder why I ever spent money on expensive, boxed herbal teas. And then I consider the lowly and persistent dandelion scattered here and there in my garden. My parents used to spend countless hours digging them up and discarding them every weekend. My neighbours poison them when they see them springing up. But recently I've come to learn about the wonderful taste and excellent medicinal properties of dandelion root, and I know I'll never dispose of another dandelion again. And while I offer my garden land to a neighbour so she can grow vegetables (which we share), all this 'wild' food and medicine comes without any cost or effort whatsoever. It seems everywhere I look Mother Earth is giving us everything we need to be healthy and wealthy. In these moments, when my eyes are fully open to the world around me, I feel truly abundant. And I can think of nothing as lovely or as profound as this.

I believe this feeling is the real reason why The Abundance Project is so powerful. It's not just about fruit.

POPULAR ABUNDANCE—WHAT WE HAVE MISUNDERSTOOD

The word 'abundance' has been tossed about quite casually in both self-help literature and everyday parlance, especially since the 2006 release of Rhonda Byrne's film, *The Secret*, and subsequent book of the same name. While the ideas and terminology presented in *The Secret* were not new, few would disagree that it contributed to the widespread popularisation of the term 'Law of Attraction.' Since the success of *The Secret*, the term Law of Attraction has become part of the fabric of contemporary business lingo, spirituality and pop-culture, as the process that brings 'abundance' into the lives of those who know how to master it. Some of the practical keys to that mastery include having a positive mindset, using visualisations to see your desired goal, and saying daily affirmations to help reprogram your brain towards success.

Byrne owes the fundamentals of her message to the 'New Thought' movement of the 19th Century founded by thought leaders such as Phineas P. Quimby, William Walker Atkinson and Ralph Waldo Emerson. Later, 'New Thought' was expanded upon by authors such as Wallace Wattles and Napoleon Hill[8], who have since become iconic names in 'Law of Attraction' urban lore. But while Rhonda Byrne openly credited Wattles' *The Science of Getting Rich* as one of her major influences, the presentation and underlying message in her book and film differs greatly from Wattles' book. While *The Secret* talks a lot about material prosperity, when Wattles uses the word 'rich' or 'riches' in his text, he seems to allude to something much more metaphysical. To be 'rich' does not just mean you are endowed with money and materialistic wealth, but that you possess the 'inner' riches of purpose, fulfilment, peace, love and connection with the Divine.

While some may argue that *The Secret* indeed carried a metaphysical message, Byrne's business partner, Bob Rainone, openly admitted that the film had an intentional focus on monetary gain, saying, 'We desired to hit the masses, and money is the number one thing on the masses' minds.'[9] One of the most obvious examples of this in the film is a scene of a girl looking into a jewellery shop window, pining over an expensive necklace. She visualises the necklace is hers and *voilà*—by dint of the 'Law of Attraction'—the necklace magically appears around her neck. While the decision to 'go for the money' undoubtedly helped to bring the film its phenomenal financial success, in my opinion it seriously undermined what might have brought some genuine meaning to the film, and contributed to a somewhat cheapened portrayal of both the 'Law of Attraction' and 'Abundance.'

TOWARDS A DEFINITION OF ABUNDANCE

Abundance is not so much the acquisition of things we desire, as it is the *harmonious relationship* with those things, and all things in the world. But when we create imbalances, we are not in harmonious relationship with the world. These imbalances could be anything from hoarding money or natural resources, to strip mining, to slash-and-burn deforestation, to the suppression of human freedoms.

Abundance is our natural state. I actually think that's part of the message in the story of the 'Garden of Eden.' The suffering and impoverishment we might experience in life is always the result of our creating an imbalance in either our natural world or our society. To return to Abundance, we must merely live in tune with that natural balance. On a micro level, that's pretty much what Sheffield Abundance did within their community. Imagine what is possible when the whole world takes up the challenge to return to Abundance.

If I were to define 'Abundance,' it would be this:

Abundance is our natural state of being.
We return to this state when we have the fundamental belief
that there is more than enough for all in this Universe.

This belief—that there is more than enough for all—must form the very foundation of who we are. It cannot be something we adopt on faith simply, because it appeals to our senses or our moral character. We must actually *believe* there is more than enough for you, for me, for everyone.

This fundamental belief can only genuinely arise when we have developed a deep **trust** for whatever we deem to be the ultimate force in the Universe. When we live and act in accordance with this trust, it stands to reason we would never feel any need to create imbalances for the aim of gaining prosperity.

Our trust would in turn inform our **actions** in that we would work respectfully along with the harmony and balance of Nature, never trying to bend it to our will. We would know that any attempts to upset that delicate balance would result in the ultimate loss of prosperity for all, including ourselves, even if it might appear to give temporary prosperity to some.

And because we would have this **wisdom,** we would know the difference between true wealth, and temporary wealth. We would know that genuine prosperity is Absolute and not subject to our ever-changing opinions.

And finally, our belief would fill us with **love,** humility and gratitude for all we are given. And because we would be filled with love, we would allow prosperity to come and go easily without judgement or the need to control it.

These four qualities of trust, actions, wisdom and love are the gatekeepers to the doorways to genuine Abundance. Without them, our prosperity is ephemeral. No amount of positive thinking, visualisations or affirmations can bring us to this state. Nor is it simply a matter of expressing 'gratitude' as many Law of Attraction proponents have stated. While gratitude is essential, for Abundance to enter our lives, we must pass through the doorways of all four of these gatekeepers.

UNLIMITED GROWTH VERSUS UNLIMITED PROSPERITY

Earlier in this book, I shared my view that the notion of unlimited growth in business was simply a myth. Nothing in Nature has unlimited growth. Even trees, the tallest living things on our planet, do not have unlimited growth. Rather, they have an in-built mechanism that limits the flow of water past a certain height. Some researchers believe this is a survival mechanism designed to prevent embolisms—air bubbles—which could prove fatal to a tree if it were to grow past a certain height. In other words, limited growth is in the best interests of the organism, and it ensures the long-life and wellbeing of the tree.[10] What's more, the remarkable knock-on effect of having a planet of healthy trees is the enhancement of the health, longevity and wellbeing of all other living creatures as well. This example shows us that *limited growth* is actually a quality of *sustainable abundance*, whereas attempting *unlimited* growth can threaten the very survival of an entire eco-system.

Businesses are also living things. They are born, grow, create by-products, decline and eventually die. They are part of the living mechanism we call 'society.' Because they are living things, unlimited growth is not only impossible, but to attempt to grow a business unlimitedly is detrimental to its own survival, and inevitably likely to cause socioeconomic imbalances that harm the flow of commerce in general. Technology may have opened up the potential to seemingly unlimited growth, but economists have long understood this does not lead to unlimited prosperity at a societal level. This is why anti-monopoly laws were imposed in the early days of American capitalism, and why international trade laws continue to be an integral part of global commerce.

Understood from this holistic perspective, we gain an entirely different slant on the word 'Abundance.' No longer does it mean ever-increasing profits and material opulence, but rather a state of *sustainable* wellbeing. Growth is essential, but it does not necessarily mean 'getting bigger.' Just as the biggest tree is not necessarily the healthiest or the longest living, neither is the biggest business. What constitutes true Abundance, whether in Nature, our personal lives or the business world, is a state of harmony, balance and flow that ensures our continued health, qualitative development and sustainability.

True Abundance has nothing whatsoever to do with money. For Abundance to actually *be* abundant, it must be unlimited. Money by its very nature is finite. No manmade invention can be unlimited in quality. Money can therefore never be endowed with the quality of Abundance. If we say we desire Abundance, but we are actually talking about profits, we are cutting ourselves short. Similarly, if we measure the value of our businesses solely in terms of profits and losses, we are taking a seriously short-sighted view of what our businesses actually are meant to be.

Some business owners confuse unlimited Abundance with a belief in unlimited natural resources. Many early capitalists maintained a metaphysical belief there was unlimited wealth in this world. Hence they did little to regulate the extraction of that wealth in the form of raw materials, believing the Earth would always be able to replenish herself. There seemed to be no thought given to the possibility of over-consumption. Even as recently as 2009 I attended the lecture of a very prominent UK nutritionist, wherein he said he believed the idea of 'climate change' was a big, scandalous lie. His reasoning was that human beings were extremely vain if they thought their actions could possibly disrupt the balance of something as great and Divine as the natural world.

The resources of the natural world are indeed unlimited, but *only* when they are allowed to move and transform in flow with the rhythm of Nature. The Earth is magnificently designed for continual regeneration, but when we extract more than the Earth can replenish within a given period of time, of course we will create an imbalance. It is preposterous to believe that extracting an estimated 135 billion tonnes of oil within a little over a single century[11]—when it has taken billions of years to produce—will not create an imbalance. It is equally preposterous to think that producing nearly 8 billion tonnes of carbon emissions *per year*[12] faster than our planet can possibly detoxify our air will not create an imbalance. And it's sheer lunacy to think that no imbalance will be caused by our disposing of over 50 million tonnes of 'e-waste' (disposal of electronic goods) every year[13], much of it brand new[14], with no more than 13% of it being recycled[15] (meaning 87% of it goes into landfills where it can take possibly *millions* of years to degrade and return to a natural state). And we haven't even begun to talk about plastics.

Over recent years, most of us have come to understand the folly of this kind of thinking. As any holistic practitioner can tell you, imbalances always result in disease, whether in the body, society or the planet. While there is no question whatsoever that this wonderful Earth is designed to recycle and replenish her natural resources, she does so on her own time frame, and not according to our business production schedules. Overpopulation is often cited as 'the' problem, but it needn't be if we re-educate ourselves about how to co-exist *with* our planet rather than continually fighting against her. The Grace of Abundance can only come to us when we are working in concordance with her timetable, and not our own. Without that balance, there can be no lasting prosperity. But when we get the balance right, there is more than enough for all to flourish.

CHANGING THE MEASURING STICK FOR PROSPERITY

Just as every tree is an integral component of the eco-system of our planet, each and every business—no matter how small—is an integral part of its socioeconomic system. Just as a single tree contributes to the conversion and circulation of oxygen and carbon dioxide in the world, a single business contributes to the circulation of currency, services and goods. It is through commerce that we distribute Abundance throughout society. Commerce provides the life-blood and sustenance of humanity. Using business size, profits and share values as the measuring sticks of business success is not only missing the point of the actual function of commerce, but it undermines the very sacredness of it.

Profits are manmade, and are therefore always limited. 'Prosperity,' however, is a Divine quality and is unlimited in nature. For business owners to move from the limited to the unlimited, i.e., towards genuine prosperity or Abundance, we must first adopt a new way to measure the true prosperity factor of our businesses.

Imagine you own a cosmetics company selling 'anti-aging' products aimed at women in their 30s. Using the traditional 'bottom line' as a measuring stick for success, your business might look like a very profitable venture. But what are the unseen 'holistic costs' for you, society and the planet? How do these stack up against the other expenses your accountant has calculated in your balance sheet? To get a better idea of what these 'holistic costs' might include, below is a list of questions we might ask ourselves.

First are questions pertaining to physical product itself:

- Has this product been ethically sourced and manufactured?
- What are the humanitarian costs of the sourcing and manufacturing of this product?
- What are the long-term environmental effects of the manufacturing, use and disposal of this product?
- What are the long-term health effects of using this product?
- What are the long-term economic effects on consumers who become dependent upon it?
- What are the long-term emotional and social effects on consumers?

Next, let's look at the 'holistic' benefits of your venture:

- How well does this product contribute to the ecological wellbeing of our planet and its inhabitants?

- How well does it contribute to the genuine emotional and physical wellbeing of people in general?
- How well does it help to address economic problems by creating local markets?
- How well does your company contribute to the healthy flow of commerce?
- How well does your company empower people as a service provider or as an employer?

Then, there are the questions revolving around consumption:

- How frequently would consumers need to replace their supply of this product?
- How have you created this frequency pattern—by addressing the actual practical needs of the consumer, or by creating an arbitrary pattern to meet your sales targets? (Example: the mobile phone industry has an alarmingly fast replacement rate, owing to its ongoing practice of 'perceived obsolescence' by introducing more and more features.)
- What is the environmental impact of this frequency pattern?
- How much waste are you generating, not only in your manufacturing but at the consumer end (i.e., when customers dispose of the empty package, tube, jar, etc)?
- What are the monetary costs other people (governments, sanitation, etc.) will have to pay for the manufacturing, distribution and disposal of this product?
- What indirect costs is your product imposing upon our educational or medical system? (Example: the success of the tobacco industry has come at a great cost to both the medical industry and the educational sector.)
- What are the costs in terms of human or animal life?
- What are the costs in terms of fuel miles, carbon emissions and overall quality of life?

And lastly, we have the questions about your marketing:

- What is the social and emotional impact of marketing an anti-aging cream to women in their 30s (or whatever your product happens to be)?
- How does your marketing affect not only these women, but also much younger women or girls in their teens?
- How does it affect young men or their relationships with women?
- How might your marketing message influence the outlook of future generations?
- How much does this product address a *genuine* need versus a need that has been created through your marketing?
- How well does your marketing contribute to the greater good and happiness of society?

You might argue that there is no way to find conclusive answers to many of these questions, but I would hazard a guess that you were formulating answers in your mind as you read them nonetheless. But finding definitive answers is actually far less important than the process of asking the questions. As any good life coach will tell you, it is within the questions—not the answers—that a client can frequently make the greatest shift. Questions come in a flash of insight. Answers come over a lifetime of reflection and examination. Questions bring about the inner changes needed for answers to reveal themselves and inform our course of action. Without questions, no change can take place. Ignorance is not a lack of the right answers, but rather a lack of the right questions.

If every business owner and marketer would read these questions at the beginning of any project, I believe we would start to see a very different world.

THE ABUNDANT MARKETER

As marketers, we are both the disseminators of ideas, as well as the 'callers to action.' As such, our communications have the potential to be immensely powerful and influential. We have the power to generate either Scarcity or Abundance—the choice is really up to us. Remember that famous line from the *Spiderman* movie

'With great power comes great responsibility'? Well, as marketers, we have a great power and a great responsibility. Like Spiderman, it is our responsibility to 'use our powers for good.'

How do we do that? If Abundance is not an external 'thing' but an idea, and we are sellers of ideas, how do we 'sell' the idea of a more Abundant mindset? We can, but once again it can only happen when we begin to ask the right questions:

- How much do we *really* believe this world has enough—even more than enough—for all to prosper and live joyful lives?
- How much are we *really* in touch with the rhythm and balance of our world?
- How much are we *really* committed to maintaining that rhythm and balance in our business decisions and actions?
- How much has this commitment *really* become part of our innermost values?
- How much are we *really* willing to speak out and practice these values in our work, even if it impacts our finances?
- How much do we *really* put true Abundance ahead of everything else?

If the answer to some of these questions is 'not much' or 'not yet enough,' we need to ask ourselves what is standing in our way. Is it fear, doubt, lack of self-belief? If so, what do we fear? What do we doubt? What do we believe about ourselves? What needs to change? What small thing can *we* do to start the process, if ever so slightly?

In reading these questions, you might hold your hands up in frustration and say, 'I cannot answer these questions. I'd have to completely abandon everything I've ever done in my business and marketing. How am I supposed to make a living?'

If you have come to that conclusion, it means you have already heard some answers in your head, and they may have scared you. It's not my aim to suggest the 'right' answers, only to invite you to ask the questions. Your answers will require time, reflection and experimentation. We cannot come up with theoretical solutions and then imagine they will serve our needs. That would be tantamount to thinking there is a 'magic bullet' we can swallow to cure a long-term chronic disease. It's simply not possible.

To restore an organism to optimum health, you need to strengthen its immune system, and then let the system heal itself. When a smoker suffering from lung cancer wants to start the healing process, he must first quit smoking so his system will no longer be flooded with toxins that make it impossible to heal. The same is true of our economy. If marketers wish to start the healing process, they can simply stop the continual flooding of society with toxic messages of Scarcity that generate the social 'cancers' of insecurity, fear, instability, dependence, overspending and debt. Then we can begin the long process of restoring the lost interdependence between businesses and consumers that is built upon trust, sustainability and self-reliance, and ultimately lead our world back towards a more abundant mindset.

Complacency, resignation, helplessness and apathy can only lead us into an even more diseased state. Asking questions is the first step in any healing process. As more and more marketers ask these important questions independently, they will begin to connect with each other and ask them collectively.

It is within our collective mind that the true answers will appear. And as they do, the power of the Grace of Collaboration will also begin to emerge.

Summary: How Abundance can Heal Humanity and the Planet

I'm sure many of us have had the embarrassing experience of seeing children in department stores having tantrums when their parents refused to buy them a particular toy. While my five-year-old grandson, Percy, doesn't throw such tantrums, he does know several advert jingles and has started asking for specific toys by brand. When my daughter was little, she was no different, nor was I when I was a child. Advertising seems to have become an unavoidable part of our children's culture. As conscious parents, we might feel uncomfortable about our children's constant exposure to commercialism, by the same token I've heard many a parent worry if we prohibit our children from being exposed to the media, we will be 'depriving' them of feeling like they fit in with their peers, making them feel like outsiders.

So what happens when these children grow up? Most of us alive today were born and raised on television advertising. Are we very different today from the screaming toddler in the toy shop when we are prevented from having something we believe we simply *must* have? Of course, instead of throwing tantrums, we complain about our finances or express our anxieties about money. Or we buy whatever it is we think we need, putting it on our credit card even when we can't afford it, taking us further and further into debt. Whether we get the 'toy' or not, neither solution brings us happiness. Neither brings us Abundance.

When we find ourselves overspending or over-consuming, it's pretty safe to say we are responding to Scarcity marketing. When we are in chronic, ever-increasing debt, we are responding to Scarcity marketing. When we tolerate wastefulness in the form of unnecessary packaging, frequent discarding and replacement of things we have bought, we are responding to Scarcity marketing. When we become hoarders of money or goods, restricting the flow of our assets when it would be healthier not to do so, we also are responding to Scarcity marketing. Basically, when we are creating any kind of imbalance of wealth in our lives or in the world, we can know most assuredly that we are responding to Scarcity marketing.

But I believe there is such a thing as an 'abundant consumer.' While a Scarcity mindset generates over consumption, debt, hoarding, waste and degeneration, an Abundance mindset generates respect, recycling, good use, taking and keeping only what is needed, sharing and a healthy overall flow of life. But what it also means is that we look up and see the wealth of what we already have. Just as the volunteers who started The Abundance Project in Sheffield looked up and saw the wealth of food the world is giving us—which many of us too often choose to ignore—an abundant mindset shows us just how much we are given at every moment. Speaking for myself, Abundance, means I stop cursing my flabby thighs and thanking the Universe that I have two functioning legs that take me wherever I want to go. Instead of thinking of my eyes as 'bad' because I have to wear corrective lenses, I see how blessed I am that

I can see at all. And when the economic situation of the world around us brings financial hardship, I see it as an opportunity to learn how to find the real Abundance that I might have been ignoring in my own backyard.

When consumers en masse finally wake up to the startling truth that most of their problems with money have been due to their responding to Scarcity marketing—and that within their arms' reach lies wealth on a scale they had never before imagined—we will finally see a new era of socioeconomic reform that will bring us back to that natural state of balance and flow called Abundance.

The abundant consumer can start the wave of change in our world through what Thoreau or Gandhi might have called the 'civil disobedience' of simply not responding to what we are being told to believe or do by marketing. When we do so, businesses and marketers will have no choice but to adapt. It requires no government mandates. It requires no activism or protests. It will cost us nothing. It will give us everything.

At the risk of sounding like an aging Baby Boomer, as singer Joni Mitchell once wrote:

'We are stardust. We are golden.
And we've got to get ourselves back to the garden.'[16]

Grace #7:
Collaboration

It was 7.45 P.M. on a dark, wintry Sunday evening on Long Island. As it was my mother's custom to serve Sunday dinner in the early afternoon, our family had just finished a light evening supper of sandwiches on crusty poppy seed rolls. I finished my meal off with a glass of milk after gagging on the last (and very stale) piece of chocolate cake I had saved from my 9th birthday two weeks before. After washing my plate and glass, I rushed to my dad to make sure everything would be ready before 8 o'clock. My father assured me it would, and he went into the basement to gather the equipment I had requested from him.

I ran into the living room and turned on our massive black and white television, which stood inside a large mahogany cabinet with glossy polished doors. As was the case with all TVs in those days, the set took several minutes to warm up, and I wanted to make sure it was ready before the show for which I had been anxiously waiting all week started. I could feel my heart pumping with excitement.

The date was Sunday 9 February 1964. The show I was so eager to watch was *The Ed Sullivan Show*. That night, for the first time ever, The Beatles would be playing on live television in the United States. Long before the days of cable TV, home video recording, satellite links, YouTube or iPlayer, an estimated 73 million American viewers tuned in live to that historic broadcast,[2] an astonishing 38% of the entire population of the country at the time.[3]

My father was a design engineer for New York Bell Telephone and was always testing and designing new communication systems. One of the perks I enjoyed while growing up was having the privilege of being the only kid in town with a selection of reel-to-reel tape recorders and microphones at my disposal at any time. My father hauled up one of his heavy analogue machines just in time for the broadcast. I switched it on and placed the mic close to the television speaker, and with great delight I was able to capture The Beatles' performance on tape. Of course, the recording conditions weren't the best, and the girls in the live audience were screaming so loudly it was difficult to hear the songs, but there was something magical in that moment nonetheless. I played the recording over and over for many months, giggling every time I remembered how the lads from Liverpool shook their hair when they sang 'Ooooh' in their song *She Loves You.* Clearly, I was in love.

And I was not the only one. From that moment, it seemed the entire nation had become seduced by The Beatles, and that music would never be the same. And indeed, for the next six years until their official breakup in 1970, their fame and success seemed indomitable. After that, John, Paul, George and Ringo all continued to write and record independently. But while some of those independent releases enjoyed significant success in terms of sales, in terms of sheer *cultural impact and influence,* nothing ever came close to the collaborative efforts of the former 'Fab Four.'

THE THIRD ENTITY

It was when I studied relationship coaching that I first encountered the term 'The Third Entity.' The Center for Right Relationships, whose teachings in their Organization and Relationship Systems Coaching curriculum revolve around an understanding of 'The Third Entity,' define it as 'that which lives outside the individuals in a particular relationship system whether a work team, family, or couple.'[4] In fact, they cite the Beatles as an easy-to-understand example of 'The Third Entity' saying, 'John

Lennon, Paul McCartney, George Harrison and Ringo Starr were individuals. The Beatles is their Third Entity.'5

The Third Entity is far more than the sum of its parts, as clearly seen in the case of The Beatles. It's not that any member of the band (or their masterful producer, George Martin) was lacking in talent in any way. Nor is it a simple matter of each person having the requisite skill-sets for a successful band. A Third Entity is much, much more than that.

Consider an ocean as an example of a 'Third Entity.' The waters of the ocean can be broken down into tiny water molecules, each having the same chemical and physical properties. But it is only when they undergo the physical transformations that occur when joined together that they can actualise their potential. Separately, they can be brushed away with a stroke of the hand, and evaporated rapidly beneath the hot sun, but collectively, they can support uncountable forms of aquatic life or become tidal waves that can inundate entire islands.

Similarly, when people come together, they inevitably form a 'Third Entity.' The Third Entity exists within *every* relationship, from families to communities to businesses to entire nations. And like the ocean, this Third Entity is the result of many changes, both internally and even externally. And just as the ocean has equal potential to support life or destroy it, The Third Entity of any human relationship, large or small, also has immense power. A marriage between two people, for example, can 'make or break' the lives of that couple as well as those of their children. It can also have a tremendous impact upon their extended family, community and possibly the entire world. It is not only the individuals who are creating that impact, but also (and frequently more so) their *relationship.* Get it right, and the relationship has the power to create a wave of great happiness and positive growth. Get it wrong, and it can cause devastation.

The Third Entity is not merely a collective of individuals, but a spirit unto itself, with a mind, heart and soul. It has a character, a personality and an overall way of being. For example, when we visit a foreign land and we sense a distinct difference in our environment, we have come into contact with that country's Third Entity. Even though we might get along very well with many individuals on our journey, we might still experience what some call 'culture shock.' It is the Third Entity with whom we are experiencing that clash; it doesn't necessarily have to arise from any particular person or incident. What's even more complex is that it is also likely that this clash is most probably arising between that Third Entity and the Third Entity of our *own* culture. We are all inevitably acculturated by the Third Entities of our families, social circles, work environments, local communities, spiritual communities and nations. Because of this, it can be extremely challenging to differentiate between the 'I' and the 'we' of who we think we are.

Because the Third Entity is just that—an entity—it has a survival instinct. It is this kind of instinct that creates the paradox of how groups of people, from nations to street gangs, can be so closely loving and loyal amongst each other, while fighting to the death against other 'Third Entities' whom they perceive as a threat. But once we come to understand the power of the Third Entity, and the many, many *layers* of relationships that have informed our beliefs, opinions, feelings and behaviour, we at least have a foundation for being able to recognise and work effectively with all the Third Entities in our lives, in such a way that we can create great things *through* them.

And creating beauty that arises through the power of the Third Entity is the essence of Collaboration.

IS TEAMWORK THE SAME AS COLLABORATION?

Literally, the word 'collaboration' is from Latin origins and means 'working together' or 'working collectively.' Modern businesspeople often use the word 'teamwork' to refer to the act of working collectively. But quite often, what many people call 'teamwork' is a far cry from actual Collaboration.

Frequently, 'teamwork' means everyone 'does their bit' to serve an end result. But I've also seen the word 'teamwork' tossed about to mean that everyone within a company unilaterally follows and obeys company policy and operations as set by the company directors. I witnessed this kind of so-called teamwork many times when I worked in the educational system. Referring to such a practice as 'teamwork' is not only misleading, it is also demoralising and disempowering to the members of the alleged team. It coerces people to behave a certain way using guilt tactics, inferring that company loyalty takes precedence over personal feelings and opinions.

Back when I was a middle manager in the educational system, I found myself frequently challenging the status quo, telling my seniors I could not find it within myself to impose demands upon my staff or students I myself didn't believe were necessary or logical. I clearly remember one HR Director telling me if I harboured these objections inwardly, my staff would instinctively pick up on it and cease to follow company policy. If that were to happen, both my own staff and my senior managers would see me as a 'weak manager.' While I understood this from her perspective, it seemed that being a 'team player' meant to work faithfully to policy regardless of what I thought or felt. I had a vain notion I could be a force for change within the system, but at that time I lacked the mental and emotional skills to address this moral dilemma in any other way than to resign from my post after several years of frustration. Ironically, I truly liked and respected my senior managers, as well as most people at the college. So what was I really battling against?

The problem was that I was clashing with the 'Third Entity'—'The Company'. My relationship with The Company was as disempowering as it would have been within a dysfunctional family. There was no way for me to create, excel or produce within such a relationship, and in spite of my efforts I was never able to adjust. I started to feel a bit like Winston in Orwell's *1984*, where power, success and freedom were attained only when you finally came to 'love' Big Brother.

When the Third Entity of our businesses, or indeed of any relationship, starts to feel like Big Brother, something is seriously wrong. Systems and policies are very important, but if we allow our businesses to become merely an impersonal collection of systems and policies moving in a linear top-to-bottom direction, there is virtually no chance that change, innovation and genuine Collaboration will appear. And without these vital things, a company will always be chasing its tail, continually trying to uphold the status quo and struggling to maintain the bottom line. There's simply no time or space for innovation when a company is too busy playing catch-up and has their head buried too deeply in their books. Such a company may have employees, but it cannot possibly have teams. A collection of individuals following company policy in which they feel resigned and powerless is *not* a team, nor are the fruits of their labours the result of Collaboration.

To call a group of people a 'team,' there's got to be teamwork; and if teamwork does not mean Collaboration, the word is utterly meaningless. A genuine team is a group of people who feel empowered to create, to change and to express themselves. They are tuned into each other's talents and ideas and know how to bring out the best in one another. They are not competing against one another, but know that every other member of the team is a valuable asset to their *own* success, and vice versa. They all have a vision of 'the whole picture,' and know whatever they do to enhance the work of others will also enhance that whole. Most of all, they know implicitly that whatever they create through their combined efforts is *always* more than the sum of its parts.

All these attributes must be present in order for true Collaboration to flourish. Only when a group of people possess and practice these qualities collectively might they rightfully be called 'a team,' and the work generated by such a team might rightfully be called the result of 'teamwork.'

CREATING THE SPACE—THE STAKE

Collaboration can only arise when the group of people in question intentionally create the space for it. 'Creating the space' means both laying the intention for Collaboration, and ensuring the ongoing safety and integrity of that space. In order for that to happen, the group must share a common vision and value system, which not only informs their direction and decisions, but to which they return again and again whenever questions amongst them arise. Back when I did leadership training, we referred to this common vision and value system as 'the stake.'

There is a big difference between company systems, policies and procedures, and the stake. Systems, policies and procedures are rules that govern operations and behaviour that hopefully help to ensure consistency of ethics and production within a company. As such, they are able to be expressed concretely in writing. They also tend to move in one direction, from the top of the organisation down to its employees. A stake, on the other hand, is a dynamic, fluid entity that exists at a meta level above systems, policies and procedures. As such, it is not always so easily expressed in words, although it's extremely valuable to do so. Before I begin any project, I always take time to formulate a stake, so I know why I'm doing it in the first place. For example, my stake for the Global Wellness Circle was *'Communities create wellness.'* My stake for this book is *'To heal humanity and the planet, we must change the way we sell.'* A stake is not a mere slogan, but the fundamental belief that forms the spirit and life purpose of your team, company or project. It is a rich, living idea that evolves and becomes more vivid over time. When your team share and cultivate a common stake, they know why they are working and where they are going *together*. When they don't, they are simply following (or not following) company policy individually. Thus to create the space for Collaboration, it is essential that a stake is present, whether articulated in words or not.

DEFINING THE STAKE IN A MARKETING CAMPAIGN

Whenever I begin a marketing campaign with a new client, the first thing we do together is define the stake, although I don't always use that word. I take whatever time is needed to get to the core of why they have written their book, started their business or created their project. It's not just a matter of my learning about their product or service or even that person; it's about defining the *impact* this product or service will have upon the world. If that impact is ill-defined, it makes my job as a marketer very difficult. It's interesting how many new authors are actually quite unclear about their stake when they first come to me, even after their book has been written. They might well be very passionate and excited about their book, but they can often be quite unclear about what this book will bring to the world, and why it is important at this particular time in history.

As a marketer, I feel it is my first responsibility to help them define this, as it will inform every aspect of the marketing campaign as we work together. The stake becomes the starting point of not only the marketing materials for the campaign, it also defines the kinds of people who will be involved—the author, me, our partners and our customers.

The success of all my online marketing campaigns is based upon my network partners, who help to promote my clients' products and services. While at a practical level they do this with the incentives of either sales commissions or leads generation, the reason partners join a campaign in the first place is 'the stake.' When you have a team of network partners who share the vision and values of the project, you have a great foundation for Collaboration. They will put more energy into the campaign, and will even help 'watch your back' if things go wrong. And when you deal with online marketing, where there are so many ways technology can backfire, dedicated partners can sometimes save a campaign from sheer disaster.

Attracting such great network partners is all a matter of communicating your stake clearly. When I invite partners into a campaign, I share the vision and values of the project, rather than trying to 'pitch' it to them with glossy marketing copy. The quality of this communication is extremely important. Because I have a large network, many people also approach me to partner on their campaigns. Sometimes I refuse an invitation either because I couldn't 'feel' the stake at all, or because the invitation was filled with so much woo-woo hype I was totally put off. I don't want to be 'sold' on a campaign; I want to be *inspired* to participate. I want to feel like I *want* to be a part of the energy, the movement, the message. I want to feel I am helping create the change in the world this campaign is all about.

When we clearly communicate our stake to our partners, they become more likely to want to *step into that stake with us*. And when they do, we have successfully created the space for the Grace of Collaboration. This process is not only relevant to Internet marketing, but to any collaborative process—from corporate teams to community groups to indie bands. When the stake is used as the grounding point for a marketing campaign, everything changes. It n longer becomes a mere matter of finding something clever, witty or entertaining to hook your target audience, but rather of co-creating something that expresses truth and gives value to the world.

THE CARE AND FEEDING OF COLLABORATION

Creating the space for Collaboration is a great achievement. Holding and maintaining that space so Collaboration can thrive is an even greater one. There is an art to making Collaboration happen. Equally, there are also many ways we can sabotage it.

The first prerequisite for Collaboration is *allowing* it to happen. While that might seem obvious or even simplistic, 'allowing' is actually quite complex. In our competitive world, and reinforced by many of our educational systems, all too many of us have been conditioned NOT to allow Collaboration. We have fought for a place at the top throughout our lives. Our instincts are to hide our work and ideas until we can 'prove' them in the form of an exam, essay or publication. We worry about having our ideas stolen and not getting due recognition. We shelter our thoughts within the fortress of Competition. Given our cultural background, allowing Collaboration to happen can be a true challenge for many of us.

Thus, allowing Collaboration requires that we learn how to *trust* people in situations where we once might have seen them as potential threats to our success. This in itself is a big, big deal. But 'allowing' Collaboration also means that we trust *our own* ideas even when they still might be half-baked. It means we allow ourselves the possibility of making mistakes and looking like idiots in front of others. Without this kind of trust, there can be no creative freedom.

All of that can be pretty frightening, so obviously, allowing also requires *courage*. In his book *Permission Marketing*, Seth Godin says, 'There are only two kinds of companies: brave and dead.'[6] I would hazard a guess that many companies die at least in part because they did not manage to muster up the courage to 'allow' necessary changes to happen. Collaboration always brings about *innovation,* but for some companies innovation is a scary thing. When I worked in the educational sector, when things got tough financially, many colleges reacted by 'tightening the belt.' Programs that generated the least amount of funding were cut, and innovation of new programs was at the bottom of the list of priorities (if not off the list entirely).

Tightening the belt is the nemesis of innovation, and often has the opposite effect companies believe it will have. It might look like a practical and responsible solution, but often it's really just a knee-jerk reaction that comes from fear. Innovation can never be at the bottom of our list of priorities. It is not only necessary for companies to survive, it's also the thing that keeps our own blood pumping, and makes us want to wake up in the morning. Once you take innovation away from a business, it's as though that business is on life-support—alive but not alive. When a company finds itself in this place, it's not so much because they lost money but because they lost 'the stake.'

The next key ingredient of Collaboration is *listening*. Again this might seem like an obvious thing, but as I've learned over decades of playing music, teaching, parenting and coaching, most of us are not natural-born masters of listening. One of the more subtle aspects to listening is what some refer to as 'reading the space.' When we read a space, we are sensing the underlying mood and needs of a situation. For instance, sometimes in a group of people, one person is feeling shut out, but they do not speak up and say anything about it. Or maybe a team leader is addressing the team, but does not adequately create the space for feedback to see how his message is landing with the others. Collaboration means we are sensitive to the unspoken and call it out when it needs to be spoken. The result of this 'reading the space' is that whatever has gotten stuck will be unstuck, and whatever has gotten knocked off balance is righted.

We all know how to read the space, but too many of us don't bother to utilise this skill, for fear of rocking the boat or being 'rude.' But politeness is grossly overrated. Even co-founder of the Polaroid Corporation, Edwin Land reportedly once said, 'Politeness is the poison of collaboration.'[7] That's why to create true Collaboration we also need to *get real*. Collaboration is not about everyone making a show of getting along and being all 'nicey-nicey.' It's about being who you are and speaking what you see. M. Scott Peck says such 'nicey-nicey' behaviour actually creates what he calls 'pseudo-communities that never succeed in rising to the level of actual productivity.[8]

Getting real also requires that we move away from hierarchies. While there will always be leaders and different roles on a team, hierarchies that create barriers to clear, direct communication can lead to disastrous results, as chillingly cited by Malcolm Gladwell in his book *Outliers*.[9]

Of course, to 'get real' with others, we must first get real with ourselves. We have to do the homework of understanding all the ways we tend to get triggered and defensive, and take responsibility for this, rather than engaging in a never-ending 'blame game' with the rest of the world. In other words, until we master the first six Graces within ourselves, we don't stand much of a chance in being able to cultivate the Grace of Collaboration with others. Our first responsibility, therefore, is to honour the Self of who we really are, as opposed to clinging to the shadow of self we may have been projecting to the world for a very, very long time.

These elements—allowing, courage, listening and getting real with Self and others—form the fertile ground for Collaboration to grow and flourish. Take that fertile ground and nurture it with the gentle rain of 'the stake' and we have the recipe for magic in our businesses. When we also apply these same elements to marketing—whether within our marketing teams or in working with our networking partners—the marketing we create as a result will be fresh, honest, genuine and creative.

But the process doesn't stop there. In this era of social media, Collaboration now extends to our customers as well. In the formative stages, I get some of my best ideas for new projects from questions my readers ask me. I also get some of my best solutions from answers they give me when I ask them. But even after our marketing pieces are created, when we send them out to the world, our audience now becomes 'the space' which we must read. Sales are not the only measure. Nor should 'stickiness' (i.e., how much the public remember your advert) be the measure. The big question should be this: How much does our audience *believe* us? And not just believe us, but believe *in* us and our stake?

Yes, it all comes back to the stake. If the public do not intuitively know our stake, our marketing has failed us. The entire purpose of our marketing should be to communicate the stake to our audience.

Sales will follow of their own accord if the audience believes in and is inspired by the stake. But the stake will only be believable if it is transparently congruent with who we are as marketers and business owners. Without that congruence, our marketing will be of little substance. Thus, the greatest Collaborative element of marketing is the feedback from our audience. And if we continually receive the kind of feedback that tells us our stake is either not being heard or is deemed insincere, it's time to spend some serious time alone on the proverbial mountaintop, so we can figure out which of the Graces we are blocking within ourselves, and hence not communicating clearly.

COLLABORATION IS THE NATURAL WAY OF LIFE

Dissecting the northern and southern halves of my town of Bedford, England, runs the River Great Ouse. On just about any day I happen to walk along the River Embankment, I'll see dozens of white swans swimming about. In spite of the many signs asking people not to feed the water fowl, folks still come out with bags of bread and cake to feed the swans every day. While I don't feed them myself, I do sometimes stand and watch the swans as they scurry about snatching up food people toss out to them.

Swans have a distinct way of interacting when faced with having to 'compete' with each other for food. If two swans go for the same morsel at the same time, the one who 'loses' the race will immediately wiggle his tail a few times as an act of acknowledging the winner, and simply swim off in another direction to look for another piece of bread. Occasionally, if two swans repeatedly find themselves bumping into one another, one of the swans will lightly grab the neck of the other swan to nudge him out of the way. Again, the 'defeated' swan gives his tail a wiggle, and the whole matter is settled in less than a second. But these victories and defeats are completely transitory. The swan who was the 'loser' might likely be the 'winner' with the very same opponent just a few minutes later. In the end, all the swans swim away fat, happy and cohesive as a group. I've never seen a skinny or lonely swan on the river. Somehow they maintain a balance in their society.

I witnessed similar behaviour amongst some crows when living in India in the 1980s. One day when I was picnicking by a lake, a murder of crows gathered around a short distance away from me, obviously waiting to see if there would be any goodies left for them. Seeing them eying me, I tossed them an apple core after I had had my fill of the apple. Very quickly, one crow caught the core and flew up into the air with it. He took a bite and then dropped the core, passing it on to another crow flying below him. That crow flew up into the air, took a bite and dropped it for yet another crow. This happened over and over until there was nothing left to the apple but the stem. I found it fascinating that not a single crow attempted to steal the whole apple core for himself.

These examples go against what many of us have been brought up to believe about Nature. While early capitalism might have been founded upon the (misinterpreted) notion of 'survival of the fittest,' the truth is that Collaboration, not Competition, is our natural state. Nature is a permaculture—a system of gives and takes, and checks and balances, that ensure the survival not just of individuals, but of the whole. A tree provides a home for birds; the birds drop 'bird poop' that fertilises the tree. Trees breathe in carbon dioxide and breathe out oxygen; we breathe in oxygen and breathe out carbon dioxide. Our world, the planets, everything is based upon Collaboration. Collaboration *works*.

While Competition surely exists in Nature, if it is conducted without regard for the whole system, it will always result in an imbalance. Imagine if the crows had simply hoarded more than their share of the food at the expense of all the other crows. So too, when we humans compete without regard for the whole system, we create imbalances both in our society and in our natural world.

It is vital we remember the 'eco' in the word 'economic.' Our economic system is part of our eco-system, not separate from it. Whatever imbalances we create within our socioeconomic system will always trickle into other parts of the greater eco-system. If we create a glut of wealth in one part of the system, another will always suffer. When we act without mindfulness of the Whole, our seeming gain will never come without a hidden cost in the long-term. This is not mere New Age pop-spirituality. It's scientific fact.

It's worth taking a lesson from the swans and the crows.

SUMMARY: HOW COLLABORATION CAN HEAL HUMANITY AND THE PLANET

At a purely practical level, Collaboration in marketing brings us more possibilities: more ideas, more feedback, more support, more excitement. Whether the Collaboration arises from partners on a promotional campaign, a panel of guest speakers on a telesummit, or a discussion thread on social media, the energy that comes from the unique Third Entity of our Collaboration is greater than any of us could ever produce on our own. Collaboration makes our work easier and the results more exciting. But most of all, it becomes a perfect circle as it loops us right back around to the first of our 7 Graces: Connection.

But Collaboration in our businesses and marketing goes beyond the act of working productively with other people—it also means we work productively *with our World*. Our ultimate 'stake' in our business should always be to serve the Whole—our Planet and all living entities who share it with us. Just as we allow, listen and get real with other people, the time has come when we must also learn how to allow, listen and get real with our Planet. Only when we ask and listen carefully to what that Whole needs and wants can we become truly holistic business owners and marketers.

The Earth is calling us.

She calls us to be in relationship with her, but we have forgotten she is our Mother.

She calls us to dance to her rhythms, but we have forgotten the steps.

She calls us to sing the song of Creation with her, but we have forgotten both the tune and the harmony.

She teaches us by example every day, but we ignore her, thinking we can learn everything on our own.

She loves us, feeds and embraces us, but we forget, pillage and rape her in return.

And now, at this time in history, millions of people are ready to stop this madness, but they fear we humans have dug a hole so deep we will never be able to climb out. But while this fear serves as grave reminder of how far we have strayed from our own humanity, the beautiful truth of our situation is this:

> *Everything in this Universe is lovingly designed*
> *to return to a state of balance*
> *when we live in Collaboration with the Whole.*

Allow it to happen. Work together. Make it so.

Epilogue:
Can Marketing Heal the World?

We began this book with a question, the first of possibly hundreds more that were to follow. And as I said at the onset, I am quite sure you have formed many more questions even than I have written within these pages. This is, as I said, a book of questions, and not a manual of answers.

Appropriately then, I am now asking you to consider one final question: 'Can marketing heal the world?' Admittedly, it seems like an absurd question. You might think, *Huh? Can marketing heal the world? I thought marketing was making us ill. How could it possibly heal anything? Wouldn't the world be a whole lot healthier if we just chucked out marketing altogether?*

Now that's a question I *will* actually answer:

No.

As we've seen throughout this book, the enterprise of business is a vital part of our social structure. Without it, society would not have what it needs to survive. Admittedly, big business has gone more than a bit overboard in producing more than we need, and marketers have been their partners in crime by making us believe we need all those things. But the problem isn't that marketing as a concept is

369

simply 'wrong' or harmful. After all, how are we supposed to find out about things we actually *do* need? Marketing is simply our means of communicating we have something of value to share. But how do we make sure it remains value-driven and keeps the 'community' in 'communication'?

Well...

Imagine if all business owners and marketers were truly in Connection to their products and services, as well as to our planet.

Imagine how this would impact not only what was made and sold, but also *how* it was made and sold.

Imagine if all marketing was based upon Inspiration, with life-giving messages that fed our hearts and minds?

Imagine if marketers mastered the lost art of Invitation, and both the quantity of marketing messages was dramatically trimmed down, and the quality made so aesthetically pleasing, it became a delight for us to invite it into our space.

Imagine if Directness guided marketers to tell it like it is, and they no longer showed us only what they wanted us to see.

Imagine if Transparency guided marketers to shine the light of truth through themselves, their companies and their products.

Imagine if marketers no longer used Scarcity to provoke consumers to act. Imagine if big businesses understood that unlimited growth was not only a myth, but detrimental for everyone including themselves. Imagine if Abundance guided them both to share what was truly valuable, and never to waste, hoard or create any kind of imbalance.

Imagine if business owners, marketers and consumers worked in Collaboration with each other to ensure commerce was healthy and in harmony with the natural flow of the environment.

Any good holistic doctor understands that for a person to be in optimum health, he must eat a good, balanced diet full of nutrients and free of toxins. In fact, many holistic practitioners will treat even serious diseases like cancer purely through changes in diet.

So if by analogy commerce is the 'digestive system' of society, it stands to reason that:

Yes...

Yes, we can heal what is ailing humanity and the planet by changing the way we sell. If businesses and marketers change what they are 'feeding' the world (both in consumables and in marketing propaganda), by removing the 'Deadly Sins' and replacing them with the '7 Graces,' we can begin the detoxification process and start to restore our unhappy, weakened social body to health.

This new paradigm cannot help but bring us a higher quality of services and products. It cannot help but bring greater conscientiousness about how we utilise our precious resources—including people. It cannot help but guide us back to community and self-reliance. It cannot help but guide us back to enterprise and innovation. It cannot help but release us from fear and anxiety. It cannot help but elevate our sensitivity to each other, and make our values the more important aspect of everything we do. It cannot help but build a greater sense of self-worth in ourselves and in our children. It cannot help but bring more stability to both our economy and to the environment.

You may say that I'm a dreamer, but I'm not the only one. If you've made it all the way to the end of this book, I can only assume you have also imagined a similar world.

So how do we *do* it? How do we make the change?

Well a good place to start is by asking more questions—together.

So let the dialogue continue...

Appendices

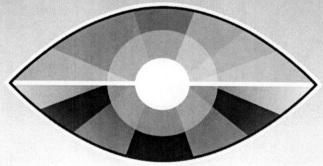

Acknowledgements
References
About the Author
Contact Information

ACKNOWLEDGEMENTS

With deep gratitude, I wish to extend my thanks...

- To the two lads in Nando's who spoke about fear, sex and humour, unknowingly kick-starting this entire project
- To all the folks in my business networks who helped me realise I wasn't meant to 'fit'
- To Allison Maslan, my first book promotion client
- To my agent, Bill Gladstone at Waterside, a voice of encouragement since the beginning of this project
- To all my marketing clients who, by asking for help, allowed me to learn more and more
- To all my friends who listened to me fumble and grumble
- To all my social media friends, followers and readers who helped me learn what worked and didn't work
- To all my blog readers who gave me feedback on my articles
- To Michael Drew, Renee Duran, Rich Gallagher, Liz Goodgold, Greg Reid and Pam Slim, who allowed me to share some of my fledgling ideas with them before I wrote them
- To Vanessa, Andrew, Charly, Katie, Callie and Kyle, the unsung heroes who kept me sane behind the scenes
- To my mastermind partners, Carol, Sorel and Lynn G., who cheered me on in the final few months of this project
- To Renee Duran (again) for the magnificent cover design
- To Jessica Keet for another fabulously proofread manuscript
- To Paula Tarrant and Shelagh Jones, who have been two of my biggest cheerleaders in this project
- To Vrinda, George and Percy, for giving me a life filled with love and laughter
- To my 2nd grade teacher who didn't take any points off my science report, even though I had drawn in a quarter-page advert for an imaginary book I wanted to write
- To everyone in the world who ever hated marketing
- To everyone who read this book...

I am truly grateful to all of you.

REFERENCES

PROLOGUE: IS MARKETING MAKING US ILL?

1. Tesla, Nikola. 1893. 'On Light and Other High-Frequency Phenomena.' Retrieved 15 December 2010 from http://en.wikipedia.org/wiki/Nikola_Tesla

PART ONE: WHERE ARE WE AND HOW DID WE GET HERE?
WHY NICE PEOPLE HATE MARKETING

1. Statistics provided directly to me during a recorded phone consultation with Caroline Edwards, ND, nutritionist at the Red Apple Clinic in Newport Wales, during a consultation on 11 July 2011.

HOW A BROKEN TV CHANGED THE WORLD

1. The Disposable Heroes of Hiphoprisy. 1992. Song: 'Television the Drug of the Nation' from album and single of the same name. Fontana Island Records.

2. In Britain, a licence is required to own a television. As of this writing, a licence for a colour TV is around £145 (roughly $235 USD) per year.

3. 'Q&A: Lehman Brothers bank collapse.' 16 September 2008. BBC News website. Retrieved 26 February 2011 from http://news.bbc.co.uk/1/hi/7615974.stm

4. 'US banks make shock status switch.' 22 September 2008. BBC News website. Retrieved 26 February 2011 from http://news.bbc.co.uk/1/hi/7628578.stm

5. Inman, Phillip. 2008. 'Hundreds of bank branches expected to close doors.' *The Guardian,* 29 September 2008. Retrieved 26 February 2011 from http://www.guardian.co.uk/money/2008/sep/30/banks.banking

6. Davis, Rowenna. 2010. 'Antidepressant use rises as recession feeds wave of worry.' *The Guardian,* 11 June 2010. Retrieved 24 February 2011 from http://www.guardian.co.uk/society/2010/jun/11/antidepressant-prescriptions-rise-nhs-recession

7. 'Bargains in closing Woolies shops.' 2008. BBC News website, 27 December 2008. Retrieved 27 February 2011 from http://news.bbc.co.uk/1/hi/7800839.stm

. 'Woolworths staff feel pain of closure.' 2009. BBC News website, 6 January 2009. Retrieved 27 February 2011 from http://news.bbc.co.uk/1/hi/uk/7813499.stm

FEAR, SEX AND HUMOUR ~ OR ~ HOW S-E-L-L BECAME A 4-LETTER WORD

1. Herbert, Frank. 2005. *Dune, 40th Anniversary Edition, Dune Chronicles Book 1.* Ace Trade Publishers. p8.

2. Emoto, Masaru. 2004. *The Hidden Messages in Water.* Hillsboro, Oregon: Beyond Words Publishing.

3. An example of chronic pain is fibromyalgia, which many metabolic specialists consider to be caused by low adrenal reserves due to or exacerbated by prolonged environmental stresses. This information was provided directly to me during a recorded phone consultation with Caroline Edwards, ND, nutritionist at the Red Apple Clinic in Newport Wales, during a consultation on 11 July 2011, but there are numerous books on the market today on adrenal fatigue that support this.

4. Held, Lisa. 2009. 'Psychoanalysis shapes consumer culture: or how Sigmund Freud, his nephew and a box of cigars forever changed American marketing.' *Monitor on Psychology,* December 2009, Vol 40, No. 11, p32. Online version. Retrieved 9 January 2011 from http://www.apa.org/monitor/2009/12/consumer.aspx

5. US Centers for Disease Control (CDC). 2001. 'Highlights: Marketing Cigarettes to Women.' From *Surgeon General's Report on Smoking and Tobacco Use 2001.* Retrieved 5 March 2011 from http://www.cdc.gov/tobacco/data_statistics/sgr/2001/highlights/marketing/

6. 'Old Smoking Ads.' Images of Lucky Strike and Parliament cigarettes ads retrieved 9 January 2011 from the now-defunct *Lemondrop* site at http://www.lemondrop.com/gallery/old-smoking-ads/1096367/

7. US Centers for Disease Control (CDC), op. cit.

8. Old Smoking Ads, op. cit.

9. *Federal Trade Commission Cigarette Report for 2004-2005.* Issued: 2007. Retrieved 5 March 2011 from http://www.ftc.gov/reports/tobacco/2007cigarette2004-2005.pdf

10. 'Virginia Slims.' *Wikipedia.* Retrieved 5 March 2011 from http://en.wikipedia.org/wiki/Virginia_Slims#cite_note-0

11. US Centers for Disease Control (CDC), op. cit.

12. Wenc, Christine. 2007. 'Smoking Is Sublime: How the Tobacco Industry Mass-Marketed the Biggest Cause of Preventable Death in the World.' A review of Allan Brandt's book *The Cigarette Century: The Rise, Fall, and Deadly Persistence of the Product that Defined America. The Stranger,*

issue June 13, 2007. Index Newspapers, LLC. Retrieved 6 January 2011 from http://www.thestranger.com/seattle/content?oid=242638

13. US Centers for Disease Control (CDC), op. cit.

14. US Centers for Disease Control (CDC). 'Fast Facts.' Retrieved 5 March 2011 from http://www.cdc.gov/tobacco/data_statistics/fact_sheets/fast_facts/

15. Ibid.

16. Webber, Andrew Lloyd and Rice, Tim. 1970. *Jesus Christ Superstar.* Album first released in the UK on Decca Records.

17. Webber, Andrew Lloyd. 'King Herod's Song Lyrics.' Retrieved 5 March 2011 from http://www.stlyrics.com/lyrics/jesuschristsuperstar/kingherodssong.ht m

18. 'Humour Therapy: Therapeutic Benefits of Laughter.' Holistic Online website. Retrieved 6 March 2011 from http://www.holisticonline.com/humor_therapy/humor_therapy_benefits .htm

19. Video: 'Life, Love and Laughter (Part 1 of 3) Dr. Lee Berk & Norm Crosby on Lifestyle Magazine.' Retrieved 6 March 2011 from http://www.youtube.com/watch?v=-uxcdKxAv04

THE RISE AND FALL OF CONSUMER CULTURE

1. Video: 'Charlie Chaplin – The Great Dictator (final scene).' Film originally released in 1940. Retrieved 6 January 2011 from http://www.youtube.com/watch?v=Rzrjg5T0cMc

2. HRH The Prince of Wales, Juniper, Tony and Skelly, Ian. 2010. *Harmony: A New Way of Looking at Our World.* London: Blue Door (Imprint of HarperCollins), pp150-151.

3. Braungart, Michael and McDonough, William. 2009. *Cradle to Cradle: Remaking the Way We Make Things.* London: Vintage Books. The term 'less bad' is used in many places throughout the book but see especially Chapter 2: 'Why Being "Less Bad" is No Good', pp45-67.

4. Madison, James. 1787. 'The Utility of the Union as a Safeguard Against Domestic Faction and Insurrection (continued).' From *The Federalist No. 10*, Thursday November 22, 1787. Retrieved 13 March 2011 from http://www.constitution.org/fed/federa10.htm

5. Kinealy, Christine. 1995. *This Great Calamity: The Irish Famine 1845-52*, Gill & Macmillan.

6. Wenc, op. cit.

7. Ibid.

8. Thoreau, Henry David. 2004. *Walden.* Originally published in 1854 under the title *Walden: or Life in the Woods.* Boston: Beacon Press; New edition, p305.

9. 'McDonald's Announces Commitment to Certified Sustainable Sources; Releases 2010 Corporate Responsibility Report.' March 9, 2011. Retrieved 20 March 2011 from http://www.aboutmcdonalds.com/mcd/media_center/recent_news/corp orate/McDONALD_S_ANNOUNCES_COMMITMENT_TO_CERTIFIED_SUS TAINABLE_SOURCES__RELEASES_2010_CORPORATE_RESPONSIBILIT Y_REPORT.html

10. 'McDonald's Annual Report 2009.' Retrieved 20 March 2011 from http://www.aboutmcdonalds.com/etc/medialib/aboutMcDonalds/invest or_relations0.Par.6540.File.dat/McD_2009_AR_Final_032910.pdf

11. 'McDonald's.' 2010. *Wikipedia.* Retrieved 20 March 2011 from http://en.wikipedia.org/wiki/McDonald%27s

12. 'How Many Hamburgers Does McDonald's Sell?' *Wisegeek.* Retrieved 20 March 2011 from http://www.wisegeek.com/how-many-hamburgers-does-mcdonalds-sell.htm

13. Saunderson, Mont H. 1944. 'Adjustments in Western Beef Cattle Production and Marketing during the War and Post-War Periods.' *Journal of Farm Economics,* Vol. 26, No. 4 (Nov., 1944), p789. Retrieved 20 March 2011 from http://www.jstor.org/pss/1232124

14. Jolly, Desmond A. 1983. 'Reasons for the decline in beef consumption: Health concerns played a part but price was most important.' *California Agriculture*, May-June 1983.

15. 'McDonald's | Our Story | Marketing | McDonald's Themes.' McDonald's Canada website. Retrieved 21 March 2011 from http://www.mcdonalds.ca/en/aboutus/marketing_themes.aspx

16. 'Burger King Advertising.' *Wikipedia.* Retrieved 21 March 2011 from http://en.wikipedia.org/wiki/Burger_King_advertising

17. 'How Has Meat Consumption Changed Over Time?' *Wisegeek.* Retrieved 20 March 2011 from http://www.wisegeek.com/how-has-meat-consumption-changed-over-time.htm

18. Matthews, Christopher. 2006. 'Livestock a major threat to environment.' Food and Agriculture Organisation of the United Nations. Retrieved 20 March 2011 from http://www.fao.org/newsroom/en/news/2006/1000448/index.html

19. Ibid.

20. 'Burger King.' 2010. *Wikipedia.* Retrieved 20 March 2011 from http://en.wikipedia.org/wiki/Burger_King

21. 'List of countries by population.' *Wikipedia.* Retrieved 20 March 2011 from http://en.wikipedia.org/wiki/List_of_countries_by_population

22. Matthews, op. cit.

23. 'McDonald's Announces Commitment to Certified Sustainable Sources; Releases 2010 Corporate Responsibility Report.' op. cit.

24. Raloff, Janet. 2002. 'Hormones: Here's the Beef: environmental concerns reemerge over steroids given to livestock.' *Science News,* Vol. 161, #1, January 5, 2002, p10.

25. Hallberg, Milton C. 2003. 'Historical Perspective on Adjustment in the Food and Agriculture Sector.' Penn State University, October 2003. Cited on the Sustainable Table website. Retrieved 4 September 2011 from http://www.sustainabletable.org/issues/hormones/

26. Kastel, Mark. 1995. 'Down on the Farm: The Real BGH Story Animal Health Problems, Financial Troubles.' Retrieved 4 September 2011 from http://www.mindfully.org/GE/Down-On-The-Farm-BGH1995.htm

27. *Diet, Nutrition and the Prevention of Chronic Diseases: Report of a Joint WHO/FAO Expert Consultation.* WHO Technical Report Series, #916. Part 3: 'Global and regional food consumption patterns and trends.' Retrieved 20 March 2011 from http://www.fao.org/docrep/005/ac911e/ac911e05.htm

28. 'Current Worldwide Annual Meat Consumption per capita.' 2010. ChartsBin website. Retrieved 20 March 2011 from http://chartsbin.com/view/bhy.

29. 'McDonald's (UK) Nutrition Counter.' Retrieved 21 March 2011 from http://www.mcdonalds.co.uk/food/nutrition/nutrition-counter.mcd

30. 'Calories in Medium Serving of McDonald's French Fries.' Third Age website. Retrieved 4 September 2011 from http://www.thirdage.com/nc/fp/21238-11554/medium-serving-mcdonalds-french-fr

31. 'Coca Cola.' Nutrition Connection website. Retrieved 4 September 2011 from http://productnutrition.thecoca-colacompany.com/products/coca-cola?packagingId=6971

32. Dalberg-Acton, Lord John. (Also known as John Emerich Edward Dalberg-Acton). 1949. *Essays on Freedom and Power*. Boston: Beacon Press, p364. Originally written in April 1887 in a letter to scholar and ecclesiastic Mandell Creighton.

PART TWO: THE 7 KEY RELATIONSHIPS
SOME WORDS ON THE NATURE OF RELATIONSHIPS

1. Donne, John. 2010. *Devotions Upon Emergent Occasions*. 'Meditation XVII,' p152. Kessinger Publishing, LLC. Originally published in 1624.

KEY RELATIONSHIP #1: OUR RELATIONSHIP WITH SELF

1. De Saint-Exupéry, Antoine. 2002 (first published in 1943). *The Little Prince*. Katherine Woods, translator. London: Egmont Books, Ltd., p65. Spoken by the Fox to the Little Prince.

2. Telander, Rick. 1990. 'Your Sneakers or Your Life.' *Sports Illustrated,* cover story. Retrieved 20 March 2011 from http://chucksconnection.com/articles/your-sneakers-or-your-life.html

3. Ibid.

KEY RELATIONSHIP #2: OUR RELATIONSHIP WITH SOURCE

1. Macy, Joanna R. and Brown, Molly Young. 1998. *Coming Back to Life: Practices to Reconnect Our Lives, Our World*. British Columbia, Canada: New Society Publishers, p21.

2. 'Source.' *The Free Dictionary*. Retrieved 24 April 2011 from http://www.thefreedictionary.com/source

3. 'Source.' *Merriam-Webster Online*. Retrieved 24 April 2011 from http://www.merriam-webster.com/dictionary/source

4. McPhaul, John. 2005. 'Rising Oil Prices: how high are they going and what are the options?' Puerto Rico Herald website, *Caribbean Business,* May 13, 2005. Retrieved 24 April 2011 from http://www.puertorico-herald.org/issues2/2005/vol09n19/CBRisingOil.html

5. 'Passenger vehicles in the United States.' 2010. *Wikipedia,* April 6, 2011 revision. Retrieved 24 April 2011 from http://en.wikipedia.org/wiki/Passenger_vehicles_in_the_United_States

6. Blanco, Sebastian. 2010. 'Report: Number of cars in the U.S. dropped by four million in 2009 - is America's love affair ending?' Retrieved 24 April

2011 from http://green.autoblog.com/2010/01/04/report-number-of-cars-in-the-u-s-dropped-by-four-million-in-20/

7. 'Motor Industry Facts 2010.' 2010. SMMT Automotive Information Services. PDF file downloaded 24 April 2011 from http://www.smmt.co.uk/reports-publications/industry-data/

8. 'Hybrid electric vehicles.' 2010. *Wikipedia*, April 21, 2011 revision. Retrieved 24 April 2011 from http://en.wikipedia.org/wiki/Hybrid_electric_vehicle#U.S._market

9. On this subject, see Leonard, Annie. 2010. *The Story of Stuff: how our obsession with stuff is trashing the planet, our communities, our health— and a vision for change.* New York: Free Press (a division of Simon and Schuster, Inc), 'Chapter 5: 'Disposal'.

KEY RELATIONSHIP #3: OUR RELATIONSHIP WITH OTHERS

1. Tennyson, Alfred Lord. 2000. Poem 'Ulysses' in *Alfred Tennyson*. Oxford University Press, US, p80, lines 18-21. Originally published in 1842.

KEY RELATIONSHIP #4: OUR RELATIONSHIP WITH OUR BUSINESSES

1. This quote, originally spoken in the 14th Century, has been translated in many different ways, all giving a slightly different meaning. This rendition of the line was spoken by The Bishop of London during his sermon at the Royal Wedding of Prince William and Catherine Middleton at Westminster Abbey on 29 April 2011.

2. Gerber, Michael. 1994. *The E-Myth Revisited: why most small businesses don't work and what to do about it.* HarperCollins, 3rd revised edition.

3. 'The Walt Disney Company.' 2011. *Wikipedia.* May 1, 2011 edit. Retrieved 1 May 2011 from http://en.wikipedia.org/wiki/The_Walt_Disney_Company

KEY RELATIONSHIP #5: OUR RELATIONSHIP WITH OUR AUDIENCE

1. Miller, Arthur. 1958. *Collected Plays.* 'Introduction,' Sections 2 and 7. Retrieved 7 May 2011 from http://en.wikiquote.org/wiki/Arthur_Miller

2. Oscar Wilde. (n.d.). *Great-Quotes.com.* Retrieved 7 May 2011 from http://www.great-quotes.com/quote/1368451

3. Ries, Al and Trout, Jack. 2005. *Marketing Warfare: 20th Anniversary Edition; Authors annotated edition.* McGraw-Hill Professional. Originally published in 1986.

. Ibid., page vi

5. Kokernak, Michael. 2009. 'Deconstructing the Commercial Pod.' Retrieved 8 May 2011 from http://www.acrossplatforms.com/by-media-type/measurement-is-deconstructing-the-commercial-pod

6. Lapointe, Joe. 2011. 'Eminem, Chrysler Hit All Cylinders for Motor City.' February 7, 2011. Aol News website. Retrieved 8 May 2011 from http://www.aolnews.com/2011/02/07/eminem-chrysler-hit-on-all-cylinders-for-motor-city/

KEY RELATIONSHIP #6: OUR RELATIONSHIP WITH MONEY

1. Thoreau, Henry David. 2004. *Walden and Other Writings.* Edited and with an introduction by Joseph Wood Krutch. New York: Bantam Dell, p117. *Walden* first published in 1854.

2. Ibid., p73.

3. 'Walden.' 2011. *Wikipedia,* March 29, 2011 edit. Retrieved 1 April 2011 from http://en.wikipedia.org/wiki/Walden

4. More, Sir Thomas. 2003. *Utopia.* London: Penguin Classics, p67. Translation by Paul Turner originally published in 1965. Written in Latin, *Utopia* was originally published in 1516.

KEY RELATIONSHIP #7: OUR RELATIONSHIP WITH MARKETING

1. Ries and Trout, op. cit., p9.

2. Ibid., page vi

PART THREE: THE 7 DEADLY SINS OF MARKETING
SOME THOUGHTS ON THE USE OF THE WORD 'SIN'

1. Voltaire. 1764. *Dictionnaire Philosophique.* Retrieved 28 December 2010 from http://en.wikipedia.org/wiki/Dictionnaire_philosophique

2. Gladwell, Malcolm. 2006. *Blink: The Power of Thinking Without Thinking.* London: Penguin Books.

DEADLY SIN #1: DISCONNECTION

1. Covey, Stephen R. 1991. Covey cites this quote from Gandhi his book *Principle Centered Leadership.* London: Simon and Schuster, p323.

2. 'Arun Manilal Gandhi'. *Wikipedia.* August 11, 2011 version. Retrieved 9 September 2011 from http://en.wikipedia.org/wiki/Arun_Gandhi. Arun lived with his grandfather for the last two years of the grandfather's life.

3. Gilbert, Steven W. 1999. 'Gandhi's Seven Blunders of the World that Lead to Violence...Plus 6.' The TLT Group, a non-profit organisation. Revised May 2008. Retrieved 9 September 2011 from http://www.tltgroup.org/GandhisList.htm

4. 'Mohandas Gandhi's "Seven Blunders of the World".' 1995. *The Christian Science Monitor,* February 1, 1995. No author or source is cited, but as the CSM seems to have interviewed Mahatma Gandhi's grandson Arun Gandhi on a number of occasions, we might assume he provided this information directly to them, but this is not confirmed on their website. Retrieved 20 December 2010 from http://www.csmonitor.com/1995/0201/01142.html

5. Gilbert, op. cit.

6. Covey, op. cit., 'Chapter 7: Seven Deadly Sins,' pp87-93. Covey refers to these as Gandhi's 'Seven Deadly Sins' and gives extensive commentary on them in this chapter. I personally prefer calling them the 'Seven Blunders of the World' as I think it's pretty witty. He also cites 'sin' number 6 as 'religion without sacrifice' rather than 'worship without sacrifice.'

7. This quote, often attributed to both Mahatma Gandhi and Mother Teresa, may have been first spoken by St. Elizabeth Ann Seton (1774-1821) Foundress of the Sisters of Charity, USA, in a speech given in the Diocese of Baltimore (retrieved 9 September 2011 from http://www.quotationspage.com/quote/33588.html). Although they do not claim Gandhi said this, this quote is cited on the Gandhi Institute website in a sidebar note as an explanation for what real 'non-violence' is (retrieved 9 September 2011 from http://gandhiinstitute.org), and has also been adopted as a slogan by many ecological/environmental groups.

8. Covey, op. cit., p90.

9. 'List of countries by carbon dioxide emissions.' 2011. *Wikipedia.* August 26, 2011 version. These statistics are from 2008 and do not include data of other greenhouse gasses. Retrieved 9 September 2011 from http://en.wikipedia.org/wiki/List_of_countries_by_carbon_dioxide_emissions

10. G., Michael. 2001. 'Rainforest Biomes.' Retrieved 9 September 2011 from http://www.blueplanetbiomes.org/rainforest.htm

11. 'Rainforest Facts.' 1996. *Raintree Nutrition.* Retrieved 9 September 2011 from http://www.rain-tree.com/facts.htm

12. Taylor, Leslie. 2004. *The Healing Power of Rainforest Herbs.* Garden City, NY: Square One Publishers, Inc.

13. Shah, Anup. 2011. 'World Military Spending.' May 2, 2011 version. Global Issues website. Retrieved 9 September 2011 from http://www.globalissues.org/article/75/world-military-spending

14. Boyles, Salynn. 2008. 'Kids' Cereals: Some Are 50% Sugar. Consumer Reports Rates Nutritional Winners and Losers.' Reviewed by Elizabeth Klodas, MD, FACC. WebMD Health News, October 1, 2008. Retrieved 28 December 2010 from http://www.webmd.com/food-recipes/news/20081001/kids-cereals-some-are-50-percent-sugar

15. The Gandhi Institute website. Sidebar note. Retrieved 9 September 2011 from http://gandhiinstitute.org.

DEADLY SIN #2: PERSUASION

1. Wakeman, Frederic. 1946. *The Hucksters.* New York: Rinehardt & Co., p24. Cited in Vance Packard's book *The Hidden Persuaders* (see below).

2. Packard, Vance. 2007. *The Hidden Persuaders.* Brooklyn, NY: Ig Publishing. Reissue with an introduction by Mark Crispin Miller. Originally published in 1957 by Pocket Books, a division of Simon and Schuster, Inc., p234.

3. Ibid., pp231-232.

4. 'What is the average conversion rate for a good landing page?' 2010. *Warrior Forum.* March 29, 2010. Retrieved 11 September 2011 from http://www.warriorforum.com/main-internet-marketing-discussion-forum/195577-what-average-conversion-rate-good-landing-page.html

DEADLY SIN #3: INVASION

1. Film: *Invasion of the Body Snatchers.* 1956. Directed by Don Siegel. Written by Daniel Mainwaring. Based on the novel *The Body Snatchers* by Jack Finney (serialized in *Colliers Magazine* in 1954). This line was spoken by the character Dr. Miles Bennell. Retrieved 11 September 2011 from http://en.wikiquote.org/wiki/Invasion_of_the_Body_Snatchers_(1956_film)

2. Godin, Seth. 2007. *Permission Marketing.* London: Pocket Books, an imprint of Simon and Schuster, UK Ltd, pp26-27.

DEADLY SIN #4: DISTRACTION

1. Palahniuk, Chuck. *Lullaby.* 2003. London: Vintage Books, pp18-19.

2. Compare the Meerkat Website. Retrieved 13 September 2011 from http://comparethemeerkat.com and http://meerkat.comparethemarket.com/home

3. According to Frito Lay (the current owners of Cracker Jack) the ingredients in the original Cracker Jack recipe were (in descending order from highest percentage to lowest) sugar, corn syrup, popcorn, peanuts, molasses, salt, corn and/or soybean oil and soy lecithin. Retrieved 14

September 2011 from http://www.fritolay.com/our-snacks/cracker-jack-original.html

4. 'McDonald's Pirates of the Caribbean Toys.' 2006. Raving Toy Mania – The Latest News and Pictures for the World of Toys. Retrieved 14 September 2011 from http://www.toymania.com/news/messages/8378.shtml

5. Pidd, Helen. 2007. *We Are Coming for Your Children.* Retrieved 28 December from 2010 http://www.guardian.co.uk/media/2007/jul/31/newmedia.advertising

DEADLY SIN #5: DECEPTION

1. Duggan, Francis. Poem: 'One Lie Leads to Another Lie.' Retrieved 2 January 2011 from http://www.poemhunter.com/poem/one-lie-leads-to-another-lie/

2. Wason, Peter Cathcart and Johnson-Laird, Philip N, 1972. *Psychology of Reasoning: Structure and Content.* Harvard University Press, Cambridge, Mass.

3. 'Food Label Fibs.' Parents Jury website. Part of *The Food Commission* (UK) Ltd, a not-for-profit company which campaigns for healthier, safer, sustainable food in the UK. Retrieved 29 December 2010 from http://www.foodcomm.org.uk/parentsjury/Food_label_fibs.htm

4. Hull, Janet Starr. 2002. 'Dangers of Aspartame Poisoning.' Retrieved 29 December 2010 from http://www.sweetpoison.com/aspartame-information.html

5. 'Food Label Fibs,' op. cit.

6. 'BBC encourages children to eat junk food!' 2003. Parents Jury website. Retrieved 29 December 2010 from http://www.foodcomm.org.uk/parentsjury/tweenies_0603.htm

7. Ibid.

8. Tryhorn, Chris. 2004. 'Tweenies swept up by Basil Brush.' *The Guardian.* 13 September 2004. Retrieved 28 December 2010 from http://www.guardian.co.uk/media/2004/sep/13/citynews.broadcasting1

9. Jones, Jenny. 2010. 'The battle for good food at the 2012 Olympics.' *Food Magazine.* Issue 87. Dec/Feb 2010. *The Food Commission* (UK) Ltd. Online version. Retrieved 28 December 2010 from http://www.foodmagazine.org.uk/magazines/

10. 'How it Works.' Streetcar website. Retrieved 17 September 2011 from http://www.streetcar.co.uk/How_it_works/

11. Havergal, Chris. 2011. 'Car club scheme moves up a gear.' *Cambridge News.* 29 July 2011. Retrieved 10 August 2011 from http://www.cambridge-news.co.uk/Home/Car-club-scheme-moves-up-a-gear-29072011.htm

12. 'Making Cash While Going Green.' 2011. Real Radio Scotland. Retrieved 10 August 2011 from http://www.realradio-scotland.co.uk/news-sport/making-cash-while-going-green/vcijj1ux/

13. Havergal, op. cit., comments by readers.

14. 'Making Cash While Going Green,' op. cit.

15. 'Locations.' Streetcar website. Retrieved 21 August 2011 from http://streetcar.co.uk/locations

16. 'Cars and Vans.' Streetcar website. Cars offered by Streetcar according to their website on 31 July 2011 were Volkswagen Polo, Golf, Touran and Transporter, and BMW 1-Series and 3-Series. While the BMWs are promoted as being low-emission and high miles per gallon, all these cars use either unleaded or diesel fuel. Retrieved 31 July 2011 from http://www.streetcar.co.uk/cars_and_vans/

17. Arnold, Chris. 2009. *Ethical Marketing and the New Consumer.* Chichester, UK: John Wiley and Sons, Ltd.

18. 'Dove Evolution.' 2006. Dove website. Retrieved 28 December 2010 from http://www.dove.co.uk/cfrb/videos/videoplayer.html#v=http://edge.dov e.com/US_en/10229/global/video/cfrb/evolution.flv. Also available on YouTube at http://www.youtube.com/watch?v=iYhCn0jf46U

19. 'Dove Self Esteem Fund.' Dove website. Retrieved 28 December 2010 from http://www.dove.co.uk/cfrb/self-esteem-fund/about.html

20. 'How brain processes what eyes see'. 2009. *Thai India News*, June 3, 2009. Quote from that article: 'Scientists have found that although visual input obtained during eye movements is being processed by the brain, but it is blocked from awareness.' Retrieved 28 December 2010 from http://www.thaindian.com/newsportal/health/how-brain-processes-what-eyes-see_100200248.html

21. University of Exeter School of Psychology. 2009. *The Psychology of Scams: Provoking and Committing Errors of Judgement.* Extensive report prepared for the Office of Fair Trading, May 2009. The researchers concluded: 'Scams cause psychological as well as financial harm to victims. Victims not only suffer a financial loss but also a loss of self-

esteem because they blame themselves for having been so "stupid" to fall for the scam. Some of the victims we interviewed appeared to have been seriously damaged by their experience' (p8). They went on further to say, 'it was striking how some scam victims kept their decision to respond private and avoided speaking about it with family members or friends' (p137). Retrieved 28 December 2010 from http://www.oft.gov.uk/shared_oft/reports/consumer_protection/oft1070.pdf

DEADLY SIN #6: SCARCITY

1. Jagger, Mick and Richards, Keith. 1969. 'You Can't Always Get What You Want.' Song from the album *Let It Bleed.* Released 5 December 1969 on Decca Records. Produced by Jimmy Miller.

2. Many sources say Audrey Hepburn died of colon cancer, while others say it was appendiceal cancer, which is a form of cancer of the lower GI tract, as is colon cancer. The words 'inoperable colon cancer' are from her official website, which has been maintained by her family members to continue her charitable legacy. Retrieved 17 September 2011 from http://www.audreyhepburn.com/menu/index.php?idMenu=55&pg=1

3. 'Audrey Hepburn's Anorexia.' Adapted from the book *Audrey Hepburn: An Intimate Portrait* by Diana Maychick, 1996, Citadel Press. Retrieved 2 January 2011 from http://www.elegantwoman.org/audrey-hepburn-anorexia.html

4. Govind, P. 2010. *Malnutrition Leading to Cancer by Some Environmental Hazards.* Retrieved 2 January 2010 from http://ijrap.net/issue-two/287-291.pdf

5. Helen Kollias. 2009. 'Epigenetics: Feast, Famine, and Fatness.' Retrieved 31 December 2010 from http://www.precisionnutrition.com/epigenetics-feast-famine-and-fatness

6. 'Scarcity.' 2010. *Wikipedia,* December 3, 2010 version. Retrieved 31 December 2010 from http://en.wikipedia.org/wiki/Scarcity

7. Tucker, Irvin B. 2009. 'Macroeconomics for Today.' Ohio: South-Western Cengage Learning. Sixth Edition, p3. Retrieved 31 December 2010 from http://books.google.co.uk/books?id=3bPkVpGnv_kC&lpg

8. 'Economics: The Core Issues.' University of Minnesota. This article is no longer available online. Retrieved 31 December 2010 from http://docs.google.com/viewer?a=v&q=cache:h1AWlLlpv8oJ:www.d.umn.edu/~btadesse/spring/econ1023/Summer2006/Lect-Chap01.ppt

9. Batt, H. William, Ph.D. 2003. 'The Compatibility of Georgist Economics and Ecological Economics.' Presentation at the United States Society for

Ecological Economics, May 22-24, 2003, Saratoga Springs, New York. Revision of an earlier paper from April 2000. Retrieved 18 September 2011 from http://www.wealthandwant.com/docs/Batt_GEE.html

10. 'The Puzzling Failure of Economics.' 1997. *The Economist*, August 25, 1997, Cover article and Editorial.

11. Pfaff, William. 1996. 'Seeking a Broader Vision of Economic Society.' *International Herald Tribune*, Saturday/Sunday, February 3-4, 1996.

12. Batt, op. cit. Massasoit (c.1581-1661) was the Leader of the Wampanoag and Pokanoket tribes. He asked this question when speaking with the Plymouth colonists whom he had befriended in the 1620s.

13. Martin (no last name given). 'Using Scarcity in Persuasion.' Erupting Mind Self-Improvement Tips. Retrieved 2 January 2010 from http://www.eruptingmind.com/using-scarcity-in-persuasion/

14. 'Economics: The Core Issues,' op. cit.

15. Leonard, Annie. Video: 'The Story of Bottled Water'. Part of The Story of Stuff Project. Retrieved 10 January 2011 from http://storyofstuff.org/bottledwater/

16. 'Hormone-Mimics in Plastic Water Bottles Act as Functional Estrogens.' *Science Daily*, March 27, 2009. Retrieved 10 January 2011 from http://www.sciencedaily.com/releases/2009/03/090326100714.htm

17. Leonard, Annie. 2010. *The Story of Stuff*, op. cit., p167.

18. Schor, Juliet B. 1999. *The Overspent American: Why We Want What We Don't Need*. New York: Harper Perennial, p81.

19. 'False shortage.' 2009. *Wikipedia*. April 11, 2009 version. Retrieved 2 January 2010 from http://en.wikipedia.org/wiki/False_shortage

20. Quelch, John. 2007. 'How to Profit from Scarcity'. *Harvard Business Review*. August 31, 2007. Retrieved 2 January 2010 from http://blogs.hbr.org/quelch/2007/08/how_to_profit_from_scarcity_1.html

21. Casima, Ryan. November 13, 2010. 'How to Reset an Epson DX4400.' Retrieved 12 February 2011 from http://www.ehow.co.uk/how_7494180_reset-epson-dx4400.html

22. Melick, Justin. December 2, 2010. 'How to Replace an Ink Pad on an Epson.' Retrieved 12 February 2011 from http://www.ehow.co.uk/how_7588289_replace-ink-pad-epson.html

23. White, Micah M. 2008. 'Consumer Society is Made to Break.' *Adbusters*, 20 October 2008. Retrieved 10 January 2011 from http://www.adbusters.org/category/tags/obsolescence

24. Leonard, Annie. 2009. Video: 'The Story of Stuff.' Retrieved 10 January 2011 from http://youtu.be/9GorqroigqM

25. Slade, Giles. 2006. *Made to Break: Technology and Obsolescence in America*. Cambridge, Massachusetts: Harvard University Press. 'Chapter 3: Hard Times', pp57-81.

26. Leonard, Annie. 2009. Video: 'The Story of Stuff,' op. cit.

27. Leonard, Annie. 2010. Video: 'The Story of Electronics: why "designed for the dump" is toxic for people and the planet.' Retrieved 10 January 2010 from http://youtu.be/sW_7i6T_H78

28. Ibid.

DEADLY SIN #7: COMPETITION

1. *The Highlander*. 1986. Directed by Russell Mulcahy. Distributed by 20th Century Fox.

2. Kohn, Alfie. 1986. *No Contest: The Case Against Competition - Why We Lose in Our Race to Win*. New York: Houghton Mifflin Company.

3. Ibid., p55.

4. Ibid., p54.

5. Ibid., p56.

6. Maurer, Robert, Ph.D., 2004. *One Small Step Can Change Your Life, The Kaizen Way*. Hardcover edition. Workman Publishing, p24.

7. Ghent, William James. 2010. *Our Benevolent Feudalism*. Originally published in 1902. Reprinted by Kessinger Publishing LLC, p29.

8. Spencer, Herbert. *The Principles of Biology (Volume 1)*. Originally published in 1864 by Williams and Norgate, London. Discussed throughout 'Part III: The Evolution of Life.'

9. 'Andrew Carnegie Quotes.' Freely quoted on the web, I have not been able to find the origin of this quote. Retrieved 20 January 2010 from http://www.brainyquote.com/quotes/authors/a/andrew_carnegie.html

10. Williams, Christopher A. 'Chemical Fertilizers Linked to Brain Cancer.' Retrieved 19 February 2011 from http://ezinearticles.com/?Chemical-Fertilizers-Linked-to-Brain-Cancer&id=1276781

11. Zandjani F, Høgsaet B, Andersen A, Langård S. 1994. 'Incidence of cancer among nitrate fertilizer workers.' Retrieved 19 February 2011 from http://www.ncbi.nlm.nih.gov/pubmed/7814099

12. Kristensen, P., Andersen, A., Irgens, L. M., et al. 1996. 'Testicular cancer and parental use of fertilizers in agriculture.' Originally published in *Cancer Epidemiology, Biomarkers & Prevention,* 1996; 5:3-9. Published online January 1, 1996. Retrieved 19 February 2011 from http://cebp.aacrjournals.org/content/5/1/3.full.pdf

13. Strauss, William and Howe, Neil. 1991. *Generations: The History of America's Future, 1584-2069.* New York: Quill (an imprint of William Morrow).

14. Drew, Michael. 2010. Video: 'Pendulum.' TEDxTalks, Calgary, Canada. Retrieved 12 October 2010 from http://www.youtube.com/watch?v=04c8e_W8jmg

15. Qualman, Erik. 2010. Video: 'Social Media Revolution' (also shown in the Michael Drew video above). Retrieved 19 February 2011 from http://www.youtube.com/watch?v=sIFYPQjYhv8

16. Peck, M. Scott. 1990. *The Different Drum: Community Making and Peace.* Originally published 1987 by Simon & Shuster. New edition published 19 July 1990. London: Arrow Books, an imprint of Random House.

PART FOUR: THE 7 GRACES OF MARKETING
SOME THOUGHTS ON THE USE OF THE WORD 'GRACE'

1. Longfellow, Henry Wadsworth. 1855. Poem: 'The Building of the Ship,' line 7. *The Literature Network.* Retrieved 25 May 2011 from http://www.online-literature.com/henry_longfellow/3797/

2. Bosworth, J. 2010. 'Syn.' *An Anglo-Saxon Dictionary Online.* T. N. Toller & Others, Eds. Retrieved 30 May 2011 from http://www.bosworthtoller.com/030025

3. 'Grace.' *Etymology Online.* Retrieved 18 February 2011 from http://www.etymonline.com/index.php?term=grace

4. 'The Graces (Charities).' Purple Hell website. Retrieved 30 May 2011 from http://www.purplehell.com/riddletools/g-cha.htm

GRACE #1: CONNECTION

1. HRH The Prince of Wales, op. cit., p304.

2. Saint-Exupéry, Antoine. 2000. *Flight to Arras.* Penguin Classics; New Ed edition (25 May 2000), p60. First published in French in 1942.

3. Cherry, Kendra. 'The Five Levels of Maslow's Hierarchy of Needs.' About.com website. Retrieved 14 July 2011 from http://psychology.about.com/od/theoriesofpersonality/a/hierarchyneeds.htm

4. 'Nuclear Family.' *Wikipedia*. June 29, 2011 version. Retrieved 16 July 2011 from http://en.wikipedia.org/wiki/Nuclear_family

5. Skoknick, Arlene. 1995. 'Nuclear Families.' Retrieved 16 July 2011 from http://family.jrank.org/pages/1222/Nuclear-Families.html

6. Godin, Seth. 2008. *Tribes*. London: Piatkus Books, p21.

GRACE #2: INSPIRATION

1. 'Ralph Waldo Emerson.' *1-Famous-Quotes.com*. Retrieved 18 July 2011 from http://www.1-famous-quotes.com/quote/2151

2. Zambrini, Lucia. 'Etymology of Inspiration.' Retrieved 18 July 2011: http://humanityquest.com/themes/inspiration/Etymology/

3. 'Spirit.' *Online Etymology Dictionary*. Retrieved 18 July 2011 from http://www.etymonline.com/index.php?term=spirit

4. Serafinn, Lynn. 2009. *The Garden of the Soul: lessons from four flowers that unearth the Self*. Bedfordshire, England: Bright Pen Books, p3.

GRACE #3: INVITATION

1. Howitt, Mary. 1829. Poem: *The Spider and the Fly*. Retrieved 23 July 2011 from http://poetry-online.org/howitt_the_spider_and_the_fly_funny.htm

2. '1870s-1940s Telephone.' *Elon University School of Communications*. 'Imagining the Internet: a history and forecast' website. Retrieved 23 July 2011 from http://elon.edu/e-web/predictions/150/1870.xhtml.

3. 'World Population Estimates.' *Wikipedia*. Statistics from United Nations Department of Economic and Social Affairs. Retrieved 23 July 2011 from http://en.m.wikipedia.org/wiki/World_population_estimates

4. Sathishkumar. 2010. 'Facebook History and Statistics in a Nice Timeline.' August 1, 2010. *TechieMania*. Retrieved 23 July 2011 from http://www.techiemania.com/facebook-history-and-statistics-in-a-nice-timeline.html

5. 'World Population Estimates,' op. cit.

6. Shiels, Maggie. 2011. 'Twitter co-founder Jack Dorsey rejoins company.' *BBC News*, 28 March 2011. Retrieved 23 July 2011 from http://www.bbc.co.uk/news/business-12889048

7. 'Twitter.' 2011. *Wikipedia*, June 29, 2011 version. Retrieved 23 July 2011 from http://en.wikipedia.org/wiki/Twitter

GRACE #4: DIRECTNESS

1. Ludacris. 2006. 'Tell it Like it Is' from the album *Release Therapy*. DTP/Def Jam Records. Retrieved 10 August 2011 from http://www.elyrics.net/read/l/ludacris-lyrics/tell-it-like-it-is-lyrics.html

GRACE #5: TRANSPARENCY

1. 'Mark Zuckerberg.' *Brainy Quote*. Zuckerberg is the Founder of Facebook. Retrieved 15 August 2011 from http://www.brainyquote.com/quotes/authors/m/mark_zuckerberg.html

2. 'Transparency.' *Etymology Online*. Retrieved 18 August 2011 from http://www.etymonline.com/index.php?term=transparent

3. This is a composite translation of many different versions of the verse from Corinthians 13:12. Some translate the word 'glass' as 'mirror.' Others translate the word 'later' as 'then.' I chose these particular words for their rhythm and the way they resonated with me personally.

4. Chaitanya Mahaprabhu. ca. 1520. *Sri Siksastakam*. Verse 1. This translation is in numerous sources, and is also a common translation I heard in many lectures when I travelled through India.

5. 'Cetas.' *Dictionary for Spoken Sanskrit*. Retrieved 20 August 2011 from http://spokensanskrit.de/index.php?tinput=ceTa&script=&direction=SE&link=y

6. Spanish mystic San Juan de la Cruz (Saint John of the Cross) lived from 1542-1591. He wrote the evocative eight-stanza poem 'La noche oscura del alma' ('The Dark Night of the Soul') in 1587 while imprisoned, and wrote an extensive commentary on it after his escape. A complete translation is available at http://www.karmel.at/ics/john/dn.html, copyright 1991 ICS publications.

7. *Katha Upanishad*. Canto 1, Chapter 2, Verse 18, line 1.

GRACE #6: ABUNDANCE

1. Culhane, Anne-Marie and Watts, Stephen. 2009. *The Abundance Handbook: A guide to Urban Fruit Harvesting*. Grow Sheffield, p5. Retrieved 21 August 2011 from http://www.growsheffield.com/images/abundbkview.pdf

2. Orwell, George. 1937. *The Road to Wigan Pier*. Victor Gollancz Ltd., Chapter 7, p72.

3. 'Sheffield.' *Wikipedia*. August 24, 2011 version. Retrieved 25 August 2011 from http://en.wikipedia.org/wiki/Sheffield

4. 'Threads.' *Wikipedia.* August 24, 2011 version. Retrieved 25 August 2011 from http://en.wikipedia.org/wiki/Threads

5. West, Derek. 2007. 'Sheffield Geography.' *Sheffield City Council* website. 17 December 2007 version. Retrieved 25 August 2011 from http://www.sheffield.gov.uk/your-city-council/sheffield-facts-figures/sheffield-profile/geography

6. 'Abundance.' *Grow Sheffield* website. Retrieved 23 August 2011 from http://www.growsheffield.com/pages/groShefAbund.html

7. Ibid.

8. 'New Thought.' *Wikipedia.* August 16, 2011 version. Retrieved 24 August 2011 from http://en.wikipedia.org/wiki/New_Thought

9. Resser, Jeffrey. 2006. 'The Secret of Success.' *Time Magazine,* Thursday, December 28, 2006. Retrieved 24 August 2011 from http://www.time.com/time/arts/article/0,8599,1573136,00.html

10. Silverman, Jacob. 2009. 'How tall can a tree grow?' *How Stuff Works,* February 23, 2009. Retrieved 25 August 2011 from http://science.howstuffworks.com/environmental/life/botany/tree-grow.htm

11. 'How Much Oil Have We Used?' 2009. *PhysOrg.com.* May 7, 2009. Retrieved 27 August 2011 from http://www.physorg.com/news160906147.html

12. 'List of countries by carbon dioxide emissions,' op. cit.

13. Zeller, Tom Jr. 2010. 'A Program to Certify Electronic Waste Recycling Rivals an Industry-U.S. Plan.' *The New York Times,* April 15, 2010. Retrieved 27 August 2011 from http://www.nytimes.com/2010/04/15/business/energy-environment/15ewaste.html

14. Leonard, Annie. 2010. *The Story of Stuff,* op. cit. Discussed in detail in 'Chapter 5: Disposal.'

15. Zeller, op. cit.

16. Mitchell, Joni. 1970. Song: 'Woodstock' from the album *Ladies of the Canyon,* Reprise Records. Copyright Siquomb publishing. Retrieved 25 September 2011 from http://jonimitchell.com/music/song.cfm?id=75

RACE #7: COLLABORATION

Satoro, Ryunosuke. Satoro was a Japanese poet. This quote appears on more than 50 websites, and is cited in at least six books. No one cites

the original source. Retrieved 28 August 2011 from
http://www.ryunosukesatoro.org/

2. 'The Beatles' First Ed Sullivan Show.' 2009. *The Beatles Bible* website.
    Retrieved 28 August 2011 from
    http://www.beatlesbible.com/1964/02/09/the-beatles-first-ed-sullivan-
    show/

3. 'Population Statistics > Population (1964) by Country.' *CIA World
    Factbooks* (2003-2011). The population of the United States was
    estimated to be around 191,889,000 in 1964. Retrieved 28 August 2011
    from http://www.nationmaster.com/graph/peo_pop-people-
    population&date=1964

4. 'ORSC™ Organization and Relationship Systems Coaching.' *CRR Global*
    website (Center for Right Relationships). CRR has a trademarked the
    term 'The Third Entity™ as it pertains to coaching. Retrieved 28 August
    2011 from http://centerforrightrelationships.com/organization-
    relationship-systems-coaching.html

5. Ibid.

6. Godin, Seth, *Permission Marketing,* op. cit., page xxviii.

7. 'Politeness is the poison of collaboration.' *BrainyQuote* website. Retrieved
    28 August 2011 from
    http://www.brainyquote.com/quotes/quotes/e/edwinland193299.html

8. Peck, op. cit. 'Chapter V: Stages of Community-Making.'

9. Gladwell, Malcolm. 2009. *Outliers.* London: Penguin Books, Ltd. 'Chapter
    7: The Ethnic Theory of Plane Crashes.' Gladwell discusses how a string
    of fatal crashes on Korean Air was the result of co-pilots not speaking in
    the face of disaster, for fear of being disrespectful to their Captain.

EPILOGUE: CAN MARKETING HEAL THE WORLD?

1. Lennon, John. 1971. Song: 'Imagine' from the album *Imagine.* Apple
    Records. Lyrics retrieved 25 September 2011 from
    http://www.lyrics007.com/John%20Lennon%20Lyrics/Imagine%20Lyri
    cs.html

ABOUT THE AUTHOR

Lynn Serafinn, MAED, CPCC is a certified, award-winning coach and teacher, marketer, radio host, speaker and bestselling author. Born in Brooklyn, NY, in 1955, Lynn was raised on Long Island. A poet, writer and musician since early childhood, Lynn studied at the New England Conservatory of Music in Boston from 1973-76, where she also began to cultivate a love for World Music and Eastern philosophy. She later completed her Bachelors in Music at the University of Texas at Austin, where she went on to do post-graduate work in Ethnomusicology, Social Anthropology and Asian languages (Hindi, Sanskrit, Bengali). In both 1980 and 1981, she was awarded the National Defence Foreign Language Fellowship, which allowed her to study language, music and spirituality in Calcutta for nearly a year, where she first met her Indian spiritual teacher. Over the next two decades, she studied ancient Sanskrit scriptures almost daily and returned to India many times. From 1997-2001, she anonymously transcribed, translated and edited many of her teacher's works for a major New Age publisher.

Lynn's career as a professional musician spanned more than three decades, and she has been everything from a symphony violinist and opera singer, to a member of world fusion, synth pop and electronic dance bands, to a 'chill out' radio DJ. Throughout the 1990s, she jointly ran an independent record label and electronic recording studio in Phoenix, Arizona, during which time she managed the marketing, distribution and graphic design. She also co-wrote and produced over 100 tracks including a number-1 trance hit under the artist name 'Overlords of the UFO' in 1994.

In 1999, Lynn moved to the United Kingdom, where she began teaching music technology at various colleges in London. After completing a Masters degree in Adult Education and Distance Learning, she developed several virtual learning environments, and worked as an e-learning mentor for other teachers. In 2005, she was awarded the Microsoft UK Innovative Teacher of the Year Award for her work in Further Education.

After working as the Assistant Director of Performing Arts at Bedford College, she left the educational sector to start her own business as a coach. She trained at the Coaches Training Institute and is a Certified Professional Co-Active Coach (CPCC), as well as a graduate of the Co-Active Leadership Program. She also studied Organization and Relationship Systems Coaching (ORSC) through the Center for Right Relationships. Her coaching practice won the Best of Bedford Business Awards in 2007, and was also voted one of the 'Ten Most Loved Businesses in Bedford' in 2008. Passionate about re-establishing our connection with the Earth, she began volunteering for the Transition Town Network in 2009, for which she received the Bedfordshire Businesswomen's Award for her work within the community.

In 2009, Lynn published *The Garden of the Soul: lessons from four flowers that unearth the Self*, which became a bestseller by dint of her unique marketing strategies that focussed upon connection rather than hard-sell. This established her reputation as a marketer and social media expert, and led the way for many other mind-body-spirit authors to ask her for help in marketing their books. Lynn has since worked with dozens of holistic business owners and authors—both self-published and those with major publishers. Every one of her launches has achieved bestseller status, many reaching number 1. Lynn also created Spirit Authors, a membership site offering training and support for mind-body-spirit authors. She is also known for her weekly 'Garden of the Soul' radio show and other online broadcasts, and has interviewed hundreds of holistic authors and speakers.

Lynn's eclectic approach to marketing incorporates every element of her background—her vast professional experience in the music industry, her work as an educator, her study and practice of spirituality, her work as a coach, her passion for the environment, her years of writing, and (most of all) her work with all those sensitive souls who came to her for help because they simply couldn't stand marketing.

Now a dual British-American citizen, Lynn resides in Bedford, England. Her daughter, Vrinda Pendred, is also a bestselling author and founder of Conditional Publications, publishing books by authors with neurological conditions such as autism, OCD, bipolar disorder and Tourette syndrome.

Lynn is also grandmother to a beautiful grandson named Percy, who loves to dance like Michael Jackson.

ALSO FROM LYNN SERAFINN

The Garden of the Soul: lessons from four flowers that unearth the Self

A Mind-Body-Spirit Bestseller

Bright Pen Books
ISBN13: 9780755211265

Said to be *'as spiritual as Deepak Chopra and as magical as Paulo Coelho,'* The Garden of the Soul takes the reader on a daring and magical journey through birth, death, love, art, spirituality and transformation in an eloquently poetic and unforgettable way. While gritty enough to grab reality by the horns and present some of the most frequently avoided topics of human experience, Lynn also shows us a highly crafted writing style that pushes the creative envelope for what can be done within the context of a personal memoir, blending it with a magic and unique metaphoric language that speaks directly to the heart.

'...a magical adventure toward deeper understanding of the relationship between Self and the world.'
                         ~ ALAN SEALE, author of *The Manifestation Wheel*

Scan QR code to **find the book on Amazon.**
~ OR~ go to http://delivr.com/1amto
Also available on Kindle, iPad and other eBook formats

Scan QR code to receive a **FREE 50-minute audio** of LIVE performance of a story from the book, read by the author.
                         ~ OR~ go to http://delivr.com/1aoig

THE GARDEN OF THE SOUL RADIO SHOW

Popular weekly show exploring personal empowerment, life purpose, balance of mind, body and spirit, and how to tap into the inner hero that lies within every human being. Since January 2009, Lynn Serafinn has hosted hundreds of distinguished guests including bestselling authors, coaches, healers, artists, motivational speakers, social reformers, community leaders and others who are actively making a positive and inspirational impact upon the world.

Hear the show live (and join our chat room)
Wednesdays at 6 P.M. UK, 1 P.M. Eastern, 10 A.M. Pacific

Scan QR code to find the show on **BlogTalkRadio.**
~ OR~ go to http://blogtalkradio.com/lynn-serafinn
Also on iTunes, Podcast Alley and many other services

SPIRIT AUTHORS

Spirit Authors is an online Virtual Coaching and Learning Experience where established, new and aspiring authors in the mind-body-spirit genre can find everything they need to make their publication a success. Created by author, coach, Lynn Serafinn, there are reasonably priced online courses available, and a collection of extremely helpful (free) articles on the Spirit Authors blog, packed with information about writing, self-publishing and marketing your book.

Scan QR code to visit the **Spirit Authors blog.**
~ OR~ go to http://spiritauthors.com/category/news
Be sure to subscribe to receive all Lynn's great info articles.

Scan QR code to receive **5 FREE podcasts**
on writing, publishing and marketing your book from
18 top industry professionals.
~ OR~ go to http://delivr.com/1aono

SPIRIT AUTHORS COACH
BOOK PROMOTIONS

We unlock #1-selling mind-body-spirit authors through authentic, humanity-based book promotions. The '7 Graces of Marketing' form the foundation of our Mission Statement, and underpin everything we do.

We offer full-service Amazon bestseller launches, as well as online platform building, both before and after your launch. If you are getting ready to publish a self-help/mind-body-spirit book sometime within the next year, contact us to see whether we might be able to help you. Please contact us 6-8 months in advance of your publication date.

All mind-body-spirit and self-help authors equally welcome, from first-time self-published authors to established authors from major publishing houses. We also help holistic and mind-body-spirit businesses create their online presence and marketing strategies.

*'I was truly blessed when I found Lynn Serafinn...**my book reached #1** in US and Canada due to Lynn leading the way.'*

> ~ **ALLISON MASLAN**, author of #1 seller: *Blast Off! Your Surefire Success Plan to Launch Your Dreams into Reality*

*'Lynn brought with her a **team of enthusiastic professionals** who worked hard to make my book launch **a huge success. The book hit #1 in the US, Canada, UK and Germany**...She literally **puts you on the map** of bestselling authors. My publisher, **Hay House, was impressed**...I recommend Lynn to anyone who is **serious about becoming a bestselling author.'***

> ~ **ROY MARTINA, MD**, author of #1 seller: *Emotional Balance: The Path to Inner Peace and Harmony*

Scan QR code to visit the **Spirit Authors Coach website.**
~ OR~ go to http://spiritauthorscoach.com
There, you will also find a PDF describing our services.

CONNECT ON SOCIAL MEDIA

Twitter
@LynnSerafinn
@7GracesMarketng (that's not a typo)
@SpiritAuthors
@GardenOfTheSoul

Facebook
LynnSerafinn
7GracesOfMarketing
SpiritAuthors
GardenOfTheSoul

LinkedIn
Lynn Serafinn

YouTube
gardenofthesoul

RECEIVE OVER 10 HOURS OF AUDIO

Find out what some of today's most dynamic thought leaders have to say about the 'The 7 Deadly Sins' versus 'The 7 Graces of Marketing.'

Scan QR code to receive **7 FREE audios** with 20 world-class speakers at 'The 7 Graces of Marketing Telesummit.'
~ OR~ go to
http://the7gracesofmarketing.com/free-telesummit

CONTACT LYNN

Scan QR code to contact Lynn Serafinn about speaking engagements, book promotions, bestseller launches, media appearances or just to say hello.
~ OR~ go to http://spiritauthors.com/contact

Lightning Source UK Ltd.
Milton Keynes UK
UKOW031457091111

181770UK00003B/13/P